Logic & Art

ESSAYS IN HONOR OF
NELSON GOODMAN

NELSON GOODMAN

Logic

&

Art

ESSAYS

IN HONOR OF

NELSON

GOODMAN

Richard Rudner

and

Israel Scheffler

EDITORS

THE BOBBS-MERRILL COMPANY, INC.
Indianapolis and New York

Contents

[vii]

Art & Representation

Logic & Language

Implication & Modality

Preface

This volume is dedicated to Nelson Goodman on the occasion of his sixty-fifth birthday in 1971. It consists of sixteen papers by students and colleagues united in their admiration for his philosophical achievement and their appreciation of his intellectual example.

Goodman has made path-breaking contributions to central areas of philosophy. In theory of knowledge and the analysis of experience, in the examination of language and the logic of systems, in philosophy of science and the interpretation of art, every work of his has revealed not only the novel solution but also the uncommon perspective; every new effort has displayed characteristic brilliance and equally characteristic penetration and radical insight.

He has, moreover, achieved wide influence as a teacher whose passion for exactitude, dedication to fundamentals, systematic conscientiousness, and exploratory verve have strengthened the highest standards and deepest conceptions of philosophical effort.

We present this volume to him with affection and with congratulations on his sixty-fifth birthday, and we offer him our good wishes for the future, as he continues his work.

R.R.; I.S.

Science & Mind

ONE

Space-Time

and

Individuals

J. J. C. SMART

SINCE MINKOWSKI it has been customary to think of the physical world as a four-dimensional space-time manifold. When we think in this way, the Lorentz transformations of special relativity are seen to be merely a matter of rotation of axes in space-time: the space-time manifold is itself independent of our particular space-time axes (or spatial and temporal frames of reference). The four-dimensional way of thinking was of course available prior to the special theory of relativity, and it is possible that as metaphysicians we ought to have regarded it as a good thing even then. However the non-invariance in special relativity of lengths and periods of time, as well as of many dynamical quantities, seems to make the four-dimensional point of view more imperative. It is the purpose of this paper to defend the

[3]

four-dimensional picture of the world as (in the present state of knowledge) giving us the best clue to the metaphysical truth.[1]

The ordinary, or common sense, or, as I shall call it for convenience, the "Strawsono-Aristotelian" or "SA", view of the world differs from the four-dimensional "Minkowskian" view in that a physical object, such as an orange, is a *three*-dimensional thing that *endures* through time. However this enduring through time is not thought of as implying that the thing has a temporal dimension. To be *at* a time is to have a certain temporal *property*, just as being red is to have a certain color quality. The orange does not extend through time: it is the *whole* orange, not just a temporal "slice" of the orange, that is at a given time. Again, according to the SA scheme, the *whole* orange can be spherical at one time and ellipsoidal at another time, and can move from one place to another. An SA object thus does not have purely three-dimensional properties such as being spherical or ellipsoidal: it has more complex properties, such as being *spherical at such and such a time*. (For if it had the simpler properties, it would have incompatible ones, such as being both spherical and ellipsoidal.) On the Minkowskian view objects (such as temporal parts or "time-slices" of oranges) can have the simpler properties, such as being spherical. Considerations of this sort can lead one to view the SA picture, with its resolute desire not to treat objects as temporally extended, as a theoretically awkward one. Our common-sense conceptual scheme, viewed from a Minkowskian vantage point, can seem to be a rather odd one.

Other philosophers, however, obviously feel very differently. For them it is the four-dimensional world view that is the odd one. Thus in his introduction to his collection of British Academy lectures, P. F. Strawson refers to the four-dimensional way of thinking as "fanciful philosophical theorizing", though it claims "to derive respectability from physics".[2]

---

[1] Part of an earlier version of this paper was read to the Conference of the Australasian Association of Philosophy, August 1969, as the first part of a symposium with Professor Bernard Williams. I am indebted to Professor Williams for his comments, some of which have made the present paper less bad than it was, even though I have not come round to agree entirely with his general point of view. I am also indebted to Professor A. N. Prior for some comments that he made in correspondence, after reading the earlier version, and that led me to expunge some erroneous passages about tense logic.

[2] P. F. Strawson, ed. *Studies in the Philosophy of Thought and Action* (New York: Oxford University Press, 1968), 5.

Perhaps neither way of talking is "fanciful": perhaps the two ways are inter-translatable. Thus when the Strawsono-Aristotelian might say that the orange changed at about midday from being spherical to being ellipsoidal, the Minkowskian could say that time-slices of the $orange_4$ before about midday are (tenselessly) spherical and time-slices of the $orange_4$ after about midday are (tenselessly) ellipsoidal. I have put a subscript "4" below the word "orange" in the latter part of the sentence to show that the word "orange" in Minkowskian is not quite the same as the word "orange" in SA terminology. In fact it would seem that "orange" can not be defined in terms of "$orange_4$", though complete SA sentences containing "orange" are perhaps inter-translatable with complete Minkowskian sentences containing "$orange_4$". For example oranges are correctly said to move or to be at rest, whereas it is nonsense to talk of four-dimensional space-time objects as moving or as at rest. When in SA language we say that two oranges are at rest with respect to one another, in Minkowskian we say that two $oranges_4$ are parallel to one another (lie along parallel world lines). Similarly, to say that one orange is moving relatively to another is equivalent to saying, in Minkowskian, that appropriate segments of their world lines are inclined to one another. In this paper I shall sometimes put the subscript "4" under words that take on a "four-dimensional" sense in the way that "orange" does, so as to avoid objections such as that oranges are the sorts of things that can be at a point of time, as a whole, and so are not four-dimensional solids. On other occasions, when it seems too inelegant to put them in, I shall leave the reader to imagine the subscripts when he feels the need.

One is tempted, then, to ask what is the relationship between the SA orange and the Minkowskian $orange_4$. However this would be very misleading. Someone who, like myself, is inclined to believe physics in a realist way, would be inclined to see the world in terms of Minkowskian objects, and to deny the existence of the SA ones. Now even though sentences ostensibly about SA objects could be mapped onto sentences ostensibly about Minkowskian objects, we do not need to acquiesce in an ontology that contains *both* sorts of objects. From the Minkowskian perspective, SA objects are like the virtual classes of Chapter One of W. V. Quine's *Set Theory and its Logic*,[3] at least insofar as talk ostensibly of SA objects can be translated away in terms of talk about the Minkowskian ones. (Compare

[3] Cambridge: Harvard University Press, 1963.

the way in which sentences ostensibly about virtual classes can be translated into sentences containing predicates instead of class expressions.)

From the SA perspective, of course, it may go the other way: it will be the Minkowskian sentences that are like the sentences ostensibly about virtual classes. However to take this line would seem to be to reject the explanatory power that comes from taking Minkowski's interpretation of special relativity in a *realist* way. From the point of view of a realist philosophy of science, we must surely agree with Minkowski that "henceforth space by itself and time by itself, are doomed to fade away into mere shadows, and only a kind of union of the two will preserve an independent reality".[4] The only way to avoid this would be to have a merely *instrumentalist* interpretation of special relativity, much in the spirit of Einstein's pre-Minkowski paper "On the Electrodynamics of Moving Bodies", which was rather operationist in tone, and was written at a time when (as he indicated in his autobiography)[5] Einstein was much influenced by Hume and Mach. It is no part of my intention in the present paper to go into the defense of scientific realism against operationism or instrumentalism, and the correctness of a *realist* interpretation of special relativity must be taken as a presupposition of my general argument. However I wish to point out one difficulty that special relativity seems to pose for the SA conceptual scheme, and that perhaps applies even when this is allied to instrumentalism.

We have noted that an SA object is not (say) spherical *tout court*, but is spherical *at a time*. Thus the SA scheme is tied to the notion of a present instant at which the whole SA object possesses certain properties. Since the advent of special relativity, however, it has become clear that there is no absolute simultaneity. Two parts of an extensive SA object might, for example, simultaneously have the same color with respect to one set of axes and have different colors with respect to a different set of axes. (Looking at the matter Minkowski-wise, points A and B in Figure 1 on a space-time object might be simultaneous with respect to one set of axes, and A and C might be simultaneous with respect to another set of axes. Let A be red, B red, C green.)

---

[4] H. Minkowski, "Space and Time", in *The Principle of Relativity, A Collection of Original Memoirs on the Special and General Theories of Relativity,* by H. A. Lorentz, A. Einstein, H. Minkowski and H. Weyl (New York: Dover, Inc., 1924), 75.
[5] P. A. Schilpp, ed. *Albert Einstein, Philosopher Scientist* (New York: Harper Torchbooks, 1959), 53.

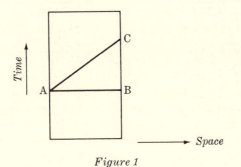

Figure 1

So with respect to what axes must the Strawsono-Aristotelian think of an object as being "all at once"? A natural answer might be: a set of axes with respect to which the object is at rest. This would appear at first sight to remove ambiguity. However what about an extensive Strawsono-Aristotelian object rotating rapidly on its axis? And what about a complex of SA objects all moving at different velocities relative to one another?

Well, then, to echo Strawson's disparaging comment, what is "fanciful" about the metaphysics of the physical world as a four-dimensional manifold? Let us see what arguments can be put on the other side, and in particular, let us look at the arguments of P. T. Geach in the paper[6] alluded to by Strawson, and which are directed against the view of the world as a four-dimensional manifold.

"Some of the arguments used in its favor are distinctly odd", says Geach. Well, maybe they are, but so long as *some* arguments are good we do not need to worry about rejecting the bad ones. Thus I would agree with Geach that the mere fact that "we can represent local motion in a graph with axes representing space and time"[7] does not prove anything much. But Minkowski does not use this weak argument, and I do not wish to use it either. It is true that in popular exposition Minkowski says, "We will try to visualize the state of things by the graphic method. . . . With this most valiant piece of chalk I might project upon the blackboard four world axes . . ."[8] and so on. But his *argument* is not the analogy with graphs. His argument is that only space-time entities are invariant and their laws covariant: one cannot get invariance or covariance by taking space

[6] P. T. Geach, "Some Problems about Time", in P. F. Strawson, ed. *Studies in the Philosophy of Thought and Action.*

[7] *Ibid.* p. 176.

[8] Minkowski, "Space and Time", p. 76.

[7]

and time separately. And it is sensible to take invariance and covariance as a touchstone of reality.[9]

Another argument, which Geach says is "odd", is Quine's, from an apparent consilience between quantificational logic and space-time physics. I would agree with Geach that Quine goes too far when he says that "the four-dimensional view of space-time is part and parcel of the use of modern formal logic",[10] since, as Geach points out, Quine elsewhere shows how quantification theory can be applied to the analysis of arguments in ordinary language, and even (if due caution is exercised) to some of those arguments that contain tenses and other indicator or egocentric expressions. Nevertheless, it is very natural to see a consilience between quantification theory, with its tenseless "is" in "there is a . . ." or "∃x" on the one hand, and Minkowski-type physics on the other hand.

Of course besides the "modern logic" mentioned by Quine, there have recently arisen systems of "tense-logic". In accordance with these, I suppose that the friends of tenses might use a tensed "is" of quantification, which of course would not be the present tense but would be the universal tense "was, is or will be" (or else, as Prior does, they might use "there is a" in a present tensed way, and then introduce the notion "it was, is, or will be the case that there is a . . ."). However this seems to me to be an unnatural way of going on. This is partly because I see no reason why temporal matters should be imported into logic. To turn one of Geach's arguments against Quine against Geach himself, could we not conceive of a physics of the future in which not only space and time but also space-time was shown to be one of the myths of primitive twentieth-century science and metaphysics? And might not *logic* still survive? Moreover, logic has most importantly been used to formalize such subjects as number theory and set theory, in which a tenseless idiom seems appropriate. Hence those who wish logic to be applicable to *all* subject-matters, whether temporal or atemporal, will not wish for temporality to be imported into the very structure of logic. The reason why tense logicians wish to import time into logic seems to be that they correctly see the connection between logic and the concept of truth, and they also espouse the ancient and mediaeval notion of a proposition as something whose truth-value can vary with time. However this ar-

[9] See Max Born, "Physical Reality", *Philosophical Quarterly*, 3 (1953) 139–150.
[10] W. V. Quine, "Mr. Strawson on Logical Theory", in *The Ways of Paradox and Other Essays* (New York: Random House, 1966), 145.

gument can be reversed. We can argue from the inappropriateness of bringing a special subject matter like time into logic to the necessity to reject this ancient concept of a proposition and of truth.[11] What is needed to avoid this ancient philosophy of logic is to recognize tenses as token-reflexive or egocentric expressions.[12]

We do not need to claim that the tensed interpretation of the quantifier is actually incompatible with special relativity, though

[11] To future generations it may well seem as odd that time distinctions were once imported into grammar (*via* tenses) as now seems to modern eyes the interesting phenomenon of periphrastic verbs in certain Australian aboriginal languages. Thus in Aranda, by means of repetitions and suffixes, verb forms may be modified so as to express extremely complicated ideas. In his *Aranda Phonetics and Grammar* (*Oceania Monographs*, No. 7, Australian National Research Council, 1942) pp. 108–109, T.G.H. Strehlow gives the example of descriptions of a mountain kangaroo eating. Various modifications of the verb "to eat" give, respectively, "descended eating", "descended-slowly-eating-all-the-while", "wandered-on-away-from-us-eating-on-its-way", and several even more complex variants on the verb "to eat". In a way this is more sensible than tenses (which Aranda also has) because to descend-slowly-eating-all-the-while is to do a unitary sort of action, different from just eating, whereas to eat tomorrow is to do the same sort of thing as to eat yesterday. However when in English we say "eating while slowly descending", we are doing something rather analogous to a Fourier analysis, and the scientific advantages of this are obvious. One day, perhaps, the scientific advantages of getting time distinctions out of verbs will seem equally obvious.

[12] It is not necessary for the present purposes to decide what the best account of these is, so long as it is agreed that there is no particular mystery about an utterance's being able to refer to itself. Reichenbach's theory (in his *Elements of Symbolic Logic*) has been influential, but has certain weaknesses, of which I have learned from Mr. Dene Barnett of the Flinders University of South Australia. Barnett has devised an ingenious account, which interprets the body of the speaker as a part of the total symbol of which the word "I" forms another part. There is no mystery that a complex consisting of the letter "I" plus your body should be a different symbol (and refer to a different person) from a complex symbol consisting of the letter "I" plus my body. Compare the case of a word in inverted commas. In a quotation expression the inverted commas do not themselves denote, but together with another expression they denote that other expression. Similarly, according to Barnett, the word "I" does not denote, but taken together with another nearby object, the speaker's body, it denotes that other object, namely the speaker's body. In line with Barnett's theory, we might make our basic egocentric expression "I now", of which a time-slice of my body, at the time of utterance, forms a constituent. Then "past" can be rendered as "earlier than I now", "future" as "later than I now", and so on. In his *Past, Present and Future* (Oxford University Press, 1967), pp. 12–15, A. N. Prior has pointed out that for certain tenses, such as future perfects, more than one "reference point" is needed, but perhaps these could be handled in terms of "the first reference point referred to by me now", "the second reference point referred to by me now", etc.

tense logic does need modification to take account of it. (A. N. Prior has mentioned postulates for relativistic tense logic due to N. B. Cocchiarella.)[13] But the simplest course in formalizing the Minkowski theory would seem to be to avail oneself of ordinary quantification theory in which the "there is a . . ." is tenseless. But be this as it may, we do not have to depend on the argument that the four-dimensional world view is forced upon us by modern logic: the best reasons for accepting it are reasons of physics.

Geach proceeds to attack another view which he alleges is part of the Minkowski way of thinking. He attributes to the Minkowskian the view (1) that change is an illusion and (2) that it is a changing illusion. Hence he has no difficulty in convicting his opponent of contradiction. Now the Minkowskian *can* accommodate the facts of change. Thus when the Strawsono-Aristotelian may say "the orange changes from spherical to ellipsoidal", the Minkowskian can say: "an earlier time-slice of the orange$_4$ is round and a later time-slice of the orange$_4$ is ellipsoidal". The Minkowskian is *not* asserting the existence of a "static world": he would have to say, of what the Strawsono-Aristotelian would call "a static world", that all time-slices of it were exactly similar. Consider another form of change, namely what the Strawsono-Aristotelian would call the "propagation" of a signal from place P at time t to place P' at time t'. (Remember that the four-dimensional counterpart of an SA place is not the neighbourhood of a point but of a line.) The Minkowskian would describe this "propagation" in different terms, namely as the *lying* of a four-dimensional object (whether a photon or a message stick$_4$) along the world line joining (P, t) to (P', t'). (In the case of the photon we have the curious fact that the space-time interval between (P, t) and (P', t') is zero.) The signal is not *propagated through* space-time since motion through space-time would have to be with respect to a hyper-time. The signal *is* (tenselessly) along a line in space-time. It is true that many books and articles use the misleading term "propagate" even in a four-dimensional context. However such locutions can nearly always be rendered harmless by appropriate mental adjustments on the part of a clear-headed reader, such as by interpreting "propagated from . . . to . . ." in the four-dimensional context as meaning no more

[13] See A. N. Prior, *Past, Present and Future*, p. 177. It is perhaps worth commenting that if tense logic is modified in order to fit relativity theory, this distorts common sense language and makes tense logic less useful for *another* of its purposes, which is to formalize the *grammar* of ordinary tensed discourse.

than "lying between . . . and. . . ." What is *not* so good is when advocates of the Minkowski world mix in dualistic metaphysics, illegitimate notions of time travel and of "consciousness crawling up world lines". Consider the remark by H. Weyl: "We travel along the world line of our body with 'screened off consciousness' ".[14] But no such bad metaphysics should be foisted onto other philosophers who wish to defend the space-time world picture. All Weyl needed to say was the aseptic remark that any perceptual awareness or memory (which I myself would identify with a space-time chunk of a brain$_4$) is an awareness of earlier space-time entities. If one thinks consistently in the four-dimensional manner one comes to *reject* loose talk of movement of consciousness or of time travel of consciousness. Now most people do seem to be subject to the metaphysical illusion of an absurdity (flow of time, advance through time), perhaps because of a misunderstanding of egocentricity, token-reflexiveness, tenses, etc. However the description of this absurdity need not itself be done absurdly: the illusion of the septic sort of change may involve change, but this need only be aseptic change, i.e. the sort of change that can be described four-dimensionally in terms of non-similarities of time-slices of the brain of the metaphysician who has the illusion of time flow.[15]

Geach seems to me to be even more unfair when he suggests that the four-dimensional view implies fatalism. He refers to one of John Buchan's novels, in which the characters "get a glimpse of the future, with no power to change it". If fatalism is the view that we cannot change the future, then it seems to be either trivial or absurd (according as to whether we interpret "we change the future" as contradictory or nonsensical). Suppose that I decide to do A rather than B. Then *whatever* our metaphysics, whether SA or Minkowskian, we ought to agree that A was our future. Our future was *never B*, because A was what we eventually did. To talk of changing the future is as silly as to talk of changing the past. But *ordinarily* fatalism is the view that what we do does not have any causal effect on what happens. This view is obviously false, and is so just as much from a Minkowskian perspective as from an SA one. Causal rules can relate space-time chunks to one another just as well as they can relate SA

14 H. Weyl, *Philosophy of Mathematics and Natural Science*, (Princeton, N.J.: Princeton University Press, 1949), 194.

15 I am assuming materialism. A dualist could describe it in terms of non-similarities of time-slices of the one-dimensional entity which is the "soul" of the metaphysician.

[11]

events. The fatalistic soldier believes that he will be killed, or not killed, no matter what he does. His view is false, because if he does pop his head out of a slit trench and gets his head shot off, his death *is* caused by his action of popping his head out. In space-time language, his world line and that of the bullet intersect, whereas if his world line were to coincide a bit longer with that of the deep interior of the slit trench it would be a longer one thereafter![16]

Geach, as might be expected in so subtle a philosophical logician, is more interesting when he goes on to attack the Minkowskian way of talking as involving "an erroneous analysis of propositions into subject and predicate".[17] Geach proposes to analyze "while" not as a temporal predicate but as a sentential connective. He considers some examples such as "McTaggart in 1901 was a philosopher holding Hegel's dialectic to be valid, and McTaggart in 1921 was a philosopher not holding Hegel's dialectic to be valid".[18] He then goes on to say that if we regard "McTaggart in 1901" and "McTaggart in 1921" as designating two individuals, "then we must say that they designate two philosophers: one philosopher believing Hegel's dialectic to be valid, and another philosopher believing Hegel's dialectic not to be valid". I do not agree that the Minkowskian need talk like this. Surely the most natural way to interpret "philosopher" four-dimensionally is as the whole four-dimensional individual from birth to death, and then McTaggart in 1901 and McTaggart in 1921 would not be two different philosophers but two different temporal parts of one philosopher$_4$ (philosopher stages, in Quine's terminology).[19] Then we can say that "believing Hegel's dialectic to be valid" and "believing Hegel's dialectic not to be valid" could be construed as dispositional predicates applicable to different temporal parts of McTaggart, just as "magnetized" and "unmagnetized" can be construed four-dimen-

---

[16] Bernard Williams has suggested that what the person who confusedly says "we can change the future but not the past" is trying to express is that causal chains run from past to future. This brings us to the so-called problem of "the Arrow of Time", which I think is less misleadingly described as that of the temporal asymmetry of the world, or at least of our cosmic epoch of it. I see no reason why this should not be considered within the context of the four-dimensional world picture: indeed if it is, as I believe it is, a deep problem of theoretical physics, it had *better* be so considered.

[17] "Some Problems about Time", p. 182.

[18] *Ibid.*, p. 183.

[19] W. V. Quine, *Word and Object* (Cambridge, Mass.: Massachusetts Institute of Technology Press and New York: John Wiley & Sons, 1960), 51.

sionally as dispositional predicates applicable to different temporal parts (iron bar stages) of the same iron bar. Of course Geach's example is "a philosopher believing that Hegel's dialectic is valid", and as Geach says, only a philosopher, not a temporal slice of a philosopher can be a philosopher believing that Hegel's dialectic is valid. But, despite Geach's refusal to allow us to amend the predicates (perhaps to "is a temporal stage of a philosopher believing that . . ."), I do not myself see why we should not take such a liberty. Geach says, "The whole ground for treating, for example, 'McTaggart in 1901' and 'McTaggart in 1921' as designating two different individuals was that we seemed to find predicates true of the one and false of the other". This reason seems to be unconvincing, because a sensible Minkowskian will claim that he has grounds which are quite other than those mentioned by Geach, namely consilience with the space-time world of special relativity, and besides that, a metaphysically neat picture, epitomized perhaps in Nelson Goodman's calculus of individuals.[20]

I might mention yet another way which is open to the Minkowskian when construing the proposition about McTaggart. Instead of taking "McTaggart in 1901" and "McTaggart in 1921" as designating two individuals, let us have two predicates "believes in 1901 . . ." and "believes in 1921 . . ." applicable to the one four-dimensional individual McTaggart. (To believe in 1901 is of course to have a certain dispositional state of its "around 1901" part.) Indeed ultimately *all* distinctions should be made by means of predicates, if we have a Quinean language that has *no* designating expressions, but only variables, quantifiers, and predicates. We can agree with Geach that temporal predicates which contain mention of dates are dispensable. (Geach considers the example of people on a cloud-bound planet who are not able to keep dates or tell the time.) What is in question is merely the *topology* of space-time, and thereby some (perhaps wholly nonmetrical) notion of earlier and later.

According to Geach, the statement that one event is simultaneous with another is not to be analyzed as saying that the two events are at the same time as another. For, he argues, we could not introduce ways of telling the time unless we already had a concept of simultaneity. "A physicist", says Geach, "may protest that he simply cannot understand 'at the same time' except via elaborate stipulations about ob-

---

[20] See Nelson Goodman, *The Structure of Appearance*, Second Edition (Indianapolis: Bobbs-Merrill, 1966), 46–61.

serving instruments", and Geach continues, "his protest may be dismissed out of hand, for he could not describe the apparatus, except by certain conditions' having to be fulfilled *together*, i.e. simultaneously, by the parts of the apparatus".[21] Geach holds that the basic notion of simultaneity is that of "while", which is a sentential connective, not a relation word. The study of "while", he argues, belongs to *logic*, and a physicist who casts doubt upon such a notion is sawing off the branch upon which he is sitting.

But this branch sawing is going on all the time in science, and scientists are very adroit in not sitting on the branch just when it is sawn. They sit on a higher branch. Thus from the vantage point of special relativity we can see that, strictly speaking, no two spatially separated events are simultaneous with one another independently of a frame of reference, though our ordinary common sense notion of simultaneity is workable, within the limits of observational error, when either distances or relative velocities are fairly small, for example in the observation of laboratory instruments.

The Minkowskian would wish to disentangle a temporal function of the word "while" from a conjunctive function of the word. He would say not, for example, "he runs while I walk" but "he runs and I walk and his running is simultaneous with my walking". Here the conjunctive function of "while" is taken over by the first "and", and the simultaneity asserting function is taken over by "is simultaneous with". "His running" could be taken here as referring to a certain running stage of the four-dimensional he₄, and "my walking" could be taken as referring to a certain walking stage of the four-dimensional me₄. That is, we replace talk of SA *processes* by talk of four-dimensional chunks of things, and let "is running" be a predicate applicable to just those four-dimensional chunks that are the four-dimensional equivalents of the things in process (people running).

Geach, of course, will have none of this, because he holds that "we need to get events expressed in a propositional style, rather than by using name-like phrases". He suggests therefore, that we should say "Wellington fought Napoleon after George III first went mad", and not "George III's first attack of madness is earlier than the battle of Waterloo". This is indeed an interesting suggestion, but I see no reason for the Minkowskian to accept it: indeed the Minkowskian had better *not* accept it, or Geach is very likely to have him properly on the hook. The Minkowskian must use something like Goodman's cal-

[21] "Some Problems about Time", p. 185.

culus of individuals, in which simultaneity, or being earlier or later than (if necessary with respect to some frame of reference), relates four-dimensional entities. Thus to say that my army service is earlier than my career as a teacher of philosophy is to say that the army serving chunk of me is earlier than the philosophy teaching chunk of me. I see no difficulty in adapting my talk in this sort of way, even though it may be at some cost to literary elegance. I suggest that talk of processes gets replaced by talk of four-dimensional chunks, and that talk of events gets replaced by talk of boundaries between different temporal chunks: thus the event of my demobilization is four-dimensionally to be thought of as a boundary between an army serving chunk of me and a later non-military chunk of me. Some events may be vaguely defined borders, of course. Thus the event that is my becoming grey haired is the rather vaguely defined boundary between a (now far distant) dark haired chunk of me and a later grey haired chunk of me. There is no more difficulty about vaguely defined temporal boundaries then there is about vaguely defined spatial boundaries, such as the boundary between arid and non-arid regions of a country. Also there is in special relativity a sense of "event" in which an event is more like a point than a boundary, as when we talk of the space-time *interval* between two events. Here "event" could be construed as an arbitrarily small four-dimensional part of a thing, much as in Newtonian mechanics a particle is an arbitrarily small bit of a three-dimensional thing.

Being a materialist, I hold that all processes, even for example processes of thought, are four-dimensional, and that all events, even, for example, acts of thought, are boundaries between four-dimensional chunks, or perhaps, alternatively, are arbitrarily small four-dimensional chunks. But dualists can readily adapt this for their own purposes, and construe processes of thought as *one*-dimensional segments and acts of thought as boundaries between these one-dimensional segments.

Clearly, then, if "earlier than", etc., are predicates relating space-time entities, these cannot relate events in the sense in which an event expression, as Geach puts it, "goes proxy for a clause". I do not deny that Geach is right in saying that in ordinary language there is such a sense of "event": for example he points out that in 1918 we might assert or deny or doubt the Kaiser's death, *i.e. that* the Kaiser is dead.

Geach concludes his paper with some more peripheral matters, which I shall not discuss. I have suggested that we regard a process

[15]

four-dimensionally as a space-time individual (usually part of a larger, more extensive individual, of course). I am here using "individual" in the sense of Goodman, not of Strawson. Thus consider the following very simple example. A rubber ball is bouncing on an elastic floor. Looked at four-dimensionally, the process is this:

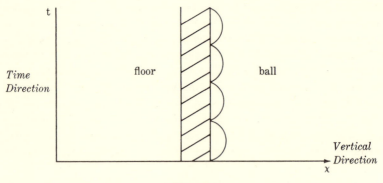

Figure 2

Looked at four-dimensionally, again, a brain process might be thought of as a vast cat's cradle of world lines ("world lines" meaning here not geometrical lines but the thin four-dimensional worm-like solids which are particles). Here I am permitting myself to think classically: the quantum mechanical picture would of course be less picturable. Since quantum mechanics has to be Lorentz invariant, it also supports the Minkowski point of view, unless perhaps the difficulties of giving a realist interpretation of quantum mechanics lead us to espouse an instrumentalist philosophy.

We cannot, of course, expect brain physiologists, for example, to talk in terms of Minkowski space-time. They talk in the language and with the grammar that comes naturally to them, which they have learned as children. There is no reason why scientists and philosophers should not follow Berkeley, and frequently "think with the learned, and speak with the vulgar".[22] Let me take some sentences from books on brain physiology and the like. (1) "There are neurons at all depths within the cortex that give rise to axons leaving the cortex".[23] This requires practically no translation at all. Minkowski-

[22] Berkeley, *Principles of Human Knowledge*, § 51.
[23] D. A. Sholl, *The Organization of the Cerebral Cortex*, (London: Methuen, 1956), 59.

wise we must of course think of the axons not as approximately lines in three-dimensional space but as planes in four-dimensional space. "Give rise to" has to be interpreted in a tenseless and non-causal manner, but this is no problem. (2) "The ten-per-second cycle of the alpha rhythm . . . ceases when the subject opens his eyes".[24] Something like this might do: "Shut eye stages of a person have ten alpha rhythm peaks per second and open eye stages have no alpha rhythm peaks". (3) "The surface membrane of muscle fibers is certainly permeable to chloride ions".[25] Here the translation is again very easy: "Chloride ions sometimes *intersect* surface membranes of muscle fibers", where the chloride ions and the surface membranes are four-dimensional solids.

Problems in physics are commonly stated in SA terminology, even when the solution is worked out Minkowski-wise. Consider this problem, from a text book:

> An excited atom, of total mass m, is at rest in a given frame. It emits a photon and thereby loses internal energy ΔE. Calculate the exact frequency of the photon, making due allowance for the recoil of the atom.[26]

We might say, pedantically in Minkowskian language, something like the following:

> AB is an early atom stage, every time-slice of which has mass m and it lies parallel to the Ot axis of a given frame. BC is a later time-slice of the atom stage. The difference between the internal energy of a time-slice of AB and that of a time-slice of BC is ΔE. BP is a photon stage, connected to AB at B, so that angle $ABP =$ 1½ right angles. (I here assume the unit of time to be such that the velocity of light is equal to unity.) Calculate the frequency of the photon stage, making due allowance for the fact that angle PBC is slightly greater than half a right angle.

The advantages of "talking with the vulgar" are obvious, but these cut no metaphysical ice: a sufficiently pedantic philosopher can translate into Minkowskian if he wants to. To take another example, we sometimes find problems in relativity theory about rotating fly wheels.

---

[24] *Ibid.*, p. 94.

[25] See Bernard Katz 'Nerve Impulse', in *The Physics and Chemistry of Life* (A *Scientific American* book) (New York: Simon and Schuster, 1955), 239.

[26] See W. Rindler, *Special Relativity* (Edinburgh: Oliver and Boyd, 1960), 108.

[17]

According to the Minkowskian, a rotating fly wheel is a helical sheaf of particles.

I think that the problem of replacing SA talk in the biological sciences by Minkowskian language is often very difficult and awkward, leading to artificial constructions. But equally, it would hardly be possible to calculate the nautical almanac using the general theory of relativity. It is known, however, that Newtonian mechanics provides a pragmatically more convenient and sufficiently accurate approximation in most cases (the perihelion of Mercury aside). But no one who accepted general relativity (and here I am not of course wishing necessarily to imply that it *should* be accepted since general relativity is so much less well tested than is special relativity) would regard the pragmatic convenience of Newtonian methods as in any way impugning the superior *metaphysical* truth of general relativity. (The contrast between truth and pragmatic convenience is one that has been stressed by Paul Feyerabend in many of his writings.)

Perhaps it is going too far to say that the SA conceptual scheme is essentially *false*. A lot depends on how much we import into it. If the conceptual scheme implies that there are events that are absolutely simultaneous with one another, then it does imply a falsehood. As I indicated earlier, I suspect that the reason why the SA scheme might have to be rejected is its apparent reliance on a notion of absolute simultaneity, when it is implied that even an extensive object can be given to us "all at once" at a moment of time. According to special relativity, only events at the same point of space can be absolutely simultaneous. However let us suppose that an austere SA language might be all right, because translatable into Minkowskian. Thus "this orange will become more elliptical" translates into "later time-slices of the orange$_4$ are (tenseless) more elliptical than earlier ones, some of which are (tenseless) later than this utterance". Even if the translations can always be carried out, we may still be inclined to think of the SA scheme as metaphysically false. Compare the way in which statements ostensibly about "virtual classes", but Platonistically construed, would be regarded as false by a nominalist, even though he would agree that statements about virtual classes could be mapped on to statements employing only quantifiers, variables, predicates, and truth functional operators. Again, let us suppose that many statements ostensibly about witches could be "translated" into statements about schizophrenia. Truth of the latter would not, in a sense, confer truth on the former. We might ask what is the relation between a witch and a schizophrenic. In a sense, there is no relation, because there are no witches. In another sense, it is of course identity: that is, the very same objective situation that *causes* a believer in witches to say "that's a witch" may be what causes a believer in schizophrenia to say "that's a schizophrenic". (Here it will be obvious to many readers how much I have been influenced by some of Paul Feyerabend's writings.) Similarly, an SA object *A* may be the same as a four-dimensional Minkowskian object *B* in the sense that the very same objective situation that causes a Strawsono-Aristotelian to report the existence of an *A* may cause the Minkowskian to report the existence of a *B*. This is without prejudice to the metaphysical questions of whether *A*'s, or *B*'s, or both, or neither, really exist.

It may well be that the ordinary conceptual scheme of the permanent-in-change, which partitions reality into space and time separately, a space that somehow *endures* through time, is *in practice* inescapable to us. Evolution by natural selection can well have programmed our brains so that we have an innate tendency to perceive the world in this way. After all, it is the *local present* that is of paramount importance to an animal that is about to leap onto its prey, and the brains of animals are very largely computers to organize leaping onto prey and plucking of fruits, and so on. That is, they have evolved as decision-making devices, not as organs of scientific contemplation. No wonder the (local) present seems in the forefront of consciousness, since (almost by definition) it is the local present that is involved in decision and action. (One might ask whether brains might not have evolved rather differently, however, if we had been animals moving with near-light velocities, and perhaps signalling to one another in practically important ways.) So *perhaps* scientists will always, in their laboratories, have to talk in terms of the common sense conceptual scheme (or "the manifest image" of Wilfrid Sellars)[27] even though what they say has also (by a sort of double vision) to be thought of four-dimensionally (in what Sellars calls "the scientific image"). I do not know whether this view that the manifest image is inescapable is true or not, but even if it is true, it is compatible with the *metaphysical* correctness of the four-dimensional view. It is quite possible that we have been programmed by natural selection to a false but useful way of perceiving the world, and that it is only in our studies, when we read Minkowski, and so on, that we can overcome this sort of original sin. The example of Newtonian mechanics and the

[27] See Wilfrid Sellars, *Science, Perception and Reality* (London: Routledge and Kegan Paul, 1963), Chap. 1.

nautical almanac shows that truth and pragmatic value need not go together, and it is pragmatic value for which natural selection selects. Alternatively, it is possible that one day, even in their homes and laboratories, scientists will not only think but also talk Minkowski-wise, and say such things as "at (x, y, z, t) approximately a time-slice of John Smith perceives (tenseless) a time-slice of Mary Jones". It depends on which hypothesis is true: the Sellarsian hypothesis that (roughly speaking) we have been programmed with original sin, or the Feyerabendian one that we have merely been indoctrinated into error by nannies, Oxford philosophers, and the like.[28] But even if the answer favours Sellars, it has no more bearing on the question of what the world is really like than has the fact that within special domains it is convenient to use false theories when it is known that they enable us to predict phenomena in these restricted domains to a sufficiently high degree of approximation.

[28] Cf. my remarks in my paper "Conflicting Views about Explanation", in Robert S. Cohen and Marx W. Wartofsky, eds. *Boston Studies in the Philosophy of Science* Vol. II, pp. 157–169 (see especially pp. 168–169) and Paul Feyerabend's comments, *ibid.* pp. 223–261 (see especially top half of p. 235 and pp. 246–251).

TWO

Empirical and Conventional Elements in Certain Numerical Laws

BERNARD R. GRUNSTRA

Introduction

IN ORDER TO discuss numerical laws, which are based on measurement results and of importance to measurement theory, it is necessary to say a few words about measurement.

A measurable property is one attributed to things in virtue of certain intricate structural relations they bear to one another. The network of these relations is similar in part to that which obtains among numbers /2,7,14,15/. The formulas used to describe the one network bear a formal resemblance to those used to describe the other. Measurement begins by establishing these similarities, and it

This paper is based in part on work supported by National Science Foundation Grant NSF 1G 65-16 to the University of Pennsylvania. I express my appreciation to R. D. Luce and D. N. Langenberg, who kindly read a rather different earlier version, and to Nelson Goodman, who years ago suggested measurement theory as a field worthy of study.
Numerals placed within / / relate to references following this essay.

proceeds by exploiting them through a set of scaling rules which constitute a functional rule for assigning numbers to empirical things. A specification of the rule (as by choice of unit) constitutes a scaling or mapping function which in effect determines a class of numerical formulas as empirically significant of the relations associated with the property name. Measurability does not depend on scaling, but measurement depends on measurability and, in a reasonable usage, on scaling as well.

The property balance-mass is an example of what N. R. Campbell regarded as a fundamentally measurable property /1,2/. This is because relations of interest to us, through which it is marked a measurable, are such as can be reported, using a suitable rule, with the numerical equality and inequality formulas governing addition. Campbell did not point out, but others have since /5,7,15/, that the same empirical relations can be mapped into other numerical relations, e.g., those expressed by formulas governing multiplication. Though it matters which we do, there is nevertheless a clear sense in which it is conventional to think of adding weights to a balance pan as adding to, rather than as multiplying, the mass effect of what is there. The extensivity relations, as we might call them, admit both of additive and multiplicative scalings, among others.

Numerical Laws

Typically a set of empirical entities stands in many more than one measurement-structured relational network. Some of these networks may be considered to be associated with some one property, as is the case with the two-pan balance, substitution balance, spring balance, etc., relationships that provide alternative ways of measuring mass. Other of these networks are associated with other properties, e.g., density, volume, temperature, pressure, viscosity, and so on. Often we find conditions under which interesting correlations obtain between the empirical relationships of entities in networks relevant to one property and the empirical relationships of those same entities in networks relevant to one or more other properties. These correlations may be captured for us in what Campbell and others have called numerical laws, e.g., $V = RI$, $M = DV$, $PV = kT$, $s = \frac{1}{2}gt^2 + vt + s_o$. Once this is done, the scaling assignments for, and ultimately the empirical relations of, a network relevant to one such property can be had from the scaling assignments relevant to others. Since this is the effect of a measurement of the first property, one speaks of having measured the property derivatively, through a numerical law.

Numerical laws are often held to be among the most important kinds of scientific law, to the achievement of which measurement is often regarded as merely auxiliary. In view of this it is of some interest to investigate the kinds of empirical correlation reported in numerical laws, and how the forms of these laws are related to empirical matters and to the choices made in measuring properties. In this paper some basic points are made relative to these problems, primarily through the study of two of the simplest sorts of numerical laws. Ohm's law is an example of one that Campbell alleges involves three fundamentally (extensively) measurable properties, and which therefore permits the derivative measurement of what can also be measured fundamentally. The familiar relation of density, mass, and volume is an example of a law in which, Campbell tells us, only two of the three properties are fundamentally measurable, so that the third is measurable only derivatively. Both laws have been called definitions —of resistance and of density, respectively. For that reason both are particularly relevant to investigating the interplay of the empirical and the conventional. Of course such a limited consideration cannot claim comprehensiveness, yet the results may be expected to have more general application.

The empirical-conventional contrast is a nest of problems in its own right. For our purposes it will do to say that the empirical is that which is characteristic of the way things are, while the conventional is that which is determined by our (inventive) decision in reporting the way things are. We shall not discuss what it means to distinguish the way things are from our reporting of them, nor the conventionality of reporting itself, nor the relative arbitrariness of some decisions and the relative constraint of others. Taking the concept for granted we shall try to indicate some of the respects in which numerical laws might be constituted in part through convention.

Ohm's law will be studied first. We shall ask what empirical matters it is reporting to us, what is presumed about the identity and measurement of its relevant properties, how much its form is determined by empirical matters if the usual measurement of those properties is presumed, and what influences those conventional choices that remain to be made. The density relation will be discussed in a similar way. Then we will consider the bearing of the difference between ordinal and transordinal measurables on conventional delimitation of law forms. Finally we will note the interaction of conventional decisions about law forms and about the measurement of the individual properties involved.

Ohm's Law

Ohm's law will be cited in the specialized form that applies to direct current electrical circuit elements that are "pure resistances" (no batteries, generators, motors or other seats of non-electrostatic electromotive force) : "The ratio of the voltage (potential) difference between two points on a conductor to the current flowing through it between these points is a constant (at fixed temperature) known as the resistance." This is usually symbolically written: $V = RI$. This equation is often supplemented with information about the "units" used in the measurement of the several properties.

We wish to ask what this law is telling us about what. It cannot be the primary function of Ohm's law to disclose something about the number system, of course. The talk about constants and ratios has to do with numbers at least some of which are scaling values. The alliterative variables of the equation refer us to the same. We ought to be able to decode the equation and read a message concerning empirical matters.

OHM'S LAW AS REPORT OF PROPORTIONAL COVARIATION

Let us suppose we have additive scaling values for various "pure resistance" conducting objects x helping to constitute various circuits n in respect both of voltage (difference) and current. If we tabulate and examine the results, we find that some of the objects x are such that in all of a wide range of circuits in which they are employed the ratio of the voltage and current values is the same. The remainder of the "pure resistance" objects are such that the ratio of the voltage and current values is not a constant over circuits except perhaps over a very narrow range of these values. If for the moment we separate off the latter as "anomalous" and consider only the "normal" objects x, we can summarize our tabulation with the following formula:

(1) $(x)(n)((x$ is a normal object $\cdot\ n$ is a circuit $\cdot\ x$ is
ingredient to $n) \supset V(x,n)/I(x,n) = V(x)/I(x) = c(x))$,

where $c(x)$ is constant over n but is in general dependent on x. This formula can be considered the primary basis of Ohm's law.

[24]

In terms of it we can see that Ohm's law is significant at least of a "joint covariation" of the "(relative) locations" of objects in each of the two extensive networks achieved for voltage and current. At the risk of laboring the obvious we enlarge a bit on what we are being told by (1) : For a given object in various circuits the order of those circuits in terms of a current operation is the same as their order in terms of a voltage operation. Furthermore, if one such circuit is operationally twice another in respect of voltage, it is twice another in current too.[1] If object a is voltage-equivalent to object b in circuit m, but thrice object b in current; and if a is in circuit n twice object b in voltage; then a is six times b in n in respect of current. Many other such empirical facts are reported or implied with the help of (1). Let us call such covariation "(operational) proportional covariation". As objects that are alike in having voltage may differ greatly in the specific voltage they have, so objects alike in having the proportional covariation property differ greatly in the specific proportional covariation they have. While an object's specific voltage is associated with its location in an extensive voltage network of relations, at this point we have mentioned no means to say how greatly objects might differ in specific covariation, or even to order them in this respect.

RESISTANCE AS PROPORTIONAL COVARIATION

OF VOLTAGE AND CURRENT

It is reasonable to suggest that the resistance of x is simply the specific proportional covariation of x.[2] But if resistance is even an ordinal property (i.e., if objects are quasi-serially ordered[3] in resistance), the concept of proportional covariation will have to be augmented to permit the identification. Indeed if Campbell is right that resistance is an independent extensive measurable, then in place of (1) we should be able to get the following formula, much closer to Ohm's law, as an empirical result:

(2) (x) (n) (x is normal and ingredient to $n \supset R_j(x) =$
$c_{ijk} V_i(x,n)/I_k(x,n)$),

---

[1] The words 'twice' and 'thrice' refer to empirical extensive relations which under an additive mapping make these terms appropriate.

[2] The discussion takes for granted that the concept of resistance is not exhausted in resistance value (nor that of voltage in voltage value.)

[3] Quasi-serial order is order in which several objects may occupy the same rank /8/.

where i, j, and k index independent scalings for voltage, resistance, and current respectively, and c_{ijk} is a constant dependent on these scaling choices. Equation (1) is a numerical law, but to represent proportional covariation as described so far, an indefinite variety of functions of $V(x,n)/I(x,n)$ could be substituted for the latter. Hence (1) is a conventional choice, in its form. Similarly, if we try to represent both the suggested putative definition of resistance and a definition of a resistance scaling as well in a formula, we might employ:

$$(3) \qquad r_j(x) = V_i(x)/I_k(x),$$

where j merely reminds us of the specific pair of scalings i and k. Obviously this formula is as much, and as little, a response to facts as (1) is a report of them.

A NARROWER BASE FOR A DEFINITION

Before we attempt to augment the proportional covariation concept, we briefly consider two competitive suggestions for a foundation of a definition of resistance. The first is that the resistance of an object be defined as the voltage drop across it for some specified current through it (i.e., as its voltage network location when it has a specified current location). This suggestion has to reckon with the fact that while various reference or unit currents have been used or proposed, none has been singled out as especially significant for the characterization of resistance. Moreover various objects are attributed resistance for which the current achievable without their destruction is much smaller than historically proposed reference currents.

A BROADER BASE FOR A DEFINITION

A second suggestion is that the resistance of an object in any given circuit is just the concurrence of its voltage and current locations in that circuit. According to it, we would perhaps describe normal objects as having a linear resistance characteristic, while anomalous objects have any of a variety of non-linear resistance characteristics. This proposal does not square with some familiar usage, in particular that which, in representing the resistance of an object as a "constant ratio", clearly has proportional covariation unsophisticatedly in view. On the other hand, for objects not having constant V/I values over a wide range of circuits, one nevertheless often speaks of resistance. Sometimes one says, "The resistance of these objects is (such-and-such) a function of the current through them," or the like. And sometimes, with no attempt to specify a function, one simply calculates the V/I ratio of the object in a given circuit and calls this the resistance of the object in that circuit.

In evaluating the conflicting usage, we must consider the significance of associating "resistance" with V/I ratios. Why does the V/I ratio seem so pertinent, even for objects for which that ratio is not constant over circuits? Why does not the VI product seem pertinent, as it also is not constant over circuits? Surely this is because of the important class of objects exhibiting the proportional covariation reported in (1) and grounding (2). It is this base which makes important the V/I ratio rather than the pair V,I associated with a given object, even for an anomalous object.[4] Nevertheless, we must distinguish between a property and that which makes it important. No doubt we have the right if we wish to call the mere concurrence of a single voltage and a single current "resistance". If we call this the broad sense of the word, then this paper will avoid this broad base for the resistance concept and stay with proportional covariation.

PROPORTIONAL COVARIATION CONVENTIONALLY AUGMENTED

We turn now to the question of augmenting the proportional covariation concept (henceforth often abbreviated to 'PC'). It seems clear that one can distinguish an empirical relation of equivalence in PC that is distinct from equivalence in either voltage or current or both. It is that which would be inferred for a pair x,y from a variety of comparisons of x with y and of each with other objects. These could include observing that x matches y in voltage in any circuit in which it matches y in current, for whatever current. They could also include the matching of objects not equivalent in either voltage or current (as in a suitable operation using a current balance with unequal moment arms).

One cannot distinguish empirical ordering and combining for PC. Here one must decide, among different ranking and combination phenomena which seem to be equally good candidates, those that shall be regarded as relevant to PC. Because of the competition one can perhaps think of the choice as more conventional than those char-

---

[4] If we can write $V = c'(I)^2$ we may also write $V = (c'I)I = R'I$, assimilating the first equation to $V = RI$. But 'R'' does not represent the same kind of covariation as 'R'.

acteristic of concept formation generally. For order those rankings are chosen that give the same order as that of the V/I ratio associated with the objects. These include, for example, the voltage rankings for objects having the same current, whatever the current. For relevant mode of additive combination, those phenomena are chosen that involve combination objects that have a V/I ratio equal to the sum of the V/I ratios of the combined objects, for whatever voltage and current. This mode of combination is series connection.

We consider now what is happening in our judging these rankings and combinings relevant to PC. Again we shall be content with a rough account, sufficient to give the idea. With the use of certain specified circuits, series connection, supplemented with ranking and matching operations, makes possible the establishment of an extensive measurement structured network. Whatever the property we should consider associated with this network, it can thereby be measured independently of voltage and current. The evidence base for equivalence and disequivalence among objects in respect of the series connection property (henceforth often abbreviated to 'SC') is drawn from matchings, rankings and combinings whose testimony is interdependent. (E.g., if x clearly "precedes" y in SC then it cannot be equivalent to y.) The operations that provide PC matchings and dismatchings as an evidence base for PC equivalence inferences are the same as a part of those employed in SC investigations (and are equally independent of voltage and current measurement). Hence the evidence base classes intersect and, although the PC base class includes no rankings or combinings, as an empirical matter both testify to the same equivalence class memberships. For example, an object z which is inferred to be SC-equivalent to the SC-sum of x and y is empirically found (inferred) also to be PC-equivalent to the SC-sum of x and y. It is on this account that SC is judged relevant to the measurement of PC, and may be used along with it to constitute the concept of resistance.

The augmentation of PC with SC is conventional, though obviously not in the sense that on the empirical level SC does not exist or is only the ad hoc correlate of a network of numerical relations of instrumental value in disposing over empirical voltage and current relations. Quite to the contrary, series connection is among the modes of combining objects that figure prominently in useful circuit construction. The augmentation is conventional first in the sense, common to all empirical concept formation, that it need not take place at all. Secondly it is conventional in the sense that PC might be considered the augmenting rather than the primary factor, and sometimes is. Thirdly it is conventional in the more interesting sense that *PC* might have been associated with other modes of ranking and combining, and in particular with the important mode of parallel combination. After all, a voltage-current proportional covariation is a current-voltage proportional covariation. The same equivalence class memberships are indicated by the parallel connection network as by the series. Convening to see series connection as relevant to *PC*, we find (2) as an empirical result (with '*R*' referring to *SC*), on account of which we convene to let '*V/I*' remind of *PC*. Reciprocally, convening to let '*V/I*' represent *PC* we are moved to convene also to see series connection as relevant to *PC* in order to make (2) the proper empirical equation. But all of this goes through just as well if we convene to represent *PC* with '*I/V*', substitute '*I/V*' for '*V/I*' in (2) and understand '*R*' to refer to the parallel connection property.

RESISTANCE AS PROPORTIONAL COVARIATION INDEPENDENTLY
MEASURABLE THROUGH CONNECTION PROPERTIES

Having said these things, one can conjecture that the proper way to look at the matter is to see not only *SC* augmenting *PC* to constitute the resistance concept, but the parallel connection property too, and no doubt some others of importance which we'll make no attempt to characterize. *SC* augments *PC* by providing an order and a mode of extensive combination. Parallel combination augments it by providing, along with further equivalence criteria, an "inverse order" and a mode of "reciprocal combination". These constitute an independent, measurement-structured network which, with respect to its associated property resistance, is not extensive but is able, suitably scaled, to provide the same numerical map with respect to resistance.[5] The third kind of conventionality in the augmentation of *PC*, therefore, amounts to this: that *SC* has been chosen to provide what it provides and parallel combination to provide what it provides, and not the other way around. But for our purposes this kind of conventionality now loses its interest, since it concerns only the choice of an appropriate word, where appropriateness is determined by a theory about what is happening in circuits. The decision to provide all that is provided in the concept of resistance shows conventionality of the first kind again.

[5] This network illustrates non-extensive (relative to resistance, not to conductance) paraordinal and transordinal relations.

[29]

CONVENTIONAL ELEMENTS IN VARIOUS READINGS OF OHM'S LAW

In a sense, Ohm's law summarizes all that has been said in the previous five paragraphs. A formula expressing the law has therefore a heavy burden of information to convey. The usual Ohm's law equation probably succeeds only by being discreetly but multiply ambiguous.

We can illustrate this with the help of Equation (2), whose consequent we rewrite here for convenience:

(4) $$R_j(x) = c_{ijk}V_i(x,n)/I_k(x,n).$$

Equation (2), suitably interpreted, we regard as expressing Ohm's law. Equation (4) we treat merely as an elliptical version of (2), deferring for a moment the question whether it can be understood as a definition. Then we can distinguish several utilizations of the equation.

(i) Equation (4) reports essentially what (1) reports: an empirical voltage-current covariation (by reporting an empirical constancy of ratio). 'V' represents voltage location, 'I', current (and each its respective scaling assignments as well).

(ii) Equation (4) reports the empirical identity of independently assessed SC and PC equivalence classes (on the basis of which SC may be judged relevant to the measurement of PC). 'R' represents SC and also its independently inferred values, 'V/I' represents PC and also its independently inferred values.

(iii) Equation (4) reports the empirical covariation of three independent sets of property locations. 'R' represents SC and its independent values, 'V' and 'I', voltage and current respectively, and their independent values.

(iv) In any of the above three cases the various assertions are empirical inferences from various evidence bases. Used reportively to relate independent "best inferences" the equation would not be true in most cases. Yet in the absence of systematic error one finds one can make the equation true by emendations which are of the same order of magnitude as the uncertainty in a best inference. In accord with the evidence strength of each independent base, one allows the various independent bases to determine proper location or equivalence class assignments for each property in such a way as to make the equation true. In reportive, as over against projective use, therefore, the three cases above do not exist as live options. A reportive version of each case can be achieved in the manner indicated, but we illustrate in terms of a general reportive version of Ohm's law that draws on

[30]

all three cases. On this version Equation (4) reports the judgment that voltage, current, SC, and PC phenomena constitute a common class in the sense that inferences concerning voltage, current, and SC locations and concerning PC equivalence class memberships may be based on evidence drawn from all these phenomena. 'R' stands for the fully augmented resistance concept, 'V' and 'I' for concepts of voltage and current augmented in appreciation of the overarching measurement network recognized in our judgment. These symbols also stand for "best values". The latter are achieved for each property by taking account, in a way weighted by relative evidence strength, of the best independent value achieved for that property and the best independent values of other properties.

This last version of Equation (4) is probably the most general version of Ohm's law. Although there is a sense in which it is conventionally true, the non-directedness of the mutual constraints (apart from the effect of evidence-strength weighting) indicates that the equation is not functioning as a definition for any property or property value.[6] Instead we are recognizing an integration of networks and in effect adopting a single scaling rule for all three properties. This rule contains elements drawn from the scaling rules applicable to the individual properties supplemented by the requirement that the given equation form be strictly satisfied. Equation (4) can no doubt be read as a definition of the resistance of x. To do so requires reading 'V/I' as indicating the fully augmented resistance concept and so is a bit awkward. However, to read (4) in this way does not seem to catch Ohm's law very well.

EMPIRICAL CHARACTER OF OHM'S LAW

The empirical character of (4) is not prejudiced by the indicated conventionality. The empirical character is shown in the fact that series connection procedures make possible sorting of objects into distinct classes within each of which the members stand in extensive relations to one another.[7] One of these classes is the class of normal objects. The extensive relations of a class of anomalous objects are among the

---

[6] Were it not for practical differences, in that resistance is "attached" to objects and current is not, we might treat current as a voltage-resistance proportional covariation.

[7] E.g., suppose four objects intersubstitutable in a specific circuit, two (unknown to us) normal, two anomalous (same covariation law). In other circuits the two normal will balance, and the two anomalous, but not generally one of each.

[31]

phenomena characteristic of another kind of covariation than proportional. To identify the normal class as such is to discover empirically that series connection equivalence classes are the same as those achieved by taking ratios of V and I values. But this sameness means, to talk of scaling values for convenience, that the differences between independently assessed values and those obtained by conventional supplementation of them are of random error size.[8] This, of course, is just what is meant by the empirical satisfaction of an equation.

CONVENTIONAL EVALUATION OF THE OHM'S LAW CONSTANT

It is apparent that the form of (4) depends on scarcely mentioned conventions concerning the scaling rules employed for the individual properties. These will be further considered at the end of this paper. At this point we wish to inquire how additional conventions operate to fix a value or values for c_{ijk} and thus determine what versions of the law will alone be found in use. Three ways of doing this come to mind at once.

In the first place one can merely decide that a certain law shall have a certain standard version, featuring a specified multiplying constant. Conventional groups of scalings (each scaling applicable for a different property) have been distinguished on the basis that if the scalings employed for the various properties involved are all drawn from a single group, each of one or more law equations will have some standard version. Such a group is known as a "system of units", because for additive scalings the specification of the unit (the entity or equivalence class of entities assigned the number one) selects a specific scaling. Only a relatively small number of distinct systems of units have found any considerable employment. Thus the name of any given law is associated with a small number of standard versions.

A second conventional way of limiting versions consists in defining the unit for one property, with the help of a particular version, in terms of values assigned an entity on specified scalings for the other two properties. (This is not necessarily implied by the convention just discussed.) For example, suppose that the volt-unit scaling for voltage and the ampere-unit scaling for current already belong to a conventional system of units for wider reasons than their contribu-

---

[8] When for the convenience of simplicity one requires satisfaction of equations such as $s = \frac{1}{2}gt^2$, $T = k(L/g)^{\frac{1}{2}}$, and $h = (a^2+b^2+c^2)^{\frac{1}{2}}$, irrational numbers enter scaling duty, as best value estimates. Because of law linkages one's effective scaling rule may be monstrously complicated.

tion to a version of Ohm's law. Then we might specify a (new) unit of resistance, the ohm, as instanced in any (pure resistance) conducting element between whose end points there obtains a potential difference of one volt while a current of one ampere is flowing through it.[9] To do so reduces (4) to:

$$(5) \qquad R_j(x) = V_i(x,n)/I_k(x,n).$$

As in the case of (4), (5) is a constraint upon the assessment of the various scaling values it relates for various objects x and circuits n. It is the result of removing the constant c_{ijk}, which depends on neither x nor n, from the mutual adjustment process.[10]

If we make a definition in terms of a single version of an equation, not just for the ohm, but for units of resistance generally, we have a further incorporation of convention in the utilization of laws. In the present case we might stipulate that the unit of resistance is to be any entity that passes unit current at unit voltage drop across its terminals, both units being drawn from a common system. This convention limits standard versions to one, and may be what some have in mind who speak of Ohm's law as a definition.

The Density Equation, $M = DV$

DENSITY AS PROPORTIONAL COVARIATION IN
MASS AND VOLUME

The density relation, $M = DV$, Campbell describes as a formula in which two of the properties are measurable fundamentally, while the third, density, is measurable only derivatively (through $M = DV$ in fact). By an argument similar to that used for resistance, the density of an entity can be presented as basically a specific proportional co-variation between mass and volume network locations. This covariation is exhibited by all the entities constituted "homogeneously" by the same "material" or "substance" as that which homogeneously constitutes the entity in question. It is such that we can write,

---

[9] If we select some object as unit, improved measurements can force us to work with, say, $V = 1.0001 \, RI$.

[10] The triple covariation of voltage, current, and resistance is a fourth property, no doubt, but an uninteresting one. It takes on identical values in all normal objects and for all circuits. All are the same in respect of this property.

(6) $(x)(y)((x$ is a substance $\cdot\ y$ is a sample of $x) \supset$
       $f(M_i(y,x)/V_k(y,x)) = C(x))$,

where $C(x)$ is constant for all samples y of x, but in general varies
with x, and where f is any of a great variety of well-behaved functions.
The quasi-serial order of objects in respect of density, together with
any "transordinal" stucture, must be supplied, if these are to be had
at all, by augmentation of the proportional covariation concept.
Equivalence classes can be determined for this property, however,
perhaps even independently of the measurement of mass and volume.
(For example, consider a balance whose moment arms are in the ratio
1 : 2 and are tipped with cups of identical construction, two on one
arm and one on the other.) What we lack, if Campbell is right, is a
class of extensive phenomena that can be seen as relevant to proportional covariation phenomena. Without it we have no way to determine
the unit function as uniquely appropriate (within a multiplying constant) for f in (6).

DENSITY AS SINKABILITY

Campbell seems to think of density as primarily a "sinkability" property. We infer equivalence for intercomparable samples of substances
which neither sink nor rise in one another, order from less to greater
according as samples sink in few or many other samples, respectively.
The empirical identity of the sinkability quasi-serial order and that
of mass-volume covariation provides a way, if I understand Campbell
correctly, to measure the former through the latter property. However the covariation has no order of its own. We must either see him
as proposing a conventional augmentation of concept, or as identifying sinkability order with the order of M/V values conventionally
chosen to represent proportional covariation. If we choose the former
then we can look at the matter the other way around from Campbell
and find the order of sinkability relevant to the ordering of proportional covariation because of identity of independently assessed
equivalence classes. This works only over part of the domain of objects
having density, but otherwise is a reasonable augmentation. Still, it
does not provide an extensive augmentation, of course.

LIMITED EXTENSIVITY

While there seems to be no candidate for a relatively unrestricted
mode of combining objects with respect to mass-volume covariation,

[34]

one can in fact establish networks of extensive or approximately extensive relations over restricted domains of substances with various operations of limited utility. For example, let small, hollow, light, but rigid spheres be formed by some uniform manufacturing process (no worse than insisting on uniformity in constructing balance arms). Let amounts of the same gas be admitted to two of these and let them be tested for equivalence in density by balancing each against the other on a pan balance. (The measurement of mass is not presumed.) Now let the gas from one sphere be forced into the other, say by displacement with a liquid in which it is little soluble. This is a "two", and we find another by admitting an amount of the same or some other gas into one of the spheres, testing for equivalence as before, and so on. A procedure for liquids would use an equal-arm balance with a pair of identically constructed cups suspended from the knife-edge on one side and a third cup of the same construction on the other side. This apparatus would permit us to find a "two" substance in density given two "one" substances (or two samples of a "one" substance.) It would also permit us to add non-equivalent substances in respect of density. Variation in the moment arm ratios or in the number of equivolume cups would permit more sophisticated assessments. The procedure could also be extended to machine-shaped solids.

Obviously an indefinite number of other operations can be devised which have about the same claim to be relevant to extensive assessment of mass-volume proportional covariation without presuming the prior measurement of mass or volume. As a class, however, these operations are characterized by their limitations. They apply to a subset of the domain of the covariation property, or they employ modes of combination of considerable complexity but little practical utility outside a measurement operation. It would be imaginable but limited and esoteric use of two liquids (centrifuging?) that made significant that mode of combination which has them filling separate identically constructed containers. On the other hand, where modes of combination for given volumes of solids or fluids are in common use, as in mixing and alloying, one finds no ready way of construing the combination as addition in respect of covariation. The combining of objects readily seen as addition in voltage-current covariation is simply achieved, of pervasive utility in a great variety of electrical circuitry, and of interest essentially throughout the domain of normal objects. By contrast the extensive density relations appear utterly contrived and ad hoc.

[35]

MIXED EMPIRICAL/CONVENTIONAL RESTRICTION OF EQUATION FORM

Nevertheless, where an additive mode of combination has enough practical use to occur now and then outside a measuring operation, it comes to contribute to the density concept. It is advantageous to reflect the extensive relations rather than to ignore them, and more conventional to do so than in the resistance case only to the extent that it is less widely useful. But where it is useful the ordinary form (within a multiplying constant) of the density relation appears as an empirical result. Elsewhere, many more practical modes of combination could be as transparently represented, if less simply, in equations of quite different form.[11] For simplicity, we conventionally choose for our general equation that which in the specialized cases is required for factuality (given certain other conventions of course) and not just for simplicity.

The density relation becomes, in elliptical form:

$$(7) \qquad D_j(x) = C_{ijk} M_i(y,x)/V_k(y,x).$$

A BROADER BASE FOR A DEFINITION

Equation (7) is similar in many respects to Ohm's law. The constant C_{ijk} can be conventionally evaluated in ways much like those already explained. Furthermore, just as the significance of 'resistance' can be broadened so that it applies to an anomalous object while in a particular circuit in view of its voltage and current locations in that circuit only, so the significance of 'density' can be broadened so that it applies to a sample of a nonhomogeneous substance in view of the mass and volume locations of the one sample. When this is done, the symbol 'D' may come to be used to represent a mass-volume correlation (over samples of a substance x at different locations in a medium, or samples at different temperatures or pressures, etc.) quite different from those for which M/V turns out to be a constant over x. By this means the equation describing the covariation that does exist is assimilated in form to the density relation, $M = DV$.

CONTRAST BETWEEN DENSITY RELATION AND OHM'S LAW

The chief difference between the density relation and Ohm's law lies in the fact that density, unlike resistance, is not for practical pur-

[11] Of course to choose simplicity here would be no more scandalous than to choose it where scaling an extensive network. There too we could employ complex formulas.

poses a transordinal measurable over its domain. The possibility of a limited independent extensive assessment of density restricts the form of the equation. Over a considerable subset of the domain, however, no such independent extensive assessment would ever be carried out. Hence best values for density would be determined simply by taking the ratio of best values for mass and volume. There might well be covariation-relevant matching or ranking operations in use which might be independently influential in determining best values for mass and volume, and covariation itself might sometimes be independently assessed for equivalence. But these could at most speak to the relative order and identity of those values. This is only to say again that as a practical matter, the form of the density relation is not empirically constrained over the whole domain, and it does not have empirical instantiations over the whole domain. It is a conventional relation in a stronger sense than Ohm's law, whose conventionality is consistent with its having empirical instantiations only.

At first sight this seems a bit strange. For simplicity, let us suppose density is unproblematically ordinal. An ordinal property can be independently ordinally scaled, and the choice allowed by an ordinal scaling rule indicates that the set of ordinal scalings constitutes a group in which any two members differ by a monotonic transformation /7,14/. Suppose one now wishes to restrict this choice by requiring that a law equation in which the property figures have a stipulated form. The logic of such a restriction in some respects does not differ from that of the restriction on the scalings of the Ohm's law properties designed to make the multiplying constant unity. In both cases one can look at the situation as though a single scaling rule were created for all the properties involved.

But with this similarity between the two cases goes a notable difference. In the Ohm's law case resistance scaling values for all objects are, through extensive relations, linked to that of any one object in such a way that defining the unit of resistance in terms of the other units fixes the constant with value one for all objects. But where we have only ordinal relations for a property, its scaling values are linked only as to order, and we must fix the scaling value for each object separately in terms of the law equation. Requiring the satisfaction of the equation destroys the independence of the ordinal scaling except in respect of relative order of the numbers. The mutual dependency indicated by this exception keeps the equation from expressing a sheer definition for the value of the ordinal measurable, although it may express such for the values of one or more specified objects.

[37]

Law Forms and Extensive Measurability

EXTENSIVE RELATIONS MORE THAN MEANS FOR SCALING ORDINAL

Campbell apparently did not think of an ordinal property as independently measurable at all. He seems to have believed that an ordinal property becomes something worth thinking of as measurable only by association with the object- (or substance-) dependent constant in a numerical law (i.e., with the covariation property of two extensive measurables). One can see some point to this. A covariation property, or an ordinal property associated with such, is linked with extensive properties in such a way that some facts about objects in respect of the latter are empirically implicated by facts about these objects in respect of the former. This gives the ordinal property an importance beyond that of its own order structure. Moreover for this reason the numerical law provides a non-*ad hoc* rule for scaling an ordinal measurable that does not require a separate scaling decision for each newly investigated object, as an ordinal scaling rule does. Nevertheless where order relations are of practical interest, and reasonably well-defined, there is point to an ordinal scaling, even in the absence of an association with a covariation of extensive measurables. This is particularly true if there is an association with a covariation of, say, other ordinals. Insofar as Campbell's view represents more than a terminological decision, it seems to represent a lack of appreciation of the significance of ordinal structures (and of non-extensive structures generally).

On the other hand, some have taken positions which, insofar as they in turn are not terminological variants, tend instead to minimize the significance of transordinal structures (and non-ordinal structures generally).[12] The view of Brian Ellis /5/ is a notable example. He seems to regard ordinal relations as not only necessary to all measurement but peculiarly definitive of what is meant by measurement. Transordinal relations he treats as if they were relevant only to the kind of procedures used to assign numbers reflecting order. He realizes that the extra-numerical import of a law like Ohm's law consists in more than the covariation of three different ordinals. However in attributing the surplus meaning to scaling procedures, he virtually relegates covariation in extensive structures to something of merely

---

[12] This paper is not concerned to consider all the types of measurement or order structures that have been distinguished. (See: /3,4,10,11,13,14,15/.)

instrumental importance. But both extensive structures and covariations among them are often of great practical importance to us in their own right, and not just as a means of implementing our interest in ordinal structures and covariations. When they are, they are part of what we describe through our measurement conventions, and not just ingredient to those conventions (in a sense in which ordinal relations are not /6,7/). In particular, where one has no more than a covariation of orders, the practical utilization of a form like that of Ohm's law equation is not a convention open to us in general.

COVARIATION OF ORDINALS

Take the case of three properties P, Q, and R whose orders exhibit a regular covariation. Let the covariation of orders be that which one would expect from three extensive properties so related that $P = QR$.

$$x \ominus_P y \supset ((x \ominus_Q y \supset x \ominus_R y) \cdot (x \oslash_Q y \equiv y \oslash_R x))$$
$$x \ominus_Q y \supset ((x \ominus_R y \supset x \ominus_P y) \cdot (x \oslash_R y \equiv x \oslash_P y))$$
$$x \ominus_R y \supset ((x \ominus_P y \supset x \ominus_Q y) \cdot (x \oslash_Q y \equiv x \oslash_P y))$$
$$x \oslash_P y \supset ((y \oslash_Q x \supset x \ominus_R y) \cdot (y \oslash_R x \supset x \oslash_Q y))$$
$$x \oslash_Q y \supset (x \ominus_R y \supset x \oslash_P y).$$

If all three properties have merely ordinal measurement structure, then if each is independently ordinally scaled we would not expect $P = QR$ to be satisfied. However we might think to supplement our scaling rules by requiring the satisfaction of this equation, perhaps by defining the Q value in terms of the P and R values. This requirement turns out to be of dubious utility.

Let w, x, y, z be four of a group of objects already investigated and scaled such that $P = QR$. Also let

$$P(y) = 56, \ P(z) = 45, \ Q(w) = 4, \ Q(x) = 2,$$
$$Q(y) = 10, \ Q(z) = 12, \ R(y) = 9, \ R(z) = 7.$$

Where a is an entity being newly investigated, let z be both P- and R-precedent to a and the latter to y, and let x be Q-precedent to a and the latter to w. Finally, suppose there is no object already investigated that falls between x and w in Q. Then any triple of scaling values for a such that $45 < P(a) < 56$, $2 < Q(a) < 4$, and $7 < R(a) < 9$ will satisfy each of the independent ordinal scaling rules and the order covariance reflecting numerical statements (e.g., $P(x) = P(y) \supset [(Q(x) = Q(y) \supset R(x) = R(y)) \cdot (Q(x) < Q(y) \equiv R(y) < R(x))]$). But no such triple will satisfy $P = QR$. Alternatively, if $Q(a)$ is chosen to satisfy $P = QR$ it must lie between 5 and 8 in value, and so

[39]

cannot correctly represent to us the fact that a is Q-precedent to w unless we are willing to rescale parts of one or more the three networks. The general need to rescale to obtain satisfaction of $P = QR$ makes the requirement pointless in practice. The conjunction of the numerical statements reflecting order covariance expresses the law obeyed by the entities and is the appropriate numerical law equation for this case.

The state of affairs is the same if one has two ordinal properties and one extensive, for all covariations are of orders only. It seems that what is important to the practical conventional utilization of an equation of form $P = QR$ is a covariation in extensive relations.[13]

Law Forms and Scaling Rule Type

As we mentioned in the introductory paragraphs of this paper, extensive relations can be scaled additively or multiplicatively (and not alone thus). The effect is the same as if we had a single overarching scaling rule in which multiplicative and additive scalings were among options to be exercised by this or that conventional specification of the rule. Such options are obviously more consequential than the options of unit specification allowed by the additive rule itself. The physical combinations which on one option are mapped into numerical sums on the other are mapped into products. Hence the scaling rule specification conventionally determines the form of the numerical equations used to express relations within individual measurement networks. Reciprocally, of course, our preference for a certain map can conventionally decide for a certain mapping option rather than another.

A scaling rule specification also conventionally determines the form of the numerical equations used to express covariations among locations of objects in each of several networks. Let independent additive scalings of three networks lead to an empirical equation of form $P = kQR$. Now let the additive rule for P be replaced by a multiplica-

---

[13] This covariation might possibly be mediated through a covariation in ordinal properties derivatively measured. We cannot discuss here whether other transordinal relations than extensive would serve; /9,12,14,15/ are relevant. Similarly we must neglect the so-called "associative" or "vicarious derived" measurement, as in that of temperature by length /5,11/. It is of interest because the form $P = Q$ could apparently be realized conventionally for two ordinals.

tive rule. A "sum-mapped" value $P(x)$ is related to the "product-mapped" value $P'(x)$ by the functional rule, $P(x) = logP'(x)$.[14] Accordingly the form of the law equation becomes $logP' = k'QR$, where again the value of the constant is subject to further conventional restriction. From the standpoint in which we have alternatively specified the same rule, both of these forms would be legitimate variant versions, just as a choice of additive scaling unit yields variant versions differing in the value of k (or k').

But again the convention can work the other way. If we decide to employ one form of law equation rather than another of the same empirical import, we are making a choice akin to restricting k (or k') to the value one. As the preference for a certain scaling rule specification determines the form both of the equations expressing individual property relations and of those expressing covariations among properties, so preferences for certain forms of both sorts of law equation operate to limit conventionally the rule specifications we employ.[15]

---

[14] We are not speaking hypothetically. To map multiplicatively is equivalent to mapping additively and transforming. Kindred transformations are in regular use.

[15] One is reminded of the debate over the conventionality of the metric of space. Spatial intervals cannot be compared for length except by mediation of relations (near and remote) among objects (or energy distributions). On the other hand, one's interest in the latter is the only reason for being interested in the former. It is the interconnection between object-extensive relations (near and remote) and various object-covariation relations than can alone be of empirical interest. Hence a change in "the metric of space" can be regarded as a special case of a change in scaling rule for the property "object-length" (presented as a function of spatial location). In general, changes in scaling rules might complicate network equations but simplify covariation equations, or vice versa. Hence overall system economy might conceivably lead us to accept a non-standard scaling rule (i.e., a "non-standard metric"). Pythagoras's Theorem and law equations relating length to angles, areas, volumes and non-spatial properties show that for millenia we have been willing to complicate "metrical" relations (with irrationals) in the interest of system economy through simplification of "geometrical" and non-spatial relations, entirely apart from the question of relative location in space. These considerations open the door to suggesting non-standard scaling rules for other properties where a gain in system economy could result.

References

1. Campbell, Norman Robert, *Physics: The Elements* (New York: Cambridge University Press, 1920. Republished as *Foundations of Science* (New York: Dover, 1957).

2. Campbell, Norman Robert, *An Account of the Principles of Measurement and Calculation* (New York: Longman's, Green, 1928).

3. Coombs, C. H., *A Theory of Psychological Scaling* (Ann Arbor: Ann Arbor Publishing, 1952).

4. Coombs, C. H., *A Theory of Data* (New York: John Wiley & Sons, 1964).

5. Ellis, Brian, *Basic Concepts of Measurement* (New York: Cambridge University Press, 1966).

6. Grunstra, Bernard R., Review of Brian Ellis, *Basic Concepts of Measurement*, in *Philosophy of Science* 34 (1967), 288–291.

7. Grunstra, Bernard R., "On Distinguishing Types of Measurement", *Boston Studies in the Philosophy of Science*, Vol. V, Cohen, Robert S., and Wartofsky, Marx W., eds. (Dordrecht: D. Reidel, 1969), 253–303.

8. Hempel, Carl G., *Fundamentals of Concept Formation in Empirical Science*, Vol. II, No. 7 of *International Encyclopedia of Unified Science*, Neurath, Otto, and others, eds. (Chicago: University of Chicago Press, 1952).

9. Luce, R. Duncan, "On the Possible Psychophysical Laws", *Psychological Review* 66 (1959), 81–95.

10. Luce, R. Duncan, and Tukey, John W., "Simultaneous Conjoint Measurement: A New Type of Fundamental Measurement", *Journal of Mathematical Psychology* 1 (1964), 1–27.

11. Ross, Strange, *Logical Foundations of Psychological Measurement* (Copenhagen: Munksgaard, 1964).

12. Rozeboom, William W., "The Untenability of Luce's Principle", *Psychological Review* 69 (1962), 542–547.

13. Rozeboom, William W., "Scaling Theory and the Nature of Measurement", *Synthese* 16 (1966), 170–233.

14. Stevens, Stanley Smith, "Measurement, Psychophysics, and Utility", *Measurement: Definitions and Theories*, Churchman, C. West, and Ratoosh, Philburn, eds. (New York: John Wiley & Sons, 1959), 18–64.

15. Suppes, Patrick, and Zinnes, Joseph L., "Basic Measurement Theory", *Handbook of Mathematical Psychology*, Vol. X, Luce, R. D., Bush, E. R., and Galanter, E. H., eds. (New York: John Wiley & Sons, 1963).

THREE

The Consequences

ROBERT J. ACKERMANN

IT IS MY intention in this paper to discuss utilitarianism, and to offer some reasons why it cannot be regarded as a completely satisfactory normative theory of ethics. I do not think that this is a simple matter of utilitarianism being right or wrong, but of its having a much more restricted scope of application than utilitarians have claimed. The way I would like to put my major contention is this. I define a decision strategy for a class of decision problems as a *global* strategy if and only if any decision problem in the class can be solved by applying the strategy to the details of the particular problem. A decision strategy is a *local* strategy if and only if it can solve some but not all of the decision problems of the relevant class. My contention is that utilitarian theories provide at best local strategies for wide classes of moral-decision problems for which utilitarians have claimed successful global strategies.

Lashing out like this at a popular theory has the difficulty that my criticism is directed at a fairly amorphous target. There are many varieties of positions that describe themselves as utilitarian. What should we take as the consequences of regarding oneself as a utilitarian? Historically, utilitarians have been much attracted to the idea that scientific method may be applicable to moral problems. Most utilitarians have held that the problem of which action in a given set of alternative actions in a moral-decision problem is a right action, can be solved by the same kind of objective scrutiny that they take to characterize scientific investigation. To solve the problem, one determines the consequences of the alternative actions, and that one (or one of those) that entails the greatest measurable aggregate goodness among the alternatives is the right action. Utilitarianism is thus marked by a belief that moral problems about which action is right have correct solutions, and that there is a global strategy applicable to finding the solution of any particular problem. The differences between utilitarians reduce to differences about procedures for measuring the aggregate goodness of alternatives. One historical measure is to find the alternative that has the greatest aggregate happiness for the greatest number, a measure that depends upon some further characterization of what is to count as happiness. If a man claims to be a utilitarian, and produces his measure and his strategy, it should be possible to calculate his solution to various hypothetical problems. That this is far from vacuous is seen by the fact that an intuitionist or emotivist could hold that he might respond to unpredictable intuitions or attitudes in new circumstances, so that no global strategy predictive of actual assessments of moral-decision problems would be applicable.

Utilitarianism defines a right action apart from all matters of practical application. In practice, we cannot measure the actual goodness consequent to each alternative in many situations calling for a moral decision. A moral agent, however, cannot be blamed for choosing an action that has the best consequences that it is reasonable for him to expect in the actual circumstances. Because of the difficulties in estimating consequences and their value, utilitarians have held that a moral agent sometimes ought to do something (on the basis of the information available to him) that is not right (on the basis of the utilitarian definition). This distinction enables the utilitarian to partially dodge the enormous difficulties standing in the way of successful application of his theory as a practical guide to moral decision. In this paper I agree to largely overlook the practical difficulties, and stick as closely as possible to the utilitarian's favorite stamping ground of sharply defined, hypothetical cases—cases where we know the alternatives and their consequences with complete theoretical precision.

If all the consequences of the alternatives in a moral-decision problem are to be comparable on a utilitarian analysis, so that the notion of a right action can be defined, we must have some sort of single measure of the goodness of various consequences which can be applied. One possibility is that this measure depends on a single criterion, such as the amount of pleasure enjoyed by human beings. No suitable candidate for such a criterion has been proposed, however, and I think that criticism has pretty well shown that the measure of goodness of alternatives must depend on a number of criteria which the measure must somehow combine to provide comparisons of the value of the consequences of various alternatives. Yet there is a considerable problem in supposing that such a measure can be found. Suppose there are several criteria for evaluating consequences. Then the alternatives in a given situation will, at least in some cases, be *ranked* differently according to the individual criteria. Given this fact, it may even be possible to show that no measure providing comparisons of the alternatives that combine the individual criteria can exist. The technical problem involved is quite analogous to well-known technical problems encountered in attempting to frame so-called social decision functions, such as the problems engendered for rational social decision functions by Arrow's Impossibility Theorem. In the social decision case, the conflicting rankings of given alternatives by individuals cannot be conflated by a rationally defensible principle into a group decision, given certain plausible properties of the individual rankings.[1] In the utilitarian case, a similar problem arises. Conflicting rankings of alternatives may exist when we consider such criteria as total consequent happiness and the equable distribution of that happiness. It would seem that the individual would have the same difficulty in reaching a coherent personal solution as a society might have in reaching a group decision provided that certain properties were true of his preference rankings of various alternatives by means of different criteria. This objection to utilitarianism can be put by saying that a utilitarian measure can be regarded as an internalized group decision function with all of the constraints that are known for such functions. To have an effective global strategy, utilitarianism

---

[1] An interesting recent exposition and discussion is to be found in Y. Murakami's *Logic and Social Choice* (London: Routledge, 1968).

would have to show that the difficult circumstances could not obtain in actual moral-decision problems.

Utilitarianism as a branch of economic welfare theory has an interesting comparison with moral philosophy in this connection. How are certain limited quantities of economic goods to be best distributed among a group of people? For anyone in a position to choose and implement such distributions, this problem must be regarded as a moral problem, or at the very least as a problem with moral components. Utilitarian theory had to be abandoned because economists reached the conclusion that the interpersonal utility comparisons required to make "greatest happiness" or "best consequences" operational could not be given an objective characterization. The assertion that some distribution of economic goods is to be considered preferable to alternative distributions must depend upon some moral assumptions which are taken up as part of the theory suggesting the distribution. It is interesting to observe that global utilitarian theories should have been abandoned in this rather technical context even though they remain as serious contenders in moral philosophy. I suspect the reason is simply this. In economic theory, the obvious measures of the goodness of distributions of goods have led to unacceptable consequences for global strategies that pretend to be value-free. Some distributional problems can be solved in a fairly straightforward way, but many cannot—and their solutions depend on the economist taking a view about what is to be preferred that is morally substantive.[2] Hopes for global strategies in ethics seem to have been kept alive solely by the relative vagueness of the notion of moral goodness.

Utilitarianism holds that nothing but the measure of the goodness of the *consequences* of the alternatives is to have decisional force in suitable problems. In the face of difficulties with describing a suitable measure, utilitarians have often retreated to an indirect argument for the tenability of some form of utilitarianism by arguing that alternative moral theories must give transparently incorrect solutions to certain kinds of moral-decision problems which utilitarianism seems to be able to handle. It is possible to describe putative moral decisions in which an agent must choose between an act that he finds morally reprehensible on traditional grounds, but that has lots of good consequences, and an act that is not morally reprehensible, and

---

[2] See pp. 1–13 of J. de V. Graaff, *Theoretical Welfare Economics* (New York: Cambridge University Press, 1957) for a typical discussion.

has pretty poor consequences. A situation can be described in which allowing an evil agent to die would have better consequences than allowing him to live. If this represents the actual situation, the utilitarian argues that permitting the death is preferable to preventing it, no matter what our intuitions may dictate. We can let this stand for the sort of case from which the utilitarian argues the patent inadequacy of other theories. What is not so often noticed is that the utilitarian who wishes to argue from moral situations which he can describe must give some consideration to the question of whether the situation as he describes it could be an actual moral-decision problem. If he does not, the danger is obvious: we can often describe things from which amazing consequences can be drawn just because the thing couldn't exist due to the fact that its description violates an appropriate notion of logical or physical possibility.

For the purposes of discussing the worth of alternative moral theories, it has always seemed to me to be a mistake to concentrate on fantastic examples. By fantastic examples, I mean cases where a moral agent must choose between murder and murder, or from any set of alternatives each of which he regards as morally reprehensible. I think there is a sense in which such examples, even if they could be actualized, could not represent more than a tiny fraction of the moral-decision problems that exhaust our moral lives. A man wired up to some infernal device that must kill either his wife or his mother depending on some decision which he can control so as to determine the identity of the victim, but which he cannot postpone, has our complete sympathy. It's hard to see how we could blame him in retrospect for whatever he does.

Another familiar, fantastic example is the one involving the woman who is asked to become the mistress of a Gestapo agent in order to save the life of her husband. I don't know why Gestapo agents should be taken on trust by moral philosophers, but they often seem to be. An agent who would scrupulously make such a proposal stretches the bounds of credulity. But even so, we want to know more about this woman. If she already is, as was once said, a loose woman, the moral problem just evaporates. And what about her husband. Is he to be taken as so impoverished of sentiment that he couldn't understand and forget in better circumstances? These considerations suggest that a dozen distinguishable movies could be constructed presenting slightly different moral problems and slightly different reasonable solutions to the problems in each. It is hard to see how any of them could establish just the problem suggested by the brief description of the situation. The description does not give a problem that is definite enough to have a clear solution.

A positive step toward handling fantastic examples can be made if we take into account the patent possibility that not every decision between alternatives with moral value that may confront a moral agent has to be regarded as a moral-decision problem. A decision to be made between alternatives, each of which is intrinsically reprehensible, or involves a certain consequence that is morally reprehensible, may simply not be a moral problem. I want to suggest that it is best regarded not as a moral problem. The reason for this is that the problem has no solution that is acceptable to the agent. It should be pointed out that this situation is somewhat different from a situation in which an agent chooses an action having the least evil among the relevant set of alternatives as the right action. We may consider for purposes of comparison a mathematician whose problem is to prove that the square root of two is an integer. This agent has a problem, but to call it a mathematical problem is misleading, since the problem has no acceptable mathematical solution. The closest integer is no more correct than any of a set of reprehensible acts. In view of this, I think that fantastic examples do not require close discussion as test cases for distinguishing moral theories. We will not regard them as cutting much for or against utilitarianism. There is a sense in which they may indeed cut against the global strategy of any form of utilitarianism that holds that any set of alternative actions having moral value constitutes a moral decision problem, but we are about to observe that not even utilitarianism can adopt a view this permissive about the range of moral problems. We will therefore simply pass over fantastic examples. There is a sufficient difficulty in talking about what the range of alternatives is in quite humdrum but morally essential cases.

The range of alternatives in a given moral situation cannot be simply the set of logically possible futures (in any sensible notion of logical possibility) for any interesting moral theory. To begin with, this set will be typically infinite. This means not only that the moral agent could not examine them all (even in principle) but also that the notion of that alternative with a measure of goodness as high as any may not be well defined. We might always be able to construct logically possible futures with a greater measure of goodness than any that have been specified. Defining the right action would then fall into the same class of activities as defining the greatest integer. Both definitions must fail to single out a unique object or a set of objects having the requisite property.

Utilitarians seem typically to be committed to a definition of a right act which is based on the supposition that the set of physically possible alternatives and their physically possible consequences is the set of moral alternatives to be considered. This is a considerable restriction of the logically possible, but it is far from clear that similar difficulties do not arise. Physically possible alternatives still seem typically to be infinite, and it is not clear that the physically possible alternative with the greatest measure of goodness is a well-defined notion. In view of this fact, it does not seem that the utilitarian is free to describe a set of alternatives that he thinks exhausts the physical possibilities as though it could single out a theoretically precise moral decision problem.

Non-utilitarians seem typically to have supposed that the set of relevant moral alternatives in a moral-decision problem lies at least partly within the decisional control of the moral agent. To begin with, the alternatives may be just those that he is willing to take as the possible moral actions (given his background and beliefs) relative to the situation. On this basis, a non-utilitarian can consistently hold that murder is never a moral alternative for certain moral agents, and that the utilitarian has simply chosen too wide a class of possible alternatives for describing moral-decision problems. The importance of this point can perhaps be explained by an analogy. A coach may have winning as his primary goal, and yet we may very well respect and admire a coach who will not explore certain lines of behavior for his team on the grounds that they violate the intent of the game, if not the rules. In such a case, the probability of winning simply doesn't interest him. Similarly, a moral agent may be interested in maximizing goodness under some measure, but he may not be interested in maximizing goodness by taking any action that entails certain kinds of consequences for other human beings.

With respect to the utilitarian claim that no other theory can handle certain kinds of examples, we see that this conceals at least an arguable claim about what should be taken as the proper set of alternatives confronting a moral agent. Consider the murder case again. More concretely, let us suppose a moral agent to have been in a position to let Hitler drown, or to have tossed him a life-ring, with certain consequences alleged to follow from each. Using a distinction introduced before, a utilitarian may claim that the right act was to permit the drowning, but the agent ought to have tossed the life ring due to his state of understandable ignorance. But we can reject the whole problem as relatively meaningless. It's also possible that if these alternatives had existed, then the agent who let Hitler live saved a man who crowded out a more efficient but politically less ruthless dictator who would have eliminated human life with a developed nuclear device. The indirect defense of utilitarianism which depends on examples that are too hot for alternatives theories to handle seems to depend on an uncritical use of a certain notion of alternative possibilities which can well be challenged. In giving such examples, the utilitarian often seems to restrict physical possibilities in a manner that is at least as, if not more, mysterious than the decisional restrictions adopted by the non-utilitarian.

I am nowhere claiming that consequences are never the test of right and wrong—they are a complete test only where consequences are all that matter. This remark should be interpreted within the utilitarian conception of what measurable consequences of actions must be if utilitarianism is not to be trivialized. For example, if "good consequences" can comprise that certain intentions are carried out, or that certain people continue to respect the agent, utilitarianism (on such a construal) could be accepted by nearly every philosopher except an outright moral skeptic. Quite often, it can be shown that features other than measurable consequences matter a great deal in the context of a moral decision. This suggests that even an improved defense of some utilitarian position can be shown to offer at best a local strategy. To avoid puzzling abstractions, I want to sketch out a rather definite moral problem. We can imagine that Jones, a professor of philosophy, faces a crucial vote on an important issue in the next department meeting. I take it that this example is close enough to actual academic experience to be shown possible by having been actualized. Jones should examine the consequences of his possible vote for proposal *A* (let us call it) or his failure to vote for proposal *A*. In an actual case, however, Jones may realize that hearts have hardened to the point where the vote will go heavily for proposal *A* no matter how he votes, or how he argues for his vote. We let this be the actual circumstances surrounding the vote. In utilitarian terms, it doesn't matter how Jones votes on the proposal if it will pass anyway. If there are no consequences of this group-decisional kind, are there any consequences that matter, or should we regard Jones as free to make a moral decision by flipping a coin? Let us suppose further that Jones has only two close friends in the department, and that they take opposite sides on proposal *A* for what they regard as important reasons. Jones may feel compelled to offer an explanation of his vote to his friends. He will then have to think the matter through, even though he knows that a reasoned explanation of either vote will retain both friendships. I like to think of Jones as feeling compelled to think through the issues involved because proposal *A* is about something important, even though he can't influence its adoption one way or another. It is important to realize that a case against the general claims of utilitarianism is provided if such situations can arise, and I believe that they do arise fairly frequently. In such cases, the consequences cancel out in the utilitarian sense, but a moral problem remains because of the nature of the issues involved and the character of the agent. Perhaps then we should not define what act ought to be done, or what act is right, relative only to a set of alternatives, but relative to a set of alternatives and a given moral agent. I think that such a relational view is forced by the phenomenology of the moral situation, and that if it is, consequentialism must be only a partial account of moral decision, an account that can at best apply only to morally identical agents facing morally identical decision problems, or perhaps to agents that are morally identical given some moral decision problem.

I am well aware that everything said to this point is applicable only to what I will describe as classical forms of utilitarianism in which it was thought that utilitarianism could be established by rational argument as the best normative theory of ethics. In its classical forms, utilitarianism held that rational argument could establish the truth of some principle of utility and an associated measure which could lead to an objective solution of the widest class of moral decision problems which would not do very much harm to considered intuitions about moral value.[3] That the current climate of philosophical opinion is not particularly suited to classical forms of utilitarianism can be fairly easily established. In the rest of this paper, I want to discuss two current forms of non-classical utilitarianism. One of these

[3] I have not taken into account the recent controversies about the equivalence or lack of equivalence between act utilitarianism and rule utilitarianism. My remarks are directed primarily at forms of act utilitarianism. If rule utilitarianism is equivalent, no special treatment is required. If, as I suspect, rule utilitarianism is not equvalent, some additional remarks would be required to discuss rule utilitarianism. I think that rule utilitarianism in many forms is not compatible with the principle of utility in any recognizable form, but I do not intend to pursue that here. The interested reader may restrict my remarks to act utilitarianism where it seems required.

holds that a suitable principle of utility can be adopted on various meta-ethical grounds even though rational argument from plausible facts is insufficient; and the other holds that the measure of goodness to be associated with a principle of utility may be irreducibly subjective. Both of these non-classical forms will diverge from classical utilitarianism on a number of substantive points.

Let us examine the first non-classical form on the basis of the following passage:[4]

> [It is] open whether the utilitarian (either act utilitarian or rule utilitarian) is to be thought of as an intuitionist, or emotivist, or a naturalist. He could be any one of the three since, given a certain version of the principle of utility, say "actions are right in so far as they tend to produce the greatest happiness of the greatest number," this could be held to be either (a) a judgment by intuition, (b) an expression of attitude, or (c) an analytic truth. So a decision for, or against, utilitarianism does not commit one to any particular position with regard to intuitionist, emotivist, or naturalistic theories of ethics, and similarly intuitionists, emotivists and naturalists are equally free to accept or reject the principle of utility.

This is a curious passage which I regard as symptomatic of muddles consequent upon taking the contemporary distinction between normative ethics and meta-ethics as though it were clear. A plain reading of this passage suggests, for example, that a naturalist is free to reject an analytic truth. But apart from such minute and easily countered criticism, there remains the obvious fact that this passage sketches a set of logically possible theories of ethics all of which seem to have some unattractive features as a total moral philosophy. In what follows we will discuss just the case of the emotivist-utilitarian, although similar discussions can be constructed for the other positions. It seems to be a considerable problem, in discussing a position like that of emotivist-utilitarianism, whether the distinction between meta-ethics and normative ethics clarifies much of anything, and even whether this distinction is itself coherent. I want to discuss these issues briefly before returning to the main thread of my argument.

A few philosophers have suggested that the distinction between

---

[4] Philippa Foot, *Theories of Ethics* (New York: Oxford University Press, 1967), p. 15. I choose this passage because of the overall excellence of Mrs. Foot's contributions to moral philosophy. It is consequently quite revealing that the distinction should appear unchallenged in her explanation of the organization of this anthology.

normative ethics and meta-ethics is roughly similar to that between science and philosophy of science.[5] I'm going to treat this as the leading candidate for the rationale since it appears fairly frequently in discussion and is the only candidate I know of that points to another distinction which seems relatively unproblematic. A brief examination of this suggestion may therefore prove useful. To begin with, the relationship between science and philosophy of science is itself not clear enough to illuminate the distinction between normative ethics and meta-ethics in any useful way. Suppose, for example, we take it that science provides certain data in the form of theories, explanations, predictions, and so on; and the philosophy of science, proceeding from clear intuitions about the relative status of some of the data, attempts to provide criteria for distinguishing acceptable theories from non-acceptable theories, and so on. On such a basis (and it seems a nearly consensus view in philosophy of science at this level of generality) it would seem by analogy that it would be the object of meta-ethics to provide criteria for evaluating the theories provided by normative ethics. But the common pattern of books on moral philosophy does not support this. Where the analogy suggests that the results of meta-ethical speculation should be used to evaluate such normative theories as utilitarianism, the reader finds instead a blank. Meta-ethical positions are simply not used to evaluate the results of normative ethics, ruling out specific normative theories as untenable. This is very strange. One would expect from an independent characterization that a normative deontologist, who found the meta-ethical arguments for emotivism convincing, would feel embarassment, yet no hints of this are encountered in the typical textbook on moral philosophy.

More positively, if we are to take an analogy between philosophy of science and ethical theory as promising, we must deal with the following problem. The institution of science has provided some relatively fixed points for initiating philosophical speculation. Some contemporary opinions can be set down as crank, or as ill-informed, and this is a helpful guide in choosing paradigms. There is also the important fact that certain historical theories have been decisively repudiated. The fact that theories of the structure of science are intended to rule out repudiated views is often overlooked, because the discussion of rival views is often directed only to the problem of their

[5] See, for example, Richard Brandt, *Ethical Theory* (New York: Prentice-Hall, 1959), 7.

fit with paradigmatic cases of good science. It is a profound error to take philosophy of science as descriptive of scientific behavior. If it were merely descriptive of good (as opposed to bad) scientific behavior, it would still be strongly normative. The problem of choosing paradigm moral judgments is extremely complicated, but if the analogy between distinctions is to be worked out, it seems that we need to attack it. However, this runs counter to the denial made by many philosophers that the philosopher has any differential advantage or expertise in making sound moral judgments. If meta-ethics is indeed supposed to be independent of particular moral judgments in this fashion, then it seems clear that no interesting analogy between meta-ethics and philosophy of science can be worked out.

An analogy might better be found between moral philosophy as it has been practiced and older forms of general epistemology issuing in such positions as naive realism, sense data theories, and so forth. The starting points are reminiscent of each other. In both cases, the problem is not to form judgments, whether perceptual or moral. These occur naturally in abundance. The problem is to evaluate these non-institutionalized judgments by finding criteria for sound judgment, and for resolving conflict between judgments which may arise in sufficiently vague or sufficiently novel circumstances. The development of such a philosophical position is nearly independent of any particular judgment in both cases, and examples have the same artificial quality unless one attempts to understand them in terms of personal experience. If this suggested parallel is worked out in detail, it would seem once again that no foothold is provided for the distinction between normative ethics and meta-ethics. The subject matter remains the naive judgments actually expressed by people, and the philosophy consists in an attempt to find reasonable grounds for evaluating these judgments, so that the philosopher can in principle find the means to construct coherent sets of moral and epistemological data.

Ethical theories can be regarded as attempts to find suitable structures for representing coherent sets of moral judgments expressed by a single individual over a period of time. On this simple basis, traditional positions in moral philosophy can be given a rather different outline from that engendered by the distinction between normative ethics and meta-ethics referred to in textbooks. To obtain an outline, we might simply ask how revisionary of an agent's expressed opinions given in the data of moral judgments a moral philosophy should be. Thinking this through, we might obtain a spectrum of theories like this:

Egoism, emotivism, intuitionism, naturalism,
catholicism, utilitarianism.

In this spectrum, *naturalism* and *catholicism* are used as short labels
for positions that have been frequently discussed in recent literature.
Such a spectrum obviously requires a considerable defense and analysis, and as it stands it seems clear that particular versions of these
general positions might be ordered somewhat differently. It does indicate, however, that emotivism and utilitarianism can provide contrasting answers to the same sort of question. Are there questions
other than the extent of revision that might be raised about the positions indicated? It would seem that such problems as those raised in
connection with cognitivism and generalization can be significantly
raised with respect to each position on the spectrum. The idea here is
that we can ask with respect to each theory what judgments (or what
terms in them) are appropriately regarded as cognitive, and to what
judgments in the data generalization arguments can be legitimately
applied. This approach seems to me to be much more realistic with respect to the complexities faced by each theory in the total range of
expressed moral judgments.

Returning to the original thread of argument, let us suppose that
the distinction between meta-ethical and normative theories can be
made out. In order to suggest more strongly that the distinction does
not lead to a description of morally coherent theories, even though it
may lead to a description of logically viable positions which one may
argue for, let us examine more closely any form of normative utilitarian theory that is held in conjunction with an emotive meta-ethics.[6]
When a philosopher holding such a total position finds someone who
disagrees sharply with him on a moral judgment (for example about
whether Jones should vote for proposal *A*), does he deny that the
principle of utility could be wrong? That is, does he admit that it
might be reasonable to take things other than consequences and their
worth into account? If so, his position collapses into a kind of emotivism when that theory is taken as normative. In other words, he admits
to basing his position on certain attitudes and accepts the fact that
ultimate disagreements in attitude are possible. This position seems

[6] This view is held in one form by J. J. C. Smart, *An Outline of a System
of Utilitarian Ethics* (Charlton, Australia: Melbourne U. Press, 1961).
Smart argues that his utilitarian system can be seen as following from a
sentiment of generalized benevolence. At the same time (pp. 40–41) he
argues that particular moral intuitions cannot yield counter-examples to
utilitarian judgments.

[55]

not to entail the sort of global strategy promised by classical utilitarianism. The other horn is obvious. If the principle of utility must be the grounds of arbitration, then he hardly accepts it on the basis of an attitude, no matter how carefully supported his position may be by subsidiary arguments. We can compare this mongrel moral position to one that could arise in epistemology. A philosopher tells us that with a probability of .90, he thinks that Leibniz's Law is an analytic truth. Does he think that it's an analytic truth, or doesn't he? The mongrel positions are difficult to refute, but this does not seem a source of strength, it seems to be a consequence of vagueness of commitment.

Now let us turn to a consideration of the other form of non-classical utilitarianism, that form in which the measure of goodness for alternatives is taken as a subjective measure. We will call a measure subjective if the goodness of the consequences of the alternative actions in some situation is not determined by a measure that can be applied by the theorist in an objective manner, but depends on what the people affected by the consequences of the alternatives *take* as the goodness of the consequences.[7] Clearly, subjective measures run into serious difficulties with respect to problems that arise when people's assessments clash in the sense that one finds a good consequence just where another finds a bad consequence.

One solution to this problem is to incorporate a principle of justice into the principle of utility invoked. Thus one might require that the assessment of each person affected be treated equally with the assessment of each other affected. The difficulty is that it is not clear how to apply such a principle in particular cases. Here is an interesting recent example. In many communities, it requires a majority of two-thirds to pass certain bond issues. These voting laws are now being challenged by parties who want to pass bond issues and contend that such voting laws violate the one-man, one-vote guideline. A *no* vote on a bond issue is not counted equally with a *yes* vote since it requires two *yes* votes to equal a *no* vote. There seems to be no way of avoiding a troublesome problem which is equivalent to the problem of making interpersonal comparisons of utility in order to adjudicate such disputes. It may even be so that not all such cases can be adjudi-

---

[7] A subjective measure is adopted by Jan Narveson, *Morality and Utility* (Baltimore: Johns Hopkins Press, 1967). See, in particular, p. 91 where *utility* is defined as whatever is thought to be intrinsically good by those affected (except for what they take to be morally good).

cated solely on rational grounds, but require instead to be settled in finer detail by decisions made in the courts.

It cannot be shown that a measure of interpersonal utility comparisons cannot be found, but there are some good reasons to doubt that there are very many hopes for such a measure. Another analogy between philosophical theories of science and ethical theories may prove useful in this connection.[8] In the philosophy of science, it has been seen for many years that the positivist criterion for accepting scientific theories is inadequate, and the criterion that allows acceptance of any theory not incompatible with all of the facts is too permissive. As a consequence, many philosophers struggled to find *the* measure of acceptability—simplicity, cost of conceptual revision, falsifiability, evidential fit, and so forth, that they felt might provide a justification for choosing a single hypothesis from among an appropriate range of alternatives in any context. Each of the proposed criteria will work effectively in certain circumscribed ranges of choice, but they are each easily counter-exampled in their particular forms as global acceptance strategies.[9] Further, there seems to be no hope for finding a master function that is in some sense a weighted sum of individual criteria. The analogy suggests that searching for a single measure and a global strategy for evaluating 'good consequence' will eventually be seen to have been the pursuit of a familiar kind of philosophical will-o'-the-wisp. There consequently seems no good reason to take non-classical subjectivistic utilitarianism seriously until it can actually produce a workable measure for the evaluation of consequences.

[8] I have explored some structural analogies between science and ethics in two previous papers, "Normative Explanation", *Philosophy and Phenomenological Research* 24 (1964), 522–529, and "Consistency and Ethics", *Proceedings of the Aristotelian Society* 1968–1969, pp. 73–86.

[9] The range of alternative scientific theories can be narrowed down (and is narrowed down in practice) by the operations of entrenchment. I suspect that the range of moral alternatives in a moral-decision problem is narrowed down by a similar mechanism. This may be the precise way in which the physical possibilities get cut down to a manageable problem, and the mechanism may depend in typical cases solely on the perceived alternatives that have been utilized in the past record of moral decisions in the agent's society. I think in this way it may be possible to trace a rather subtle use of one of Nelson Goodman's seminal ideas. I would like to express my appreciation to the editors of this volume for inviting me to share in honoring the originality and exactitude of Goodman's important contributions to philosophy and logic.

FOUR

Metaphors for
the Mind

COLIN MURRAY TURBAYNE

For having now my method by the end
Still as I pull'd, it came.
                    JOHN BUNYAN

The Problem

OUR EVERYDAY talk concerning the mind is rich in metaphor and analogy. We say that someone's mind is "shallow" or "deep", his intellect "strong" or "weak", his understanding "narrow", his imagination "vivid", or his judgment "biased". We say that someone "handles" his concepts with competence, or that another "ransacks" his memory for a "lost" thought. Our talk is far more metaphorical than we realize until a speaker destroys the abstractions and exposes the concrete meanings, even if ludicrously: "Although Smith is equipped with a brilliant, razor-sharp mind, nevertheless it is extraordinarily shallow and completely closed, and he fails to exercise it"; "Jones handles his concepts and his pen with competence"; and "Robinson is

The basic research for this paper was done during tenure of a Guggenheim Fellowship in 1966.

[58]

engaged in ransacking his memory and his suitcase". But these mixed metaphors and category mistakes serve not only to disclose the presence of metaphor in our use of such adjectives and verbs to refer to characteristics and operations of particular minds; they serve also to suggest the presence of a hidden analogy in our use of such nouns as "mind", "intellect", and "understanding". We use these nouns as if they denote *things* on the analogy with such nouns as "body", "hand", and "brain".

The use of figurative language in reference to this subject, however, is not confined to laymen. In their accounts of the nature of the human mind and its operations, philosophers also resort to the use of metaphor and analogy. They do so because their subject matter is obscure, confused, and extraordinarily complex. I notice that they use these devices in three main ways.

In the first way, the philosopher, like the layman, uses various metaphors or analogies unsystematically to illustrate the nature of mind as a whole or different aspects of it. Aristotle, for example, used these figures in an attempt to elicit the passive and the active aspects of the mind. The former he called "the place of ideas" (*topos eidon*),[1] and he claimed that "what the mind thinks must be in it just as characters may be said to be on a writing tablet on which as yet nothing actually stands written".[2] The latter he compared to a creator (*poietikos*), to a first principle (*arche*), and to light (*phos*), whose essence is activity (*energeia*).[3] More concretely, he said that the mind "is analogous to the hand (*cheir*), for as the hand is a tool (*organon*) of tools, so the mind is the idea (*eidos*) of ideas".[4] Descartes, puzzled by the problem of the mind's relation to the body, speculated that the mind "resides in" its body like "a pilot in his ship",[5] while Hume supposed that "the mind is a kind of theatre where several perceptions make their appearance, pass, re-pass, glide away, and mingle in an infinite variety of postures and situations".[6] The collection of such illustrations from the account of any one theorist resembles, in the idioms appropriate to metaphor, a mixed metaphor. Here we can readily discern the presence of metaphor or anal-

---

[1] *De Anima* 429a.
[2] *De Anima* 429b.
[3] *De Anima* 430a.
[4] *De Anima* 432a.
[5] *Meditations on First Philosophy* II.
[6] *A Treatise of Human Nature*, Bk. I, Part iv, sec. 6.

ogy, and we can be sure that the theorist himself is aware of its presence. Aristotle did not claim that the mind is a writing tablet or a hand, literally speaking; Descartes that it is a pilot in a ship; or Hume that it is a theatre in which the particular perceptions play their parts.

In the second way, the philosopher develops and sustains one of these metaphors or analogies to make what can be presented as a theory. He specifies various features of his illustration so that they make a system. This system constitutes, in the idioms appropriate to metaphor, an extended or sustained metaphor and, in the idioms appropriate to theories, a model. Plato, for example, who held that "anything of real importance can hardly be set forth except through the medium of the model" (*paradeigma*),[7] described how the method proceeds: "We take something that is less well known and compare it with something else that is better known, and out of the comparison there arises one true notion which includes both of them".[8] But on many occasions he also showed how it works. In the *Phaedrus*, for example, he tried to exhibit the nature and resolution of moral conflict by likening the mind to the composite nature of a charioteer (reason) driving a pair of winged horses, one obedient (spirit), the other disobedient (desire). In the *Republic*, with much the same purpose, he compared the mind to a political community divided into a ruling class, an executive class, and an artisan class. Having specified these features in his model, he was able to deduce parallel features in the thing modelled, and then to confirm their presence by other means.

Of these two ways the second is far more interesting both to the author and his readers. This is so because on the part of the author it involves a whole series of acts of creation tersely described by John Bunyan with reference to his own conception of life as analogous to an adventurous journey, an analogy that he extended and sustained throughout a whole book:

> *For having now my method by the end,*
> *Still as I pull'd, it came.*[9]

Because this method is described, the reader is able to see into the works, as it were, of the author's mind, to see both sides of the com-

---

[7] *Politicus* 277d.
[8] *Politicus* 278c.
[9] *Pilgrims Progress* I.

parison or the paradigm, and to test whether the vehicle is adequate to carry its freight. Here once again both the author and his readers are fully aware of the presence of analogy. Plato did not claim that the mind is a state, literally speaking.

The third way differs from the second roughly as a metaphor is said to differ from a simile. The comparison or paradigm in the literal sense, is no longer overtly made. Instead of saying, for example: "The rulers and guardians are to the state as reason and spirit are to the soul", the author merely says: "Reason rules the soul while spirit guards it". He even omits to add: "metaphorically speaking". This way resembles the second, however, in that the collection of assertions constitutes a system corresponding to the original extended metaphor. Now an effective metaphor, invented by a genius and extended by him to make an entire theory, tends to pass into another stage of its life. It passes from conscious metaphor into unconscious myth, from make-believe into belief. The passage is made more rapid if the machinery of the comparison is hidden either by the inventor or by his followers.

Now a main problem in the philosophy of mind, it seems to me, is the problem of bringing to the surface these extended metaphors submerged or partially submerged in the accounts of the influential metaphysicians of the past.[10] In this way we can discover the nature of the conceptual scheme with which we operate. This is a problem of peculiar interest and difficulty requiring detective skill. The clues provided are found in the finished vocabulary of the theory that has come down to us. Strictly speaking, the vocabularies of the original model and the thing modelled should be different, but in practice the vocabulary of the former rubs off onto that of the latter. All this is a problem of analysis. Its solution is found when, having become to some degree aware of the metaphors involved, we proceed to reuse them instead of being used by them. But there is another main problem, one of synthesis. Having brought to the surface the submerged metaphors, need we use the same ones? If we are aware, we can stop and think. We can choose our metaphors. We are no longer duped citizens of the city-state of Oz but the Wizard of Oz himself. In our search for the best possible metaphors we can either use the old ones or, if these are worn out by overuse, invent new ones.

---

[10] Colin Murray Turbayne, *The Myth of Metaphor* (New Haven: Yale University Press, 1962). Revised edition (Columbia, S.C.: University of South Carolina Press, 1970).

The Mind as a Subject Owning Predicates

Far more deeply entrenched in our conceptual scheme than such representations of the human mind as a theatre, as a pilot in his ship, as a charioteer driving two horses, and as the composition of the ruling, executive, and artisan classes of a political community, is the conception in which the mind and its states and operations are represented in the idioms appropriate to a fundamental feature of grammar, specifically to the subject and the predicate of an indicative sentence.

So elementary is the subject-predicate distinction in grammar, known to us all from our first lessons in analysis and composition, that one hardly needs to specify its main features. Traditionally four features of this model dominate our modern conception of the mind. First, the human mind is represented as a particular thing or substance which, on the analogy with the subject of a sentence, has embedded in it the ideas of self-subsistence, of completeness, and of independence. Thus it is able to stand alone. Second, the states and operations of this thing, the mind, are represented as activities or qualities or attributes of it which, on the analogy with the predicates ascribed to a subject, are incomplete, dependent beings having need of the support given them by the subject. Third, just as the same predicate can be ascribed to many subjects and many predicates can be ascribed to the same subject, so the same characteristics can be possessed by many minds and many characteristics can be possessed by the same mind. Thus these characteristics, being recurrent entities, are universals. Fourth, the paradigm of a subject-predicate sentence is a proper noun followed by a verb in the active voice or by the copula and an adjective, as in "Socrates thinks" and "Socrates is wise". This distinction, built into the model, parallels the distinction in the theory between the operations or activities of the mind and its states.

In modern times Descartes' theory is the paradigm of the traditional application of the subject-predicate model. Nevertheless, just as a sleep-walker uses his legs to walk without knowing that he does, so Descartes used this model. This is seen more clearly in the *Third Set of Objections*, where he was pressed by Hobbes, than in the *Meditations*. He used the model to demonstrate the immortality of the human mind. All he had to do, he thought, was to show that the mind is a pure substance, and thus that it is complete and stands alone. Accepting the axiom that no predicate can stand alone, but that it must belong to a subject, he drew the parallel: "No activity, no attribute can exist without a substance in which to exist".[11] Then, admitting that "we do not apprehend the substance [mind] itself immediately through itself, but by means only of the fact that it is the subject of certain activities",[12] and interpreting thought as an activity and an attribute, he concluded: "It is certain that no thought can exist apart from a substance [the mind] that thinks".[13] Accordingly, his famous argument *Cogito ergo sum* is elliptical for *Cogitatio est, ergo res cogitans est* which, in turn, abbreviates the argument just presented. His ulterior conclusion was that the human mind or soul is a "pure substance", i.e., "even if all its accidents change . . . nevertheless it still remains the same soul. . . . From this it follows that the mind is immortal by its very nature".[14]

Since the time of Descartes, philosophers of mind have worked within the same framework. They have presented their theories as different interpretations of the same model—as different pictures inside the same frame. A well-known contemporary example is P. F. Strawson, who, in his book *Individuals*, defends a subject-predicate conception of the human person.[15] Unlike Descartes, however, he also defends the traditional doctrine, i.e., the parallel between the subject-predicate distinction in grammar and the substance-attribute dichotomy in ontology. He does this by showing that the parallel depends upon "the crucial idea of completeness" present in subjects and substances (called by him "particulars") and absent in predicates and attributes (called by him "universals").[16] The problem in the philosophy of mind that he tries to solve he presents in a Kantian style: Given that we can and do identify persons, i.e., we distinguish one person, including ourselves, from others, what is the nature of a person presupposed by this? Or what conception of a person *must* we hold?[17] His solution is an extended application of the subject-predicate model. In one passage he summarizes his solution: [In order for any person] "to have the idea of himself, *must* he not have the idea of the subject of the experiences, of that which has them"?[18]

---

[11] *Third Set of Objections* II.
[12] *Ibid.*
[13] *Ibid.*
[14] *Meditations* II.
[15] *Individuals* (London: Methuen, 1959), chap. 3.
[16] *Individuals*, chap. 6.
[17] *Individuals*, p. 87.
[18] *Individuals*, p. 88.

Although he uses the same subject-predicate model as did Descartes and his followers, his interpretation of it is different. Whereas Descartes conceived a person as a composition of two subjects, mental and material, each owning its own mental and material predicates, respectively, Strawson conceives a person as one subject owning both mental and material predicates.[19] In this fashion, Strawson gives his solution to the problem of personal identification: A person must own observable material predicates; otherwise we could not pick him out from others.

Although I have said that the theories of Descartes and Strawson represent two of the many different applications of the same model or paradigm, it should be noted that such idioms as "model", "paradigm", "analogy", etc., are foreign to their accounts. Descartes, it seems to me, although he used such terms as "subject" as well as "substance", was unaware even of the existence of the parallel between grammar and ontology. In this he is typical of the majority of philosophers. Strawson, on the other hand, although he uses such terms as the grammatical "subject" and the ontological "particular" interchangeably, is fully aware of the parallel. His exhibition of the two sides of the parallel constitutes a main merit of his account, enabling us to perceive the presence of either a weak or a strong analogy or to tell whether the vehicle can carry its freight. But for him the parallel between the subject-predicate distinction and the substance-attribute or particular-universal dichotomy is more than an analogy or model. The presence of a model suggests and allows for the possibility of an alternative model, but Strawson's whole argument—according to which if we have the idea of a person, then we *"must"* have the idea of a subject of experience—manifests the same a priori character as does that of Descartes. It seems to me then that while we should adopt Strawson's starting point, the facts as they are commonly agreed to be, we should ask not "What theory must we hold?" but rather "What theory provides the best explanation?"

If I am right in treating the subject-predicate distinction as a model or paradigm, then this model should have been invented by someone, by some great sort-crosser, probably from the very remote past, who made overt a comparison not previously made. This, so it happens, is the case. To my knowledge, Aristotle was the first to make explicit the subject-predicate distinction in grammar:

[19] *Individuals*, p. 104.

A subject (*hypokeimenon*) is that about which anything is predicated but which is not itself predicated of anything else.[20]

He was also the first I know of to draw the parallel substance-attribute or particular-universal distinction in ontology by defining it in terms of subject and predicate:

> Some things are universal, others particular. By the term 'universal' (*katholou*) I mean that which is of such a nature as to be predicated of many subjects; by 'particular' (*kath hekaston*) that which is not thus predicated. Thus *man* is a universal, *Callias* a particular.[21]

Although I suppose it would be generally assumed that these distinctions were accepted by Plato, in my view they were foreign to his thinking. Some scholars, however, have argued that Plato did draw them.[22] At any rate this parallel between the distinctions became a traditional doctrine in Western philosophy. As we have seen, it was this parallel that Strawson defends and uses as a basis for his theory of persons. There are, however, several other parallels to the subject-predicate distinction in Aristotle's ontology, for example:

> (i) the distinction between matter (*hyle*), about which things are predicated although it is predicated of nothing, and form (*eidos*)
> (ii) the distinction between potency (*dynamis*) and function (*energeia* or *entelechia*)
> (iii) the distinction between passive mind (*pathetikos nous*) and active mind (*poietikos nous*).

In order to make this last distinction, he used the distinctions in (i) and (ii) apparently as analogies: "Since each class of things in nature, like nature itself, has (1) matter, i.e., a potency to become any particular within the class, and (2) a creative cause that makes the things actual—cf. the relation of art to its material—this same pair of distinct factors must likewise be present in the soul".[23] Thus while passive mind is analogous to a subject, the active mind—that which is permanent or indestructible—is analogous to a predicate. This view,

---

[20] *Metaphysics* 1028b.

[21] *De Interpretatione*, chap. 7.

[22] J. L. Ackrill, "Plato and the Copula" in R. E. Allen, ed., *Studies in Plato's Metaphysics* (London: Routledge and Kegan Paul, 1965), 207–218, originally published in *Journal of Hellenic Studies* (1957).

[23] *De Anima* 430a.

unlike the first parallel mentioned, has not become a traditional doctrine. Central in our tradition is Descartes' view in which the permanent or indestructible mind itself is a subject or substance, while thinking is a predicate or attribute of it.

Now that I have elicited the main features of the model, let us consider some of its inadequacies. *First,* I notice that it breaks an important rule in the use of models. The features of the model should be, as Plato prescribed, "easier to make out" than those of the thing modelled; but the supposed antithesis between subject and predicate, far from being distinct, is blurred. Aristotle himself made it so by laying down that while a subject can never be a predicate, a predicate can be a subject, e.g., " 'Animal' is predicated of the species 'man' ".[24] Transferring this asymmetry to the theory, we get the confusing consequence that not only is the mind a substance but also are thinking, imagining, walking, etc.—activities usually regarded as attributes of the substance mind or predicates of the person. As new substances or particulars, they can now stand alone. This consequence is not what the theorist wants. The history of science, however, records many cases in which the model is modified to fit the theory. Usually this involves making the model more complex. In this case it is made more simple. It was Russell who showed how to repair the subject-predicate model. He argued that a predicate can never stand alone: "When it seems to occur as a subject, the phrase needs amplifying and explaining." Thus such a sentence as Aristotle's "Man is an animal" is analyzed into two sentential functions, "(x) (if x is a man, then x is an animal)",[25] in which each function maintains the subject-predicate form and the trespassing predicate "man" is restored to its proper place. In this way, generally adopted by logicians, the symmetry between the model and the theory is preserved. However, the subject-predicate distinction is one of grammar or syntax, not of semantics. Grammatically "man" can function as a subject just as well as "Socrates" or any proper noun.

Second, I notice that what might be considered the model's most ingenious feature, viz., the "completeness" of subjects and the "incompleteness" of predicates, cannot be established. Russell tried to defend this difference in his *Philosophy of Logical Atomism* in 1918, and it has been adopted since by Strawson as "crucial".[26] Russell

[24] *Categories,* chap. 5.
[25] "The Philosophy of Logical Atomism" in R. C. Marsh, ed., *Logic and Knowledge* (London: Allen and Unwin, 1956), 205.
[26] *Individuals,* p. 12.

claimed that in order to understand a subject, such as "This" in "This is red", we need only to be "acquainted with the particular", but that in order to understand the predicate we need to "know what is the meaning of saying that anything is red," i.e., to "understand propositions of the form 'x is red' ". This distinction he said, answers to that between particulars and universals: "Each particular stands entirely alone and is completely self-subsistent," whereas universals are dependent entities.[27] In this obscurity he left the matter. It was Ramsey, in his *Foundations of Mathematics* (1931), who clarified it by showing that the predicate, e.g., "wise" in "Socrates is wise" is less "complete" than "Socrates" merely because it "collects" a narrower range of propositions of the form "x is wise", while "Socrates" collects a wider range, i.e., any proposition in which "Socrates" occurs. But of course, this constitutes no "crucial" difference. This is so because, as Ramsey noted, our decision to use substantives to define ranges of propositions in one way only is a matter of custom and of our common interests. We could use them as we now use adjectives. In which case the distinction between "Socrates" and "wise", between subject and predicate and accordingly, between substance and attribute or particular and universal are "of a subjective character and depend on human interests and needs".[28]

Third, I notice that an important feature of the model fails to appear in the thing modelled. We identify the subject of a sentence just as immediately as we identify the predicate, yet this is not duplicated in the theory in which the substance itself, whether it is a mind or a person, is not an object of acquaintance. Hume pointed out that he could never "catch" himself, the elusive subject of his experiences. All he could catch were the experiences. But Descartes had already exposed the weakness of the parallel by admitting that mind substance is known only through its attributes. Similarly, Strawson, although he insists that if we can identify a person, then we must conceive him as a subject owning predicates, nevertheless fails to make use of the concept of subject when he explains how we do identify a person: We identify a person, not by picking out the subject, but through predicates which we assume must be ascribed to a subject. From this I conclude that since the subject part of the model admittedly sheds no light upon how we identify minds or persons, it can be dropped without any real loss.

[27] *Logic and Knowledge,* p. 201.
[28] *Foundations of Mathematics,* p. 129.

Fourth, I notice that yet another prominent feature of the model fails to appear in the traditional theories. According to the model, the same predicate, say an adjective or a verb, can be ascribed to many subjects. Translated to the thing modelled this surely means that mental states or personal characteristics, being recurrent entities, are universals. But the theorists do not make the correct translation. Instead they turn these states and characteristics into particulars. For example, Strawson claims that "it is logically impossible that a particular state or experience in fact possessed by someone should have been possessed by anyone else".[29] Translating back to the model we get the confusing consequence that the predicates of subjects are subjects. It is true that Aristotle had laid down that predicates could function as subjects, but he denied that a subject could be a predicate. His denial continues to be accepted doctrine. From this it seems to me that if the theorists find that mental states or personal experiences are particulars, they must either discard the subject-predicate model or repair it beyond recognition.

Fifth, extending the last point, if the same predicate can be ascribed to many subjects, it is shared by them. Translating this to the thing modelled we learn that my mental states or personal experiences can be shared by other minds or persons. But in general, subscribers to the subject-predicate theory deny this. Cf. the statement of Strawson given above. Translating back to the model, we get the confusing consequence that the predicates of a subject can be ascribed only to it. Once more it seems to me that the theorists must either discard the model or repair it drastically. In fact, they have resorted to an auxiliary model, viz., that of private ownership of property. Strawson, for example, refers to "the fact that one's experiences, or states of consciousness, are ascribed to something which *has* them with that peculiar non-transferable kind of possession. . . ."[30] But this too is a case of drastic repair upon the original model, for ownership of private property surely is transferable. Moreover models and their auxiliaries should be made to mesh. Private properties and shared predicates constitute a mixed metaphor of the same order as "Britain has had a really heroic row to hoe in trying to keep her economic nose above water."

Sixth, the subject-predicate device, used to illustrate the mind in its passive and its active aspects, is uneconomical and confusing.

29 *Individuals,* p. 97.
30 *Individuals,* p. 98.

One would expect the subject to play some important part here, and I notice that in Aristotle's theory it does. The mind or intellect, in its passive and active aspects, is modelled upon the subject and the predicate, respectively. The active aspect he said, "must be a *logos* or *eidos*, not a matter (*hyle*) or subject (*hypokeimenon*)".[31] But in modern and recent interpretations I notice that both the passive and the active aspects are the analogues of predicates. Thus passive states of consciousness are modelled upon adjectives, while the actions or operations of the mind are modelled upon verbs. For example, although the connection with adjectives and verbs is not explicit, Descartes specifies that the only predicates of the subject mind are its thoughts which are "mainly of two sorts, the one being the actions of the soul [or volitions], and the other its passions" [or perceptions].[32] Strawson moves a certain class of personal or P-predicates to a central position in his picture. These predicates involve "doing something" and "clearly imply intention". Another class of P-predicates he calls "states of consciousness".[33] Now it seems to me that if both the active and the passive aspects of the mind are treated as predicates, then the retention of the subject is an unnecessary extravagance. Yet according to Descartes and Strawson the subject, although it plays hardly any part, is assigned the major role: unlike the minor role of the predicate it is assigned completeness, independence, and permanence.

By thus eliciting and examining the main features of the subject-predicate myth, I am able to some extent, to become "strange to the familiar". It is like taking off and examining a pair of darkened spectacles that I have worn all day without knowing that I had them on. By doing this, such statements as "The mind is a substance", "Thought is an attribute of mental substance", "Persons are subjects owning P- and M-predicates", have become for me lively metaphors —as lively as "metal fatigue", "the Iron Curtain", and "the Ghost in the Machine". Thus I can now choose either to use the subject-predicate device with awareness of its limitations and other defects, or to adopt a new one. I notice especially that there is a great imbalance in the old model with regard to activity and passivity. Within our Cartesian-Newtonian tradition, the dominant picture of the human mind is that of a passive observer receiving impressions from the

---

[31] *De Anima* 414a.
[32] *Passions of the Soul*, article 17.
[33] *Individuals*, pp. 105, 111.

outside world, while the picture of the whole self or person is that of a passive thing acted upon by external forces. Perhaps it is time to try to discard these old pictures and to make a new one.

The Mind as Reader and Writer

A promising approach to the study of the mind has been suggested recently by Paul Kolers in his article "Bilingualism and Information Processing".[34] He first makes the obvious suggestion that since one of the principal activities of the human mind is the manipulation of symbols, an investigation of the way in which we use symbols will yield some insights into the workings of the mind. Then he makes the not so obvious suggestion that an investigation of the way a bilinguist uses two sets of symbols will enable us to learn much about mental operations. He summarizes his own investigation: "A person who can speak two languages has clearly mastered two sets of symbols. Experiments that cause the two sets to interact provide important clues to how the mind works".

What interests me here is Kolers's second suggestion. If he is right, however, then the investigation can be conducted nearer home. It seems to me that a person who can read and write *one language* has clearly mastered *two sets of symbols,* and that an investigation of the way the two sets interact will provide important clues to how the mind works. In what follows I want to extend and implement this suggestion. I assume that the workings of the mind are revealed by the ways in which it uses symbols. The two main ways of using symbols are interpreting and manipulating them, and the prototypes of these operations are reading and writing. I suggest also that the workings of the mind will be revealed more fully by considering not only bilingual subjects (those who can already read and write) but subjects who are striving to become bilingual.

Let me consider that peculiar relation that obtains between the items of the written and the spoken languages of what we commonly call the same language. When as children we learn to read and write, our aim is to bridge the gap between these *two different languages.* It is strange that we now think them *one language,* for the gap between them is in some respects far wider than that between, for example, spoken English and spoken Italian, or the hieroglyphics and

[34] *Scientific American* 218: 3 (March 1968), pp. 78–86.

the Greek script carved on the Rosetta Stone. This is so because the elements of these two languages belong to two different sense realms. There is much more resemblance between the sounds **kăt** and the sounds **gătto** than between the sounds **kăt** and the marks *CAT*.

Now a primary sense of the verb "to read", according to the Shorter *Oxford English Dictionary*, is "to peruse and utter in speech", i.e., "to translate from the written into the corresponding spoken language". I notice that this happens whenever I read, although usually the utterances are silent. Psychologists tell us that even in speed reading there are minute movements of the glottis. This sense of reading is present in the Roman citizens' injunction to Mark Antony: "Read the will; we'll hear it Antony". Being illiterate these plebeians had to have the Latin document translated into the Latin tongue. Presented with this new and unknown written language, which we have to read in order to be admitted into our exclusive literate society, we are, in fact, confronted with a decoding problem of enormous complexity. However, we come already equipped with a language that is old and known, namely, our own native but artificial tongue, the spoken language. As children confronted with specimens of this mysterious writing, our aim is to break its code and to become readers or native decoders, able to translate these foreign marks into the sounds of spoken English. Our predicament is similar to that of Champollion when he began to decipher the hieroglyphics. Like him, we have to transfer our knowledge from a language that is old and known to another that is new and unknown. Fortunately, to help us in solving one of the most difficult problems of our intellectual life, we possess that all-important factor that Champollion lacked. We have a teacher, usually our mother, who can give us a lamp so that we may tread safely into the unknown. Right at the start she provides us with a Rosetta stone, a bi-lingual clue enabling us to translate the characters of this strange new language into the sounds of our mother tongue. This translation-link is the alphabet. The letters of this alphabet, *A, B, C,* which belong to the new language, we learn by ostensive definition, the way we begin to learn any foreign language. Our teacher points to the letters as she gives them their proper names, **ēi, bī, sī,** which belong to our old language. This involves the establishment of an association between entirely different things so that when tested by being *shown* a letter or a word we can *tell* its name. The process takes time and experience and repeated acts.

Then comes the most difficult part of the task, that of learning to translate written letters, when they occur in a certain order, into one spoken word of our old language. Because of the impracticality of confining reading to saying the proper names, our teacher introduces us to the convention of substituting one complex term for the many simpler terms or proper names. Thus, for example, we learn that instead of translating a group of letters by the cumbersome names ēi, pī, pī, el, and ī, we must translate by substituting the one word æ p'l. In trying to perform this enormously difficult task we are baffled by the small help provided by our translation-link, the proper names of the letters of our alphabet. Alas, only some of these names are acrophonetic! For example, when we see the characters *A T E*, the sound of the proper name of the first letter, ēi, offers a hint for the finished translation into our language, ēit. But this hint is useless in England where the marks *A T E* are translated as **et**. Finally, the name ēitʃ of the letter *H* offers no link whatsoever between *H* and its phonetic counterpart in the translation of the marks *H E R B* either in England (hɜɹb) or in New England (ɜɹb). We are baffled not merely by an enormously complex code but by one that is crazy. We cannot readily overcome the disparity between the sounds of our mother tongue and the symbols we see on the page. In English, for example, there are only 26 letters in the alphabet but more than 80 sounds. Thus one character may be translated into many different phonemes. There is nothing in the character *O* itself that tells us which translation to pick: the sound ōu represented in *GO*, or the one in *ONE*, or in *DO*, or in *GONE*, or in *WOMEN*. Conversely, many different characters may translate into only one phoneme. There is nothing in such different characters present in *TO, WOO, FLEW, CANOE*, and *RHEUMATISM*, that can tell the beginning reader to translate them into only one sound. Finally, how is the frustrated beginner to know that some characters, such as the *B* in *COMB*, the *E* in *CAUSE*, and the *H* in *HERB* do not translate into sound at all? It is easy to see why the young player loses these language games. Thus, winning the game with the *F* in *AFT, IF*, and *OFT*, we forthwith lose it with the *F* in *OF*. Able to read the combinations *MIGHT, RIGHT, LIGHT*, and *TIGHT*, the shocking truth is revealed to us when we encounter the combination *EIGHT*.

In spite of these difficulties, many of us learn to read. For some of us the learning process is shortened by letting us break first a simpler code. This is the approach of Sir James Pitman's Initial Teaching Alphabet (I. T. A.).[35] It is a simpler system than English

---

[35] See John A. Downing, *The i. t. a. Reading Experiment*, University of London Institute of Education (1964), pp. 5–25.

although it contains more primitives: Pitman has almost doubled the number of letters of its alphabet and tripled the number of vowels. Nevertheless, each letter translates into only one phoneme of our old language. Thus before we start to decipher, all the defects of our present alphabet that I listed above have been eliminated. Moreover, his alphabet provides a real translation link. All its proper names are acrophonetic. In every case the sound of the name of the character recurs in the sound of the phoneme itself. Fortunately, we can use other devices to help in counteracting the caprices of language. We rely upon analogies, prenotions, and context. Thus we learn to overlook the multitudes of typographical sizes and shapes and pass on to the translation. Abstracted from its context there is nothing in the combination *READ* that enables us to choose between the translations **rēd** and **rĕd,** but we translate successfully when it is preceded by *TO* or *HAD*. Numerous other abstractions like *TEAR, ROW, WIND, LEAD,* and *CLOSE* are tackled in the same way. Eventually, having begun as cryptanalysts, we succeed in translating any message like a native decoder.

The final stage in learning to read is, perhaps, of more interest. Having successfully bridged the gap between the two languages in one direction, we tend to ignore the bridge and to minimize the gap. We had accepted the conventions, first, of calling the letters and their corresponding phonemes by the same names, using, for example, the name "Double-U" not only for the mark *W* but for the sound it translates into; and then of doing the same thing with the combinations, using, for example, the name "apple" not only for the marks *APPLE* but for the sounds **æ p'l**. Other names are shared also, such as "letter", "word", "sentence", and, indeed, all the words listed in the dictionary. This custom is highly convenient. It saves an endless number of new names, and it constitutes a translation link—a Rosetta stone, as it were—between the members of this pair of languages. But it also enables us to forget the presence of two languages. We not only call these two languages "one language", viz., "English", but we think of them as one.

"Writing", in the primary sense, is "the use of letters or other conventional characters in order to represent significant sounds". It is, therefore, translating from the spoken into the written language. Plato used the legend of Thoth, the great inventor of writing, to make an important point: "What you have discovered is a recipe not for memory, but for reminder".[36] What we are reminded of when we

---

[36] *Phaedrus* 275a.

read is the real thing, the spoken discourse. *Writing*, then, in terms of the model, is the manipulation of letters or other conventional characters to represent and remind a reader of items in the spoken language. A concrete symbol of this basic operation that we perform upon the spoken language is the Seated Scribe. The scribe is taking dictation. Receiving a message in the primary language, he is in the process of translating it into another. Receiving, for example, the message **miseh** in plain text, he encodes it into the cryptograms of the owl, the bolt, and the twisted flax, and, according to the rules of syntax, puts them together in order in an invisible rectangle to make a well-formed formula. Thus he is able to bridge the enormous gap between the two languages in the reverse direction from reading, so that another reader can be reminded of the original. The bridge or translation link that he uses is spelling, which, like a scaffolding, is dispensable. By spelling the *names* of the items of the message he is able to bridge the gap, for these names constitute a rebus: they sound like the names of the vocabulary of the secondary language, the letters of his alphabet, which he has already learned by ostensive definition. It is, of course, accidental that the words of his metalanguage are in the same language as the original message. The characters and their syntax are conventional, being based upon a compact between him and his reader. Otherwise they could not be decoded, and there could be no language. Nevertheless, within these conventions, he has his own unconventional writing style.

These basic operations of reading and writing when appropriately interpreted, should be manifested in our cognitive operations at all age levels, even including the level of the neonate and the infant, i.e., the period which Piaget describes as "the period prior to the development of language and thought as such".[37] The mind of the infant, if we accept Piaget's own investigations, is never passively receiving, but always acting. It is properly seen as the mind of a maker or poet. For example, the infant, finding no permanent things or substances, has to make them. Piaget refers to "the initial absence of substantive objects, followed by the construction of solid and permanent objects",[38] and, by the end of the second year, to the synthesising of the different visual, tactual, oral, etc., spaces into one space.[39] All this reflects in elementary fashion the ways in which we learn to read by combining many letters into one word and accounting them one

[37] David Elkind, ed. *Six Psychological Studies* (New York: Random House, 1967), 5.
[38] *Six Psychological Studies*, p. 14.
[39] *Ibid.*

entity and by fusing or blending our two systems of symbols into one set, in our case, English. Finally, the infant mind engages in a form of writing when, in order to send a message to his mother, he resorts to "body English."

A more elaborate manifestation of the mind as reader is seen when we construct a theory of perception by interpreting the letters of the written language as visual qualities and the phonemes of spoken language as the spatial properties of physical objects, i.e., their sizes, shapes, etc., which could be known by us if we had not been gifted with sight. Here we see a point-by-point application of the model as I have described it.[40] The monolingual subject, striving to become bilingual, models a person who, until now deprived of sight, learns to "read" this new and unknown visual language. He fails to "translate" at all until the "letters" like "round", "square", etc., are "ostensively defined". The names of these "letters" from his own language form a "bi-lingual clue". Unhappily the "code" of visual language is chaotic. It is this factor that introduces visual illusions or "ambiguities" in this language. The frustrated beginner constantly "mistranslates". He learns, however, to overcome "ambiguity" by relying upon "context". Eventually he learns to "read" this language like a native "decoder", and finally manages to fuse or complicate the items of the two languages. The products of such fusions or complications of the visual and the haptic realms constitute our visible world. Thus by interpreting the model in this way, we get a theory of vision much the same as Berkeley's.[41]

If perceiving is appropriately modelled on reading, then the creative arts are appropriately modelled on writing. The analogy between writing (*graphe*) and painting (*zographia*), also drawing and sculpture, was noted by Plato, who saw these arts as forms of handicraft (*cheirourgia*). What distinguishes painting and drawing from photography is their greater flexibility or freedom from convention. Just as the writer can break some of the rules of grammar but not all, so the artist, such as the Egyptian scribe, Botticelli, and Chagall, can ignore the rules of perspective: While not free from all conventions (if so, his work could not be read), such unconventionality and other idiosyncrasies constitute his style[42] or, as the etymon indicates, manner of writing. An apparently simple but highly complex form of

[40] For a fuller account, see Turbayne, "Visual Language from the Verbal Model", *Journal of Typographic Research*, III: 4 (October 1969).

[41] George Berkeley, *Works on Vision*, ed. C. M. Turbayne (Indianapolis: Bobbs-Merrill, 1963).

[42] Turbayne, "Visual Language from the Verbal Model".

writing is sculpture. If I am right, the sculptor is properly seen as translating. He no more makes a copy of his subject than does the scribe when he encodes the spoken message into painted characters on a flat surface. Consider, for example, one of Picasso's many versions of "Head of a Woman" (1932). Just as the obvious reading of the hieroglyph I have been using is an owl, a bolt, and twisted flax (cf. the once-obvious reading of the letter *A* as a bull's head), and the correct reading is the phonetic sequence **miseh,** and through it, a crocodile, so the obvious reading of Picasso's composition is a smiling face with hard, prominent nose and soft, deeply modelled mouth, while the deeper reading is a happy blending of the male and female sexual organs, and through it, the conception of the mutual subjectivity of sexual intercourse. This is to accept John Berger's illuminating account of the work in which "its secret is a metaphor".[43] Although I present the sequence from the reader's standpoint, one has only to reverse it in order to obtain the writer's sequence from the conception to the set of cryptograms.

The preceding account of reading and writing suggests a plausible approach to the problem of how the mind acquires mastery of a language, an approach contrary to the traditional rationalist doctrine that has been resurrected in recent years.[44] According to the latter, the mind comes equipped with certain innate ideas or principles in the form of knowledge of language structure. This knowledge it applies to the mastery of its first language. It seems to me, however, that we are able to acquire this "first" language, not through knowledge of any innate ideas, but because all of us have been mastering code-breaking and encoding skills from earliest infancy. Some of us more readily broke the code of written English because we had already broken the simpler code of I.T.A. Most of us were helped to acquire our "first" language because we had already broken the code of visual language in the first months of life. A similar view is presented by Nelson Goodman in his critique of the doctrine of innate ideas.[45] Anticus queries Jason:

What we call a language is a fairly elaborate and sophisticated symbolic system. Don't you think, Jason, that before anyone ac-

---

[43] *Success and Failure of Picasso* (Baltimore: Penguin, 1965), 160.
[44] N. Chomsky, *Cartesian Linguistics* (New York: Harper and Row, 1966); *Language and Mind* (New York: Harcourt, Brace, 1968), chap. 3.
[45] Nelson Goodman, "The Epistemological Argument", *Synthese*, 17:1 (1967), 23–28.

quires a language, he has had an abundance of practice in developing and using rudimentary prelinguistic symbolic systems in which gestures and sensory and perceptual occurrences of all sorts function as signs?

Reflection upon these basic operations of reading and writing suggests a new approach to the conception of the mind. The traditional or Cartesian concept is of the mind as a thing or substratum housing attributes. A recent conception, an attempted correction of the Cartesian, is of the mind as a power or capacity to do things: "My mind does not stand for another organ. It signifies my ability and proneness to do certain sorts of things".[46] These two conceptions derive from different readings of Aristotle's distinction between mind as passive and mind as active. As we have seen, while the former stresses Aristotle's comparison of the two aspects with a subject (*hypokeimenon*) and its predicates, the latter reading stresses the comparison with power or capacity (*dynamis*) and its exercise (*energeia*). But the attempted correction is barely different from the original, for the conceptions of potency or ability and substratum are almost identical, and both imply passivity. The preceding account enables me to drop these conceptions of the mind as a combination of passive and active, of a *thing* with attributes, and of an *ability* to do things, and to replace it with a conception of the mind as wholly *energeia*, i.e., in action. Having begun with the assumption that the workings of the mind are revealed by the ways in which it uses symbols, I end with the suggestion that the workings of the mind *are* the mind, and that these workings are the ways in which it uses symbols.

[46] G. Ryle, *Concept of Mind* (New York: Hutchinson, 1949), 168.

FIVE

Other Minds

HILARY PUTNAM

Realism in the Philosophy of Mind

"EMPIRICAL REALISM" is the position that the existence of the external
world is supported by experience in much the way that any scientific
theory is supported by observational data. The empirical realist reply
to skepticism has recently been extended by Paul Ziff from skepticism
about material objects to skepticism about other minds.[1] I do not
suggest that Ziff was unaware of the need for the various qualifications that have to be made in the realist position if it is to be tenable.
However, I am not happy with the way in which Ziff states the arguments. Ziff's statements are very brief, and it may be that the features
I shall object to are ones that he would have eliminated in a longer
and less aphoristic presentation. However, here they are.

[1] "Symposium: The Other Minds Problem. The Simplicity of Other
Minds". *Journal of Philosophy*, Vol. LXII, No. 20 (October 21, 1965),
575–584.

There are two parts to Ziff's argument: what he calls the *via negativa,* and the citation of positive support. I take them up in turn.

The *via negativa* amounts to this: if I accept the hypothesis that I alone have a mind, then I must, according to Ziff, suppose that I differ from other human beings in some *other* respect, presumably a physiological respect. I can't differ from other human beings in *just* this one way, that I have a mind and they don't.

> Could the other one and I relevantly differ only in this? that I do and he doesn't have a mind. Suppose we opt for yes. Then how do we account for this fantastic state of affairs? Why do I have a mind? Why doesn't he have a mind? Do minds just come and go in the universe? Did one just happen to light in my head? Is there no bait for this bird? Say 'yes' or even 'maybe' and what can one do but resolve to accept the relation, miraculous and inexplicable, between the mind and the body, anyone's of course. For it is not as if one had or is even likely to have any coherent theory of the mind in independence of the body. (*The Simplicity of Other Minds,* p. 575)

Now, I am puzzled by this, and in a variety of ways. In the first place, I do not see why the negation of the thesis that others have minds, i.e., that all people or all normal people have minds, is that I am unique in having a mind. It would rather seem to be the thesis that some, perhaps most, people do not have minds. (I once asked Bob Yost the question, "Are there other minds?" "Not many", he replied.) Suppose I find a mole under my left arm. Must I conclude that all other people have moles?

Could the other one and I relevantly differ only in this: that I do and he does not have a mole? Suppose we opt for yes. Then how do we account for this fantastic state of affairs? Why do I have a mole? Why doesn't he have a mole? Do moles just come and go in the universe? Did one just happen to light under my arm? Is there no bait for this bird? Say 'yes' or even 'maybe' and what can one do but resolve to accept the relation, miraculous and inexplicable, between the mole and the body, anyone's, of course. For it is not as if one had, or is even likely to have, any coherent theory of the mole in independence of the body.

This is, of course, nonsense. And I think it is nonsense not because we know more about moles than we do about minds; indeed, we know more about minds than we do about moles, or at least I do. Suppose that this mole under my arm is the first mole that I have ever seen. Suppose, for some reason, I am unwilling to ask other people whether they know what it is, or whether they have ever seen one before, etc. Perhaps such questions might be dangerous in my society. I would not, in the absence of investigation, conclude either that I am unique in having a mole under my arm, or that all other people have moles under their arms. If I concluded anything at all—and why should I?—I would very likely conclude that I and perhaps *some* other people have or have had moles under their arms, but that it is not necessarily the case that everyone has a mole under his arm. I might, if I had never seen anyone unclothed, seriously entertain the supposition that everyone has a mole under his arm just as I do: perhaps the mole is just a part of the body, like the finger or the nose, albeit a part I haven't been taught the name of. I might also consider the hypothesis that most people lack moles, and that this is just a freak.

Ziff says that "talk about the mind is primarily a fancy way of talking about mental states and mental events (themselves fancy ways of talking)". It seems to me that he has himself depended too much upon this fancy way of talking; e.g., the metaphor of bait for birds. Let us talk for a moment about the problem of the existence of material objects. 'Material objects exist' is not a "hypothesis" that explains anything; and indeed 'material objects do not exist' does not explain anything either. What does explain a host of phenomena is something we might call "thing-theory"; that is, the conjunction of all the theories, hypotheses, empirical laws, ordinary empirical statements (or a suitable consistent subset of all these) that we accept, and that we employ in explanation. With some care in making explicit additional auxiliary hypotheses connecting thing-events with the events one could describe in a sensation or appearance language, one can even make out that these hypotheses, laws, garden variety empirical statements, etc., together with these auxiliary hypotheses explain the phenomena that would be described in a sensation or appearance language. Thus part of the empirical realist case is correct: These individual bundles of thing statements, together with appropriate auxiliary hypotheses connecting thing-events with "sense datum" events, do stand in the relation of *explanation* to various phenomena. A second part of the realist case is also correct: The phenomena, in turn, stand in the relation of inductive support to these thing statements and empirical hypotheses. That is to say, our experiences confirm in many cases that some theory stated in thing-language is correct, not in the sense of establishing that the theory is correct as opposed to some other theory which implies that material things do not exist, but as opposed to some other theory which likewise implies that material objects exist. In short, what has been tested is not thing-theory as opposed to "no-thing" theory, but thing-theory as opposed to *alternative* thing-theory. We have inductively established *not* that material objects exist, but that *this* account of how material objects behave is more probable than some other account of how material objects behave. More precisely, we have established that in *this* case *this* account of how *these* material objects behave is more probable than *that* account of how these material objects behave; in some other case, that such-and-such an account of how *those* material objects behave is more probable than such-and-such an alternative account of how *those* material objects behave; etc. Even the most radical skeptic could grant this much.

'Material objects exist' has not been *confirmed*. "Thing-theory" has not been *confirmed*, because really there is no such thing as thing-theory; there are only many many many many individual systems of statements about things which individually might be regarded by a logician as theories. *Thing theories* have been confirmed *as opposed to alternative thing theories*.

The skeptic would be happy to grant this much, because he could say, "Very well, then, *if* things exist, very likely the received account of how they behave is the most probable; or, at least, it is more probable than those alternative accounts that have actually been considered and ruled out. But my question is not, "Is the accepted account of how material objects behave more probable than those alternative accounts which have been considered and ruled out?" but, "Is the accepted account more probably true than that there are no material objects at all?"

I claim that, in spite of these difficulties, nonetheless there is something right with the empirical realist rejoinder to skepticism. It is true that thing-theory (pretending that the totality of all accepted thing-theories can be axiomatized as a single consistent theory) has been tested only against alternative thing-theory; but that is because no one has been able to put into the field a "no-thing" theory that would account for all, or even a good part of, the phenomena that are presently accounted for by means of thing-theory, and that would lead to different testable predictions. To give up 'material objects exist' would require giving up all of the individual laws, statements, hypotheses, etc., that *imply* material objects exist. But then what alternative explanation would we have for the phenomena in question? The inability of anyone to suggest an alternative explanation is itself our deepest justification for staying with the accepted explanations. The situation appears to me to be exactly the same in the case of psychological statements. We explain the behavior of other people as well as of ourselves by reference to desires, character traits, etc. We say that other people are on occasion egotistical, angry, suspicious, lustful, tired, sad. The question is not: Do other people have minds? but: Are other people ever egotistical, angry, suspicious, lustful, tired, sad? If we continue to use "theory" as logicians do, which is, of course, a wide deviation from ordinary usage, and say that any explanation of someone's behavior in terms of egotism, suspiciousness, anger, lust, sadness, may be regarded as a *psychological theory*, then we may say that there are many behavior facts that we can and do today explain by means of psychological theories. I do not have in mind by "psychological theories" the kind of thing Ziff referred to in his paper, that is, theories in learning theory and neurophysiology; I will come to them later. To be sure, no "psychological theory", in my sense, has ever been tested against a "no-mind" theory. This is so for the same reason that no thing-theory has ever been tested against a "no-thing" theory; no one has ever seriously propounded and elaborated in the detail that a scientist would require an explanation of a set of phenomena based upon the hypothesis that no material objects exist; and neither has anyone ever seriously propounded and elaborated in the detail that a scientist would require an explanation for a set of behavior facts based upon the hypothesis that no other person is ever tired, angry, sad, lustful, or suspicious. Psychological theory has been tested against alternative psychological theory, not against "no-mind" theory. Moreover, just as in the case of material objects, the observation reports that we ordinarily make are not neutral with respect to the issue *psychological theory* or "no-mind" theory, any more than they are neutral with respect to the issue "thing-theory" or "no-thing" theory. Although we could, if there were some reason, make guarded reports about the behavior of others which did not assume that they have minds, we do not ordinarily do so.

These facts show that our reasons for accepting it that others have mental states are not an ordinary induction, any more than our reasons for accepting it that material objects exist are an ordinary induction. Yet, what can be said in the case of material objects can also be said here: Our acceptance of the proposition that others have mental states is both analogous and disanalogous to the acceptance of ordinary empirical theories on the basis of explanatory induction.

It is disanalogous insofar as 'other people have mental states' is, in the first instance, not an empirical theory at all, but rather a consequence of a host of specific hypotheses, theories, laws, and garden variety empirical statements that we accept. These, indeed many of them, have been established by explanatory induction; but in no case was the alternative considered one that implied the nonexistence of the mental states of others; but the alternative was an alternative supposition *about* the mental states of others. It is also disanalogous insofar as it is built into the language used to make observation reports that other people have mental states. Thus two requirements for a good inductive test of a proposition are violated: that the alternative hypotheses being tested disagree with respect to the truth-value of the proposition, and that the *language* used to couch the observation reports with which all the hypotheses are confronted be "neutral" with respect to the issue at hand. It is analogous, however, in that part of the justification for the assertion that other people have mental states is that to give up that proposition would require giving up all of the theories, statements, etc., that we accept *implying* that proposition; and those latter statements do have, many of them, the kind of explanatory role that the inductivist stresses. It is also analogous in that many empirical theories are accepted today precisely for the two reasons that (a) they, or theories that presuppose them, provide plausible explanations of many phenomena, and (b) no alternative is today in the field.

If this is right, I think we can see what the difference is between "other people have minds" and "other people have moles". The supposition that other people have moles under their arms is not implied by the various explanations that I give of their behavior. If I say that other people do or don't have moles under their arms, or that most do or that some do, it makes no difference to anything. But if I say that other people do not have minds, that is if I say that other people do not have mental states, that is if I say that other people are never angry, suspicious, lustful, sad, etc., I am giving up propositions that are implied by the explanations that I give on specific occasions of the behavior of other people. So I would have to give up all of these explanations.

But if a body of theory has genuine explanatory power, we do not give it up unless an alternative is in the field. (This is Newton's famous "rule 4", in fact.) It is therefore up to the objector, in the case of the thesis that others have mental states, to provide an alternative explanation for the behavior of other people. It is the fact

[83]

that no such alternative explanation is in the field, along with the undoubted explanatory power of the accepted psychological theories, that constitutes the real inductive justification for the acceptance of the accepted system.

Fortunately, Ziff accepts all this. Indeed, he himself says,

> To these hypotheses, still others must be conjoined. What is in force and active here is not a single silly hypothesis, that there are other minds, this naively supposed to be somehow based on an unexplored analogy. Instead one is confronted with a complex conceptual scheme. The fact that there are other minds is an integral part of that scheme and presently essential to it.

Ziff, however, says, "one is not restricted here to a *via negativa.*" Let us examine, then, Ziff's positive argument, which is, unfortunately, even more briefly stated than his negative argument. Ziff's positive argument is an inductivist one in an almost pure form. What he says is that if I assume that others have minds, and that "others" includes animals (rats, etc.), and that the mind and brain stand in a significant relation, and to these hypotheses I conjoin "still others", which he does not state, then I obtain a conceptual scheme which "draws support from a multitude of observations and experiments". Ziff gives two examples. The first example, is, unfortunately an explanation of the behavior of some rats that does not contain a single psychological predicate. The explanation is:

> the control of feeding behavior is located in two "feeding centers" in the lateral hypothalamus and two "satiety centers" in the ventromedial hypothalamus. Destruction of the satiety centers resulted in overeating and obesity, while stimulation of these centers was followed by cessation of eating.

Since this is an example of an explanation of behavior using a theory that does not contain a single psychological predicate, it cannot be regarded as confirming psychological theory at all.

Ziff's second example is an experiment of Lashley and Franz (1919) which may be summed up by the sentence: "There are many indications that animals in a problem box situation experiment with many solutions." Since "experiment with many solutions" is a borderline example of a psychological predicate (it is borderline because there are computing machines that can experiment with many solutions, but to which we would not today attribute mental states), this second example is at least dimly relevant. It seems to me that it is only Ziff's scientism that makes him go to such recherché examples, when

[84]

every day we explain the behavior of people and animals in a way that involves psychological predicates, in their primary uses, all over the place.

I do not wish to quarrel with Ziff's examples, however. Undoubtedly, we can find explanations of individual pieces of behavior that contain essential and paradigmatic occurrences of psychological terms. I am a little unhappy about the statement that "our conceptual scheme *draws support* from a multitude of observations and experiments". This is the language of theory-testing and confirmation. And I have already suggested that the existence of the mental states of others is not really the conclusion of an explanatory induction, even though there is a sense in which we can give an inductive justification for accepting that proposition. We speak of a theory as having "support" or "confirmation" only when it has been the survivor of an experimental test, and it cannot have been the survivor of an experimental test if no alternative was ever in the field—not even the "null hypothesis". To say that the existence of the mental states of others *draws support* from experiments and observations is to make the status of that existence appear much weaker than it is. Fortunately, Ziff does not say this. But in saying that "our conceptual scheme" draws support from experiments and observations (which is, of course, quite true, if "our conceptual scheme" is the whole system of psychological propositions we accept, as I take it Ziff means it to be), and then adding "the existence of other minds is an integral part of that scheme and presently essential to it", there is the danger that one leaves the impression "the existence of other minds" likewise is something in connection with which one has "support from experiments and observations". The existence of the mental states of other people does not "draw support" from experiments and observations, nor does it "not draw support". It is, as Ziff himself says, "a fact of the day". And if someone asks "How do you know?" the answer is *not*, "By the following experiments and observations", but, "What alternative do you propose?"

All these criticisms should not obscure the essential agreement between myself and Ziff, and our common disagreement with the modish treatment in terms of "behavioral criteria", "how the words are learned", etc. Ziff and I both agree that "what is in force and active here is not a single silly hypothesis", but "a complex conceptual scheme". Ziff and I both agree that the complex conceptual scheme, or parts of it, provides explanations, in a quite standard sense of explanation, for behavior facts. The fact that psychological statements

[85]

are used to *explain* behavior is at once obvious and completely neglected both by the traditional philosophers who talk about an "inference by analogy" and by the contemporary philosophers who believe that the existence of mental states can be logically (or linguistically) inferred from that of behavior. To put it crudely, the "inference" to the mental states of others is what has been called an "inference to the best explanation"—or it would be, except that it isn't an inference! (It isn't an inference because, to repeat, no alternative is or ever has been in the field.) Where we differ is in our attitude towards the argument that "if only I have a mind, then there must be some other relevant difference". For Ziff this seems to be a central part of the story, whereas I am suspicious of this argument, and inclined to think that even if it is correct, it is not very important. Let me now turn from my examination of Ziff to an examination of his critics.

Shoemaker's Criticisms of Ziff

In this section I want to take up Sydney Shoemaker's criticisms of Ziff.[2] (Shoemaker's criticisms are advanced more as questions and difficulties than as decisive objections; I shall treat them here, however, as if they were meant to be decisive objections.) Shoemaker's criticisms are two: that Ziff does not account for how we learn to use the words, and that knowing that behavioral criteria entitle us to apply psychological predicates to other people is part of knowing the meaning of those psychological predicates. At bottom, these are the same criticism: what is being suggested is that knowing the meaning of psychological predicates *involves* knowing that behavior entitles us to apply them to other people; and that this *must* be so because otherwise it would be impossible to learn the words. What is being presented, then, is the conjunction of a fashionable claim about the *logic* of psychological predicates with the already-disreputable argument that the claim must be correct because "how else could we learn to use the words?" Since I have discussed this position in detail in two previous papers, I shall be much briefer here, and shall concentrate on points that I did not go into in those papers.

In my previous papers I presented models for the use of language

2 "Symposium: The Other Minds Problem. Comments". *Loc. cit.*, pp. 585–587.

which make it clear that language-using is at least logically possible even if words are not criterion-governed in the sense in which Malcolm, for example, assumes they must be. These models are mathematical models, and as such they were necessarily (given the present state of our knowledge) extremely over-simplified; but I believe this does not affect the validity of the point. In general, the way language-use works, according to one of these models, is as follows:

The speaker's use of a given word, be it a psychological word or any word, depends upon a number of factors: for example, upon the set of sentences containing that word that he accepts; upon the stimulus meaning of those sentences that have stimulus meaning, together with the speaker's history of past stimulation; upon the inductive and deductive logic that the speaker consciously or unconsciously accepts; and upon the speaker's system of values and preferences. If a speaker changes his inductive logic, for example, then this will affect what empirical sentences beginning with a universal quantifier he will accept (actually, it will affect what empirical sentences of *any* form he will accept; but we may suppose that the most immediate and striking effect will be upon the acceptance of universal quantifications). If the change is very drastic, then we may even want to consider it as tantamount to a change in the *meaning* of the universal quantifier; more precisely, there are logically possible deviations from the present use of language such that it would be arbitrary whether to count them as changes in the *meaning* of the universal quantifier, or to say that the *meaning* of the universal quantifier has not changed but that the inductive logic has changed. Similarly, there may be situations in which we can say either that a man uses a psychological term, say, "jealous", incorrectly, i.e., that he assigns to it an unusual meaning, or that he assigns to it the same meaning as does everyone else, but that he accepts a very different set of sentences. More precisely, there are logically possible situations in which it is arbitrary whether to say that someone means something unusual by "jealous" or to say that he has a very unusual set of beliefs about jealousy.

It should be clear that in such models there is not, strictly speaking, any such thing as "the meaning" of a given word, and hence the question "in what can the meaning of a psychological word consist, if not in a set of criteria?" has no force. (Although "anti-essentialistic", in this sense, such models are neutral with respect to the existence or non-existence of a sharp analytic-synthetic distinction. In the language of these models, that is simply the highly technical issue, whether there is a set of privileged sentences involving a given word such that a change in one of *those* sentences *has* to be counted as a change in the meaning of that word.)

I make these much-too-brief remarks only as a reminder of the "non-criterial" view of language. With this in mind, let us consider the question whether someone could understand the meaning of a psychological word, say "angry" without knowing that certain forms of behavior entitle one to apply that word to another person.

The question is ambiguous. If the question means, could someone who did not even know that certain types of behavior are thought to entitle one to say that another person is angry be said to know the meaning of the word *angry*, then the question does not have to do with entitlement relations; it has to do with knowledge of the beliefs of the community as to entitlement relations, and it has to do with the bearing that that knowledge or lack of that knowledge could have on knowing or not knowing "the meaning" of the word "angry". If, on the other hand, the question is, could someone who lacks the knowledge that the behavior of other persons entitles one in certain circumstances to say that those persons are angry—not that this is believed to be so, but that it *is* so—be said to know the meaning of the word "angry", then the question does really have to do with entitlement relations and their relation to meaning. Let us take the first form of the question first. The first form of the question comes to this. Could someone learn the meaning of the word "angry" without at the same time learning that certain particular forms of behavior are thought to entitle one to say that another person is angry? This breaks down into several subquestions. One subquestion is, must one learn the meaning of words? Could one be born just being able to speak the language? Another subquestion is this, if one learns the meaning of words from other speakers, not from robots, phonograph records, moving pictures, etc., must one acquire the meaning of psychological words by learning that certain behavioral indicators are normally taken to entitle one to apply those words to another person? A third subquestion is, suppose one learned the meaning of the word "angry" from other speakers, and one learned to use the word partly by applying it to others on the basis of behavioral indicators; if those behavioral indicators were *not* what we regard as indicators of anger at all, would it follow that "angry" did not have the *meaning* that *we* ascribe to it?

All of these questions are extremely hard. I find it very strange that anyone should feel confident about answers to these questions, especially about the modish answers, and even stranger that anyone should regard it as a defect of the realist rejoinder to skepticism that it avoids these questions. Since space is short, let me simply say dogmatically what I think is the answer to these questions. First, I think it is not a logical truth that language must be learned. It may be that at some time in the future we shall all speak a single world-language, and if that language does not undergo change, it might even be possible to produce humans who will be born speaking the language, without having to go through any process of language acquisition at all. In the second place, if one does learn one's native language, and one does learn to apply psychological words to other persons, I think this does not absolutely have to be on the basis of behavioral indicators. It could be on the basis of neurophysiological or other theory, and I think that it would not necessarily follow that the terms had a different *meaning,* at least not provided that they had their ordinary reporting use. Third, even supposing that psychological words are learned on the basis of behavioral indicators, and even supposing that those indicators are very different from the ones we use, I think it does not follow that those words necessarily have a different meaning from that of our culture. We all know the story about people who are supposed to grimace when happy and smile when sad. If the people in those cultures spoke English, I think it would not be correct or customary to say that the words "happy" and "sad" have a different meaning when used among those English speakers. If one of those speakers sees Jones grimace and says, "I see that Jones is happy today", it's not that he uses the word "happy" with a non-customary meaning; it's just that he believes, and, indeed, has good reason to believe, that people normally grimace when they are happy.

At this point, however, a certain puzzle arises, or rather seems to arise. If I can say that people who grimace are "happy", that people who smile are "sad", then couldn't people learn to use any psychological word in any circumstances whatsoever? And if they could, in what would the *sameness of meaning* of the psychological word possibly consist—used in those circumstances by those people, and used by us in what we regard as normal circumstances for the application of the word? I think that it is just this line of thought that leads such people as Strawson and Shoemaker to think there must be quasi-logical relations between facts about behavior and assertions about the mental states of other persons. And I think that in this line of thought there are two separate confusions to be distinguished. In the first place, I cannot arbitrarily say of just anyone under just any circumstances that he is happy. If I say of someone who grimaces that he is happy, this is because I believe that the state that I call *happiness* is one that *could* lead to that behavior under *some* circumstances, and that those circumstances obtain in the case in question. If it were deeply imbedded in my psychological theory that under no circumstances can a person who grimaces be happy, then I might be disinclined to say that the meaning of "happy" was the same even in the culture described a few moments ago and in our culture. It does not follow, however, that there is any behavioral sign that could not be a sign of happiness, or any behavioral sign that could not fail to be a sign of happiness. It only follows that a given behavioral sign can be a sign of happiness in some circumstances only if the people who take it to be a behavioral sign in those circumstances have appropriate other beliefs, habits, customs, etc., in connection with happiness. It is *not* odd, in certain circumstances, to believe that one's neighbors grimace when happy; but it is more than "odd", it is strongly semantically deviant, to suppose that one's neighbors *dislike* being happy. Even this, however, may not be impossible. The fact that it is strongly semantically deviant to believe that one's neighbors dislike being happy does not mean that under no conditions can one believe that one's neighbors dislike being happy; it only means that one would have to tell a considerable story to succeed in convincing us that there was such a belief, with no change in the meaning of "happy" involved. Even if it were actually analytic that one cannot, or cannot always, be averse to being happy, notice that this analytic relationship is not a relation between any psychological state and a behavior indicator, but between two different psychological states.

In sum, a person who is obviously a native speaker of (correct) English could fail to know that people who scream are usually in pain, that people who smile are usually happy, and so on, and it might still be the case that he knew the meaning of all of these words and used them with the same meaning that we do. That is to say, normal English speakers, when given sufficient information about the kind of culture that *this* speaker comes from, might decide to account for the difference in what he says as owing not to any difference in the meaning of words, but simply as owing to a difference in the behavior that he is accustomed to. No inference of the following form can be valid: Jones knows the meaning of the word "pain"; Jones knows that if someone winces, screams, writhes, etc., normally, one is entitled to conclude that he is in pain. One of the most pathetic aspects of twentieth-century philosophy is the persistence with which philosophers have attempted to breathe life into this particular dead horse.

Suppose, now, that someone has grown up in our culture and knows exactly what we take to be behavioral indicators of pain, anger, jealousy, lust, etc. Let us now suppose that he becomes converted to philosophical skepticism, and he decides that in fact none of these indicators *entitle* us to say that someone else is in pain, is angry, jealous, lustful, etc. It is only, according to him, that we *think* these indicators entitle us to say these things. Should we say of this man, as many philosophers want us to say, that he is making the following logical blunder: denying the very *criterial* relationships (between molar behavior and mental state) upon which the customary understanding of psychological terms depends? This is balderdash. In order to know the meaning of a term, I need not talk exactly as my neighbors do, or even assent to the propositions to which they assent. At most it is necessary, and I doubt if it actually is necessary, that I assent to the propositions that are normally taken to be "evident", "obvious", etc., unless I have some reason for not doing so. "I don't believe that other people are conscious, or, at any rate, I don't believe that we *know* that other people are conscious", is a perfectly good reason for refusing to accept the entitlement relations that most people accept. It may, of course, be *crazy* to believe that other people aren't conscious, and it may even be crazy or silly to believe that we don't know that other people are conscious; but that is exactly what we should say in this case—that the assertion is silly, or crazy, or foolish, etc.—*not* that the speaker is making a logical blunder or using words with a different meaning or anything of that kind.

At this point we come, I think, to the vital nerve of this whole dispute. If the skeptic—the man who talks in the way I just described —does not contradict himself, if he does not use the words with a different meaning, then in *what* does this *sameness of meaning* consist? We take it that seeing someone writhe and moan, etc., entitles us to say that that someone is in pain; the skeptic does not. Yet we are both supposed to have the same *meaning* of the word "pain". In what does this *meaning* consist?

As a crude oversimplification, we may suppose that it consists in this: a shared disposition to use the word "pain" (or whatever psychological word may be in question) in a certain way. If we take it that this disposition must be as *specific* as a disposition to conclude that someone is in pain when he writhes, moans, screams, etc., obviously one cannot share the customary meaning of the word "pain" and not share the disposition to conclude that someone is in pain when he writhes, moans, screams, etc. To be sure. But it seems to me absurd to suppose that the linguistic disposition shared by people who use the word "pain" correctly is that specific. The disposition is rather a disposition to use the word "pain" in various ways, depending on various things, and depending in part on what sentences containing the word "pain" one accepts. If we know that a man is a very consistent skeptic (of course, no one is), then what will count as showing that he misunderstands the word "pain" may be quite different from what will count as showing that I, who am not a skeptic, do not use the word pain with the customary meaning.

My position is circular. I do not regard this circularity as a defect. I argue that the skeptic's beliefs, or rather the sentences by which he expresses his beliefs, are not semantically deviant on the ground that he talks just the way normal people would talk if they had to express *those* beliefs. But this assumes that there are beliefs here to be expressed, not, as it were, pseudo-beliefs. I count the skeptic's beliefs as beliefs precisely because I see no reason to count the sentences that he utters in expressing his putative beliefs as in any way semantically deviant. This is circular because the argument is that the skeptic's total usage of psychological words is not semantically deviant, because it is just the usage that one would expect if one had to express certain beliefs that the skeptic has. But this assumes that certain key sentences used by the skeptic to express those beliefs are not semantically deviant, and this is just what many linguistic philosophers challenge today. The reason I am not perturbed by this "circularity" is that it is a circularity only as long as operational constraints are not considered, and in empirical science operational constraints must be considered sooner or later. The decisive fact is that the sentences the skeptic utters are not regarded as linguistically deviant by native speakers other than those with a philosophical axe to grind.

I don't mean to say that the native speaker necessarily has available to him such technical notions as "semantically deviant". The native speaker doesn't have available such notions as "grammatical" and "ungrammatical" either, at least not in the sense in which linguists are now using "grammatical" and "ungrammatical." However it is easy to find out if native speakers think there is something linguistically wrong with a sentence, at least in a large class of cases (I don't deny that there are cases in which it is unclear whether what is

wrong with a sentence is regarded as linguistic by native speakers).
It is also easy to find out that in many cases what speakers think is
wrong about a sentence is simply the way it is formed, e.g., an adjective should precede rather than follow the noun it modifies, or a word
is pluralized incorrectly, or something of that kind. In such a case, we
have no hesitation in saying that those native speakers regard the
sentence as "ungrammatical" even if they don't actually put it that
way. Do native speakers, however, regard the skeptic's sentences as
ill-formed, or ungrammatical? Clearly they do not. Do they regard
them as involving violations of the use of words? Clearly, they do not.
What most speakers say about sentences by skeptics is that they involve a silly belief, or a crazy belief, or a belief that isn't worth discussing—or, in some cases, a belief with which they agree. In short,
the overwhelming majority of informants regard the skeptic's sentences as correctly *expressing beliefs*.

Am I saying that sentences should never be counted as semantically deviant unless the majority of informants regard them as
deviant? No, I am not saying that. I am aware that in many cases
native informants will fall into disagreement about precisely this
kind of question, and that is the sort of case in which it is appropriate
to let considerations of theoretical advantage decide. I doubt, however, if there are any cases in which the linguist should go against the
unanimous agreement of native informants. I think in the case of the
skeptic's sentences we are as close to unanimous agreement as we
ever are in linguistics—that there is nothing wrong with the *language*
that the skeptic uses. It seems to me virtually unimaginable that
considerations of theoretical advantage could override such a powerful consensus. Fortunately, we do not need to discuss whether they
ever could or not. For I think it is easy to see that they do not in this
particular case. To see this, just ask yourself: In what cases *do* we
override the intuitions of some native informants? We do so when
there are not direct, but indirect, operational constraints at work.
That is to say, even if the informants do not agree at first hand that
a certain usage is linguistically deviant, still, if we say that that
usage is linguistically deviant it must be because it fails to correspond to certain statements in our grammar or in our semantic theory.
Those statements, in turn, must at some point be empirically supported. It may be that in simpler cases than the one at issue informants do clearly mark as deviant usages that violate those statements
in our grammar or semantic theory, and that this justifies us in accepting those statements as descriptive of the language and using

them to decide disputed cases. All this is ABC, of course. If it is granted, then, that the skeptic's sentences cannot be ruled out as semantically deviant on the basis of direct linguistic evidence, i.e., on the basis of the testimony of informants, the question becomes, can they be ruled out indirectly as semantically deviant on the grounds that they violate norms of language? What are these norms of language, and what is the evidence that they function as such in the language? The answer is that the supposed norms of language have the form that certain behavioral criteria entitle one to say that other people are, as it might be, egotistical, angry, happy, sad, tired, jealous, etc. But what is the evidence that these are norms of language? The evidence is that if a person is confronted with a clear case of another person who is angry—with someone showing unmistakable signs of anger, or egotism, or joy, or whatever—and fails to note that the person is angry, he may be suspected of not knowing the meaning of the word. At first blush, this is very convincing, but only at first blush, for we see when we look more carefully, that the person is only suspected of not knowing the meaning of the word "angry", or whatever, if he is unable to give a reason for not agreeing that the subject in question is angry, or whatever, or if we are unaware that he possesses such a reason. Suppose he can offer a reason. Suppose he says, as it might be, "That's not the way angry people act". If he's wrong— if, in fact, *that* is exactly the way in which angry people act—then the suspicion that he does not know the meaning of the word "angry" is strongly increased. But it still does not amount to logical necessity, for if it turns out that that is not the way in which angry people act *in the speaker's culture,* then the suspicion that the speaker does not know the meaning of the word "angry" lapses, and is replaced by the conviction that what the speaker does not know is how angry people behave in *our* culture.

Similarly, if the speaker refuses to agree, and has the reason to offer, "That's only behavior, and no amount of behavior entitles one to apply a psychological predicate to another", then again the suspicion that he does not know the meaning of the word "angry" lapses, and is replaced by the conviction that the speaker is a skeptic. At this point, it becomes apparent that the logical behaviorist position is just as circular as the position that I advocate; for the norms of language, or alleged norms of language, to which the logical behaviorist appeals in trying to establish the skeptic's sentences as semantically deviant are not in fact then norms of language in the usual sense, or if they are, the empirical evidence that they are is no better than the direct empirical evidence that the skeptic's sentences are semantically deviant. But we agree that the direct empirical evidence was *against* the thesis that the skeptic's sentences were semantically deviant, which is why it required some kind of indirect argument to establish this in the first place. Both positions, then: mine and the logical behaviorist's, are circular; I can break out of my circle by appealing to the overwhelming consensus in the linguistic intuitions of native speakers; whereas the logical behaviorist can appeal only to the overwhelming consensus in the philosophical opinions of committed logical behaviorists.

Plantinga's Objection to Ziff[3]

Plantinga's objection to Ziff's argument is that there *is* an alternative hypothesis in the field. The one that Plantinga mentions is the familiar hypothesis that there is a demon who has created all beings other than me without minds, and who causes them to act exactly as if they did have minds for the express purpose of fooling *me*. Plantinga is aware of the usual replies, that this hypothesis is less *simple* than psychological theory, that it is *parasitic* upon psychological theory, etc. The difficulty he sees with these replies is that they depend upon notions of complexity, parasitism, and so on, which are today far from clear. In a sense, I agree with Plantinga. I think that the notions of simplicity, plausibility, parasitism, and so forth, are indeed far from clear, and I am not optimistic about prospects of making them clear in the foreseeable future. I think that to a large extent when scientists talk about accepting a theory because the theory is plausible or not ad hoc, or simpler than another, they mean a variety of different things. Ziff expresses the conventional view that there are "factors" of "completeness, coherence, and simplicity" which are "the hallmarks of a sound theory", and I am skeptical and inclined to think that "simplicity", "parsimony", "completeness", are today just words that we use to cover our ignorance. What seems to me the case is that the actual procedure of science depends upon balancing two desiderata: on the one hand, we try to put the accepted theory under maximum strain, that is to say, we try to maximize *a priori* plausibility and probability; theories that seem to us too wildly implausible, we do not even bother to test.

[3] "Symposium: The Other Minds Problem. Ziff's Other Minds". *Loc. cit.*, pp. 587–589.

What do plausibility and probability (I hate talk of "simplicity") really depend upon? In part, probability may itself be a matter of previous inductive inference; to what extent this is so is being explored, both within inductive logic and within mathematical statistics. This question is closely related to the whole question of the applicability of so-called "Bayesian" models, both for confirmation theory and for decision theory. Beyond this, it seems clear that plausibility and probability have something to do with the accepted science and metaphysics of a given time. Teleological explanations seem plausible to an age that is steeped in teleological philosophy; mechanistic explanations will seem plausible to an age that is steeped in mechanistic philosophy. But exactly how sociological considerations affect the priority ordering[4] of hypotheses is something that we know little about. Glib explanations of scientific preference for one explanation of given phenomena over another in terms of "the metaphysics of the time" tend to be cases of *post hoc propter hoc*. It is easy to explain the acceptance of one theory over another in terms of a disposition to accept that theory over the other. I suspect that in the last analysis not only inductive logical and sociological factors will have to be invoked, but also biological factors, if we are to understand how humans actually arrive at a priority ordering of hypotheses. Very likely we shall have to be able to solve the problem of "artificial intelligence", and to simulate the human ability to construct and select inductive hypotheses, before we shall have any real understanding in this area. But I disagree with Plantinga in one important respect. It may be that pointing out analogies between the acceptance of thing-theory, or the acceptance of psychological theory, on the one hand, and explanatory induction, on the other, is pointing out an analogy between what is unclear and what is equally unclear, as Plantinga urges; but I do not agree that even so it is valueless.

The decisive point is this: that there is a difference between scientific belief and arbitrary belief, even if scientific belief depends in part on ordering of hypotheses, which is, in some sense, "arbitrary". If scientists simply ranked hypotheses in some arbitrary way, and then accepted the hypothesis highest-ranked no matter what observations might tell them, scientific belief would *really* be utterly ar-

---

4 The idea that rational men "rank" hypotheses according to "plausibility", "implausibility", etc., is employed in what follows as a useful methodological fiction. Of course, what one encounters in real life is not a fixed "priority ordering", but rather changing intuitive judgments which are themselves dependent upon context, factual knowledge, argument, etc.

bitrary; but that is not what the scientist does. If the scientist simply accepted some ordering of hypotheses, and then proceeded to accept the highest-valued hypothesis which was not yet falsified by empirical data, but he did not make any special attempt to gather falsifying data, still, in large part, scientific belief would be arbitrary; for, it is the case with a great many theories that one is not likely to come across falsifying evidence unless one tries to find it. But neither of these descriptions is an accurate description of the scientific method. The scientific method is the method of testing one's ideas in practice; of subjecting them to maximum strain; of accepting only beliefs that have succeeded in practice. The element of arbitrariness still comes in, in that one cannot possibly test all beliefs, and in that at any given time there will be infinitely many beliefs that cannot be ruled out on *deductive* grounds, that is to say, on grounds of incompatibility with observation. So some kind of priority ordering has to be used, and it is true that if our implicit priority ordering is unfortunate—in the sense that the hypotheses that are true of the actual world are located at an impossibly vast "depth", while the hypotheses that are above them in the priority ordering are extremely bad—then by using the scientific method we shall never come to the truth about the world. Once one has pointed this out, it is clear, I think, how science differs from dogmatism even though there are arbitrary and authoritarian elements in science. That science is not sheer dogmatism and authoritarianism is not, of course, any proof that science will work, or even that science is any more rational than any other method. The problem of the justification of induction, if it is a problem, still remains.

But let us return to Plantinga. According to Plantinga, explaining our knowledge of the existence of other minds in terms of the scientific method is explaining the obscure in terms of the more obscure. What is admittedly obscure about the scientific method is the basis of the intuitive priority ordering of hypotheses that scientists actually employ; to admit that that is obscure is not to admit that every feature of the logic of theory testing is obscure. I have been arguing, in effect, that we know enough about the scientific method today to make this sort of analogy enlightening, and that indeed the detailed understanding of just how the priority ordering of hypotheses is arrived at will be unlikely to contribute much to this argument. Having said this, one should say one or two more things about Plantinga's specific example of the demon hypothesis. First of all, I grant what is often disputed, that the demon hypothesis represents a logical possibility. It is perfectly imaginable that other people should be mere "dummies" controlled remotely by some intelligence I know nothing of. But I do not grant that this hypothesis is "in the field". For a hypothesis to be in the field, it is not enough for it to represent a possibility that we can imagine; it must meet two further conditions. It must be elaborated, the details must be worked out to a certain degree, various questions which naturally occur to one must be answered, and, secondly, it must not be too *silly* to consider. This hypothesis, the demon hypothesis, has obviously never been elaborated in any detail at all, and it obviously is too silly to consider. This is the point at which the skeptic boggles. Is this not dogmatism, is this not authoritarianism, to rule out a hypothesis *a priori*, on the ground of some kind of an intuitive judgment, whose basis we know little of, to the effect that it is "too silly to consider". The answer again is "no". For, even if the demon hypothesis is too silly to consider, i.e., too far out on the priority ordering for scientists to consider it necessary to test it, still one is *allowed* to test it if one wants to. One of the features of the scientific method is precisely that one is allowed to disagree with one's colleagues with respect to what is too silly to consider. If I really believed that other people were dummies, then it would be up to me to try to find some testable difference that that might make, and to try to construct some test to show that it is correct. But what if it is built into the hypothesis that I cannot succeed —that the demon, or the remote intelligence is far too clever for me to discover how he works, or by what mechanisms his "dummies" work? This is to ask, what if it is built into the theory that it has exactly the same testable consequences as some theory that is more plausible? The answer is, if someone with malice aforethought constructs a theory that has this feature, he will succeed in constructing a theory that is not logically false, but is such that by its very construction would always be irrational to believe. It is not *a priori* that such a theory is false; but it is *a priori* that it could never be believed rationally. But then, Plantinga would of course point out, everything is going to depend on the judgment that the hypothesis is indeed "deeper down" in the priority ordering, "less plausible", "less probable", "more ad hoc", or something of that kind than the vast constellation of hypotheses that we have called "psychological theory". How do we know that this is so? Or, if it is so, as a matter of fact about the actual intuitive judgments of scientists, how do we know that those intuitive judgments are rational?

This is a difficulty only in the sense of being *the* difficulty that constitutes the problem of induction. To raise the problem, how do we know that the intuitive priority ordering of hypotheses actually employed by scientists is *the rational* priority ordering of hypotheses (if there is such a thing), is precisely to raise the whole issue of the justification of induction, at least if "induction" is understood as we have been understanding it in this paper. It seems to me, then, that Plantinga, playing the role of the skeptic, can remind us that the scientific method depends on regularities in what we all consider to be silly hypotheses, in what we all consider to be ad hoc hypotheses, in what we all consider to be plausible hypotheses, in what we all consider to be probable. He can remind us of the enormous role played by agreement in our judgments in the normal inductive method of science, and to do this is no mean contribution. But reminding us of this, and reminding us how little we understand this, is not showing that there is something concerning which knowledge is impossible.

SIX

Origins of
Problem Solving
Strategies in
Skill Acquisition

JEROME S. BRUNER

THE TRADITIONAL topic of this paper is the development of human
sensory-motor skill in infancy. But a close analysis of the early acquisition of human skills leads one in time to a reconsideration of the
concept of skill and its relation to problem solving in the broad, of
which skill acquisition is one manifestation. The exercise ahead will,
consequently, take us far from the usual setting in which problem
solving is studied. And this is perforce the case. For problem solving

Presented at the XIX International Congress of Psychology, London, July
1969.
        The research reported here was supported by grants to Harvard
University, Center for Cognitive Studies, from the National Institute of
Child Health and Human Development, Grant No. R01 HD-03049; The
National Institute of Mental Health, Grant No. 1P01 MH-12623; The
Carnegie Corporation, Grant No. B-3233; and The National Science Foun-
dation, Grant No. GS-1153.

in human infancy has little to do with getting cannibals and missionaries across imaginary rivers or with solving either mechanical puzzles or mathematical conjectures. Yet, I think this detour into infancy may prove of some use, for there are forms of strategy to be observed in infancy that may tell us much about the origins of later intelligent behavior.

The typical problem solving of the infant has to do with the use of hands, of eyes, of bodily orientation, etc., in dealing with things and people. At first glance, these seem exclusively like matters of perception, of attention, of manipulation and locomotion, of social interaction—and their maturation and development. But it is precisely in the *use* and *coordination* of these processes for the attainment of goals that we encounter the earliest problem solving. When such problems are solved, we properly speak of the child as having achieved a skill. The mastery of a skill thus turns out to be equally well described as a case of the infant developing strategies for using information intelligently in choosing among alternative modes of responding. The only presupposition is that, in fact, the infant is *capable* of alternative modes of responding, and that is a fairly easy matter to demonstrate, as we shall see.

"A strategy refers to a pattern of decisions in the acquisition, retention, and utilization of information that serves to meet certain objectives, i.e., to insure certain forms of outcome and to insure against certain others".[1] In fact, we infer the rule of a strategy from a sequence of acts, and while it is of great interest whether a subject can "report" or be "conscious" of his strategy, reportability or consciousness are certainly no more required features of strategic behavior than is a reportable knowledge of the rules of grammar necessary for the production of grammatical speech. Indeed, many studies of problem solving and concept attainment indicate precisely that even intelligent adults often use strategies without awareness and give very muddled accounts of what they are doing.

A striking feature of a strategy, once mastered, is that it can be applied to a wide variety of contingencies, its underlying rule being generic with respect to the stimuli that are relevant and the responses that are permissible. It has, so to speak, a transfer principle built into it. The try-out strategy for dealing with multiple alternatives, "win-stay-lose-shift"[2] can be, and is in fact, applied to a wide variety of

[1] J. S. Bruner, J. J. Goodnow, and G. A. Austin, *A Study of Thinking* (New York: John Wiley & Sons, 1956), 54.
[2] *Ibid.*

choice-situations in spite of a limited setting of first mastery. Such instant generality characterizes many early strategies used by children in gathering information, e.g., studies by Potter or Mosher, reported in Bruner, Olver, and Greenfield.[3] "Direct transfer" of a strategy seems to be dependent on *comprehension* or *recognition* of the requirements of a task. It is reminiscent of the productivity or generativeness of a language's syntax, in the sense that once a rule for forming a grammatical sequence has become part of one's competence, a vast number of sentences or rule-bound strings can be generated with no further learning. Similarly, once having mastered the elements of chess, a vast number of different games can be played. So too with sensory-motor skills: learning to ride a bicycle, we have learned them all—perhaps even at one-sixth Earth's gravity. We shall want to examine this feature of productiveness of strategies, skills, and language in examining early problem solving to see whether the communality is deep or trivial.

The Structure of Skill

In characterizing the structure of skill, we must first make a sharp distinction between what the Russian physiologist Bernstein[4] calls *activity* on the one hand and *movement* on the other. Activity requires the coordination and regulation of movement in the attainment of some particular objective. A mosquito is to be slapped, a ball is to be thrown, or a screwdriver is to be turned—these are activities involving the coordination and direction of movements. At very least, the carrying out of such an activity requires a system containing an effector which is to be regulated, a control source that conveys to the system the specifications of the act intended, a receptor that registers the course of the act, a comparator that estimates the discrepancy between intended act and act thus far accomplished, and a feedback device that converts the discrepancy computed by the comparator into regulatory signals to the effector. In short, there is a feed-forward signal from the control source specifying intention, a discrimination

[3] F. A. Mosher and J. R. Hornsby, "On Asking Questions", in J. S. Bruner, R. R. Olver, P. M. Greenfield, *et al.*, *Studies in Cognitive Growth* (New York: John Wiley & Sons, 1966).

[4] N. Bernstein, *The Coordination and Regulation of Movement.* (New York: Pergamon Press, 1967).

of present state, a comparison of present achievement with intention, and feedback based on that comparison. This is the essence of regulated activity. It is a familiar enough biological model, one that is renowned from the work of von Holst and Mittelstaedt[5] and of Sperry[6] on plasticity of behavior, and is referred to most often as the reafference principle. In any case, it provides the means by which a nervous system distributes information both in order to govern anticipation and to compute regulatory feedback.

What of "immature" skills or the presumably "unskilled" behavior of the infant? How can these be characterized? There is a large and in many ways useful literature on skill acquisition during infancy and childhood, but it is preoccupied with normative problems and with "developmental diagnosis", and the nature and growth of skill *per se* are forgotten. What we know of adult skills is highly suggestive— particularly the work of the Cambridge group inspired by Sir Frederic Bartlett—Craik, Welford, Broadbent, Mackworth, Poulton, Crossman, and others. Craik[7] early argued that human skill involved three functions—a perceptual function, a translatory function, and an effector function. The system comprising the three could be viewed as a reckoning device, the task of the translatory system being to devise an effector output that would be appropriate to invariant features of a display picked up by perceptual functioning. The objective of such skilled activity is to bring about a change in the signal or display parameters according to some criterion. As Welford puts it in his recently published book,[8]

> The functional unit of performance does not typically consist merely of perceptual processes leading to motor responses, but of attempts by the organism to bring about modifications in the situation in which it finds itself. . . . The unit of performance extends from a signal to a modified signal and . . . response or action is merely a link between these two. The way of looking at [skilled] performance has two important consequences. First, it places the main emphasis on perception and decision and thus

[5] E. von Holst and H. Mittelstaedt, "Das Reafferenzprinzip", *Naturwissenschaften* (1950), 37, pp. 464–476.

[6] R. W. Sperry, "Physiological Plasticity and Brain Circuit Theory", in *Biological and Biochemical Bases of Behavior*, H. R. Harlow and C. N. Woolsey, eds. (Madison, Wisconsin: University of Wisconsin Press, 1958).

[7] K. W. J. Craik, *The Nature of Explanation* (Cambridge, England: Cambridge University Press, 1943). (Reprinted in 1952.)

[8] A. T. Welford, *Fundamentals of Skill* (London: Methuen, 1968), 196.

makes the essential matrix of behavior cognitive. Secondly, since actions merely bridge the gap between one perceptual situation and another, they can vary substantially without the *functional* unit of performance having to be regarded as different: the central mechanisms are capable of producing a range of actions the details of which are matched to the precise requirements of the occasion so that the same end may be achieved in slightly different ways.

Skill, then, requires a capacity for perceiving and comprehending the nature of a task and constructing according to rule a response appropriate to achieving a change in the environment.

When we turn now to consider infancy, there are several alternative ways of looking at immaturity—be it immaturity of skill, of problem-solving strategies, or of voluntarily directed activity in Bernstein's sense. We may look at the level of intention or feedforward in the sense of whether a program exists that can guide and coordinate constituent acts. Or we may find immaturity on the level of the comparison required between intention and actual output—inadequate, ill-timed, or noisy feedback. Or we may find it at the level of perception and comprehension of the requirements of a task. Indeed, some aspects of immaturity can also be attributed to insufficient development of the effector system, although this is interesting psychologically only because such effector immaturity might, in the presence of an appropriate intention, evoke revealing compensatory activity designed to bypass an inadequate effector. Such instances exist in infancy as they do in aging, though in the former case they are "compensations" for capacities not yet attained, and in the latter for capacities that have been lost. The former type of compensation is not as absurd as it may first appear, as we shall see.

Any early human skill, I shall argue, is initially performed in an awkward but recognizable form that expresses a preadapted program of action. It is frequently the case that such initial performances run off without feedback. Thus, initial attempts to take hold of a visually presented object often betray a kind of ballistic or impulsive property, suggesting that the first effort at achieving an objective is aimed and fired, though not regulated in passage. Often, the early, preadapted version of what is to become a highly regulated skill, takes the form of a relatively undifferentiated motoric "holophrase", as with the infant "reaching" for an attractive object by a general raising of the arms, pointing of the fingers toward the object with prolonged gaze and a working of the tongue and mouth for which the object is

[104]

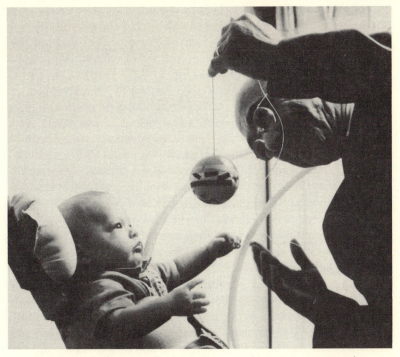

Figure 1. A three-month-old infant, reaching for an attractive object, raises his arms, points his fingers toward the object, and shows typical mouthing behavior. (Courtesy of Ted Polumbaum, PIX, Inc., New York.)

eventually destined.[9] An example of such behavior is contained in Figure 1. From this position there may later differentiate a swiping response toward the object, the hand being shot toward the object quite accurately though ballistically.[10] No startle occurs when the hand shoots through the visual field in this fashion, and character-

[9] I have seen a three-month infant, foiled in his effort to mobilize hands and arms for a reach, lean forward to try to take the object with his mouth —a pattern one sees months later when an object is presented within reach while both the infant's hands are full. Direct mouth-taking is obviously an ancient pattern, very common in G. gorilla. *Cf.* H. Knobloch, and B. Pasamanick, "The Development of Adaptive Behavior in an Infant Gorilla." *Journal of Comparative and Physiological Psychology* (1959), *52* (6), 699–704. Also, *cf.* A. H. Riesen, *Primate Growth and Development*, a film (New York: Appleton-Century-Crofts Library, 1967).

[10] J. B. Alt, *The Use of Vision in Early Reaching.* Unpublished honors thesis, Department of Psychology, Harvard University, 1968.

istically the hand is fisted by the time it reaches the object, suggesting a reafference signal preceding the act. Such data suggest the pre-existence of a program of action or intention or feed-forward, well before the development of the other features of voluntarily controlled action.

Opportunity for practice of such "immature" action appears to have three notable effects: modularization, differentiation, and re-placement. As with adult performance, repetition has the effect of making the action, however immature, more uniform in both timing and pattern. We may refer to this process as *modularization,* for it is upon the achievement of some degree of predictable uniformity of response that the action pattern in question becomes amenable to be-ing fitted into larger sequences of behavior directed to other, more temporally remote objectives. Coordination of power and precision grips—holding a larger object immobile with one hand while using the pincer-grip of the other to contact a small object attached to it—gradually becomes uniform, and once it does it becomes imbedded in a longer act that involves "strumming" and/or "pulling" the smaller object rather than simply contacting it with a pincer grip. It is modu-larization that permits newly mastered subroutines to be integrated into acts controlled by more sustained intentions. What was once self-sustained now becomes integratable into larger sequences.

The second process is *differentiation.* What was originally "holo-phrastic" or even ballistic, now begins to differentiate into parts, to allow the influence of feedback control. Pauses now develop within the sequence, and the impulsive appearance of the act diminishes. For example, reaching and taking an object is initially an almost seamless carrying out of an intention to bring the object to the mouth, and the sequence goes off with no pauses. Indeed, the act can be disorganized at virtually any point by inserting a finger or nipple into the child's mouth. With practice, pauses appear. A finger in the baby's mouth results not in disorganization, but in the temporary stopping of the act at the next pause point. It is this slow differentiation that renders the act more plastic, more amenable to the process of being "con-structed" to the requirements of the task. To use a linguistic analogy again, as an act becomes more differentiated and plastic, it becomes more context sensitive and can be altered appropriately to fit into dif-ferent sequences—as mastered phonemes or morphemes can be modi-fied to an appropriate allophone or allomorph to fit a phonological or sentence context.

Note that the processes of modularization and differentiation both presuppose an enormous amount of initial *perceptual* functioning and considerable translatory power to guide even the initial pattern of action. In the initial stages of skill development, we can find no evidence of deficit in perceptual functioning, although we encounter considerable deficit in organizing stimulus events *over time* into signals for the guidance of serial action. The usual picture is of an infant, beset by intention, gazing intently, but powerless to mobilize a response. This, by the way, is a pattern found in no other organism during immaturity, a matter of great evolutionary interest that we must pass over until another occasion.

Finally, practice and the perfecting of a skilled action sequence eventually leads to its *replacement* by a new and cruder action sequence. This is indeed very puzzling, for, in fact, the perfected act is leading to even more reinforcement as it becomes appropriately shaped to the requirements of a task. We shall see many instances of this phenomenon in a later section of the paper. To put the matter very briefly, it may well be that with better control achieved through modularization and differentiation, the infant's information-processing capacities are freed so that new modes of task analysis can take place and lead to the output of response patterns in terms of new action programs.

What is characteristic of initial skilled performance is the sharp restriction in degrees of freedom that is imposed upon the action in question, a point that has been made much of by Bernstein[11] in his analysis of skill acquisition in adults. It is this reduction in degrees of freedom that gives to infant behavior its characteristically stiff, awkward quality. An example suffices. Observe a six-month-old's hands and fingers when they are idly in contact with an object with no visual surveillance present. They move about deftly, indexing tactual irregularities, hands orienting this way and that.[12] It appears to be palpation without an objective or, perhaps, as Zinchenko[13] suggests, a form of scanning in the service of modelling the environment. But observe the same infant reach for an object under visual guidance. The fingers now are spread wide open, stiffly and fully extended, the bodily orientation is by midline aiming, and the reach is more likely

[11] *Op. cit.*

[12] Cf. J. S. Bruner and B. Koslowski, "Descriptive Analysis of the Hands Used as Tools in Manual Problem Solving." In preparation (Center for Cognitive Studies, Harvard University, 1969).

[13] V. P. Zinchenko, "Aspects of Orienting Movements of the Hand and Eye and Their Role in the Formation of Motor Habits". Translation by Dan I. Slobin of an article in *Voprosy Psikhologii* (*Questions of Psychology*), (1956), *6*, pp. 51–52.

than not bisymmetric. There is no shaping of the hand to the dimensions of the object, no anticipatory finger closure. Grace is absent. This is an initial feature of strategic performance that we would wish to note in passing, to reconsider more concretely later—the infant's way of achieving what Welford[14] calls "economy of decision", cutting down the number of invariant features to be taken into account in early performance.

Once the initial achievement of modularized, differentiated subroutines has occurred, the process of skill acquisition becomes increasingly one of combining and adjusting already available constituent acts into increasingly appropriate, variable, and more extended sequences of directed action. These in turn become the modifiable subroutines in still more extended goal-directed sequences of activity. Let it be clear, however, that many of these more complex and extended instances of manual intelligence are also preadapted or innate, though they cannot appear until skill in the manipulation of the world has achieved a certain level. It is an anomalous position, yet we must propose that the expression of some innate activity patterns depends upon prior learning!

There is one crucial point that has to be made here. The construction of new action patterns for the achievement of more remote goals depends not only upon the combination process just described, but crucially upon the capacity of the infant to hold an intended objective invariant while the process of construction is going on. As characteristic of early skilled behavior as its awkwardness, is its openness to distraction by other features of the environment impinging upon the infant. Indeed, it is often the case (as in the study of Bruner, Bruner, and Kahneman),[15] that it is difficult to describe the initial and terminal points in the actions of a seven-month-old using a cup in a rich stimulus setting. The unit of analysis under these circumstances extends from the impingement of one distraction to that of the next. It is an aspect of the kind of "planning control" that Luria[16] locates in the frontal lobes and that has been so brilliantly described by him[17]

[14] Op. cit.

[15] J. S. Bruner, Blanche M. Bruner, and Irah Kahneman, "A Study of Cup-use in Three Infants, 7 Months, 14 Months and 21 Months of Age", Eighth Annual Report of the Center for Cognitive Studies (Harvard University, 1968).

[16] A. R. Luria, "The Origin and Cerebral Organization of Man's Conscious Action". An Evening Lecture to the XIX International Congress of Psychology (London, 1969).

[17] A. R. Luria, Higher Cortical Functions in Man. Translated from the Russian by Basil Haigh (New York: Basic Books, 1966), and Human

and by Rylander.[18] Luria contends (personal communication) that it is impossible to diagnose a frontal or prefrontal tumor in an infant who has not passed the age we are describing.

One last point before turning to data and observations. It has to do with the effect of practice or "learning" on the acquisition of new skills. The principal point made thus far is that, *once a primitive or awkward version of a performance has occurred,* practice has the effect of leading to its modularization and differentiation and eventual replacement. But it is difficult to specify what role, if any, practice serves in *producing* a *new* pattern of action. This is, again, something of an anomaly, for at most one can say (as we shall see) that practice may have the principal effect of either increasing the kind of comprehension necessary for a leap ahead or for increasing processing capacity—as in the Bryan and Harter studies[19] of telegraphy in which mastery of *letters* surely could not account *directly* for the next step of shifting to *words* as units. Indeed, we have already commented on the fact that learning may provide the vehicle for subsequent expression of a preadapted pattern. What seems crucial in infant and adult alike is the growth of comprehension of task requirement—what may properly be called means-end analysis—and about the role of learning in this, we know very little.

Perhaps there are two ways in which learning operates to produce *new* skilled patterns that go beyond those mentioned. One is akin to "trial-and-error" or serendipity. The child, by accident, hits on a solution and recognizes it as such, repeating it appropriately afterwards. This type of learning is rare if not absent in the first six months of life. Mostly, such accidents are not utilized for the guidance of later behavior. A second form of learning "new skills" is provided by imitation, but this again is highly circumscribed and is a topic better treated elsewhere.[20] Neither "accidental" nor "imitative" learning, in my view, accounts for more than a small fraction of newly acquired skills.

Brain and Psychological Processes. Translated from the Russian by Basil Haigh (New York: Harper & Row, 1966).

[18] G. Rylander, "Personality Analysis Before and After Frontal Lobotomy", *The Frontal Lobes, Proceedings of the Association for Research in Nervous and Mental Disease.* Vol. XXVII (Baltimore: Williams & Wilkins, 1948), 691–705.

[19] W. L. Bryan, and N. Harter, "Studies in the Telegraphic Language: The Acquisition of a Hierarchy of Habits", *Psychological Review* (1899), *6*, pp. 345–375.

[20] *Cf.* K. Kaye, Unpublished doctoral thesis, Harvard University, 1970.

Experiments on Skill Acquisition

To illustrate the points we have considered, let me use three experiments on skill acquisition from our laboratory at Harvard. The first involves the use of the hands under visual guidance to take possession of objects. The second depends on the use of an innate response—sucking—but for new and arbitrary ends: to bring into and hold in focus a moving picture. The third involves direction of the oculomotor system by anticipation.[21] In the second and third studies, the effector function—sucking and eye-movements—are highly perfected: the task is to organize effector output in a fashion consonant with available information. In the first study, control of effectors is shaky and, in the youngest infants, of very recent origin ontogenetically.

In the first study, fifty normal infants served as subjects, equally divided into five ages: four-five months, six-eight, nine-eleven, twelve-fourteen, fifteen-seventeen. A small toy is handed to the right or left hand. When it is taken, a second toy is immediately presented on the side of the full hand. If not taken after fifteen or twenty seconds, the second toy is shifted to the midline. A third and then a fourth object is presented at the midline if the child has taken and retained preceding objects handed to him. When, at any point in the four presentations, the child indicates clearly that he will not take the next object, the trial is ended. Each infant received four trials, half begun with the left hand, half with the right.[22]

The youngest group of infants, four to five months of age, are at the beginning of their manipulatory careers. Their preoccupying task is to take possession of a simple object consistently, and the use of this response sequence as a module in a more inclusive sequence is almost ruled out by the degree of concentration required to get hold of the object. At the same time, the act of taking possession is dominated by the intention of getting the object to the mouth. Some indication of the growing mastery of simple "taking" on the part of infants at the different ages is provided by Figure 2, indicating the percentage of children in different age groups able to grasp and retain the first object presented on all four trials. Figure 3 tells the

[21] The first study was a collaborative enterprise of the author and Karlen Lyons and Judith Simenson, the second was conducted by Ilze Kalnins, and the third by Alistair Mundy-Castle and Jeremy Anglin.
[22] J. S. Bruner, J. Simenson, and K. Lyons, "The Growth of Manual Intelligence: I. Taking Possession of Objects". In preparation, Center for Cognitive Studies, Harvard University.

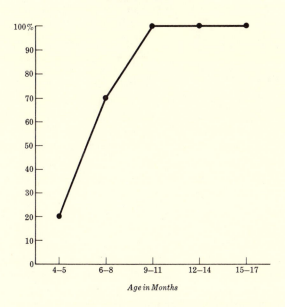

Figure 2. Percentage of infants able to grasp and hold first object on all four trials.

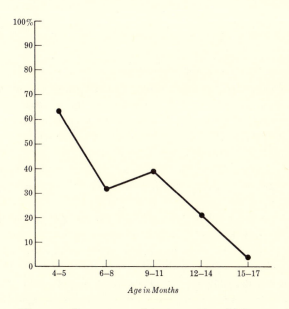

Figure 3. Percentage of instances in which an object is brought to mouth in "two-object" task.

[111]

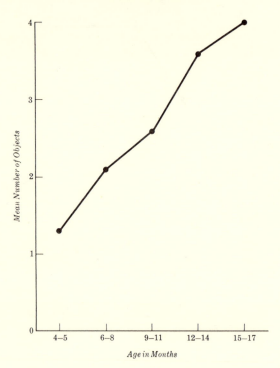

Figure 4. Mean number of objects taken and held on best trial.

other part of the tale: the percentage of instances in which the infants of different ages took the first object to the mouth as a second object was being presented—in effect, sealing off the response from inclusion in a longer act. It is not surprising, then, that the older the child, the more successful his performance—as judged by the number of objects he was able to take over on his best trial (Figure 4).

But the linearity of this function is totally misleading, for the infants at different ages used quite different strategies or programs for achieving their success. It is not just the decline in the infant's preoccupation with the simple task, or even receding preemption of the goal of mouthing, but the qualitative change in strategies that is crucial. The second object is presented on the side of the hand already grasping a first object. Note that it is rare for infants under a year of age to reach across the body midline for an object—possibly a means of keeping complexity and conflict reduced by regionalizing the reaching space—so that the filled hand must be emptied in order for the

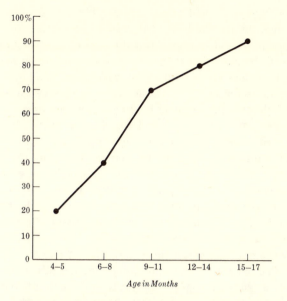

Figure 5. Percentage of infants who transferred an object from one hand to the other in order to free the first hand to reach for another object.

second object to be taken. Dropping the first object or putting it in the mouth seem not much help, for the dropped object may itself become a target for the reach, and mouthing most often brings reaching to a halt. The solution is to put the first object into the free hand at the midline, and reach with the hand thus freed. It is such an automatic subroutine for the adept human adult that we forget how slowly acquired it was. Figure 5 presents the percentage of children at each age who effected a hand-to-hand transfer of this kind on at least half of the trials. In effect, it is this constituent routine of transfer that makes possible coping with two objects. Even at that, it is a difficult routine to employ proactively, anticipating a second object's coming by transferring in advance. No children under six months showed such anticipatory transfer, only a tenth of those between six months and a year did so, and only slightly more than half between a year and a year and a half. We shall encounter the issue of anticipation again in a later study to be reported.

But hand-to-hand shift does not deal with the problem of three objects. Functionally speaking thus far, the infant's numeration system is one-by-mouth and two-by-hands. The task is now to go to "many" and, as we shall see, the mediating routine for this leap ahead is "deposit and storage". But it comes in its own time. Given a third object, the most that the youngest infants could do was to break off and not reach at all, or to drop the two objects being held and start all over again. By six months, the strategy changes as the constituent routine of simple reaching and holding is better mastered. Now the child reaches out with a full hand for the new object, but we were mindful of this possibility, and the objects are too big to get two in a hand. So the infant may content himself with banging the new object on the old. At nine months, however, there appears a new routine that incorporates older skills: deposit an object at some depot point like the crook of the arm, and take the new object with the freed hand. More than half the infants in the age range nine to fourteen months do this, and virtually all over that age do so.

Note the effective strategic combination of transferring and depositing. The efficacy of the combining rule depends, however, upon mastery of a crucial recognition rule: the distinction between "to be possessed" and "already possessed". That is to say, the child must *leave* in storage those items that have been placed there. Figure 6

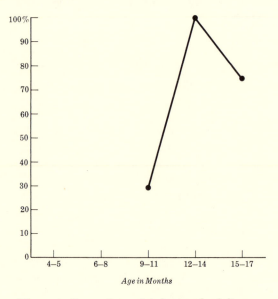

Figure 6. Percentage of infants who left more than half of the deposited objects in storage until the end of trial.

[114]

illustrates the difficulty of applying this rule. We take the proportion of infants who left in storage over half the objects deposited on their most successful trial. Plainly, the achievement of this delay capacity or discriminative capacity is slow in maturing. Many children are as tempted to repossess the deposited object as to take possession of the newly presented one.

What does practice do for the child? Certainly practice within the half hour of the experiment does nothing to improve *effectiveness*. Figure 7 contains "learning curves" for the different age groups. There is surely no learning in terms of the number of objects children were able to take up in the four successive trials. Performance, to be sure, becomes modularized in the sense of becoming smoother, faster, and more uniform. But each child stayed mostly within the confines of the strategy that he initially employed. When a new strategy emerges, it does so in full if rough cry, then to be smoothed by practice and rendered into a building block for more extended directed sequences. It is the emergence of new strategic features like

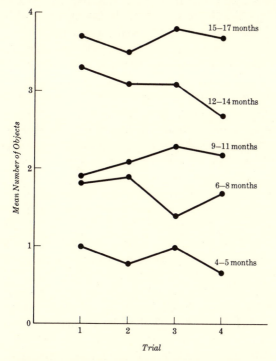

Figure 7. Mean number of objects taken on successive trials.

those just described that leads to the striking series of steps upward at each age. An exception to the stepwise rule of skill acquisition may seem to be present in the mastery of anticipation and of delay. Anticipatory shifting of an object, once it occurs, is "strengthened" by practice—but that is true only *after* it first appears. So too with delay in removing an object from storage, once it is put there. But again, the improved delay occurs after the first delay has occurred, marked as it is by conflict as to whether to repossess the just deposited object or to take a new one.

Consider now a quite different situation, one in which the infant uses a response that is, if anything, more perfected than it will ever be in later life—sucking. Here we need not concern ourselves with *whether* the response has to be mastered, but rather with *how* it is handled in order to alter an environmental event. A very brief description of Kalnins's experiment does not do it full justice, but will serve our purpose. Her infants, ranging from five to eleven weeks of age came twice a week for six weeks to our laboratory for six-minute sessions in which they sucked on a recording pacifier while watching a lively close-up color film of an Eskimo mother playing with her child. The film sequence was known, from earlier projects, to be interesting to infants of this age. All children began with a calibration session in which the picture's focus was changed randomly throughout for a predetermined schedule. Then followed eight test sessions in which there was a contingent link between the sucking and the focus of the picture. For some infants in all of the sessions sucking drove the picture out of focus, for some it brought it into focus, in either case holding it either in or out if rate of sucking exceeded 1.3 sucks per second. For some babies, the first test sessions were out-of-focus sucking, the later in-focus, and for others in-focus sessions were followed by out-of-focus. All infants ended with three sessions in which the projected film was going in and out of focus with no relation to the infant's sucking—more non-contingent trials.

Recall one thing about sucking. It is a highly organized pattern, structured in bursts of a signature length for particular babies. Bursts are interspersed with pauses as in Figure 8.

With this much background, let me mention the first findings: *length of burst* is scarcely affected at all by its consequence in the focus of the picture. Bursts tend to be slightly, but only slightly, longer for sucking into focus than for sucking out. Bursts, not sucks, are the constituent modules. What *does* change, and it does so immediately and drastically, is the length of pauses *between* bursts, or, put in another way, the number of bursts per unit time. Pause length for

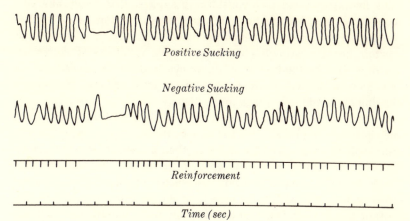

Figure 8. A typical burst-and-pause pattern in a thirteen-week-old infant.

in-focus sucking varies from three to four seconds; for sucking out of focus, pauses double to about seven to eight seconds. The change from suck-in to suck-out or vice versa takes place virtually immediately, although over a number of trials the infant may become more efficient in the sense of lengthening pauses that produce a focus and shortening those that produce defocusing.

Note one last important component of this skilled performance, one that goes beyond sucking and pausing. The infant can either *look* at the screen before him or *avert* his gaze. Compare those instances where sucking has produced full focus, and those where sucking has produced blur. In focus, close to full time is spent looking at the picture; in blur, slightly less than half time. So too with pauses. Where pauses produce clear focus, the picture is watched almost constantly; where they produce blur, again the baby looks away about half the time. Note that in the non-contingent sessions, the infant also looks when the picture is in focus and looks away when it is not—regardless of whether he is sucking or not. Stechler[23] has used the apt expression "obligatory attention" to characterize the young infant's attraction to stimuli organized in certain ways—face-like objects, concentrically organized displays, optimally complex patternings, etc. *Cf.* [24,25,26,27,28].

[23] G. Stechler, & Elizabeth Latz, "Some Observations on Attention and Arousal in the Human Infant", *Journal of the American Academy of Child Psychiatry* (1966), *5* (3).

[24] R. L. Fantz, "The Origin of Form Perception", *Scientific American* (1961), *204* (5), 66–72.

[25] Peggy R. Koopman and Elinor W. Ames, "Infants' Preferences for

The findings we are now considering suggest that there may be a complementary feature to such attention in the form of a kind of "obligatory aversion" in which the infant "actively" looks away from certain negative stimuli—blur in this case, violations of expectancy as in extinction trials,[29] or stimulus overload.[30,31] We speak of such aversion as "active" in the sense that the infant shows resistance in having his head turned back to the display.

In sum, the infant sucks in all conditions with modular bursts of characteristic length. He regulates outcome in two ways. If sucking leads to desired clarity of focus, then pauses are kept to a minimum length and the picture is watched. If, on the other hand, sucking leads to defocusing, the infant lengthens his pauses, looks during these pauses, and averts his eyes to avoid the defocused picture. The infant performs in this fashion virtually immediately and when conditions change to the obverse, the shift in responding is a step function rather than a gradual change. Three components—sucking, looking, and pausing—are sequenced in a fashion to fit the requirements of a task. The principal instrumental component, because it is so strongly and innately organized, does not change characteristics much, but *how* sucking is *used* changes in a most striking fashion. With respect to *looking,* it is carried along by the stimulus events— the rule being to look at focus and avert from blur. The infant then adapts to the task by deploying the one resource that is under voluntary control—pausing. Two fixed patterns, sucking and obligatory at-

---

Facial Arrangements: a Failure to Replicate". Presented at Biennial Meeting of the Society for Research in Child Development (New York, 1967).

[26] M. Hershenson, "Visual Discrimination in the Human Newborn", *Journal of Comparative and Physiological Psychology* (1964), *58* (2), 270–276.

[27] J. Kagan, and M. Lewis, "Studies of Attention in the Human Infant", *Merrill-Palmer Quarterly of Behavior and Development* (1965), *11*(2), 95–127.

[28] W. Kessen, "Sucking and Looking: Two Organized Congenital Patterns of Behavior in the Human Newborn", *Early Behavior: Comparative and Developmental Approaches,* eds. H. W. Stevenson, E. H. Hess, and H. L. Rheingold (New York: John Wiley & Sons, 1967).

[29] Yvonne Brackbill, "The Smiling Response and its Resistance to Extinction as a Function of Reinforcement Schedule", *Dissertation Abstracts* (1957), *17,* p. 175.

[30] Bruner, Bruner, and Kahneman.

[31] T. B. Brazelton, and J. S. Bruner, Research reported in the *Ninth Annual Report of the Center for Cognitive Studies* (Harvard University, 1969).

tention, are then rendered quite flexible and a complex task is handled with remarkable subtlety in spite of the instinctive or reflexive apparatus on which it depends and despite the fact that the infants are between five and eleven weeks.

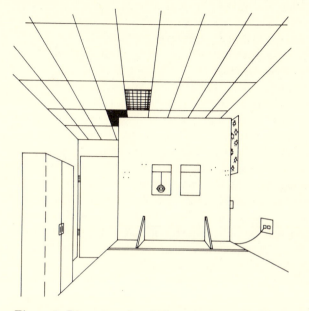

Figure 9. Diagram of window apparatus. (From Mundy-Castle and Anglin, 1969.)

We come now to a study carried out by Mundy-Castle and Anglin[32] that deals with a specialized form of skill much like visual tracking, save that the stimulus to be tracked is not always present. In effect, the task is simple, at least on the surface. The infant sits upright in a supporting chair at 18 inches distant and midway between two small windows, each 11 × 12 inches, separated by a strip three inches wide, cut in a large screen, 4½ ft. high × 4 ft. wide (Figure 9). Into one window a "hyper-stimulus" ball[33] is lowered, remaining there for six seconds, then moving up and out of view for three and one-half seconds, at which point another ball begins its descent into

[32] A. C. Mundy-Castle, and J. Anglin, "The Development of Looking in Infancy", Presented at Biennial Conference of the Society for Research in Child Development (Santa Monica, California, April 1969).

[33] J. S. Bruner, "The Growth and Structure of Skill", *Motor Skills in Infancy*, K. J. Connolly, ed. (New York: Academic Press, in press).

the other window. The cycle continues as long as necessary in this way. The balls and other alternative stimuli were pretested to assure that the objects used would interest infants in the age range studied —ten days to five months.[34]

Plainly, the infant's performance is premised upon his appreciation of space-time relationships, of such concepts as recurrence and permanence, and other quite classical Piaget-Michotte cognitive structures. But whereas in the two preceding studies the infant's *instrumental* activity produced a change in the environment, in the present case the environment remains unchanged, the infant simply repositioning himself to bring the display to perceptual mid-field. No effector needs to be mastered, as in reaching, nor need an arbitrary relationship between action and consequence be grasped, as with sucking and focus. The task is, so to speak, as purely cognitive as possible. In view of the fact that the outcome of the performance is not a change in the environment, one may properly argue that the task does not require "skill" in Welford's sense,[35] though it is surely an "activity" as Bernstein intended the phrase.[36]

Let me, before discussing response patterns in this study, review a few things about infant perception of "locus", for this is in a proper sense a study of anticipation of locus, and one's conception of locus will determine where somebody looks. Objects appear from earliest possible testing to have a locus in an "objective" space. A study in progress in our laboratory by Aronson and Rosenbloom shows that if an infant is looking at his vocalizing mother (who is behind a soundproof glass partition, her voice carried by a stereophonic system into the baby's chamber), he will show marked disturbance if her voice is displaced so as to appear to come from other than her visual locus. Such disruption occurs as early as twenty days of age, which is the youngest age thus far investigated. Babies, moreover, can keep track of objects that appear and disappear—as behind screens—and the work of Bower[37] as well as Gardner's work now in progress suggests

[34] The devising of this apparatus went through a long and tedious evolution, dominated by the original hope that lights shining through a translucent screen could be used for stimuli and thus readily controlled for distance between them, differences between them, time relationships, etc. The ambition to build an apparatus that was both tidy and flexible in stimulus control had to be sacrificed when it was discovered how important were movement and parallax as elements of attraction in infant attention.

[35] *Op. cit.*

[36] *Op. cit.*

[37] T. G. R. Bower, "The Development of Object Permanence: Some Stud-

that even at four to six weeks they can track an object through disappearance behind and reappearance beyond a screen if the disappearance is governed by a simple trajectory and a constant velocity, and if the length of the disappearance does not exceed a certain critical time (the value of this critical time is still quite uncertain but is almost surely affected by the visual structure of the task). In short, the infant has not only some grasp of the "concept" of locus, but also of "path" between loci—each concept constrained by specialized conditions.

The last point to be made is that from the point of view of fixations of the eyes, young babies and old adults and all between, land their saccades and rest their gaze preferably on a sharp contour.[38,39] This is probably as primitive a response of the oculomotor system as there is and, as is well known, can be traced down the vertebrate series by the use of nystagmus producing displays consisting of a movement of sharp contours across the visual field. The relevance of these points will be apparent in a moment.

The response of the infants to the task set by Mundy-Castle and Anglin can be characterized by "stages", each representing a somewhat different strategy for dealing with recurrent regularity in the environment, each governed by a somewhat different form of economy. There is little question that from the point of view of effector capability, the youngest baby could have done what the eldest babies did. At ten to fifteen days (the youngest age studied), the infant rests his gaze on a sharp contour at the edge of one of the windows, and his fixation may dwell around there for thirty seconds at a time with only small deviations from the contour. Usually, but not always, gaze shifts to the region of the ball when it appears, and may rest there only a second or two of the six seconds that it is in view. During this first stage, the violation trials used have no discernible effect. A violation trial is one in which the pattern of simple alternation is broken, and it never appears more often than once in twenty trials. The window contour is the base to which the gaze then returns, to return to the ball momentarily as it begins its withdrawal upward, then back

---

ies of Existence Constancy", *Perception and Psychophysics* (1967), *2* (9), 411–418.

[38] N. H. Mackworth, and J. S. Bruner, "How Adults and Children Search and Recognize Pictures", *Human Development* (1970), *13*, pp. 149–177.

[39] C. B. Trevarthen, "Report of Research on Coordination of Head and Eye Movements", *Eighth Annual Report of the Center for Cognitive Studies* (Harvard University, 1968).

to the edge. During visual contact with the ball, there is more likely to be a transient disruption of breathing, a stilling of limbs, and a momentary reduction of sucking if a pacifier is being used—all suggesting heightened attention. If the contour used is the exterior one, then the infant attends only to the ball that appears in that window. If it is an interior one, he will favor the window it bounds, but not exclusively.

With growth, dwell-time on the ball itself increases, and less time is spent on the "base contour". That the base contour has special significance is attested by the infant's resistance to having his head moved physically from its position while his gaze is disposed on it.

A second stage begins at about thirty days. It is marked by fixation on the ball more exclusively, staying with it while present and shifting to the second window only when it disappears. Recall that this involves anticipation, for by shifting when the ball disappears the infant arrives at the second window before the ball has fallen there. On violation trials, the second-stage baby is "caught out" by the shift, and though he may swing back to the window just left, he often shows disruption for several trials after. A characteristic growth heralding the end of the second stage is cross-looking, a quick glancing to the opposite window in the midst of a long fixation on the ball.

This cross-looking is the dominant mode of the third stage, beginning usually by fifty days or shortly after. At first, cross-looking occurs principally during the three and one-half seconds when the ball is not present in either window and may constitute a search strategy. Later, the cross-looking may occur at any time in the cycle, and even occurs momentarily when the baby is fixed on a ball in one of the windows.

The later phases of the third stage exhibit two features. The first is an increased tendency to track the object upward out of sight and in some cases even to follow an assumed trajectory up, over, and down to the upper edge of the opposite window. The second is a tendency to extend cross-looking, while the balls are not present, to other features of the room not intended to be part of the experiment. The imposition of an assumed path and widened cross-looking became increasingly common from fourteen to sixteen weeks onward, when fixation times also become shorter and more adult-like in tempo. The balls now are given less fixation time, and other objects relatively more. Finally, the whole experimental arrangement becomes virtually unmanageable at about four months. For one thing, the babies appear to be bored by the relatively poor visual fare and are searching the room for fixable cues, but perhaps more important, the ball now evokes a new response beyond looking—namely, *reaching*—and the ball as displayed is close enough to sustain the reaching but too far to be touched—its distance being approximately eighteen to twenty inches from the infant's sternum.

Several features of this developmental pattern are already familiar from the two preceding studies. One is new and deserves special attention. It is the elaboration of the concept of locus that is so central in the formulation of the infant's tracking plans. The locus of the event to be traced (or "kept track of") seems initially to be defined operationally as the position of an intermittent feature (the appearing and disappearing ball) in reference to a persistent feature (the simple contour of the window). It would seem as if the infant required a simple and predictable visual structure from which to operate in order to sample variable or less predictable events. Gradually, the time given to fixating the less predictable ball increases, until the infant looks at the ball exclusively. He looks at a ball so long as it is present, then after a brief "blank" period he shifts to the other side when a ball appears there. He is successively monitoring two positions where the ball appears. But there is no sign that any heed is paid to the other position from the one he is in.[40]

The two positions seem to achieve simultaneous "existence" when the infant begins cross-looking to monitor the second position while looking at the ball in the first position. Position then becomes a locus. The infant also now shifts to the second position on or just before the disappearance of the ball in the first, awaiting its reappearance. Locus now is literally a place where an event may occur.

Once this achievement has been stabilized, a new mode of operation begins. The infant connects the loci where events occur with an assumed path that takes its direction from the movement of the disappearing and reappearing object. It is at this point that the child's fixation times begin to approximate those of the adult and become less stare-like. Perhaps more processing capacity is made available through anticipation, through the extrapolative use of a path, and through better structuring of loci. In any case, the infant becomes

---

[40] When two balls are presented simultaneously, as has been done in some preliminary observations, the infant at this stage shows some tendency to get "stuck" on one of them for longer periods of time than an older infant. These observations are being carried out more systematically.

increasingly capable of "taking in the situation" with a flurry of quick fixations.

What is so striking about this course of growth is the extent to which it involves the "maturing" not of sensory or motor capacities (the necessary sensory and motor constituent routines are present in the younger ones). What develops is a skill for processing information and using that information to govern a sequence of goal-directed behavior. What the infant is mastering and elaborating are those cognitive substrata of skill to which Welford refers. They are concepts like independent object, predictable succession, locus, connected loci, path of an absent object, recurrence.

We have said nothing explicit about the effects of learning or experience in this experiment. In this respect, the visual scanning system is especially interesting. Without wishing to raise the issue of eye movements in the formation of cell assemblies and phase sequence as Hebb has defined these,[41] I would only point out, as Yarbus[42] and Mackworth[43] have already done, that when something new has been learned conceptually or spatially, the scanning pattern of the eyes reflect it immediately. What is required is not receptor or effector capacity, which is there, but a cognitive model of the visual world that permits regulation of activity.

Some Conclusions

In what sense can we say that the phenomenon called "strategy" in problem solving is first revealed in the initial skill acquisitions of infancy? We have proposed that overt skilled performance that requires the attainment of objectives by the deployment and control of effectors on real objects in real time represents the expression of an internal competence rather than the acquisition of specific responses. Skilled action involves the appropriate combining of constituent subroutines under the guidance of "feed-forward," anticipatory control and with regulatory feedback for correction. The competence involved in the guided combinatorial performance of skill is, we would hold,

[41] D. O. Hebb, *The Organization of Behavior: a Neuropsychological Theory* (New York: John Wiley & Sons, 1949).

[42] A. L. Yarbus, *Eye Movements and Vision* (New York: Plenum Press, 1967).

[43] N. H. Mackworth, "Eye Movement Studies", reported in the *Sixth Annual Report of the Center for Cognitive Studies* (Harvard University, 1966).

homologous to the competence observable in directed problem solving. In the case of skilled action, the objective is to produce in the environment a change of a specific kind within specifiable limits of space and time. Where problem solving is concerned, one generally works not so much with real objects in real space and time, but with representations of the real world, however these may be coded.

That there are enormous difficulties between the two domains—the constraining world of objects in contrast to the more readily transformable representations of real events—nobody would deny. Nor could one deny that the operations of problem solving are, similarly, less constrained than those of sensory-motor skill, and not simply by virtue of the absence of immediate space-time-gravity parameters on the objects of thought. As Piaget points out in one context,[44] and Bartlett in another,[45] representation involves symbolizing the world of events, freeing them of unidirectional action (Piaget's famous reversibility argument), and making them subject to logical and linguistic operations rather than just physical, manipulative ones. Problem solving "in the head" is not simply "internalized action". What is being urged here is that skilled, goal-directed action is based upon the same or a homologous competence that underlies problem solving and that this competence is there to be inferred from the opening weeks of life.

At several points in the discussion, we have likened the combinatorial generativeness of human skill to the syntax of a language, and indeed it is upon the distinction between competence and performance that we have rested the claim for "instant transferability" of human manual skill. There are striking parallels, yet it is difficult still to specify in any usefully precise ways the homology between the syntax of language proper and the ordering principle that governs the construction of skilled sequences of action. We are not much further along this track than Lashley was at the time of his often quoted Hixon Symposium lecture.[46] Yet I urge that we continue to look for the deeper similarities between, say, human manual skill and linguistic competence, and particularly for any hint about like patterns

---

[44] J. Piaget, *The Origins of Intelligence in Children*, translated by Margaret Cook (New York: International Universities Press, 1965).
[45] F. C. Bartlett, *Thinking: An Experimental and Social Study* (New York: Basic Books, 1958).
[46] K. Lashley, "The Problem of Serial Order in Behavior", in *Cerebral Mechanisms in Behavior: the Hixon Symposium*, ed., L. A. Jeffress (New York: John Wiley & Sons, 1951).

of early acquisition. We have been at pains to explore some of these in the body of this paper.

Finally, strategies of both skill and thought share the property of being indirectly aided by practice, and indirectly only. Professor Bartlett once remarked, "It is not practice but practice *the results of which are known* that makes perfect".[47] Practice perfects a way in which one already does something. But it is by virtue of that perfecting that the capacity for more elaborate processing is freed, and new skills or new solutions qualitatively different from what went before can be brought to bear on the task. Indeed, some of the new skills and new solutions may even have an innate or preadapted basis. With respect to thought, this is taken to imply a Kantian position, and where the theory of skill is concerned, an ethological one. Be that as it may. Indeed, initial learning may be necessary in some instances for such innate behavior patterns to be expressed. In other cases, the new skills are made possible by the existence, not of preadapted patterns reflecting our phylogenesis, but by the operation of more powerful rules of comprehension backed up by the means for generating performance to match the requirement of what we come to comprehend. In a word, when one examines closely—indeed, microscopically—the acquisition of early human manual skill, one is struck at how little of what one observes conforms to the stereotyped idea that "responses" are "acquired". Rather, it is an underlying skill or competence that is triggered into being by experience. Once skill is acquired, a variety of behavior performances can be generated that singly or in combination fit the unique exigencies of the environment.

Observing the onset of skill in the infant of the human species leads one to deep doubts about whether the conception of stimulus and response is not, after all, an artifact of our methods of studying adult subjects. It is an old point, made decades ago by Dewey in his Presidential Address to the American Psychological Association.[48] But it is striking today as it was then. In observing the growth of behavior, a stimulus cannot be taken out of the context of the action upon which it impinges. Nor can a "response" be arbitrarily isolated from the web of related competence of which it forms a part. I believe that ideas like skill, competence, and strategy will, perhaps, lead us to consider again the underlying structure of human action and the mode of its acquisition.

[47] Welford, *Op. cit.*

[48] J. Dewey, "The Reflex Arc Concept in Psychology", *Psychological Review* (1896), *III*, pp. 357–370.

Art & Representation

SEVEN

The "What" and the "How":

Perspective Representation

and the

Phenomenal World

E. H. GOMBRICH

PHILOSOPHY THRIVES ON argument. Thus I hope it will not be taken as a breach of decorum if a contribution to a *Festschrift* attempts to clarify a point of disagreement between the recipient and the author. In *Languages of Art*[1] Nelson Goodman has persuasively argued against J. J. Gibson and me that "the behavior of light sanctions neither our usual nor any other way of rendering space; and perspective provides no absolute or independent standard of fidelity". The first question which this statement invites is "Fidelity to what?" It is to this question that this essay has initially to address itself, before it can attempt to introduce some fresh arguments into the ancient debate about perspective.

Some time ago, while vacationing in the Austrian Alps, my

---

[1] Indianapolis: Bobbs-Merrill, 1968, p. 19.

eyes fell on a picture postcard that showed a splendid view of the upper reaches of the Inn valley towards the Swiss frontier. It looked as
if it would be worth seeking out the place from which the photograph
had been taken. Since I neither doubted its fidelity, nor was unaware
of the behavior of light, I took a map and a ruler and attempted to
plot the vantage point by the direction of the river and the parts of
the vista visible on the picture. We then set out with the card and
the map and were rewarded by the beautiful view. Not quite, though:
we saw the valley along the same axis, but the card proved that certain
distant mountains had also been visible to the camera which showed
less on our horizon; the photographer must have stood a little higher,
at a spot where it was too late for us still to climb. But this discovery,
of course, did not shake our confidence in the method of plotting the
spot. On the contrary, it was due to that method. Whatever we may
mean by "ways of rendering space" we all rely on photographs or
topographical views to tell us *what* objects in space can be seen from
a given point. Clearly, we also know that the relationship between
maps and such pictures is reversible. Just as a picture can be located
on a map, so a map allows us to construct a picture.

Let us imagine a law case that depends on the account of a witness who claims to have seen through the hole in a fence, one night,
how the window of a house opposite was lit up and the accused took an
object out of a chest of drawers. There would be two methods for the
defense to check this claim. One would correspond to my walk: he
could take the jury to the spot and demonstrate *ad oculos* that the
chest in question could not be seen from that spot by anyone. But such
a procedure would not be necessary if the plan and elevation of the
house and the fenced garden were exactly known. In such a case it
would be easy to work out exactly how much of the room could be seen
from the hole in the fence. We need only draw such straight lines from
the point from which the witness claims to have watched across the
window into the room to specify exactly what objects can have been
visible to him and which were occluded. Should he change his story
and now claim that he saw the movement through a mirror on the wall
of the room, or merely its shadow cast by the lamp on the ceiling, this,
too, could be worked out with relative ease. Nor will the situation
change dramatically if we allow our hole in the fence to have been
large enough for the witness to have watched with two eyes. The disparity of the information that was transmitted by the two retinas is
of vanishing relevance at the distance that interests us here. And even
if we alter the story and let the witness claim to have walked to a

given spot where he had freedom of movement, we can still say exactly what he can or cannot have seen from any given point, even if he used binoculars or turned them round to increase his field of vision. To return to the abstract proposition on which agreement should be easy: given an accurate map of any three-dimensional array and indication about the transparency and refraction indices of all the bodies in this array, any other visual aspect of this array can be mapped indicating which features would be visible and which occluded for an observer at any point of the map. It is a transformation for which a computer can be programmed, and it is precisely this transformation that traditional one-point perspective performs.

The famous demonstration by Brunelleschi of the newly discovered laws of perspective (Figure 1) can indeed be formulated in this

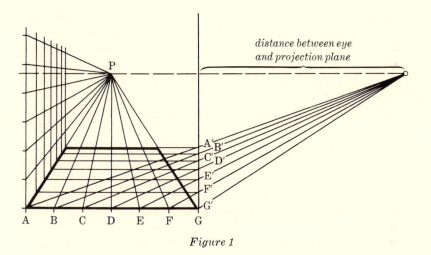

Figure 1

way.[2] The architect took up his position inside the Florentine Cathedral at a given distance from the open door and showed that he could map out exactly what of the baptistery and the other buildings opposite could be seen from where he stood. If he placed a grid or a net

[2] I have discussed this famous episode from a slightly different angle in "From the Revival of Learning to the Reform of the Arts: Niccolò Niccoli and Filippo Brunelleschi", *Essays in the History of Art presented to Rudolf Wittkower*, ed. Douglas Fraser, et al. (London: Phaidon Press, 1967), 81–82. It has been discussed from other points of view by Rudolf Krautheimer, *Lorenzo Ghiberti* (Princeton University Press, 1956), and John White, *The Birth and Rebirth of Pictorial Space* (New York: Thomas Yoseloff, 1958).

[131]

in front of the open door, he could make his prediction increasingly precise and specify exactly what of the view would appear in which of the squares of the net—at least down to the margin of binocular disparity. To eliminate this margin he could always resort to a peephole, and thus he was able to put his theory to the test that a knowledge of euclidean geometry and of the "behavior of light" alone sufficed to construct an image in a peepshow which matched exactly the vista of the buildings opposite the cathedral door that could be obtained from the spot he had selected. If he chose to draw this image on a flat panel opposite the peephole, the laws of geometrical projection would come into play which state that planes parallel to the picture plane—for instance the central facade of the baptistery—would appear in the projection as reduced in size but similar in shape—parallels remaining parallels and identical windows identical windows. The same laws also postulate that it would be different for solid bodies. A sphere, for instance, would only project as a circle when seen head-on along the central axis. As soon as it was shifted to the side of the axis, its projection would deviate from the circular form and approximate an ellipse. Not that this fact invalidated the peepshow experiment. For through the peephole the lateral ellipse on the flat board would be seen foreshortened and therefore "corrected" into a circle.[3]

The oddity of such distortions has been used ever since to question the claim that perspective projection shows us the world as we see it. We do not know if Brunelleschi ever made such a claim. What is relevant is rather that perspective allowed him to map what was seen through that door. If that claim were spurious, we would not now find the piazza swarming with tourists equipped with all kinds of cameras to record and remember the sights they see. For the camera is so constructed that it also maps this information on a flat plate or piece of paper, and that the resulting image obeys as far as possible the laws of projection, minor distortions which are discussed in the literature on optics being "corrected" to make parallels come out parallel.

Is this how we see the world? It is an odd and indeed a misleading question.

Nelson Goodman is certainly right when he protests that the behavior of light does not tell us how we see things. It is doubtful

[3] Cf. Gezienus ten Doesschate, *Perspective, Fundamentals, Controversials, History* (Nieuwkoop: B. de Graaf, 1964), which seems to me the most balanced and authoritative treatment of this subject.

whether, standing in the cathedral, Brunelleschi could take in more than a fraction of the vista at a time; he had to change his focus and since the area of focussed vision is very small, he had to sweep his eye across the opening thus obtaining a succession of different images, rather than one. This is true even though Brunelleschi was careful to select a relatively narrow field of vision which could be taken in without turning the head.[4] The situation becomes much less tractable when we leave the inside of the cathedral and return to our Alpine scenery. Old-fashioned guidebooks sometimes contain fold-out panoramas from such points of vantage that allow us to identify what we see. The representational accuracy of these diagrams is as easily checked as was our picture postcard. The triangular mountain above that ridge is Mount A., the steep rock on its right belongs to the range of B., and the three houses down in the valley stand on the outskirts of C. which happens to be hidden from us by the slope on which we stand. But here we come at last to a crucial point, for if we claim the same fidelity for the panorama that we have claimed for the picture postcard we are caught in the very contradiction Nelson Goodman had in mind when he denied any objective standards in these matters. For clearly a series of picture postcards do not add up to such a panorama. We can easily check this if we take a series of photographs of the wide vista, turning the camera till we have recorded the whole view. If we then want to join them together, fitting their edges where the vistas overlap, we quickly discover that the result deviates from the fold-out panorama. The panorama was a strip, bounded by parallels, but our composite picture fans inwards, the groundline forming the circumference of a polygon, each individual photograph having to be cut to the shape of a trapezoid, converging towards the horizon. If we wanted to take in the sky, say the cloud formations, the relation would be reversed and the lines would diverge downwards. Not that all this is surprising. The map of a panorama could not be projected onto a flat piece of paper. It could only be accommodated on the inside of a sphere with the horizon as the equator, and other features distributed accordingly. One could imagine such a panorama drawn inside a trans-

---

[4] Like other authors, Nelson Goodman appears to think that the eye must be strictly stationary. This is not correct, as Doesschate has shown (*op. cit.* chapter XII) and as the reader can verify if he places himself inside a room and attends to the view appearing through a window. A change in the direction of his gaze may blur this view but will not change it. As soon as he turns his head, of course, other things will come into the view in the window, for the head is pivoted on the neck, and any turning means a lateral displacement.

parent globular shelter on a mountaintop, which would indeed match the outlines of all features of the view as we stand in the center and turn on our heels, at least if we are willing to make the minor adjustments demanded by binocular disparity (negligible for distant views) and by the asymmetries of our body.[5] No doubt, such a panorama too could be drawn from a map by a computer.

Are, then, both methods right? Can it make sense to claim "fidelity" for perspective as a record of what can be seen from a fixed point by a stationary observer, and at the same time to accept the demand that a correct map of what is seen from a given point when we turn our head must be curved? It is certainly true to say that to project the world in which we look round onto a flat plane is to distort it. In this situation the map of the horizon labours under the same difficulties as does the map of any part of the globe.[6] In projecting it onto a plane we must compromise the accuracy of geometrical relationships. The larger the area covered, in both cases, the more noticeable will these distortions become. They hardly matter in the map of a town, but they do affect the shape of a continent. *Mutatis mutandis* this also applies to our mapping or photographing vistas. The wider the angle that is taken in, the more the fidelity of the picture will appear to be compromised; the smaller the section, the smaller the distortion.

But the plea that the distortion in a perspective picture is "only a little one" will hardly satisfy its critics. The rival claims of the curvilinearists[7] and the straightliners in perspective which have led to a new Battle of the Books cannot be shrugged off in this way. It is obviously Nelson Goodman's conviction that both can make out an equally good case, which has led him to his relativist conclusion.

And yet, we must pause to ask what it is we are really trying to map when we draw a panorama. We are certainly not confronted with a real spherical object such as the globe, but rather with an apparent one, such as the vault of heaven. It is because we tend to relate the distant view to this imaginary vault that we so strongly feel the need for a spherical map. Unlike the map of the curved surface of the earth, therefore, it will be an attempt to map appearances rather than

[5] See note 4 above.

[6] See Ralph M. Evans, *Eye, Film and Camera in Color Photography* (New York: John Wiley and Sons, 1959).

[7] For the problem of curvilinear perspective see also Kenneth Adams, "Realism in Painting", *Discovery* (July 1962), and my comment in the subsequent number of that Journal.

reality; it will seek to record the "how" rather than the "what" and this, admittedly, is not solely determined by the behavior of light.

I hope that this distinction alone may explain why I remain an unrepentant straightliner, but at the risk of monotony I should like to restate my case in a form that may perhaps further the argument a little. I must, for this purpose, return to the eyewitness story of the room observed through a window. Theorists of perspective have always been fond of rooms with checkerboard floors and walls (Figure 1), and we may imagine the place of the alleged crime even more perfectly patterned with all the walls and the ceiling covered by the grid. I hope it will be agreed that our knowledge of the behavior of light will tell us exactly which squares will be visible and which occluded by the walls of the house, the furniture in the room, or any other feature from where the witness saw it. This mapping, furthermore, would certainly have succeeded if he drew the observed fact onto a flat paper. Indeed this map would have coincided with a tracing of the view he could have made on a vertical transparent plane while keeping his eye still. It is true that he might equally have chosen to make the tracing on a curved plane, say on a bow window, and provided he had kept his eye still, the two tracings would coincide from that point of view. So, by definition, would also the straight lines of the patterned room.

"We know all that", the curvilinearist would reply", but it does not alter the fact that our visual space is curved". It is a reply that has gained some superficial plausibility by Einstein's discoveries, but much as I have had to read, as an art historian, about methods of "rendering space", I have still failed to grasp what this is supposed to mean. If light rays are bent in gravitational fields so that stars appear to be displaced, occlusions will no longer occur along straight lines, and the mapping of the constellations will have to be revised. But nobody has claimed, to my knowledge, that occlusions here on earth are not the consequence of light moving along straight lines, and it is in these I am interested rather than in "space".

I admit that the example of the room is somewhat weighted as an ideal case, particularly if we look at it head on as in the standard diagram. But my argument would not be affected if, instead of one room, we would imagine a whole expanse of a facade with all its windows lit up, for even then one point perspective would tell us how much of each room was visible from the point. What would be disturbing in such a larger map would only be that it becomes increasingly unrealistic. Who would glance at windows sideways or upwards, and how much would he then see anyway? It is for this reason that wide-angle snapshots look so strange; they do not remind us of a possible experience, the inspection of occlusions in one direction.

But what is important is that these same occlusions would also have to be entered on the curved map. If we should really keep the eye on the same spot while moving—by no means an easy feat and one that would involve us in walking in a circle—the windows projected on the inside of the globe would still reveal the same aspects through the windows, though their images would now differ in size and be curved.

The standards of fidelity of the two informational maps would be the same, precisely because neither of them represents "space" but things in space of which no stationary view can give us complete information. What we took for a room in the first example, after all, might have been a stage setting or an "Ames Room" with a sloping or even a curved floor, and what we took for a large chest of drawers, occluding six square foot units, might have been small and oddly shaped. Outside the range of binocular disparity it is only movement that allows us to detect such tricks—the very tricks of perspective. Rotation of the eye on one spot would not suffice here either.

What is characteristic of the experience of space, I believe, is precisely the feeling that we *can* move and test the various aspects of things. We ought not to be surprised that this experience cannot be recorded on any one informational map; the wonder is rather, as we shall see, that perspective renderings appear less rigid than they are.

Even so, we may grant for argument's sake that rigidity is untrue to our experience of a world in which we can turn and move, and we might do justice to this objection by having the original map drawn, not on a rigid surface, but on some elastic material, a piece of rubber that could be stretched or contracted. Using this expedient, we could then take our map and adjust it to the panoramic circle, curving its straight lines without upsetting its information content.

But would we really have been well advised on our trip in the Austrian Alps to copy our picture postcard onto a sheet of rubber before setting out to identify the view? It showed us *what* could be seen from that spot. No device could fully show us *how* we would see the view.

It is this inability of any representation, of course, that prompts Nelson Goodman to dismiss the claims of perspective. He reminds us of the well-known fact that photographs offer their surprises and disappointments to those who have seen the view: "Pike's Peak dwindles dismally in a snapshot" (*Languages of Art,* p. 15). It is as familiar and as justified a complaint as the corresponding stricture that "the photograph of a man with his feet thrust forward looks distorted" (ibid.).

Apparently, then, we would have to manipulate our elastic map considerably to approximate our phenomenal world; we would have to extend the area of the peak and contract the spot with the feet thrust forward. Here, however, one could not but agree with Nelson Goodman that none of these operations would be likely to be very successful; there are indeed no objective standards by which it should be done. For our phenomenal world is not only "elastic", it is in constant movement. There is the change of focus and of accommodation; there is the distortion due to astigmatism and other flaws in our vision; there is, above all, the effect of our own movement which stretches and dissolves the informational map into a fluctuating succession of images. Within this flux of events we selectively single out points of interest, and this attention in its turn acts perhaps as magnifying glass extending the map here and blurring the shrinking areas elsewhere. Whether this phenomenal world of ours can be more easily described, let alone represented, than can the elusive images of a dream, is indeed an open question; and Nelson Goodman is right when he insists that it nowise "looks like" a picture drawn in perspective or in any other way.

I believe it is J. J. Gibson who has most fully explained why we shall never succeed in thus pinning down our visual sensations.[8] Our senses, in his terminology, are "perceptual systems": they exist to process the stream of information that reaches us from the world; and they are exceedingly well attuned for this task. It is for this reason that he has proposed what I have elsewhere called his "Copernican Revolution",[9] the theory that it is futile to ask how we construct the world out of our sensations, because it is in fact the invariant three-dimensional world that is given to us. What the child and the unsophisticated—and presumably the animal—responds to is the world out there. Concentration on our visual sensations is a product of reflection which was largely due to the development of the pictorial arts. There may be difficulties in the way of this formulation, but I am sure it comes closer to the truth than does the traditional account. But if it does, we shall have to reformulate the problem of perspective representation, without, if possible, dismissing it as irrelevant.

[8] James J. Gibson, The Senses Considered as Perceptual Systems (Boston: Houghton Mifflin, 1966).
[9] "The Evidence of Images", in C. S. Singleton, ed. Interpretation, Theory and Practice (Baltimore: Johns Hopkins Press, 1969).

I have attempted precisely this in *Art and Illusion*[10] when I suggested the paradoxical formulation that the world does not look like a picture but a picture can look like the world. The standard of fidelity, to use Nelson Goodman's terminology, is asymmetrical. Philosophically it may look monstrous to say that while *a* is unequal to *b*, *b* equals *a*, but it is this monstrosity I have proposed and should like to defend and reinforce. The world, we have seen, never looks like a picture mainly because we move through the world and in doing so we are guided by the transformation of aspects that occurs all around us. Moving towards a door, the shape of the door remains invariant but its size changes; moving past a table, its aspects change in a predictable manner. Predictable to our perceptual system but not to our awareness. Few people could describe, let alone draw these transformations which depend, of course, on the behavior of light. But it is this melody of change, as Gibson has shown, that allows us to perceive the invariants and to inform us of the shape of things in our surroundings in an unambiguous way. From this point of view it makes no sense to ask whether we see straight lines as curved or straight. We perceive them as straight if they are straight; though we all can play interesting games if we try for once to attend to our sensations: Moving in a car along the road we can see the roadside swing round past us in a complex curve, due to the fact that the parallactic shift is much greater in our proximity than it is further along. If we focus on a point on that road somewhere in the middle distance, we shall see the road pivoting around that spot which has become our temporary reference point. These are experiences that always accompany our movement, but few people may be aware of their character. They have no need to know them.

I would suggest that the same is true of the dwindling of "Pike's Peak" and of the so-called distortion of proximal objects, in other words, of all the phenomena that have been subsumed under the term of the "perceptual constancies". As long as psychology talked in terms of visual sensations, these were described as somewhat anomalous adjustments which the mind carries out in viewing the visual field. The mountain 'looks larger' than it should, the feet smaller. But as soon as we adopt Gibson's approach, this formulation will not do. The feet always look the size and shape they are, and even the distant mountain looks large because it is large. And yet it would be clearly wrong to attribute the size from which the constancies deviate simply

[10] New York: Pantheon Books, 1960), 329.

to the whims of perspective. Though painters may have been among the first to be aware of that effect, we can all experience it without resort to drawing or to a psychological laboratory. For the so-called constancies may be described as the degree of unexpectedness of what will occlude what in our field of vision.

Take two oranges of unequal size, or two unequal coins, and try to hold one so as to precisely occlude the other. It will not be very easy to fix this place without trial and error, for we are normally not much concerned with these relationships in our line of sight. If we then move the occluding shape sideways so that both objects can be seen side-by-side, we tend to experience a shock of surprise, for the smaller one will persist to 'look' small, though we have just found that their images must be equal. There are many variants of this experiment, from drawing the view on a windowpane to measuring the size of one's mirror image on the mirror's surface. Each of these experiences, familiar to every painter still trained in the skill of perspective, will tend to confirm the feeling of unreality with which we look on relations of occlusion.

Why are we so rarely aware of them? Is it not because normally they are of little practical relevance? In reaching out for the orange on the table I adjust my hand to its real size which I shall soon be able to test. The fact that in the course of this movement my thumb may for a moment occlude its total width is of no significance and is 'gated out'. J. J. Gibson may well be right in his surmise that nobody could be interested in the relative sizes of images in the plane before painters investigated them. Even the painter, however, tries for obvious reasons to avoid those extremes that Nelson Goodman has referred to —the oversize hand or foot. Why are they avoided? Once more the explanation suggests itself that in real-life situations we rarely have occasion to attend to such occlusions. If a small object cuts out a large part of our field of vision, we simply shift our head and are rid of the obstruction. It is only where our movement is impeded, as when we sit in a theater and are bothered by the size of the hat of the lady in front that we notice the laws of perspective that make it obscure half the stage. Even so it is not quite true that such occlusions will always look unrealistic. In the motion picture the rapid enlargement of an object can make us duck.[11] We are attuned to the behavior of light, even though we do not know it.

[11] See my paper "Visual Discovery through Art", *Arts Magazine* (November 1965), now reprinted in James Hogg, ed. *Psychology and the Visual Arts* (Baltimore: Penguin Books, 1969).

Indeed it seems to me that some of the constancy phenomena described in psychological literature can best be interpreted in the light of the role that expectations of movement and therefore of transformations play in our processing of visual information. Take the well-known experiment by Robert H. Thouless which aims at measuring what he calls "Phenomenal Regression to the Real Object".[12] The subject was asked to look from a given point at a circular coin lying on the surface of a table and to select from a series of graded ovals the one he thought would match the foreshortened coin. It was found that the shape selected always deviated in the direction of roundness from the shape calculated on the basis of projective geometry. It looked as if the coin were tilted towards the observer.

In Thouless terminology the appearance was a compromise between the real object (which is circular) and the real projection (which is a steep oval). I have argued elsewhere that the term 'real' here is perhaps a little misleading. What the experiment shows is that we tend to anticipate the effect of an inspection movement. If we wanted to find out the shape of an object, we would either turn it in our hand or move in relation to it, till we got it into full view. Somehow this expectation colors our awareness of what we see to such an extent that even the demand to find out which cardboard shape would match or occlude the object in question fails to elicit the correct response. After all it is a complicated demand: we must predict when and how an unfamiliar piece of cardboard held vertically would coincide in its outline with a familiar coin on the table over there. Real life never poses this question, while real life often makes us carry out inspection movements. Thus we generally underrate the degree of tilt because it will soon right itself.

The Thouless experiment reminds us to what an extent our perspective representation on the flat rubber sheet would have to be pulled about to adjust to these various influences on apparent size and apparent shape. The distant coin not only looks larger but also rounder than it "should", just as Pike's Peak not only looks taller but also steeper than it turns out to be when you measure its slope against an occluding pencil. The case against the phenomenal world looking like its projected picture on a plane is indeed even more formidable than Nelson Goodman has made it.

[12] Robert H. Thouless, "Phenomenal Regression to the Real Object", *British Journal of Psychology*, 1931, vol. 21, reprinted extract in M. D. Vernon, ed. *Experiments in Visual Perception* (Baltimore: Penguin Books, 1966). I have discussed this experiment in *Art and Illusion*.

But these arguments overlook a fact which we neglect at our peril: the picture, too, is part of the phenomenal world, and if the phenomenal world bends, turns and twists, so surprisingly does the perspective representation. It is possible to show that we do in fact tend to pull it about, and that the degree to which we do it is generally ignored or at least underrated.

I feel that Nelson Goodman's diagram on page 18 of *Language of Art* is a case in point. He looks for fidelity in the demand that the picture and the view of a high tower should match, and finds that this could only happen in eccentric and unrealistic situations. The illusionistic painters of Baroque ceilings might not have found them quite as absurd as he implies, but that is beside the point. What matters is that pictures are not visually as inert as he seems to postulate. For as I have also tried to argue elsewhere, the so-called distortions due to the constancies and other effects also apply to pictures painted in perspective.

Take the Thouless experiment. I would predict that a painted coin or plate represented as lying on a table would also obey the law of "phenomenal regression to the real object", which I would interpret as an anticipated inspection movement.[13] Indeed it might be possible in this way to devise a measurement for the degree of illusion experienced in front of a painted still life and to examine the influence that fidelity to the "behavior of light" may have on this automatic reaction. One thing has been shown, perspective representations do lead to that surprise at occlusion which I have described as an aspect of the constancies.[14] A pair of dividers shifted from the foreground of any picture postcard to the features near the horizon will convince the reader that even in pictures we rarely estimate the true extent of diminution with distance.

But naturally the constancies not only operate in the picture, they also operate *on* the picture. If it is true that coins anticipate our inspection movements, this must also be true of paintings. It has often been said and repeated that a picture in perspective will look right only when seen exactly from the center. It is curious how this myth could survive into an age in which persons sit in the cinema, in front of the television set or the projection screen when their friends show snapshots of their holidays without much caring to avoid a slight

[13] For a demonstration see R. L. Gregory, *Eye and Brain* (London: Weidenfeld and Nicolson, 1966), 172.
[14] See *Art and Illusion*, p. 304, and my papers quoted in notes 9 and 11.

angle. They know that the picture will look normal, thanks to the constancies.[15]

I believe this phenomenal correction to be both more interesting and more complex than writers on this subject have generally allowed, for if we think the matter through we come to rather startling results.

The first of these results follows from the postulate that pictures seen obliquely will tend to "right themselves" in anticipation of our inspection movement. If this could be verified, it would follow that if we stand in front of a large mural, looking sideways and looking up and down to take it all in, its surface would begin phenomenally to buckle and curve according to the direction of our gaze. That sharp contrast between the flat perspective projection and the spherical panorama would lose much of its phenomenal reality. A wide panorama of the ocean, for instance, with its horizon painted quite properly as a straight line, might appear phenomenally and almost unnoticeably to curve around us as we turn our head.

But this consequence of the fact that pictures also belong to the phenomenal world must be seen as superimposed on another effect which would at first appear to pull in the opposite direction. I refer to the notorious phenomenal shift in the orientation of objects represented in perspective pictures. I have discussed this intriguing phenomenon twice, once in *Art and Illusion* and again in a later essay on *"Perception and Visual Deadlock"*, but I have never been satisfied that my explanation was exhaustive.[16]

It was based, above all, on what I called the "negative test" of consistency. In a painting, an object with a pronounced aspect such as a foreshortened gunbarrel, a pointing finger, or a human eye will continue to show the same aspect from whatever side we look at the picture. If these objects were not painted, but real, any move on our part would of course show them from a different side and reveal a different aspect; since we fail to produce this change, we instinctively assume that the object is still pointing at us and must therefore have moved. The effect is stronger where the object concerned is seen thrusting

---

[15] No less a mind than Einstein addressed himself to this problem in a letter to M. H. Pirenne quoted by Doesschate, *op. cit*, p. 158. He speaks of the beholder "easily compensating for the distortion on condition that the visual angle . . . is small". This "compensation" is precisely the constancy phenomenon. I hope to show further below that other factors also play their part.

[16] In *Meditations on a Hobby Horse* (London: Phaidon Press, 1963).

outward from the picture, because such an object would change its aspect more rapidly than would another, further in the distance. Thus the knife handle in our diagram (Figure 2) will appear to move more than the face of the clock in the background.

Figure 2

I know now that this explanation is incomplete, but it points at least to one important element in the theory of representation which is rarely discussed explicitly—I mean the difference between objects of pronounced orientation (such as a gun or a clock), objects of indistinguishable orientation (such as a sphere), and objects of unknown orientation (such as a tree whose branches may grow in any direction). Once we realize that a perspective projection might correspond to an infinite number of different arrays in space, it also becomes clear that the configuration on the plane will unambiguously correspond to an object of known shape and orientation only when it belongs to the first of these categories. We can tell where the painter stood in relation to a building or even a pointing gun barrel on the assumption that the building is bounded by a rectangle and the gun barrel was straight. We cannot know the same of a tree or a rock unless we are familiar with its shape or—and this is a complication I prefer to omit—if the additional cue of light and shade brings in another element of orientation.

Now this ignorance of ours as to the real array the painter had before him makes us also more tolerant towards a change of configuration on the picture plane. If it does not correspond to one thing, it may plausibly suggest another.

It is armed with this knowledge that we must try to tackle the problem of the intriguing change in perspective pictures as we walk past them. When in *Art and Illusion* I attributed this "internal movement" in the picture to the way in which "we contribute some of the imagined movement from the store of our own explanation", I was certainly wrong. The movement is real enough. It is of course the result of the foreshortening of the picture as we look at it from the side.

How this foreshortening operates on the plane is a simple matter of projective geometry. If we keep our eyes at the height of the picture's horizon while we move sideways, the line of the horizon itself will shrink but not change in orientation, but lines parallel to the horizon will increasingly converge from up and down towards our vanishing point. The frame will be the most oblique but all oblique lines inside the picture will both get shorter and steeper as the area of the picture contracts. (Figure 2) Thus the proportion of every configuration will change and become narrower, the horizontals being more affected than the verticals.

Now perspective is a system of representation in which the orientation and relation of lines is given a particular significance. Lines converging towards the vanishing point of the picture are understood to be at a right angle to the picture plane, and the orientation of other foreshortened objects of known shape is seen in relation to this system.

When it is said that a perspective picture only "works" when the beholder's eye is fixed precisely at the point from which the array was drawn, it is tacitly assumed that only then will the beholder see precisely what the painter saw, and how he saw it. The first is correct, the second doubtful in any but extreme cases of contrived trompe'loeil. But the way in which pictures adjust to other viewpoints suggests that there is no need for the painter's vanishing point and the beholder's to coincide for a plausible or possible view of a three-dimensional arrangement of things to emerge. If trees appear taller and narrower, and even persons somewhat slimmer, well there are such trees and such persons. If the young lady on the poster (Figure 3, pp. 146, 147) who extends her arms to embrace us seems, when seen from her right, to have become asymmetrical, her right arm being longer than her left one (which is further away from us), we need not even suspect her of being misshapen; we need only assume that the arm further away is not shorter but more foreshortened, and the convincing character of the picture is restored. Does not "more foreshortened" also mean that the arm is turned a little more towards us? Of course it does mean precisely this, and so, as we walk along the poster, the lady will go on smiling at us and her arms will turn towards us, not because we 'project' or imagine this movement, but because the unnoticed transformations on the picture plane carry this significance.

The complexity of this transformation is naturally somewhat confusing, but one theoretical point must be made. If a picture is so constructed as to have its vanishing point in the center, as indicated in our diagram (Figure 1), its oblique position will resemble the side-wall of our diagram; this means that the vanishing point will now appear to be along the line D', that is, it will have moved from the center towards the opposite frame. Note that this movement is only relative to the picture. For while we shift our position, the area of the picture will inevitably seem to contract, and this contracting movement will shorten the apparent length of the horizon on which the vanishing point has now become a little eccentric. What accounts for the strong impression of movement, however, is not this slight dislocation of the vanishing point on the picture plane, but its imaginary position on the far-distant horizon. It is towards this ideal point that the orthogonals of the perspective construction are converging, and it is the apparent shift of their orientation that makes for that veering movement which naturally appears to affect the foreground most of all.

At the same time, the narrowing of the whole picture leads to the predicted increase in steepness, and to a relative lifting of the horizon, as if the ground were sloping upwards. The road leading from the horizon outwards towards the center of the picture which abutted onto the frame at a right angle will now form an obtuse angle on the side on which we stand and will thus appear to be leading towards us, QED.

One thing, perhaps, should be added. The actual transformations and shifts affecting every configuration on the plane clearly are of a complexity that not only defies description but also perception at one go. Hence our tendency to select some point of reference in relation to which we see the 'movement' of the other features, much as we saw the lateral road swinging round a focussed point during real movement. Here is one of the subjective elements that accounts for the feeling that the movement is carried by particular features of interest, the road leading towards us, the gun or the eyes of the portrayed. It is these we take as points of reference, and here what I have called the negative test may well apply. But it is all the more important to stress that the movement as such, the change in the angle relative

Figure 3

to the frame, and therefore the change in the degree of foreshortening is real and not imaginary.

The objectivity of these transformations which I have never seen fully described[17] is easily demonstrated by the simple expedient of photographing pictures or diagrams from various angles.

It is interesting and amusing from this point of view to scrutinize art books which show interiors with pictures on foreshortened walls, or similar murals in churches. They will confirm the varying tolerance of different objects to this kind of transformation. Roads leading into the distance fare best, of course, because the shift of the vanishing point simply shifts their apparent direction. Round buildings are also relatively unaffected, because their elongation is not felt

[17] The only systematic discussion I know is in the brief chapter X of Doesschate, *op. cit.*, who treats it from the point of view of distortion.

Figure 3 (continued)

to be disturbing. It is different with symmetrical facades parallel to the picture plane, for being closer to the horizon than the lower frame, their bounding lines will be less converging, and so they will appear to have shifted towards the beholder while their central feature has become eccentric.

The few effects here described certainly do not exhaust the way we tend to process and change the phenomenal aspect of a painting seen in perspective. Other tendencies may exert their pull: for instance, the relative importance of objects, or the familiarity of aspects or shapes, such as letters which we always scrutinize for their invariant rather than their changeable features. All these elements get into the mill which churns and transforms the information from the visible world, and they do so because of what Thouless has called the effort after meaning, the desire to make sense of what we see.

[147]

But does not this effort presuppose an expectation? Does the way we look at perspective pictures not depend on a certain amount of conditioning? It probably does. It is unlikely that an observer who had never seen such pictures would "see" all the transformations I have attempted to describe. But would that prove that Nelson Goodman or even G.ten Doesschate are right in calling one-point perspective only one of many possible ways of mapping the world? I doubt it, for if I am right, perspective is not only uniquely successful in mapping *what* we see from a given point; the rich and elusive *how* we see perspective renderings may also be unique.

Could other systems of representation elicit the same complex and manifold type of reaction? Questions such as these are more easily asked than answered without experiment. But one experiment has been performed. I refer to the course of historical development that has led to the evolution of perspective representation. It seems to have impressed those who saw it as "better" than other methods, and whether we regret this or not, even the Japanese adopted it when they learned of its existence. How can we explain this undeniable success of perspective if it were only another mapping method that must be learned to be decoded? Is it not more plausible to think that there is indeed something compelling in the trick even though it achieves genuine illusion only in such special cases as in peepshows, on the perspective stage, or on illusionist ceilings seen from the right place?

I have suggested elsewhere that what perspective renderings do more easily is to unsettle our perceptions.[18] However difficult it may be in any individual instance to say "how" we see a perspective representation, such a representation may still be an exception to J. J. Gibson's postulate that we see the objects of our surroundings precisely as they are.

Pictures constructed on the tightly knit system of perspective (which is imitated by the camera) tend to resist this process. It takes a special effort and much unlearning of reactions to see them merely as things. The very way they dissolve and transform themselves approximates them to that elusive experience we describe as the phenomenal world.

If proof were needed of this elusiveness, it would lie in the types of transformation I have here tried to classify and analyze, for though they may all occur simultaneously, they are logically in contradiction with each other—much as is the panoramic and the static

[18] See note 9.

view, or the experience of Pike's Peak as it is and as it appears to be.

To sum up, I have attempted to separate three ways in which the perspective picture is stretched or transformed: The first corresponds to the Thouless effect of the constancies and demands that objects in paintings that are drawn as tilted will appear slightly more turned to the beholder than they are really represented. The second, which should be based on the same tendency, would demand that the picture itself, frame and all, would appear less foreshortened than it is; and yet the third, which is the most important and the most interesting, is precisely based on the objective and unnoticed transformations in the plane which are due to this foreshortened view. Introspection suggests that the three actually co-exist peacefully. As our attention shifts in its search for meaning, all the pulls and counterpulls that shape our phenomenal world come into play in the processing of pictures. Maybe it is precisely this paradoxical type of transformation that points to the connection between fidelity and the behavior of light, and therefore to the limits of relativism in representation.

EIGHT

Pictures, Representation, and the Understanding

MARX W. WARTOFSKY

I AM TEMPTED to subtitle this paper "Meditations on a Dinner Plate", partly out of respect for Gombrich's essay, "Meditations on a Hobby-Horse"; partly out of a disenchantment with the British preoccupation with pennies and their elliptical looks; and partly out of the conviction that a philosopher is likely to do better on a good meal, than on a pocketful of small change.

It should be clear from all this that I shall be concerned in this paper with a famous (or infamous) philosophical shape: the circle, which allegedly appears elliptical when viewed obliquely. I propose to examine and to uphold the thesis that the tilted circle, which is supposed to appear elliptical, in fact *appears* circular; but that we represent it as elliptical in our pictures in order to *make it* appear circular; and therefore, that talk about elliptical appearances is talk about how we represent what we see, and how our seeing is affected by our canons of representation. In short, we picture what we understand, when we represent tilted circles as ellipses in our pictures. So we may be said to see what we see by way of our picturing, when we claim to see a tilted circle as as ellipse. All this is packed rather densely here, and I hope to unpack it so that it becomes clear, and so that any sense of paradox or perversity will vanish.

The philosophical proponents of elliptical looks are the sense-datum theorists, from Moore, Broad and Russell, through Price, Ayer, and their elliptoid American counterparts. What I want to claim is that the sense-datum theorists, in talking about elliptical looks, have literally taken leave of their senses, and have constructed for us what is in fact a philosophical counterfeit—a fiction of the understanding —which has been passed off on an unsuspecting populace as true sensory coin. In rejecting, or at least reinterpreting their claims, I hope to generalize from the discussion of ellipses and circles to a thesis concerning the part played by representations and pictures in our knowledge of the external world.

Now, beyond these opening remarks, some brief background: The argument from illusion, on which much of sense-datum theory builds, runs something like this: When we look at a plate or a coin from any angle off the normal, what we know to be a round or circular object appears elliptical. Since the elliptical appearance cannot in fact be part of the surface of the object, and since such appearances change as we move about, while the object or its so-called "real shape" is sup-posed to remain the same, what appears to us cannot be the real shape of the object, but rather a sense-datum, or a series of such sense-data. In Price's elaborate construction, we are introduced to families of such sense data, some of which are so-called nuclear sense data, con-stituting standard solids and some of which are parts of distortion series of this family. Russell's version talks of a *space of perspectives*, in a frankly geometrical construction, which relies very little on sense-data as appearances, but relies rather on the laws of geomet-rical optics and of perspective transformation. Early Ayer, of *The Foundations of Empirical Knowledge*, reduces the sense-datum theory to a "manner of speaking" in which there is allegedly no difference in the facts which sense-datum talk and material-object talk are both about, thus evading an ontology of sense-data. But all are taken with elliptical looks as somehow given or known by acquaintance.

Now let us ask a very unphilosophical question: What are the facts of the perception of tilted circles? How could one tell what a tilted circle appears as? Plainly, we all know what it means for it to appear as an ellipse, and all of us would presumably exhibit our visual sophistication by *representing* or *picturing* such tilted circles as ellipses. Thus, it has been very easy to become the victims of the naiveté of our sophistication, and to concur that, after all, what is given in perception (as anyone can plainly see) is an elliptical appearance. We can, after all, "see" the ellipse, even though we "know" it is a tilted circle. Thus, the classical view held that it was some perceptual judgment which preserved shape constancy, "interpreting" or "correcting" the elliptical appearance. Helmholtz, for example, spoke of this as an *unbewusstes schluss,* an unconscious inference or judgment. But how is one to tell *what* appears, from which such an inference, conscious or unconscious, is made? Just looking and seeing apparently will not do, if the inference is unconscious, or if it necessarily intrudes on the looking, for then one can never get an "uncorrected" or "uninterpreted" appearance. And unless one has an independent mode of access to the appearance, one is in fact making a hypothetical inference *to* the appearance, rather than making an inference *from* it; that is to say, one is performing what Peirce described as an abductive inference to "elliptical looks" as a premise from which it would follow (on the additional premise that the perceptual judgment that preserves shape constancy is an inference) that the real shape is circular. But if there is no independent mode of access to the appearance, or to what is "given" as a sense-datum, then (1) it cannot be "given" in any perceptual sense, but only in the judgmental sense of a hypothetical premise, and (2) there is no logical reason why the premise should be that the "given" shape is elliptical, rather than square, or triangular, or pear-shaped. Each of these, through some set of transformations, will yield a circle; and any of them will do as the hypothesis from which, by the "proper" *ad hoc* transformation, we arrive at the "corrected" judgment that what we see is a tilted circle.

There obviously is some reason why we choose the elliptical shape as that which "appears"; or rather, there is a set of reasons. The set of transformations that we choose to employ is that of geometrical optics, i.e. that set of projective transformations which, when the projection is made onto a plane surface, give us the so-called laws of perspective in drawing. Such a projection would yield an ellipse from a tilted circle. Furthermore, since vision is a matter of reflected light from surfaces (which is presumably projected through an aperture with an inverting lens onto a plane surface, i.e. the retina), retinal image-formation is taken to be such a projection onto a plane surface. Our neurophysiological model of vision and of the eye, adopts this geometrical optics, therefore. This is reinforced by the fact that, were we to look at the image formed on a retina (say in an eye removed from an animal, like a rabbit), the *image* of a tilted circle would in fact be an ellipse.

But there are serious objections to such a simple view of image formation, even at the level of the neurophysiology of vision. The fact that the retinal projection is on a curved rather than a flat surface; that the so-called "surface" is really an array of highly specific neurons, which fire differentially; that so-called visual projection areas on the retina are complex rather than simple mappings of the projected light rays (i.e. that contour, edge, and slant receptors for "shape" are not simply arranged) ; and finally, that we do not "see" our retinal images with some third or inner eye—all these are well-known complications of the simple picture theory of visual perception. Thus, one could claim against the thesis that we "see" what is projected onto our retinas: first, that we just do not; and second, that this account of seeing is theory-laden, dependent on our beliefs and our knowledge of geometrical optics and the physiology of vision. Thus, seeing tilted circles as ellipses is seeing through theory-tinted glasses.

I think this is true, but it is not the whole truth. For the account of what appears to us when we look at tilted circles may be given by someone who is not theoretically committed to all this, or who knows nothing about it. Presumably, we may find a naive subject who will tell us exactly what he thinks he sees, in a relatively theory-free way.

There are several ways to elicit this response experimentally: The experimenter may ask the subject to draw what he sees, i.e. to make a picture of it. He may present the subject with a series of shapes, from among which the subject is to pick the shape that most closely corresponds to the perceived shape. He may ask for a verbal description. (This last would presumably be the most ambiguous response with regard to differences in visual shape, although differences in shape may be expressed verbally by a naive subject, uncommitted to the theory of geometrical optics, by such expressions as "x is rounder than y" or "y is flatter than x and rounder than z". But more on this later.)

From the results of a well-known set of experiments, Thouless concluded that what is seen is neither a circle nor the projected ellipse, but something in between the two. Thouless writes:

It is commonly stated in textbooks of Psychology that when we observe figures inclined to us, we see them not in the shapes indicated by the laws of perspective but in the shapes which these figures 'really' possess. Thus when we look obliquely at a circular object we see it not as an ellipse but as a true circle. While it is undoubtedly true that such an object seen in these conditions is judged to be of its true shape and also that we are prepared for motor reaction to a circular object, I do not find that experiment confirms this statement as to what shape is seen. If a subject is shown an inclined circle and is asked to select from a number of figures the one which represents the shape seen by him he chooses without hesitation an ellipse. This ellipse, however, is widely different from the one which represents the shape of the inclined circle indicated by the laws of perspective, being much nearer to the circular form. The subject sees an inclined figure neither in its 'real' shape nor in the shape which is its perspective projection but as a compromise between the two.[1]

Thus, according to Thouless, the "phenomenal shape" is not the ellipse, as the laws of perspective transformation would represent it, but a "regressed" ellipse, tending towards the "real" (circular) shape. The perceptual shape constancy, which leads us to identify the tilted circle as a tilted circle, rather than as an ellipse presented in the fronto-parallel plane, thus intrudes, according to Thouless, upon the presented stimulus-object, which Thouless identifies with the ellipse "correctly" presented as a perspective transformation according to the laws of geometrical optics.[2]

[1] Robert H. Thouless, "Phenomenal Regression to the Real Object", *The British Journal of Psychology* (1931) 21, Part 4, p. 339 ff.
[2] Thouless compares this result to Hering's experiment with light intensities. In Hering's experiment, a white disk in strong shadow is seen as brighter than an intensely illuminated grey disk, despite the fact that the retinal image intensity is greater for the illuminated grey disk. So too, in Hering's experiments with constancies of hue, a blue surface illuminated by an unsaturated yellow light, so that it looks colorless to monocular vision (through a tube), continues to look blue when seen in a surround, and binocularly, (though its saturation is less than when it is illuminated by white light.) Here too, in Thouless's terms, there is "regression to the 'real' object", i.e. to "real" brightness or intensity of a surface, or to "real" hue. (But this is more problematic, perhaps, because of the greater ambiguity of what we mean by "real color" as against "real shape", so that the reference-object or reference-properties of the perceptual constancy is not as clearly specified in the color (brightness, hue) case as in the case of shape.)

Thouless's point, of course, is that so-called shape constancy is *not* preserved, but that there is instead what he calls "compromise" between the *stimulus-shape,* i.e. the perspectival projection on the retina, and the *real shape,* for which our motor responses are cued. Thus, the "compromise" *phenomenal shape* is a "phenomenal regression to the real object". By contrast, when Thouless's subjects were asked to reproduce or to match actually elliptical disks or trapezoidal figures, there was practically no such "distortion" of the stimulus shape; that is, the ratio of long to short axes of the ellipses drawn or matched were very close to those presented.

Among the many experiments on this problem reported since then, it has been shown that as the depth-cues (e.g. light or texture gradients) or surround-cues were removed, shape constancy decreased. In effect, what such experiments do is impoverish the visual presentation of the tilted circle so that the actual visual information in the input approaches that of a presented ellipse in the fronto-parallel plane. Eissler[3] removed depth cues by monocular presentation. Langdon[4] showed that shape-constancy is inversely proportional to removal of perceptual cues, such as surround-cues. Leibowitz and Bourne[5] showed that shape-constancy varied directly with exposure duration and luminance—i.e. as visual acuity was impaired, shape constancy decreased.

Constancy was also shown to vary with intelligence and training. For example, Thouless reported that experienced artists and teachers of perspective, though they show some "phenomenal regression", match the stimulus-shape more closely. That is to say, they preserve constancy least, in their reproduction or matching of the stimulus shape. Likewise, Leibowitz, Waskow, Loeffler, and Glaser, in their study[6] ("Intelligence Level as a Variable in the Perception of Shape") showed that constancy effects were strongest for Rhesus monkeys, then decreased in order of "intelligence", among the other

[3] K. Eissler, "Die Gestaltkonstanz der Sehdinge bei Variation der Objekte und ihrer Einwirkungsweise auf den Wahrnehmenden", *Archiv für Gestaltpsychologie* (1933) **88**, pp. 487–550.

[4] J. Langdon, "The Perception of a Changing Shape", *Quarterly Journal of Experimental Psychology* (1951) **3**, pp. 157–165.

[5] H. Leibowitz and L. E. Bourne, Jr., "Time and Intensity as Determiners of Perceived Shape", *Journal of Experimental Psychology* (1956) **51**, 4, pp. 277–281.

[6] H. Leibowitz, I. Waskow, N. Loeffler, and F. Glaser, "Intelligence Level as a Variable in the Perception of Shape", *Quarterly Journal of Experimental Psychology* (1959) **11**, pp. 108–112.

groups tested (mental defectives, slow learners, first-year psychology students, and Ford scholars making up their rank-ordered groups of subjects).

In general, then, the claim of these experiments is that a tilted circle "appears" as an ellipse to the degree that visual acuity or normal visual cues are impoverished, and to the degree that "intelligence" or training intrudes upon the stimulus-input. Further, the experiments tacitly or explicitly presume to be getting at what the subject "sees" by contrast to what he is presented with, as an independently definable stimulus-object, or stimulus-shape. Thouless's distinction, between "real shape", "stimulus-shape", and "phenomenal shape" re-articulates the standard difference, in studies of perceptual constancies, between "real" and "apparent" shape, but introduces the mediation of stimulus-shape. The problem here is, of course, the independent specification of the stimulus, apart from the "phenomenal" response. Here, as in psychophysical experiments generally, the stimulus is defined within the context of some physical theory. Just as in psycho-physics, stimulus-strength is measured within some such theoretical framework as electrical energy, or luminance, or temperature, here the stimulus-shape, as projective ellipse, is "measured", or defined by the laws of geometrical optics. The "real" shape, to which the constancy is relevant, on the other hand, is defined by its tactile-motor properties, i.e. in the three-dimensional, Euclidean-Cartesian space taken to be canonical for physical objects. The plane-projections of geometrical optics are transformations of this Euclidean space, which are embodied in the laws of perspective. Further, Cartesian optics and dioptrics construct a physiological model of the eye according to these same laws. It is this model that defines the stimulus-shape, in this case, as a projective ellipse.

Now the question arises as to what defines the so-called phenomenal shape, or the "perceived" shape, which the experiments show to vary from the ellipse? It is obviously not enough to say, as Thouless does, that there is a "compromise", between the real shape which perceptual constancy ought to yield and the "phenomenal" shape. For this states the problem entirely in terms of visual stimulus-variables and some presumably tactile-motor response-variables, implying that the "compromise" is simply one between sense-modalities. But Thouless's own results, with teachers of perspective, and those of Leibowitz *et al*, suggest strongly that what intrudes here is visual *understanding*. What I shall mean here by visual understanding is a familiarity with and a knowledge of canons of visual representation.

Such an understanding is presumably acquired—it can be taught, and it can be learned. More than this, it can be induced in the experimental situation itself, by appropriate verbal cues. My argument, in short, will be that the choice of the elliptical shape as the "appearance" of a tilted circle is a function of a commonly understood canon of representation, in drawing, namely that of linear perspective. Now it would be vacuous to claim that tilted circles are drawn or represented by artists as ellipses *because* they have adopted the laws of perspective as canons of "correct" representation. This verges on tautology. (What it means to have adopted such canons, is to represent tilted circles as ellipses.) But if we are concerned with experimental subjects who are not artists, and who are asked to choose matching shapes, rather than to draw them, the question arises as to how a canon of representation in drawing operates on such presumably naive subjects. The experimental situation is worth examining here.

In all of the studies cited, the subject is asked to reproduce or represent what he sees by choosing a matching shape from among a set of such shapes. (These may be cut-out shapes, or pictured shapes). Thouless writes, for example, that the subject is asked to choose a shape that "represents the shape seen by him". Thus, the very condition for getting access to what "appears" to the subject is bound up with (1) *the subject's representation of it,* and with (2) *what he is asked to represent by the experimenter.* Thus two things are involved here, both of which conspire to produce a representation according in some degree with the canonical representation of the tilted circle as an ellipse, and therefore in violation of the preservation of shape constancy. The "regression", on my view, is not *to* the "real object", but *away* from it, and to a canon of representation.

The argument for this is as follows: (1) First, with respect to the subject's representation of the perceived shape, the very condition of representing the shape involves what one takes a representation to be. The naive view is that a representation somehow reproduces the perceived shape of the object. The logic of the experiment (and of the term "phenomenal shape") assumes this, since the subject's representation is explicitly taken to be the "perceived shape". But I would argue instead that a representation does not reproduce the "perceived shape" (whatever that may be) but rather specifies a canonical similarity (from among an infinite set of such similarities). That is to say, the representation is a conventionally adopted specification, which looks "right", or is a "proper" representation, by virtue of our

[157]

acceptance of a certain "vocabulary of forms" (Gombrich's phrase, I think). In this case, the appropriate convention is the elliptical "picture". Why then do the untrained subjects produce a "regressed" ellipse tending to the circle? There is a lot buried in this sort of question: (1) First, there is the residual assumption that what makes the ellipse the appropriate convention is some "natural" tie it has with the stimulus-image. But this, I have argued earlier, will not hold up, because we do not "see" the stimulus-image, if we mean by it the retinal-image; but also, the "picture" we have of a retinal-image is itself a "picture", though in this case a neurophysiological picture, or model, derived from seventeenth-century optics and dioptrics. Second, there is in the question the assumption that the shape-constancy which exerts influence on the visual image is a function of tactile-motor perception, and is not native to the eye, so to speak. But whatever the intermodal effects, I think this does not explain the subject's "regression to the real object". Rather, I would argue that the "compromise" Thouless speaks of is between what the subject sees (a tilted circle) and what he knows he should represent it as (an ellipse); and that the compromise is a function of skill in the use of the canons of perspective representation, i.e. in visual understanding. The argument gets complicated here by the fact that the subjects are not asked to *draw* the shape presented to them, but rather to choose a representation of it. But I would argue that these two are closely related. That is, the visual-manual skill of *drawing* the ellipse in accordance with the laws of perspective is directly related to *seeing* it in terms of such a representation. The experimental results bear this out in the following way: teachers of perspective chose shapes closest to the so-called "stimulus-shape", in Thouless's experiment. Monkeys and mental defectives chose shapes closest to the "real shape", in the experiments of Leibowitz *et al.* In neither case was the drawing skill called upon. What was called upon was the visual understanding of a canon of representation. But this understanding is in direct relation to the practice and the acquired skill of drawing in accordance with the canon. The normal subject's "index of regression" is therefore an inverse measure of this skill, on this view.[7] The subject's repre-

---

[7] Talk about "skill", or "correct" representation is taken here to be relative to a given canon—i.e., the laws of linear perspective. Cézanne's departures from this canon are not to be taken therefore as lack of skill, but rather the deliberate choice of another canon. The same thing is true, I think, of all those art forms that "violate" the laws of perspective, e.g., Romanesque painting, or classical Chinese or Japanese drawing and painting.

[158]

sentation is therefore, in general, a function of his visual understanding, defined in this case by his practical knowledge of the laws of perspective; this "knowledge" defined, further, as his ability to draw shapes in accordance with this canon; and directly related to this, his ability to choose from among a set of shapes the ones that are in closest accord with this canon. Therefore, the subject may be said to "see" by way of his picturing.

(2) Second, however, what the subject chooses to represent is also a function of what he is asked to represent by the experimenter. Here, the analogy between impoverishment of the visual presentation by removal of perceptual cues, and impoverishment of the visual presentation by verbal cues, is significant. In the experiments by Eissler, Langdon, Leibowitz, and Bourne cited above, luminance, duration of exposure, surround cues, etc., were controlled in such a way that the stimulus-input of the tilted circle approached more and more closely that of an ellipse. But a similar effect can be induced by verbal directions to the subject, deliberately, or inadvertently. If the subject is asked to represent the "shape" that is presented to him, or to match the "shape" he sees by choosing from among a set of two-dimensional, abstracted "shapes", cut out or drawn, then what is being elicited is already an abstraction from the visual field. The question "what is the shape that you see" or the direction "choose a matching shape" already impoverishes the visual field, by directing attention to an abstracted part of it, just as decreased luminance or exposure time do. If I name the object, for example, and ask the subject simply to "draw the dinner plate you see before you", I would venture the guess that a less elliptical figure would be drawn, in most instances, than if I asked the subject to "draw the shape of the top of the dinner plate". This latter question impoverishes the perceptual field, and directs the subject to remove surrounding cues "subjectively" or "intentionally", so to speak, rather than removing them objectively, as in the other experiments. The artist, trained visually to fix upon the abstracted property "shape", and trained in perspective drawing, will be able to approach the so-called "stimulus-shape" in his representation, precisely because the abstracted property he is fixing on is defined by the same laws of geometrical optics that define the "stimulus-shape". But this is part of the history of the development of the laws of perspective, about which more needs to be said than can properly be said here. Suffice it to note that "shape", apart from the "real object" (of which it is only one property, and a very complex one at that), is already an abstraction, selected as much by

the history and development of our representational and picturing activity, as by what is presented to us in the visual field.

The untrained child, drawing a tilted circle, preserves constancy, on the other hand. The child's drawing of a plate on a table looks something like this: (Figure 1).

Figure 1

Neither the trapezoidal foreshortening of the rectangular table, nor the elliptical foreshortening of the circular plate, enters into the representation. But note what happens when the "proper" representation of the table in perspective is combined with the shape-constancy preserving circle (Figure 2). We would "read" this picture as that of a plate standing upright on its edge on the table. The surround cues of the table, its grain, its shortened rear legs, all work against the visual understanding of the plate as lying *on* the table. So too, in Figure 3

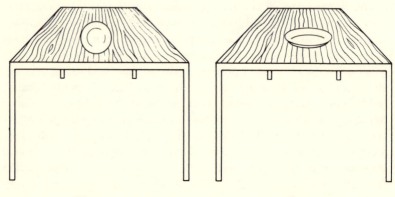

 Figure 2   *Figure 3*

we see the ellipse as a tilted circle, given the perspectival surround-cues of the table, etc., whereas if we were given simply the abstracted shapes of a rectangle and an ellipse (Figure 4), no such interpretation would be given. Figure 5 *suggests* an interpretation like that of

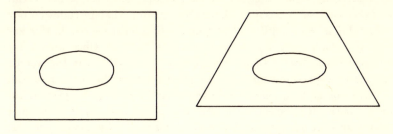

Figure 4   *Figure 5*

Figure 3 but less forcefully so, since "table" cues, (legs, grain), and "plate" cues (thickness of edge, etc.) have been removed. Through all this, what is working most powerfully is the convention of representation which maps three-dimensional objects onto a plane surface. This is a very complex transformation. But we take it without difficulty, because the canon is so well established. (So too, we accept unflinchingly the radically divergent canons of representation which give us Popeye, Mickey Mouse, and the huge-headed children in the comic strips "Peanuts" or "Miss Peach".)

The secret of our acceptance in these exceedingly odd cases is familiarity, not simply with this or that character as drawn, but with a style, or a style-complex. But in the case of the "correct" drawing of the projective ellipse, our familiarity is somehow normative in a different way. Or so it would appear. No one would argue that any human being could be constructed as Popeye is, or as Charlie Brown is. Yet, caricature yields resemblance, and even insight and unique depiction. But in the case of "correct" perspective representation, we take the canon to be veridical, and not simply an accepted convention. On my argument, the two cases are similar. Yet, I think, everyone would feel that the perspective representation is actually "closer to the way things really look", or further still, that it *is* the way things look. This is, if not an epistemological fact, certainly a cultural fact, and it needs coping with. But to cope with it properly, I would have to go into the status of the canons of perspective drawing more fully than I have in the suggestions made thus far. This is the burden of a continuation of this essay, still in work.

[161]

To summarize thus far, however: I argue that in normal perception of objects, and in the normal *praxis* which is the context of this perception, shape-constancy is the correct account of what we see. We see tilted circles as round, i.e. as tilted *circles,* and not as ellipses. Only by abstraction do we separate the shape from the object, so that it can be taken as itself an object of perception. But what intrudes on our doing this is the condition of communicating what we see, in this abstractive way, by means of a representation of it. Once we are required to *represent a shape,* we are already caught up in the web of canons of representation—and in particular, in the modern world, we are bound to a canonical framework derived from geometrical optics, both with respect to our models of the physiology of vision, and with respect to our representations of what we see, by way of pictures. The same geometrical optics that gives us the ellipse as a retinal image of the tilted circle gives us the laws of perspective which direct us to represent the tilted circle as an ellipse.

But if this canon is so pervasive, then in our "acceptable" mode of representation, we "read" the elliptical representation *as* a tilted circle, thus effecting a re-transformation in our seeing of pictures, which is the inverse of the transformation we effect in making the pictures. That is why we draw circles as ellipses *in order to make them look circular;* and that is why, if we were to draw tilted circles as circular, they would look wrong to us.

This bespeaks an important fact: that a theory as historically recent as geometrical optics is, or as perspective drawing is, has become an integral part of our visual understanding, or of our visual "common sense", so much so that it affects our seeing. In a subsequent study, I propose to show how this took place; and also to show that we are able to entertain alternative and radically different canons of representation at the same time.

[162]

NINE

On Seeing
What We
Shall See

RICHARD RUDNER

WE MAY cut in on a certain broad syndrome of epistemological difficulties by first attending to what looks like a much narrower problem in aesthetics.

1
The Relevance of "Whodunit"

When it is discovered that a painter in the Low Countries has been producing almost undetectably fraudulent "Vermeers" and for some years has been successfully peddling them to even the most discriminating of connoisseurs, the world of painting (except perhaps that segment of it consisting of the artists themselves) suffers a certain agitation. Dealers, critics, and museum officials eye their collections nervously.

Now, it would appear that whatever apprehension exists stems from concern with financial investment, or reputation or *amour propre;* for the paintings are, presumably, just the paintings they have always been. Their *aesthetic* impact or import, it would seem, should remain unchanged.

What we have just noted here about the case of the fraudulent "new" Vermeers applies equally to the more usual cases of fakes or copies of already authenticated originals. And, of course, we needn't be distracted by any suggestion of wickedness. The quite legitimate reproduction business continues to make great strides. Thus, *Newsweek* (1969), in a story in its art section, reported

> . . . something close to perfect reproduction has been developed by Guenther Dietz, a 48-year-old goateed German living near Salzburg. Recently, when prominent art experts and museum curators from all over the world examined Dietz's reproduction of an abstract sketch by Swiss artist Otto Bachmann at the Munich International Council of Museums Convention, they could detect theoretically no difference between the original and the Dietz duplication. Theodore Rousseau, vice director and curator in chief of New York's Metropolitan Museum, considers Dietz's work so good that "they can't be called reproductions. They should be called facsimiles." . . .
>
> When his process for high-speed, mechanized mass production is perfected, eventually everyone could own a "masterpiece." "Dietz is now known only to the initiated," a prominent German art critic wrote. "But it is only a matter of time until this quiet revolution will rock the artistic world."

Suppose now, we were to be confronted with a reproduction so "good" that there is to the naked eye no perceptual difference whatever between it and the original. How should we regard it? Shall we construe any effect, which our knowledge that it is not the original has on us in our contemplation of it, as a "legitimate" or as an "illegitimate" aesthetic effect? In this case, since the picture is not masquerading as an original, it would seem that no *moral* disquietude ought to disturb our experience of the work.

Our decision here really seems simple enough. The facts that the original is chronologically prior, that *it* was touched by the hand of the artist, and that *it* costs more money, seem scarcely to furnish a legitimate or reasonable basis for finding it aesthetically more valuable than the reproduction. If there is no difference to be seen between the two, would we not be correct in concluding that we should aesthetically value the reproduction precisely as we would or do value the original?

Consider the fact that from the viewpoint of *purely aesthetic* valuation a reproduction might, in falling short of fulfilling its purpose, do so in at least two quite distinct ways: it might turn out to be aesthetically worse than the original, as in the case where some subtle differences in hues which contributed to the impact of the original are lost in the reproduction; or, it might turn out to be aesthetically better than the original, as in the case (no doubt, rare) where, say, the reproduction process lends a brilliance to some of its hues, thus enhancing some of its pictorial merits in a manner that the artist might not have been able to attain. In the first case, we ought to disvalue, relatively, the reproduction; not because it is a poor *reproduction*—although indeed it is—but because it is a *worse picture* than the original. In the second case, however, by the same token ought we not to disvalue, relatively, the *original*?

There is a tension and a puzzle here which, in one form or another, has dogged aestheticians at least from the time of Plato. One important aspect of it has to do with aesthetic *evaluation*. When we learn that an art work is unoriginal or, more narrowly, that a painting is inauthentic,[1] we tend *on that account* to disvalue it—even though, on inspection, we can't tell the difference between it and the original—or, even though we may have found intense aesthetic gratification in it previously.

By habit, conformity or cultivation it has come to seem unreflectively right to most of us not to value an unoriginal art work—say a copy of some fine famous painting—as highly as we value the original. But some puzzlement arises when we consider that we would want to say of the painting, which we have just learned to be a copy, that it was the *same art work*, the same particular painting, it had been the moment before we became aware of that peculiar relationship it happens to bear to another particular painting. This peculiar

[1] Failure to be *authentic* (e.g., being a copy of, or being a reproduction of, or being a fraudulent version of) does not, of course, exhaust the ways in which a painting (or for that matter any art work) might fail to be original. I am here not distinguishing among various types of unoriginality, it is here not in point to do so; not because there aren't important and illuminating distinctions to be made, but rather because the very general considerations I am leading up to below will, if cogent, apply equally to all forms of unoriginality or inauthenticity in art.

characteristic, "being a copy" of the work in question, seems a remote characteristic—in important ways different from those that *are* patently characteristics of its "aesthetic surface" and whose relevance to the determination of its aesthetic worth is undisputed. May we not thus be engaged in some subtle philistinism (something like being unsubtly influenced in some other cases by price) when we negatively evaluate art works because of their unoriginality?

Perhaps it isn't just perversity that leads so many people to benignly regard artists who perpetrate frauds. Sometimes the argument given is to the effect that if, for example, the fake Vermeers cannot be established as fake without the use of special technical apparatus of various sorts, then the work *should* be valued precisely as we would evaluate a newly discovered, authentic Vermeer. Indeed, perhaps a stronger, more general point is suggested in the following brief interlude:

"Here is a painting. What do you think of it?"

"Who painted it?"

"Never mind who painted it, you dolt! What do you think of it?"

We thus, often look askance at a man who must first peer at a signature before he makes an aesthetic judgment—as though in some manner he'd had his aesthetic sensibilities crippled.

But the tension in our rational inclinations sets in again on further reflection. The arguments are *not* all on the side of the ostensibly tough-minded who disparage as philistine considerations of "whodunit?" Isn't it, after all *aesthetically* significant that the original painting *has* certain characteristics (which we might, following Goodman,[2] call *autographic characteristics*) relating it peculiarly to its "original" painter? The original is related to certain of its painter's activities in ways that distinguish it from the copy. Barring some theory of internal and external relations, such autographic characteristics are as much, and as objectively, characteristics of the original as are its color qualities. More particularly, the objection that authenticity, unlike color, is not a characteristic that may be seen on *initial* presentation, may come to seem rather uncompelling on reflection. We remember that a painting, and especially a good painting, may often have many "painterly" or pictorial characteristics that also become apparent only after repeated viewings—character-

[2] Nelson Goodman, *Languages of Art.*

istics about which there is no doubt whatever concerning aesthetic relevance.

Similarly, on the side of the putative philistine, appears the rejoinder to a more complex objection—an objection that gets us somewhat deeper into our problem. The *objection* that elicits this rejoinder is that considerations of originality or authenticity are matters that depend upon acquiring "extraneous" evidence or coaching, in any case, considerations that fall under the category of "extraneous" knowledge. Originality or authenticity (the objection continues) is unlike even the most complex or subtle characteristics of the "aesthetic surface" in the sense that such autographic characteristics do not become manifest (in the kinds of case at issue here) just on account of, and even after, repeated viewings. It is not clear though that this objection isn't met by the following rejoinder: "Extraneousness" per se cannot render a characteristic irrelevant aesthetically; for, at least two kinds of "extraneous" knowledge have surely not hitherto been ruled out even by most of the putative anti-philistines on grounds of aesthetic irrelevance. First, where *recognition* of objects (i.e., subjects) in a painting contributes to its aesthetic *impact,* extraneous information about such subjects, or about our conventions of representation of such subjects, appears to be required. Second, where recognition of subjects is not obviously in point, we can still not ignore the well-established fact that in the context of appreciation of even "non-representational" art, "extraneous" experiences, instruction, exercises and practice—*between* viewings of a painting—may be helpful or requisite for the appreciation of the complex spatial or formal relations characteristic of such a painting. Such between-viewings training, it seems reasonable to suppose, does constitute the acquisition of "extraneous" knowledge.

But perhaps the difficulty in resolving the quarrel between the philistines and the anti-philistines on the aesthetic relevance of authenticity (or on the relevance of unoriginality generally) hinges on the simplistic assimilation of the quarrel about the relevance of knowing "whodunit" to the quarrel about whether external *characteristics* (in the sense of characteristics of the painting whose possession is not determinable just on the basis of *seeing* the painting however often) are, as such, aesthetically relevant.

Now obviously the notion of an *external characteristic* is not the clearest of notions to have come down the philosophical pike (even in the recent vintage decades of unclear philosophical notions), and we shall be returning for a harder look at it below; for the time being, however, given the assumption that it is an unproblematic concept, the suggestion being made is that externality is still *not* a sufficient condition for a characteristic's being irrelevant in judgments of the *aesthetic* worth of a painting.

The import of this suggestion is *not* that the anti-philistine position is wrong in holding that unoriginality is irrelevant but only that the *externality of unoriginality* cannot plausibly be construed as a sufficient ground of irrelevance. A second point, which should not be obscured by the present considerations and a point to which we shall also recur below, is that these considerations have all been addressed to the questions of the relevance of originality to judgments of *aesthetic worth*—questions of whether being the original painting is, just on account of its being the original, *aesthetically better* than the fake. But it is important to notice that questions of whether a given characteristic is relevant to judgments of increased aesthetic worth of a painting may not be at all the same as questions of whether such characteristics are part of what is *constitutive*, regardless of worth, of the aesthetic in painting. The ambiguity of attributions of aesthetic relevance just noted may, of course, mislead us in both directions: a characteristic may not be an *aesthetically constitutive* characteristic in the sense that its presence or absence may be irrelevant to, say, a pair of paintings being aesthetic objects at all. Yet in judging the relative aesthetic *worth* of the two paintings, consideration of some such non-constitutive characteristics may turn out to be quite justifiable and thus be aesthetically relevant to the judgments of worth.

On the other hand, a characteristic like *authenticity* may be aesthetically constitutive, in the sense that it allows us to *discriminate aesthetically* between two paintings (perhaps by allowing us to say that one is regarding one of the paintings but not the other as an aesthetic object) without this implying anything whatever concerning judgments of the relative aesthetic worth of the two.

In short, what I have *so far* been delineating as the problem, raised by the quarrel between philistine and anti-philistine positions, is focussed narrowly on the relevance of unoriginality as regards *only* judgments of relative aesthetic *worth*. In section **2** I shall proffer a suggestion which I think dissolves this problem and allows both the philistine and anti-philistine to consummate what I take to be their main interests in assuming the stances they do. Still, regardless of the cogency or success of any such suggestion, it should be noted that it does not address itself to the question of *constitutive relevance* and

[168]

cannot, without some further argument, be taken to settle the question of whether originality or authenticity are *constitutive* of the aesthetic. That question, in fact, will obtrude in section **3** where it leads almost immediately to more general methodological concerns in section **4.**

2
Aesthetic Value and Artistic Value

Elsewhere[3] I have proposed that one illuminating way of taking care of difficulties, respecting judgments of value about paintings, is to construe the problem as stemming mainly from an avoidable conflation of two kinds of value judgments. In fact, I suggest that it is reasonable or appropriate to make two quite different kinds of value judgments not only about paintings but about any art works. One of these kinds I call, for lack of a better term, *judgments of artistic value* (for short, *artistic judgments*), the other, *judgments of aesthetic value* (for short, *aesthetic judgments*). Alternatively the suggestion may be taken as claiming that any art work has at least two kinds of value: aesthetic value and artistic value. The aesthetic value of a work, and hence the kind of aesthetic judgment it is cogent for us to make of it, will be sufficiently determined by our[4] aesthetic experience of the work—our response to its aesthetic properties. The artistic value of a work, on the other hand, is *not* determined by our aesthetic experience[5] of the work. Having made any particular kind of aesthetic

---

[3] In a paper entitled "Originality and Esthetic Value" delivered before a colloquium of the University of Pennsylvania Philosophy Department many years ago.

[4] The question of to whom this "our" refers may be, for purposes of this essay, innocently deferred. Its answer would neither affect nor be affected by the problems we *are* pursuing.

[5] It might be noted that this proposal is applicable not only to theories of aesthetics which hold aesthetic experience to refer in some sense to a "unique" or "monolithic" or special unitary type of experience but also to those theories in which *aesthetic experience* is held to refer to the response, however heterogeneously complex it might be, which we *in fact* make upon presentation of what we are construing to be an art work. In the latter case, the need would still remain to discriminate among *artistic* and *aesthetic* elements "within" the complex experience.

We are not, that is to say, trapped by this mode of speaking into what Goodman (*op. cit.*) calls the Tingle-Immersion theory of aesthetic experience, a theory that he attributes, in a footnote, to Immanuel Tingle and Joseph Immersion (ca 1800).

judgment is neither a necessary nor a sufficient condition for arriving at any particular *artistic* valuation of it.

A little reflection shows that artistic value, in fact, belongs not to aesthetics at all but, broadly speaking, to the realm of *ethics*; a realm I take to include prudential as well as moral valuations. Specifically, the term *artistic value* and its cognates are intended to apply in situations essentially involving aesthetic objects but which are typically ethical in character. Artistic judgments are based on our findings in the sociology and psychology of art as well as on our systems of ethics or our hierarchies of prudential preferences. Thus, if we valued the preservation of objects of art or of artistic endeavor as *goods* in our society, however aesthetically blunted we might be—valued it on the purest altruistic grounds, because we knew that others would be gratified—we would then negatively evaluate certain practices and perhaps even certain art objects whose existence might be counter-productive of such preservation. Notice that this negative evaluation could also be our artistic evaluation despite any positive *aesthetic* judgment we had made just of the art object or (since it *is* surely possible for even these to be regarded aesthetically) of the practices.

In general, and in contrast to aesthetic considerations, artistic considerations appear to be relevant whenever we want to, or need to, *do something with or about art*. Perhaps the best sense of what is intended here may be gained from an illustration.

Since I think the aesthetic-artistic distinction I have just attempted to draw extends more broadly than to paintings only (and, indeed, more broadly than to merely an adjudication of just how authenticity is to be taken account of in evaluating art works), I shall use an example of another kind of unoriginality and one from some other art than painting. The example, specifically, is intended to show a tension between apparently contrary impulses toward valuation, which is resolved by employing the distinction I have suggested.

> A friend of mine, who edits a "little" literary magazine, tells me "I have just read through a really fine short story which, as rarely happens these days, moved me deeply. It's a beautiful job, but I am going to reject it."
>
> "How come?"
>
> "It is derivative in too many important ways. I do not mean that the story itself is blatantly cribbed. But the style, mood, the tone,

and even salient thematic notions are all quite obviously bor-
rowed from Borges."

"But you say it is a fine piece?"

"It is superb."

"Tell me, would you have published it if it had been submitted
by Borges or if you had discovered it, say, posthumously, in a
cache of Borges's unpublished manuscripts?"

"Most assuredly!"

"I mean on the basis of its aesthetic merit and not because it
would have historical, or topical, or fashionable interests."

"That is what I mean, too."

In this example the distinction between artistic and aesthetic
value makes clear why there is nothing really "queer" or incoherent
about the decision the editor is making. We can agree that, in this
case, considerations of "who really dunit?" or "whodunit first?"
are aesthetically irrelevant—we can agree in short, that it is a superb
piece—*aesthetically,* highly valuable. Yet, at the same time we can
consistently endorse the negative judgment indicated by the editor's
remarks and his decision to reject the manuscript. That there might
be substantial grounds, or at least some grounds, for his negati· ·
artistic judgment in this case may be seen if we consider high   ·
probability that reinforcement of writers' imitative artistic ben﹍
iors results in the increased probability of the choice of such behav-
iors, that this renders more likely, as a consequence, a failure to
explore rich new artistic avenues, and that this in turn may lead to
the stultification of, and perhaps the eventual death of, an art genre
in our milieu. Faced with such potentially grave consequences, our
editor need not feel guilty in turning down such a manuscript regardless of the aesthetic pleasure it has afforded him. Concomitantly, of
course, no one need feel guilty about having made a *positive aesthetic*
judgment in such a situation.

The difficulties generated by cases of fraud in painting or, indeed,
in any of the arts, seem likewise amenable to fairly obvious resolution
in the light of the distinction here being made. For the distinction
leaves us consistently free to judge *aesthetically* the fake without regard to questions of who painted it and without regard for whatever
nefarious purpose it may have been painted; and yet, likewise, it
leaves us free to disapprove *artistically* of the work and the artist and
therefore to take appropriate action against it and him.

Again, for example, the distinction we are emphasizing between *aesthetics* and *artistics* enables us to see the coherence in judging Walter Gieseking a great virtuoso and yet refusing to go to his recitals, the coherence of taking Ezra Pound to be a great poet and yet approving his arrest, the coherence of not feeling guilty about our aesthetic, positive valuation of Richard Strauss's music.

Finally, the distinction between aesthetics and artistics illuminates some aspects of the history of aesthetics. In particular, it makes clearer what some writers, whose results may have made us uneasy, have *actually* been up to while purporting to be doing, or while traditionally having been taken to be doing, aesthetics. It is apparent, for instance, that Tolstoy was doing *artistics* for the most part rather than aesthetics; even though he himself was certainly not clear about this. Most of Plato's principal theses concerning art are seen to be *artistic*. And once and for all his stand on art works, which includes what we take to be obvious aesthetic sensitivity to many of the works he would most stringently have banned in his Good State—that stand, is seen to be at least systematically consistent.

In fact, it is also rather clear that historic preoccupations with the *function* of tragedy and the *function* of comedy have usually been moral or political, or socio-psychological and hence, in this context, artistic preoccupations rather than aesthetic ones. In general, all considerations of the function of art, in the history of aesthetics, turn out likewise to be artistic considerations.

We are thus able, so far, to move toward a solution of the problem about *valuing* paintings which initiated this discussion—dissipating the tension created by the abundance of patent reasons for making "opposite" value judgments, without stepping out into the murky, treacherous depths of epistemology—confining ourselves solely to the sunny, hospitable, and relatively clear reaches of value theory.

But our luck has about run out. If we are to move to an examination of the postponed problem of the *constitutively aesthetic* in painting, then we shall have to venture into darkest epistemology.

3

Merely Looking

The question of whether consideration of "whodunit" makes a relevant aesthetic difference in paintings is given its most searching scrutiny in Nelson Goodman's *Languages of Art*. Since his treatment is thorough, subtle, and provocative, and since he arrives at conclusions in this matter that I find not entirely congenial, I want here to use a detailed account of his position as an elaborate foil for expressing my uneasiness about such conclusions and for contrasting them with some alternatives. The issue, however, is here complicated on at least two counts: First, though I find difficulties at certain critical junctures in his argument and hence do not feel compelled to accept his conclusions, I am not sure that those arguments could not be (though perhaps awkwardly) patched up and then still come to be an essential part of a quite general aesthetic theory, which *as a whole* was more appealing than any rival in the field. Second, though I find difficulties in some of Goodman's conclusions about the constitutive-aesthetic relevance of factors like originality or authenticity in painting, I do not myself have an adequate alternative definition of the aesthetically relevant in painting which I can preferentially produce.

Accordingly, insofar as my own investigations and meager constructive results are represented in this section at all, they are highly tentative and insufficiently elaborated. (Indeed, the tentativeness of the investigations in this and the following sections is one of the reasons for the prudence of the title of my essay.)

Goodman's epigraph to Chapter III (entitled "Art and Authenticity") of his book will serve to reintroduce the problem to which we have been attending and have already, in one way, solved in the preceding sections of this essay. The epigraph he uses is a quotation from Aline Saarinen:

> . . . the most tantalizing question of all: If a fake is so expert that even after the most thorough and trustworthy examination its authenticity is still open to doubt, is it or is it not as satisfactory a work of art as if it were unequivocally genuine? (*Languages of Art*, p. 99).

Goodman takes this issue to be a critically important one for any theory of aesthetics. He tells us that the theoretical problem raised by forgery is even more acute than the practical difficulties forgery poses for museum officials:

> The hardheaded question why there is any aesthetic difference between a deceptive forgery and an original work challenges a basic premiss on which the very functions of collector, museum, and art historian depend. A philosopher of art caught without an answer to this question is at least as badly off as a curator of paintings caught taking a Van Meergeren for a Vermeer. (*op. cit.*, p. 99).

[173]

We'll come back to the question mentioned, but before doing so it is worthwhile noticing that the issue being discussed is not the relevance of authenticity to judgments of aesthetic *merit* in painting but rather its relevance to the *constitutively aesthetic* itself. Goodman's position here accepts this distinction, and the independence of the realms (as I have in the considerations I adduced at the end of section 1 above). He makes a particular point of this again toward the end of the book when he does focus at last on questions of aesthetic merit or aesthetic value.

> The distinction here drawn between the aesthetic and the non-aesthetic is independent of all considerations of aesthetic value. That is as it should be. An abominable performance of the *London Symphony* is as aesthetic as a superb one; and Piero's *Risen Christ* is no more aesthetic but only better than a hack's. The symptoms of the aesthetic are not marks of merit; and a characterization of the aesthetic neither requires nor provides a definition of aesthetic excellence. (p. 255).

What precisely then is the question about the *constitutive aesthetic* relevance of authenticity in painting? Consider, he says, that we have before us on the left Rembrandt's original painting *Lucretia* and on the right a superlative imitation of it.

> We know from a fully documented history that the painting on the left is the original; and we know from X-ray photographs and microscopic examination and chemical analysis that the painting on the right is a recent fake. Although there are many differences between the two—e.g., in authorship, age, physical and chemical characteristics, and market value—we cannot see any difference between them; and if they are moved while we sleep, we cannot then tell which is which by merely looking at them. Now we are pressed with the question whether there can be any aesthetic difference between the two pictures; and the questioner's tone often intimates that the answer is plainly *no*, that the only differences here are *aesthetically* irrelevant [my italics] (p. 100).

Having raised the question, Goodman begins immediately to explore its aesthetic and epistemological suggestions by noting the ways in which the question wants more and more stringent refinement.

"We must begin", he says, "by inquiring whether the distinction between what can and what cannot be seen in the pictures by 'merely looking at them' is entirely clear". (p. 100).

And he begins to ring the changes, all too depressingly familiar

[174]

to those who have been through the direct-observational-empiricist-criterion-of-meaning wars: Are we "looking" at the painting—but not "merely looking" when we use X-ray, fluoroscope, microscope, etc. Is "merely looking" to be confined to looking without the aid of any instrument. This, he remarks, would seem "a little unfair to the man who needs glasses to tell a painting from a hippopotamus." (p. 100).

Several challenging cases are delineated, but then Goodman does not wish to linger unduly over such relatively simple difficulties:

> All these cases might be covered by saying that 'merely looking' is looking at the pictures without any use of instruments other than those customarily used in looking at things in general. This will cause trouble when we turn, say, to certain miniature illuminations or Assyrian cylinder seals that we can hardly distinguish from the crudest copies without using a strong glass. . . . To specify what is meant by merely looking at the pictures is thus far from easy; but for the sake of argument, let us suppose that all these difficulties have been resolved and the notion of 'merely looking' made clear enough. (p. 101).

Yet, Goodman reminds us, even if we concede the point, even if we know well enough what we mean by *merely looking,* our troubles would be only beginning. For instance, we should still need to know who is doing the looking. Apropos of this point, Goodman remarks:

> Our questioner [of the aesthetic relevance of authenticity] does not, I take it, mean to suggest that there is no aesthetic difference between two pictures if at least one person, say a cross-eyed wrestler, can see no difference. The more pertinent question is whether there can be any aesthetic difference if nobody, not even the most skilled expert, can ever tell the pictures apart by merely looking at them. *But notice now that no one can ever ascertain by merely looking at the pictures that no one ever has been or will be able to tell them apart by merely looking at them.* In other words, the question in its present form concedes that no one can ascertain by merely looking at the pictures that there is no aesthetic difference between them. This seems repugnant to our questioner's whole motivation. For if merely looking can never establish that two pictures are aesthetically the same, something that is beyond the reach of any given looking is admitted as constituting an aesthetic difference. And in that case, the reason for not admitting documents and the results of scientific tests becomes very obscure. (pp. 101–102).

[175]

The passage just quoted at length and especially the conclusions which appear to be incorporated into the antecedent clause of its penultimate sentence, bring us to a juncture in this account that I do find puzzling—perhaps misleading. The plausibility of Goodman's point appears to rest on conflation of two questions associated with distinct, rather complex characteristics[6] of a pair of paintings. Let us refer to the paintings as R and R', and the first of these complex characteristics, as A, where

A = having been painted by Rembrandt.

Suppose, consonant with Goodman's example, we initially assume that no one can tell by merely looking at R and R' which one (if either) possesses the characteristic, A. Now consider a second characteristic (what we might refer to as a "meta-characteristic") M. Here I am "reconstructing" (I trust serviceably) the condition suggested by the italicized sentence in the passage cited just above:

M = no one ever being able to tell by merely looking at R and R' whether either possesses A or whether either possesses no characteristic that will ever enable anyone to tell them apart by merely looking at them.

The ostensible (and, if actual, harmless) redundancy is deliberate in case A should, in fact, *not* be the sort of characteristic delineated in the second alternand.

The problem Goodman's example poses, then, finds us confronted with a pair of paintings (R and R'), which have characteristics that distinguish them from each other (e.g., their respective ages) but which seem not to be visually distinguishable from each other (in the sense that we could not tell which was which if their positions were "shuffled") by merely looking at them. The question arising is can we ever tell which (if either of them) has A by merely looking at

---

[6] Here, as elsewhere in this essay, I am eschewing the grinding of any nominalistic axes in the employment of ostensibly platonistic language without any attempt to provide nominalistic analyses. Though the "nominalizability" of the discussion is not being claimed in this essay, perhaps a footnote is the appropriate place to record my belief that attempts at such an analysis would not run into insuperable difficulties. For a consideration of how nominalism may bear upon questions of aesthetics and of how nominalistic analyses might be effected, see my articles, "The Ontological Status of the Esthetic Object", *Philosophy and Phenomenological Research* (1950), Vol. 10, No. 3, and "What do Symbols Symbolize?: Nominalism", *Philosophy of Science, The Delaware Seminar*, Vol. 1, Bernard Baumrin, ed. (New York: John Wiley & Sons, 1963).

them? What Goodman appears to be saying is that this question amounts to the question of whether anyone could tell if R and R' had M, *the much more "complex" characteristic,* by merely looking at them.

But these two are surely *not* the same question! Whether we can tell by merely looking at a pair of paintings that no one *could* ever distinguish them by merely looking, is not the same question as whether such specific differences as authorship, age, micro-physical or micro-chemical constitution or any other not-now-visual-difference, can ever be ascertained just by merely looking. It is, for example, likely that R and R' will have disparate future histories that will lead them to be differentiable in the future on the basis of now-visual properties which they *do not now* exhibit;[7] it is surely possible that one will become scratched, or scuffed, or will "fade" differentially in such a way as to permit us in the future to distinguish between them by merely looking. However, it is clear that this likely eventuation is not one that can be ascertained by now *merely looking* at R and R'; rather we believe it will occur, if we do, on the basis of considerable *theoretical* knowledge and observations of things other than R and R'. Of course such *future* differences, which could at the appropriate future time be ascertained by *then* merely looking, would, many of them, be precisely of the kind that our anti-philistine would countenance as aesthetically relevant. Answering the question whether R and R' have M (i.e., the question whether anyone can tell *by merely looking at them* that they will never, by merely looking at them, be distinguishable), in the negative is thus, of course, not incompatible with holding that *every* aesthetically relevant difference between R and R' is ascertainable *by merely looking at them at some time or other.* More importantly for present purposes, it is not incompatible, contrary to the thrust of Goodman's argument, with also holding that R or R' having A *cannot* be ascertained *by merely looking* at R and R' now or at any future time.

To show that we cannot tell whether we shall ever be able to tell a pair of paintings apart by merely looking, might then be construed as showing for a given pair of paintings (say R and R') that it may be the case that we cannot ascertain by merely looking that we shall not in the future find an aesthetically relevant (e.g. a "visual") way

---

[7] The difference between, on the one hand, a not-now-visual property which a painting may now possess but we do not now know the painting to possess, and on the other hand a now-visual property that the painting does *not now* possess, is what is in point here.

of distinguishing them. When Goodman describes this situation, he does so by saying, "... no one can ascertain by merely looking at the pictures that there is *no* aesthetic difference between them". However, he also *takes this itself to be an aesthetically relevant fact* about (or an aesthetic characteristic of) the pictures. He appears, thus, to be saying that the very fact that we cannot tell whether the pictures *have M* by merely looking at them is aesthetically relevant and to conclude, thereby, that there *is* at least one aesthetically relevant characteristic that is not ascertainable by merely looking at the paintings. But to call a characteristic, like that of being unable to tell whether *M* obtains, an aesthetic characteristic seems an uncalled for or, at least an ungrounded, stretching of the notion of an aesthetic characteristic. We might just as well argue that our being unable to tell, *by merely looking* at the paintings, *how-much-it-would-cost-to-determine-at-some-later-time-whether-there-were-any-aesthetic-differences,* was itself an aesthetic characteristic of them.

Perhaps, though, we can take some steps to advance the discussion that may both simplify and sharpen it. Let us, to avoid continued awkward circumlocution, refer to any characteristic, whose possession by paintings cannot be ascertained by merely looking at the paintings, as an *A*-characteristic and any characteristic of paintings that can be ascertained by merely looking at them as an *O*-characteristic. In pursuing and refining his argument, Goodman sees at once that the notion of (what we are calling) an *A*-characteristic wants relativization. A characteristic of a painting is an *A* (or an *O*) only for some person, x, at some time, t. Accordingly the question that most cogently, in his view, poses the problem:

> ... amounts finally to this: is there any aesthetic difference between the two pictures for x at t, where t is a suitable period of time, if x cannot tell them apart by merely looking at them at t? Or in other words, can anything that x does not discern by merely looking at the pictures at t constitute an aesthetic difference between them for x at t? (p. 102).

In our, somewhat more platonistic, terms this question may be posed as, if a is an *A*-characteristic of paintings R_i to R_n for x at t, can a be an aesthetically relevant characteristic of them for x at t? Goodman proceeds to argue that certain *A*-characteristics may, indeed, be aesthetically relevant. His argument depends on *causally connecting* the results of our present (non-perceptual) apprehension of *A*-characteristics of paintings with future apprehension of perceptual, that is, *O*-characteristics, of those paintings. Thus, he tells us

> Although I see no difference now between the two pictures in question, I may learn to see a difference between them. I cannot determine now by merely looking at them, or in any other way, that I *shall* be able to learn. But the information that they are very different, that the one is the original and the other the forgery, argues against any inference to the conclusion that I *shall not* be able to learn. (pp. 103–104).

This is not just the delineation of "some possible", future-discernible *O*-characteristic as aesthetically relevant; it is, again, the much stronger claim that a present *A-characteristic is aesthetically relevant*—presumably, because it is causally connected with an aesthetically relevant future *O*-characteristic:

> And the fact that I may later be able to make a perceptual distinction between the pictures that I cannot make now constitutes an *aesthetic* difference between them that is important to me *now*.
>
> Furthermore, to look at the pictures now with the knowledge that the left one is the original and the other the forgery may help develop the ability to tell which is which later by merely looking at them. Thus, with information not derived from the present or any past looking at the pictures, the present looking may have a quite different bearing upon future lookings from what it would otherwise have. The way the pictures in fact differ *constitutes an aesthetic difference between them for me now* because my knowledge of the way they differ bears upon the role of the present looking in training my perceptions to discriminate between these pictures, and between others. [my italics] (p. 104).

In summing up these considerations, Goodman cites three reasons for the relevance of such an *A*-characteristic as authenticity:

> In short, although I cannot tell the pictures apart merely by looking at them now, the fact that the left-hand one is the original and the right-hand one a forgery constitutes an aesthetic difference beween them for me now because knowledge of this fact (1) stands as evidence that there may be a difference between them that I can learn to perceive, (2) assigns the present looking a role as training toward such a perceptual discrimination, and (3) makes consequent demands that modify and differentiate my present experience in looking at the two pictures. (p. 105).

[179]

Goodman appends a needed qualification in a footnote to this paragraph:

> In saying that a difference *between the pictures* that is thus relevant to my present experience in looking at them constitutes an aesthetic difference between them, I am of course not saying that everything (e.g., drunkenness, snow blindness, twilight) that may cause my experiences of them to differ constitutes such an aesthetic difference. Not every difference in or arising from how the pictures happen to be looked at counts; only differences in or arising from how they are to be looked at. . . . (Footnote 3, p. 105).

The relevant conclusion to which his argument comes here is that, ". . . since the exercise, training, and development of our powers of discriminating among works of art are plainly aesthetic activities, the aesthetic properties of a picture include not only those found by looking at it but also those that determine how it is to be looked at." (pp. 111–112).

With this outline of Goodman's argument before us, we may now see how such considerations of the *constitutively* aesthetic fit in or contrast with the considerations of aesthetic and artistic *value* discussed earlier.

4
What May Be Seen

In the first two sections of this essay I argued that considerations of authenticity would be irrelevant to assessments of the aesthetic (though not to the artistic) *value* of a painting. My discussion, in contrast to the argument of Goodman just examined, was *not* specifically addressed to the problem of whether *A*-characteristics (like authenticity) are *constitutively* relevant. My argument was not, for example, relevant to the context of regarding a painting aesthetically per se, i.e., regarding it, quite apart from judging its aesthetic *value* or *merit*, aesthetically as a painting whether good or bad. The distinction, between the problems of what is to be included in assessing the aesthetic value of a painting and what is to be included in determining what constitutes an aesthetic, per se, property of an object, has thus been assumed throughout my remarks to this point and, as was noted above, is assumed by Goodman's arguments as well as my own. Nevertheless, the constitutive and the valuational problems do resemble each other. It is clear, for instance, that the very same sort of tensions—those ostensibly cogent impulses to explicate in contrary ways the key concepts involved—that were resolved in one way by my arguments in the context of aesthetic *valuation,* are also present but apparently resolved in an "opposite" way by Goodman in the context of the *constitutively* aesthetic in paintings. Can both these modes of resolution be considered acceptable? If not both, which, if either, is to be favored? In particular, if considerations of "whodunit", or of authenticity, are construed to be (like considerations of price) too remote from, or too alien to, what we can "see" and *should* be assessing in judging the *aesthetic merit* of a painting, are not also such considerations, similarly, too remote from what we can "see" in a painting to be numbered among the *constitutively aesthetic* properties of the painting?

Let us begin anew by noting some of the qualifications that appear required for prima facie cogency of Goodman's thesis. Goodman includes authenticity as constitutively relevant because, briefly, he believes our apprehension of this characteristic has effects on "how" a painting "is to be looked at" and hence, presumably, on what we may come to "see" in it.[8] But some questions are raised on a closer scrutiny of this formulation.

First, we need to ask whether all ways of discriminating—i.e., all ways of developing powers to discriminate in any way whatsoever—among paintings *are* aesthetic activities. Surely not. Developing our powers of discriminating, through chemical investigations, the relative usefulness of paintings as easily combustible fuel, are for example, clearly not aesthetic activities however skillful we may be

---

[8] It may be illuminating here to remind ourselves of the following: I was led to take *A*-characteristics, like the identity of the painter, to be irrelevant to *aesthetic valuation* though relevant to *artistic valuation*—where *artistic* valuation need not include any *aesthetic* apprehension of art objects. Artistic valuation belongs rather to contexts of doing something with, or about, or in consequence of, art works or of their modes of existing and affecting or being affected by us. Goodman's argument, then might be viewed as "connecting with" my arguments just insofar as his involve showing that apprehension of, say, authenticity not only has "moral" effects (and hence is not only in the domain of *artistics*) but also has effects on what is strictly our aesthetic (morally independent) apprehension. If his arguments here *are* cogent, then my assumption, that being in the context of doing something about, or to, art works is *sufficient* for relegation to artistics, might be untenable and with the vitiation of that assumption the main basis of my argument would be removed. I am, though, not persuaded of the entire cogency of his arguments.

trained to become in this discrimination. This means, second, not only that we cannot take every activity which contributes to our powers of discriminating among pictures as, *ipso facto,* an aesthetic activity, but also, and correspondingly, that (contrary to the apparent import of the last sentence of the footnote from Goodman, quoted above) what "counts" cannot be even *all* those involved in, or arising from, how they are *to be looked at.* For surely some lookings-at, some modes of perceiving paintings (e.g., looking at them, and discriminating among them as potential clues of psychological aberration in their painters) cannot properly be called aesthetic.

We are claiming, in short, two things by way of showing the need for Goodman to formulate a more narrow thesis if he is to have a tenable one. First, we are claiming that his arguments cut too coarsely as they now stand, for they do *not* show (as they ought) that not all activities of increasing our powers of *discriminating among pictures* through reference or detection of their A-characteristics can be counted as aesthetic activities. No doubt Goodman would concede this point. The first two numbered reasons in the quotation as well as much else in his full discussion clearly suggest, in fact, that he wishes to maintain that only those A-characteristics, *whose* ("non-visual") *detection now* affects, or may affect, our future prowess at making any *perceptual* discrimination, are to be counted as aesthetic characteristics. What this thesis finally comes to is that all those A-characteristics, whose apprehension affect our ability at discriminating any O-characteristics, are aesthetically relevant (i.e., are aesthetic) characteristics.

But we have just argued that this formulation is too broad and that this may be seen when we note that not even *every* O-characteristic (i.e., visual, perceptual characteristic) of a painting is an aesthetic characteristic. Accordingly, those A-characteristics whose apprehension was causally connected only with our ability to discriminate among paintings on the basis of their *non-aesthetic* O-properties, could, themselves, surely not be counted as aesthetic characteristics.

This last consideration allows us to see more clearly that A-characteristics, even in Goodman's approach, must at most be counted as, so to speak, merely secondary aesthetic characteristics; their status as aesthetic being derivatively conferred on them by the causal connection which might be traced between our apprehension of them and our future ability to perceive those properties (not just *any* perceptual properties) that *are* the aesthetically relevant visual perceptual properties of the paintings—and, relative to any aesthetic A-properties, their primary aesthetic properties. Assume, then, that this narrow construal of Goodman's view is a faithful one, are we in a position to assess it and does it emerge as a compelling view? If we are in a better position to assess the view, still some impediments to a fair assessment of it require removal.

First of all, the view does *not*, as just noted, furnish us with a determination of just what perceptual features of a painting are to be included among its constitutive features as a painting. Since such features would, presumably, include the crucial, *primary* aesthetic properties, their characterization remains a desideratum. Again, surmounting this primary difficulty is an obvious necessary condition for removing the second impediment—i.e. the identification of the secondary aesthetic characteristics. Moreover, surmounting that primary difficulty will help take care of still a third impediment to reaching a decision about the acceptability of Goodman's view. This third difficulty is one whose consideration was waived earlier in employing the notion of "merely looking" at paintings. In particular we must inquire whether Goodman may not have conceded too much to potential opponents of his position in accepting the view that a distinction can be made between "merely looking" at a painting and other modes of apprehending it.

The determination of what are the visual, perceptual characteristics of a painting (our first desideratum) would, indeed, furnish us with a serviceable clarification of *merely looking*. For, to say that O is a characteristic of a painting, which may be discerned by merely looking at the painting, would presumably be to imply that O was among the visual, perceptual characteristics of such a painting. Knowing what the latter were, we would thus be in a position to know what could *not* be seen by merely looking at the painting. All in all, then, the problem of determining primary, constitutive characteristics of paintings emerges as one whose solution is fundamental to appraising Goodman's approach to the constitutively aesthetic in painting.

Goodman gives the problem its most explicit and sustained attention in several sections of his book other than those (on "authenticity") we have thus far been most closely examining.[9] The fact is that the problem of the constitutive O-characteristics of paintings is connected in quite complex ways with other aspects of his syste-

---

[9] The principal "other" sections referred to here are Chap. I, Sec. 9; Chap. II, Sec. 1–3; Chap. V, Sec. 4; and Chap. VI, Sec. 1, 2 and 5.

matic treatment of topics in symbolization. By the end of his first chapter (which is given over in large measure to an analysis of what it comes to for a painting to represent) it is clear that for an object *to be a painting* on his account, it must have not only "pictorial" properties, but (insofar as it is functioning as a painting—as a "pictorial" aesthetic object—rather than as, e.g., a wind break or a psychological protocol) *those very properties must also* be functioning as symbols.

We cannot, of course, begin to do justice here to Goodman's deep and intricate arguments for construing all art works as objects that function as symbols (i.e., as components in systems of symbolization, representation, or reference). What is immediately relevant to our present concern though is his view that paintings *qua* paintings are, or are constituted of pictorial symbols which denote or refer *by* "depicting" (in contrast, e.g., to linguistic symbols which denote or refer by describing). That, *qua* paintings, they refer through the mediation of their *pictorial* properties is crucial. As Goodman emphasizes,

> To say that depiction is by pictures while description is by passages is not only to beg a good part of the question [of how to distinguish between depictions and descriptions] but also to overlook the fact that denotation by a picture does not always constitute depiction; for example, if pictures in a commandeered museum are used by a briefing officer to stand for enemy emplacements the pictures do not thereby represent [depict] these emplacements. To represent, a picture must function as a pictorial symbol; that is, function in a system such that what is denoted depends solely upon the pictorial properties of the symbol. (pp. 41–42).

Our own query, concerning which *O*-properties must be the primary aesthetic properties of *paintings*, receives, then, a complex answer: they are just those of its pictorial properties which, relative to a system of denotation, are such that what is denoted in that system depends only on those properties.

Goodman at once becomes rather less opaque about how such pictorial properties might be differentiated. But though he indicates what *some* of these pictorial properties will be (e.g. colors or, perhaps, colors-at-places on the surface of the painting) he does not furnish us with a full or entirely satisfactory definition. He tells us that:

> The pictorial properties might be roughly delimited by a loose recursive specification. An elementary pictorial characterization states what color a picture has at a given place on its face.

Other pictorial characterizations in effect combine many such elementary ones by conjunction, alternation, quantification, etc. Thus a pictorial characterization may name the colors at several places, or state that the color at one place lies within a certain range, or state that the colors at two places are complementary, and so on. Briefly, a pictorial characterization says more or less completely and more or less specifically what colors the picture has at what places. And the properties correctly ascribed to a picture by pictorial characterization are its pictorial properties. (p. 42).[10]

Though Goodman does not provide us with an explicit definition of 'pictorial property', he does provide us with important insights[11] into how and why his theory opts for the constitutive aesthetic relevance of such *A*-characteristics of paintings as authenticity.

One of the importantly original results that Goodman achieves consists in showing that the problems, of the identity of art works of various sorts, are fruitfully formulable as well as solvable in a systematic framework which develops and extends certain concepts of formal syntax and semantics. Thus, coming to our more specific concerns, reflection supports the plausibility of Goodman's point that no correct instance (i.e., correct performance) of a musical composition is "any more an instance" of that work than is any other correct performance. What will determine any of these instances as correct performances is, of course, their compliance with a correct or authentic score. Notice, though, that *all accurate copies of a score are equally authentic* as scores. Accordingly the composer's own manuscripted

---

[10] Goodman is not only aware that this is a *rough* delimitation, he is also explicitly aware that it has some major shortcomings. For example, it fails to make provision for "the often three-dimensional nature of picture surfaces." (Footnote 34, p. 42.) (Nevertheless, despite its shortcomings", it has echoes of his systematic results in *The Structure of Appearance* [Indianapolis: Bobbs-Merrill] that lend the characterization depth and significance.)

Goodman, it seems, believes that "nothing very vital rests on" a precise formulation of the distinction "between pictorial and other properties" (*ibid.*); but one of my chief concerns in the last two sections of this essay is that failure to provide an adequate definition of *pictorial properties* perforce leaves uncompelling his theory of the constitutive aesthetic relevance of authenticity.

[11] These insights present a rich harvest of useful and stimulating results; the book furnishes new and searching analyses not only of aspects of discursive or descriptive symbolic systems, but also of how paintings, music, architecture, scores, scripts, diagrams, and sketches may be construed as symbols (or as involving systems of symbols) that figure in our experiences of aesthetic objects or adjuncts (like scores) of aesthetic objects.

[185]

score is (if accurate) no more genuinely or authentically "the score" than any other accurate copy. As Goodman points out, even a forgery of a Haydn manuscripted score would, if an accurate copy, be an "equally genuine"(p. 112) instance of the score. Similarly all accurate copies of a poem or novel are equally authentic or genuine instances of such works.

In contrast, authenticity or the character of being *genuinely-the-work* is *confined uniquely to the artist's original in painting*. It becomes fundamental to the theory of symbolism and aesthetics he is propounding for Goodman to insist that ". . . *even the most exact copies of the Rembrandt painting are simply imitations or forgeries, not new instances, of the work.*" (p. 113). It is in this connection that he introduces the terms 'autographic art' and 'allographic art'. "Let us" he says:

> speak of a work of art as *autographic* if and only if the distinction between original and forgery of it is significant; or better, if and only if even the most exact duplication of it does not thereby count as genuine. . . . Thus painting is autographic, music nonautographic, or *allographic*. (p. 113).

Goodman raises the perplexing problem of how precisely to account for the differences between autographic and allographic art—how, precisely to characterize those differences, and how, in particular, to delineate the important consequences these differences result in for an aesthetic theory and a theory of symbolism. His response to such questions in his elaborated aesthetic theory connects crucially with the question of whether such an *A*-characteristic as having-been-fashioned-by-the-artist-as-the-original is a constitutive aesthetic characteristic of a painting. As we know, Goodman's response to this question is affirmative. But detailed examination of that response makes it clear (contrary to the suggestion of his discussion of "merely looking") that he is not simply led to his position by considerations of the effects that our present (nonperceptual) knowledge of the "history of production" of a work may have on our future ability to make fine discriminations among the painting's *O*-characteristics. Rather, he is led to his position by considerations of how the need for theoretically usable criteria for *identity of a work* divides off contingent from constitutive properties, and selects as constitutive (for painting) such *A*-characteristics as authenticity. But this, it needs to be noted, is a selection that is thereby dictated quite independently of considerations of how our present knowledge of the obtainment of

[186]

such *A*-characteristics may have effects on how we later come to look at a painting.

Compare the problem of *identifying* a literary work over a period of time and in various places with that of identifying a painting over a period of time and in various places. In the case of the literary work, inauthenticity (indeed, even the characteristic of being a *deceitful* forgery of the manuscript) is a contingent rather than a constitutive property. The constitutive characteristics of a literary work are just those that provide for *sameness of spelling* as the criterion for being an authenticated instance of the work. "Let us suppose," Goodman suggests:

> ... that there are various handwritten copies and many editions of a given literary work. Differences between them in style and size of script or type, in color of ink, in kind of paper, in number and layout of pages, in condition, etc., do not matter. All that matters is what may be called *sameness of spelling*: exact correspondence as sequences of letters, spaces, and punctuation marks. Any sequence—even a forgery of the author's manuscript or of a given edition—that so corresponds to a correct copy is itself correct, and nothing is more the original work than is such a correct copy. . . . To verify the spelling or to spell correctly is all that is required to identify an instance of the work or to produce a new instance. In effect, the fact that a literary work is in a definite notation, consisting of certain signs or characters that are to be combined by concatenation, provides the means for distinguishing the properties constitutive of the work from all contingent properties—that is, for fixing the required features and the limits of permissable variation in each. Merely by determining that the copy before us is spelled correctly we can determine that it meets all requirements for the work in question. (pp. 115–116).

But the criteria for identity of a painting, according to Goodman, furnish a marked contrast. For paintings:

> ... on the contrary, with no such alphabet of characters, none of the pictorial properties—none of the properties the picture has as such—is distinguished as constitutive; no such feature can be dismissed as contingent and no deviation as insignificant. (p. 116).

Goodman then concludes that, if we have the Rembrandt *Lucretia* before us, the only way we can establish that it is genuine will be:

. . . to establish the historical fact that it is the actual object made by Rembrandt. Accordingly, physical identification of the product of the artist's hand, and consequently the conception of forgery of a particular work, assume a significance in painting that they do not have in literature. (p. 116).

The distinction between autographic and allographic art has importance in Goodman's systematic development of his views which, in fact, extends considerably beyond our own immediate concern here. The distinction helps to lead Goodman into a subtle and intricate theory of notation which has far-reaching ramifications not only in aesthetics but in basic reaches of philosophy of language and philosophy of science as well. The magnitude (as I hinted at the outset of section **3**) of this conceptual edifice by itself, without being directly decisive for our concern (with the question of whether *A*-characteristics are aesthetically constitutive in painting) still tends by sheer "inertia of mass" to induce acceptance of Goodman's view of painting rather than to attempt to push aside an elaborate system to which that view is essentially connected.[12] But how essential is the connection?

Suppose, we consider again a suggestion, which is put forward more than once by Goodman, that not only are the constitutive

---

[12] The intimacy of the connection between these considerations in aesthetics and some aspects of a theory of notation, may be relatively succinctly indicated in the following passage:

A forgery of a work of art is an object falsely purporting to have a history of production requisite for the (or an) original of the work. Where there is a theoretically decisive test for determining that an object has all the constitutive properties of the work in question *without determining how or by whom the object was produced, there is no requisite history of production and hence no forgery of any given work.* [my italics] Such a test is provided by a suitable notational system with an articulate set of characters and of relative positions for them. For texts, scores, and perhaps plans, the test is correctness of spelling in this notation; for buildings and performances, the test is compliance with what is correctly spelled. Authority for a notation must be found in an antecedent classification of objects or events into works that cuts across, or admits of a legitimate projection that cuts across, classification by history of production; but definitive identification of works, fully freed from history of production, is achieved only when a notation is established. The allographic art has won its emancipation not by proclamation but by notation (p. 122).

aesthetic properties of a particular art work non-identical with its constitutive properties *as* that work, but also, that the latter do not even form a proper subset of the former. In speaking of performances of a musical work, for example, he remarks that ". . . several correct performances of about equal merit may exhibit very different specific aesthetic qualities . . ." (p. 120). And he adds almost immediately, *"Thus even where the constitutive properties of a work are clearly distinguished by means of a notation, they cannot be identified with the aesthetic properties." (ibid.,* italics are mine).

Goodman nowhere fully elaborates this point but, again, what is suggested by such remarks is the possibility of drawing distinctions not only between a work's contingent aesthetic properties and its constitutive aesthetic properties, but also between its constitutive *aesthetic* properties and *other* of its constitutive properties. Assume that drawing these distinctions is *not* incompatible with his general systematic treatment of aesthetics and symbolism. This assumption, together with the considerations to which we have been giving detailed attention up to this point, would jointly support both the maintenance of the position I have been espousing—i.e., the non-aesthetic character of authenticity—and also that very illuminating part of Goodman's theory devoted to the analysis of the identity of an art work.

The feasibility of merging the views may be seen when we consider, in particular, two of the conclusions among those we have been meticulously uncovering in this and the preceding section. First, we have seen that it is not the case that every A-characteristic (whose apprehension now may be causally efficacious in affecting how we shall look at a picture in the future) can properly be construed as even a secondary aesthetic property. For, though apprehension of A now may improve my abilities to make "finer discriminations" of, say, O-properties later, these last need not be finer discriminations of *aesthetic* properties—in such cases it would be absurd to interpret the A-properties as (even secondary) *aesthetic* properties.

But these very possibilities (as well as Goodman's remarks and suggestions on the subject) alert us to the usefulness of taking systematic account of the distinction between, on the one hand, those properties of an art work that must be counted among its constitutive features for the sake of being able to give a systematic account of the identity of the work and, on the other hand, those of its properties that are the work's aesthetic properties (and which thus might be employed for identification purposes only insofar as they are in the intersection of the sets of its constitutive and its aesthetic properties).

We may, in short, *eat* the anti-philistine cake of rejecting authenticity as any aesthetic property at all, and at the same time *have* the cake of the powerful systematic devices furnished by Goodman for the analysis of problems of work-identity. And, we may accomplish this feat by construing, where this is needed, authenticity (i.e., what Goodman calls "the requisite history of production" for the unique instance of any autographic work) as a constitutive characteristic of an art work (such as a painting) *without* holding that such a characteristic is an aesthetic characteristic.[13]

In the context of the *constitutive* properties of paintings, as in the context of their valuation, there is no decisive ground furnished by Goodman's investigations that rules out holding all aesthetic properties of a painting to be among its O-properties. When he turns attention to the question of how paintings function in our aesthetic experience of them[14] the *aesthetic* characteristics he focusses on—which, in cases of paintings, determine their mode of symbolization *as representation*—fall into the realm of O-characteristics.[15] So too

---

[13] I am not, of course, suggesting that authenticity isn't, for Goodman, an aesthetic characteristic. He makes it clear enough that he so regards it. What I am saying is that he *needn't* so regard it for purposes of giving an account of work-identity in his system. More than this, I am claiming that it is patently more congruent with my *artistics-aesthetics* distinction to construe authenticity as *not* belonging to the constitutively *aesthetic* properties of works and, moreover, that I can make this construal without rejecting valuable parts of Goodman's analysis.

[14] In Goodman's systematic treatment, to experience paintings *qua* paintings, aesthetically, is to attend to them as symbolic entities of certain kinds, i.e., as entities that symbolize by representation (or depiction) rather than by description.

[15] For the full import of the crucial distinction, in Goodman's systematic account, between representational and non-representational (e.g. discursive) modes of symbolization, the reader, not already familiar with it, must be referred to the detailed and subtle elaboration that the distinction is given in *Languages of Art*. Formal ground for the distinction is laid in Chapter IV ("The Theory of Notation"). Of special importance is the concept of syntactical density (see p. 136). In key definitions Goodman uses the concept of a *determination* (of differences among syntactical marks) *which it is "theoretically possible" to make.* The concept of a *theoretically possible determination is* not fully explicated, but it obviously is intended to refer to determinations that may be made on a basis other than that of "merely looking." In the light of our analysis above, however,

we find him adverting (as mentioned above) to O-characteristics which are to be systematically "constructed" (by "rough recursion") from basic *pictorial* O-properties like colors-at-places-on-the-picture's-surface.

There is one final base that must be touched before we can bring this inquiry to a close: We have managed to put off coping with the question of *what can be seen by merely looking*—or, indeed, what can be seen by any sort of *visual* inspection. Let us see how we might (or whether we still need to) respond to this question. The positions that this essay has been espousing identify the aesthetically relevant characteristics of a painting with some of what I have been referring to as its "O-properties."

Now, there are two presupposed distinctions which may bear on the cogency of that view. One is the distinction between those properties of a painting that may be apprehended by "merely looking" at it and those properties, if any, that are not apprehendable by *merely* looking but that may be apprehended by (presumably less casual) *visual* inspection. The second distinction is that between what can be apprehended by any sort of visual inspection (i.e., what *can* be seen) and what (if anything) cannot be seen. For purposes of the present inquiry the second distinction is, in fact, by far the more important. The long lines of the argument we have been elucidating

---

this presents us with no new problem. Any "theoretical" (presumably, non-O) properties which might be involved as constitutive would belong to the non-aesthetic constitutive set.

For those already familiar with *Languages of Art* the following summary passage (though heavily larded with technical terms like 'density', 'articulation', and 'symbol scheme' from his systematic treatment) may be a useful reminder of the pivotal position the distinction occupies.

> Nonlinguistic systems differ from languages, depiction from description, the representational from the verbal, paintings from poems, primarily through lack of differentiation—indeed through density (and consequent total absence of articulation)—in the symbol scheme. Nothing is intrinsically a representation; status as representation is relative to symbol system. A picture in one system may be a description in another; and whether a denoting symbol is representational depends not upon whether it resembles what it denotes but upon its own relationships to other symbols in a given scheme. A scheme is representational only insofar as it is dense; and a symbol is a representation only if it belongs to a scheme dense throughout or to a dense part of a partially dense scheme. Such a symbol may be a representation even if it denotes nothing at all. (p. 226).

[191]

(supporting both the aesthetic irrelevance of authenticity in painting to the *evaluation,* as well as to the "constitution", of the paintings) require that not every property of paintings be an *O*-property (even where we identify *O*-properties with the very broad class of those that can be seen by any sort of visual inspection); the arguments also require that every *aesthetic* property be an *O*-property. We have, in short, been arguing both that there are *A*-properties (like authenticity)—properties that cannot be *seen* by any sort of visual inspection of the painting (though they are, like current price, determinable properties of the painting), and also that *A*-properties, non-visual properties, are not aesthetic properties. Clearly our second argument presupposes the tenability of the first.

Prima facie, it seems obvious that there are non-visual characteristics of any physical object. Prima facie, we would count among such non-visual characteristics not only auditory or olfactory properties (like giving off a metallic sound when hit by a hammer or having a pleasant odor) but also such "theoretical" properties as being shorter than the diameter of an electron and, indeed, also such "not-now" visual characteristics (of a painting) as having once been located less than 171½ miles from the house of the aunt of a teacher of my grandfather.

As I say, prima facie, there surely are non-visual characteristics of paintings. But a veritable spate of philosophers of acuity, from Kant to N. R. Hanson and Goodman himself, have taught us that we can see pretty much what we want to, or shall, see—that we see pretty much what we can be conditioned, or trained, to see. Is there no limit to that conditioning?

We may, in fact, circumvent a long discussion by putting the situation in a standard epistemological form: any tenable claim that a given object had a certain "non-visual" property, *P*, is one for which some visual evidence would be relevant. We might hold that people who claim they can *see* that this object smells nice or they can *see* that it gives off a metallic sound are presumably so accustomed, habituated, or conditioned to making inferences that associate (e.g., olfactory characteristics with *visual* ones) that they are no longer aware of making the inference. But the subtle and complex analyses, which several contemporary philosophers of language and of science (and some non-contemporaries too) have provided, have taught us that it is a mistake to try to make hard and fast (or perhaps any) distinctions between what is *perceived* (by whatever sense) and what is inferred. Such philosophers have taught us, indeed, that what is seen can be tenably described in very many different ways. The answer to the question, "What may we see when we see X?" like the answer to the question, "What is the way the world is?" is, to quote Goodman once more, "not a hush, but a chatter." The answer is, we see what we *shall* see—in the sense that there are surely alternative systems for plausibly unpacking the sense of "see" (in congruence with the legions of other concepts to which it must be related), which will allow a very great variety of (to one or another of us, astonishingly *un*visual) things to be *seen*. In principle I see no way of limiting such systems or their reach.

But there may *be* such a principle of limitation. (In the era before we had sophisticated electronic, or acoustical, or thermal sensing auxiliaries to the blind, we might have been more confident of finding such a principle; we might, for example, have rested an in-principle-limitation on the eye's physiology. Recent advances tend to make this seem more and more an arbitrary peg—the "blind" man, electronically aided, says he is *visualizing*—sensing visually.) Clearly this is a very large problem to which this essay cannot here hope to address itself. Happily, however, it need not do so. It would be very difficult to demonstrate that our requisite (rather commonsensical), systematic use of 'see', which specifically relegates authenticity to the nonvisual, is, in principle, an untenable use of the term. As we have seen, in our survey of Goodman's theory, the basic tenets of his ostensibly opposing theory are not actually incompatible with our conclusion about the nonvisual character of authenticity. Finally, the logically constructive ("roughly recursive") task of carving out the pictorial (i.e. visual) properties of paintings on a basis of "color-location" predicates is a task for which promising ground has surely already been broken. When consummated it would very likely give us a constructive means for identifying the visual properties of a painting and for showing that such *A*-properties as authenticity are not among them.

If the above considerations help make it reasonable to accept the plausibility of holding that there are properties that are *not* visual ones, the dependent thesis is likewise rendered more reasonable. On the basis of all the considerations we have reviewed, it is more commonsensical to classify *A*-properties, like authenticity, among the nonvisual than among the visual characteristics of paintings; and this decision is rendered even more acceptable by our finding that so illuminating and ramified a theory as Goodman's does *not* prevent such a classification. With these two legs of our position that authenticity is not a constitutive aesthetic property secured, we may note that *nothing* in our argument actually hinges on any further distinction between what may be seen by "merely looking" and what may be seen by any visual inspection—what *is* crucial alone is that the latter not be construed to include *seeing* such non-visual properties as "whodunit" even when we construe such properties as constitutive for the sake of making identifications.

Logic & Language

TEN

Axioms for

Functional Calculi

of Higher Order

ALONZO CHURCH

THIS PAPER is a contribution to the axiomatic treatment of the simple
theory of types, in the sense of functional calculi of third and higher
orders, up to and including order ω. This is a topic that seems to have
had relatively little attention in the logical literature, at least from the
point of view of axiomatic economy and independence of the primitives, although there exist many and detailed axiomatic studies of
propositional logic and a lesser number of studies of first-order logic.
(By Russell, Łukasiewicz, Tarski, Leśniewski, and others there have
also been axiomatic treatments both of propositional calculus as extended by adjunction of quantifiers for propositional variables and of
what Leśniewski called protothetic, two calculi which may be regarded
as fragments of functional calculi of second and higher orders.)

For references to the literature and for terminology and background material the author's *Introduction to Mathematical Logic*

Vol. I (Princeton: Princeton University Press, 1956), is relied on here. Some of the material in the present paper appeared in an abstract by the author in *The Journal of Symbolic Logic*, Vol. 21, page 218.

As regards style of the desired axiomatizations we make the following general remark. The demand for economy in primitive notations, rules of inference, and axioms is not absolute, but may be subject to other demands which for a particular purpose or in a particular connection are thought to be more important.

Especially the demand for economy is always subject to the demand for adequacy of the system formulated. And we regard adequacy as meaning not only that all the expected theorems shall result but also all the expected consequences of any assertion, even of a non-theorem—in some sense of "expected", which is appropriate in the context and which may vary all the way from a truth-definition to merely retaining the consequences of some previously known formulation. This latter requirement of adequacy might be expressed by saying that all the expected consequences of any added postulate shall result; but if it is put this way, it is then necessary to understand that a postulate is not necessarily something that will be firmly maintained, and that a postulate may even be introduced for the purpose of refuting it by showing it to have undesirable consequences.[1]

The foregoing is conclusive, in some cases, against avoiding substitution rules for variables of a particular type by the device of employing axiom schemata in the way that is explained in Sec. 27 and Sec. 30 of *Introduction to Mathematical Logic*. In particular this is clearly inadmissible in the case of the variables of highest type-class in any functional calculus of odd order[2]—with the exception of those

---

[1] This point has been made by others, against the idea that an (axiomatically formalized) branch of logic is to be identified with the class of its theorems. The writer is unable to trace the original source. See, however, the first three paragraphs of Sec. 41 of *Introduction to Mathematical Logic*.

[2] We anticipate the objection that an added postulate might be replaced by a postulate schema. If a single postulate, in the form of an assertion containing a free variable of highest type-class, is unacceptable in the sense of having unacceptable consequences, then the underlying logic ought to yield these consequences.

More loosely put, the objection to the formulation without substitution rules is that it fails to give the variables the status of variables—they could be constants for all that appears in the (syntactical) primitive basis. If with each new postulate some of the logic has to be supplied in its application to that postulate, then the original statement of the underlying logic was defective.

functional calculi that have only constants and not variables in the highest type-class.[3] In this paper we shall employ substitution rules systematically for variables of all types, partly for uniformity, and partly because we prefer to treat first from this simpler point of view the questions of economy that we here raise. We shall leave for later consideration the modifications that result if we seek at the same time to avoid rules of substitution by the device of axiom schemata (due to von Neumann) with or without the additional device of the Gödel-Leśniewski-Henkin[4] "pseudo-definitions" (so-called by Leśniewski).

In formulating a primitive basis for one of the functional calculi, it might be natural to demand separation properties analogous to the well-known separation properties of various formulations of propositional calculus which are due to Hilbert, Hilbert-Bernays, and Bernays —among them as an example the System P_H which is described in *Introduction to Mathematical Logic*, Sec. 26. It is further well known that the demand for separation properties may often conflict with the demand for economy; and it is remarkable that in (for example) the system P_H the separation properties are secured without loss of independence of the axioms. But there is of course a deliberate sacrifice of economy in the primitive notations of the system.

For a primitive basis of one of the functional calculi there is no absolute decision as to what separation properties shall be demanded. As one such property, however, it might be asked that a primitive basis for one of the pure functional calculi shall include as a part of it a primitive basis for each of the pure functional calculi of lower order; e.g. from a primitive basis for pure functional calculus of fifth order it shall be possible to obtain a primitive basis for pure functional calculus of fourth order (or indeed of any lower order) by merely deleting certain of the primitive notations, rules, and axioms without other change. Or instead of this we may make only the weaker demand, which can perhaps be more simply satisfied, that a primitive basis for a pure functional calculus of odd order shall include as a part of it a primitive basis for each pure functional calculus of lower odd order; and a primitive basis for a pure functional calculus of even

---

[3] In particular for simple applied functional calculi of first order, it is well known that the device of axiom schemata which is here in question not only is admissible but, as explained in footnote 250 of *Introduction to Mathematical Logic*, is hardly avoidable in formulations of standard kind.

[4] Leon Henkin, "Banishing The Rule of Substitution for Functional Variables," *The Journal of Symbolic Logic*, Vol. 18 (1953), 201–208.

order shall include a primitive basis for each pure functional calculus of lower even order.

Where a conflict arises between the demand for economy and such separation demands, the decision between the two may in part depend on purpose and general context and may in part be subjective. It is not the intention of this paper to make such decisions, but rather to call attention to some questions that arise and to make a beginning towards exploration of the possibilities. Such particular primitive bases as we present are mainly in the direction of preferring economy over separation properties when there is a conflict.

The first threatened conflict between economy and separation properties arises from the remark[5] that in functional calculi of second and higher order it is possible to introduce a notation f, to denote the truth-value falsehood, by the definition

$$f \to (s)s$$

If the primitive notations include $\supset$ and the universal quantifier, as is usual and natural when *modus ponens* and generalization are taken as primitive rules, then this definition of f means that the primitive notations need not include any additional connectives of propositional calculus. In particular, negation may be introduced by the definition $\sim P \to P \supset f$, or more fully,[5]

$$\sim P \to P \supset (s)s$$

The theorem $\sim p \supset . p \supset q$ is then forthcoming as a consequence of familiar theorems involving $\supset$ and the universal quantifier. In this way introduction of the universal quantifier, at the level of at least second-order functional calculus, results in a reduction in both the primitive connectives and the axioms of propositional calculus that are necessary.[6]

---

[5] Due to Russell, as explained in footnotes 225 and 226 of *Introduction to Mathematical Logic*.

[6] It is shown by Rasiowa ("O Pewnym Fragmencie Implikacyjnego Rachunku Zdań" in *Studia Logica*, Vol. 3 (1955), 208–226), crediting the result to Słupecki, that if we begin with a fragment of the implicational propositional calculus characterized by saying that its theorems are all those that remain valid when $\supset$ is replaced everywhere by $\equiv$, the rules of inference being substitution and *modus ponens* as usual, and if we then add quantification with respect to propositional variables, and laws of quantification sufficient to make $f \supset p$ a theorem, the full implicational propositional calculus will follow—and hence of course the full propositional calculus by way of the definition of $\sim P$ which is given above.

It is only very superficial reflection that could suggest an attempt to avoid the foregoing situation by the device of omitting propositional variables from among the primitive notations of the higher-order functional calculi, or by that of not allowing quantification with respect to propositional variables. For the above definition of f can of course be replaced by

$$f \rightarrow (F)(x)F(x)$$

Or if we further omit the singulary functional variables from among the primitive notations,[7] we can still make the definition

$$f \rightarrow (F)(x)(y)F(x,y).$$

and so on.

A second point of conflict between the demand for economy and that for separation properties arises in connection with the axioms of extensionality. These are the axioms

(1) $\mathbf{f(x, y, \ldots, u)} \supset_{xy \ldots u} \mathbf{g(x, y, \ldots, u)} \supset$.
        $\mathbf{g(x, y, \ldots, u)} \supset_{xy \ldots u} \mathbf{f(x, y, \ldots, u)} \supset$.
        $\mathbf{h(f)} \supset \mathbf{h(g)},$

where $\mathbf{x, y, \ldots, u}$ are n variables, all different, and of any arbitrary types, and $\mathbf{f, g,}$ and $\mathbf{h}$ are variables of such type as to make the axiom well-formed. (Hence in particular $\mathbf{f}$ and $\mathbf{g}$ are n-ary functional variables of the same type, and $\mathbf{h}$ is a singulary functional variable of such type that $\mathbf{h(f)}$ is well-formed.) Or these axioms may also be written in either of the following forms, which are equivalent to (1) if usual laws of propositional calculus and of quantifiers are granted:

(1′) $\mathbf{f(x, y, \ldots, u)} \equiv_{xy \ldots u} \mathbf{g(x, y, \ldots, u)} \supset . \mathbf{h(f)} \supset \mathbf{h(g)}$

(1″) $\mathbf{f(x, y, \ldots, u)} \equiv_{xy \ldots u} \mathbf{g(x, y, \ldots, u)} \supset . \mathbf{h(f)} \equiv \mathbf{h(g)}$

[7] In the same sense in which it is true that we can without loss omit the propositional variables from among the primitive notations, it is true that we can further omit the singulary functional variables without loss. Neither omission would seem to be a genuine economy, as there is always the question: Where shall we stop? If such economies are to be undertaken at all, it would seem to be better to follow Tarski in omitting *all but* the singulary functional variables (although below order ω this interferes with the usual separation of the functional calculi into orders). However, for our present purpose it is not necessary to say more about any of these proposed economies than that they do not interfere in any substantial way with what is said in the text, either about the possibility of defining f or about the effect of the axioms of extensionality.

It is well known that in *Principia Mathematica* axioms of extensionality of the above form (or forms) are not used. In the first edition an intensional interpretation is intended for the propositional and functional variables, and the extensional notions of *class* and *relation* are available only in the sense of Russell's contextual definitions. In the introduction to the second edition axioms of extensionality are proposed as a modification, but because this is done in the context of ramified type theory, the axioms are not entirely the same as here and their effect is quite different from that of axioms of extensionality in simple type theory.

In spite of the precedent of *Principia Mathematica,* there are reasons of some force that can be given for including axioms of extensionality in the basis of a functional calculus of third or higher order. One of these is just that the extensional interpretations of the propositional and functional variables are conceptually simpler and are often closer to an intended (especially mathematical) application; if the extensional interpretations are intended, it is better to make this explicit in the axioms and avoid indirection. A second reason is that there is a difficulty in regard to the rule of substitution for functional variables which (it seems) can most simply be resolved by allowing axioms of extensionality.

In connection with the first reason it must be pointed out that adoption of extensional interpretations of the propositional and functional variables forces adoption of a Fregean as against a Russellian theory of meaning. Indeed the intensional interpretations and the resort to contextual definitions in the first edition of *Principia* are Russell's method of dealing with the well-known puzzle about meaning which originated with Frege but is now more familiar as illustrated by Russell's example concerning Sir Walter Scott and King George IV.[8] One of the advantages of Frege's theory of meaning is

[8] Let us introduce predicates S and W, $S(x)$ to mean that x is Sir Walter Scott (that x scottizes, in Quine's phrase) and $W(x)$ to mean that x wrote *Waverley*. The predicates S and W are functional constants rather than functional variables, but it is clear that an intensional or extensional interpretation of the functional variables must go together with an intensional or extensional interpretation of any functional constants that are introduced. Since it is a fact that $W(x) \equiv_x S(x)$, the extensional interpretation identifies the denotations of S and W, so that whatever is true of one is true of the other. We may suppose, as seems likely, that King George IV believed that $S(x) \equiv_x S(x)$. On the extensional interpretation it seems to follow that King George IV believed that $W(x) \equiv_x S(x)$. But at the time of the now famous dinner it is more correct to say that King George suspected that Sir Walter might be the author of *Waverley* than that he so believed.

that it leaves us free to formulate a purely extensional object language when the purpose is extensional; then later, if we wish to deal with intensionalities, we may extend the language by introducing appropriate intensional notations.

To explain the second reason let us consider the (metatheoretic) notation

$$\overset{\vee}{\mathsf{S}}{}_{\mathbf{B}}^{\mathbf{f}(x, y, \ldots, u)} \mathbf{A} \mid$$

for substitution for an n-ary functional variable $\mathbf{f}$, where $x, y, \ldots, u$ are n different variables of suitable types. The operation on the wff $\mathbf{A}$ which this notation calls for may conveniently be explained by saying that we first make an ordinary substitution of[9] $\lambda x \lambda y \ldots \lambda u \mathbf{B}$ for all free occurrences of the variable $\mathbf{f}$ in $\mathbf{A}$ and then apply a series of contractions by which expressions of the form[10] $\lambda x \lambda y \ldots \lambda u \mathbf{B}(a_1, a_2, \ldots, a_n)$ are replaced by

$$\mathsf{S}_{a_1 \, a_2 \, \ldots \, a_n}^{x \ \ y \ \ldots \ u} \mathbf{B} \mid$$

These contractions are continued until a wff of the appropriate functional calculus is obtained, and it is this final wff which is denoted by

$$\overset{\vee}{\mathsf{S}}{}_{\mathbf{B}}^{\mathbf{f}(x, y, \ldots, u)} \mathbf{A} \mid$$

Restrictions[11] must be imposed to assure that there is no capture of variables either in the original substitution for $\mathbf{f}$ or in any of the subsequent contractions, and when these restrictions fail, the metatheoretic notation is understood simply as denoting the wff $\mathbf{A}$.

---

[9] The expression $\lambda x \lambda y \ldots \lambda u \mathbf{B}$ is not a wff of any of the functional calculi, at least not in usual or standard formulations of them. But this fact does not prevent the use which we here make of this expression in order to explain an operation by which a wff of a particular functional calculus is transformed into another wff of the same calculus.

The point is conspicuous that if we extended the notation of functional calculus by adjoining the abstraction operator λ as a new primitive, the rule of substitution for functional variables could be replaced by simpler rules of ordinary substitution, alphabetic change of bound variable, and contraction—and some of the complications in connection with the rule of substitution for functional variables could be avoided. In effect a complicated rule of inference is thus broken down into simpler ones. But we here follow the standard usage according to which an abstraction operator is not considered to belong to the notations of functional calculus.

[10] We might write this as $\{\lambda x \lambda y \ldots \lambda u \mathbf{B}\} (a_1, a_2, \ldots, a_n)$. And the braces may indeed be useful for clearness, especially if a complicated particular expression has to be written, but they are not strictly necessary, as in the context of one of the functional calculi the scope of the operators $\lambda x \lambda y \ldots \lambda u$ is determined by the condition that $\mathbf{B}$ shall be well-formed.

[11] Compare *Introduction to Mathematical Logic*, Sec. 35.

[203]

The above-mentioned difficulty in regard to the rule of substitution for functional variables arises when the wff **A** contains occurrences of the functional variable **f** as argument of another functional variable **h**, since in this case the series of contractions that are applied after substitution of $\lambda x \lambda y \ldots \lambda u \mathbf{B}$ for free occurrences of **f** will not result in a wff of functional calculus (not all occurrences of the abstraction operator λ are eliminated by the contractions). We seem to be forced to impose another restriction on the substitution operation $\check{S}$, namely that **f** shall not have in **A** occurrences as argument of another functional variable, and again to understand the result of the substitution to be just **A** itself in case the restriction fails. If axioms of extensionality are available, it is easy to see that this new restriction on substitution for functional variables is not in fact an essential restriction; to take for illustration the case in which **h** and **f** are both singulary, we can prove in consequence of the appropriate axiom of extensionality

$$\mathbf{h(f)} \equiv . \mathbf{f(x)} \supset_x \mathbf{g(x)} \supset_g . \mathbf{g(x)} \supset_x \mathbf{f(x)} \supset \mathbf{h(g)} ,$$

and either side of this equivalence can then be replaced at will by the other (with any choice of the variable **g** as different from but of the same type as **f**). On the other hand, without axioms of extensionality there is a puzzling question as to what can be considered adequate. If intensional interpretations are intended for the propositional variables and the various types of functional variables, perhaps the question can be resolved only by introducing some suitable strict or intensional implication, and some suitable strict or intensional equivalence, and stating analogues of the axioms of extensionality by means of them.

For these reasons, in formulating a primitive basis for one of the higher-order functional calculi, let us proceed on the assumption that axioms of extensionality are to be included. An effect of the axioms of extensionality may be to render non-independent some of the axioms of propositional calculus that would otherwise be used, or at least to open up new possibilities of economy in regard to propositional calculus axioms. For one very important derived rule of propositional calculus, either the principle of substitutivity of mutual implication or the principle of substitutivity of equivalence, follows from the axioms of extensionality by no more than (or little more than) *modus ponens* and substitution for functional variables. This is clearest if we suppose that the case $n = 0$ is admitted in the axiom schema (1) (or (1′)

[204]

or $(1'')$), so that we have as one of the axioms that is covered by (e.g.) the schema $(1):$[12]

(1_o) $\qquad\qquad p \supset q \supset . q \supset p \supset . h(p) \supset h(q)$

For simplicity we shall in fact suppose this in what follows. But the same results can be obtained if we suppose $n \geqq 1$ in schema (1) (or even $n \geqq 2$, etc.), and ultimately the axioms that correspond to $n = 0$ (or $n < 2$, etc.) can then be proved as theorems.

Now therefore we turn to some particular primitive bases for functional calculi as being suggested by the above considerations. We sketch the matter rather than give a fully detailed treatment. We confine attention to pure functional calculi, as for our purpose there is perhaps nothing to be gained in going beyond that. And we further confine attention, in this first treatment, to functional calculi of odd order and of order ω. (For functional calculi of even order the axiomatic basis must in any case be somewhat different; a more extensive use of axiom schemata than in the case of functional calculi of odd order is hardly avoidable, and we may hence prefer to adopt Leśniewski's "pseudo-definitions"[13] as a means of excluding the somewhat complicated substitution operation $\overset{\vee}{S}$ from at least the primitive rules and axiom schemata.)

For pure functional calculus of order ω we take the following primitive symbols: the sign of material implication $\supset$ and the brackets [ ] that go with it, the universal quantifier, the notation (composed of parentheses and commas) for application of function to argument, an infinite alphabet of individual variables, an infinite alphabet of propositional variables, and for each type of functional variables an infinite alphabet of variables of that type.

This statement presupposes the notion of a type, and must therefore be completed by explaining this notion as follows. There is a type 0, to which the individual variables belong. If $a_1, a_2, \ldots, a_n$ are any given types, there is a corresponding type $(a_1, a_2, \ldots, a_n)$ to which there belong n-ary functional variables. And since a pure functional calculus is here in question (i.e., constants are not among the primitive

---

[12] We may without loss specialize to a particular functional variable, say h, so that (1_o) is a single axiom rather than a schema.

[13] They might preferably be called comprehension axioms, as Henkin's explanation tends to suggest, though not quite explicitly. Gödel (*Monatshefte für Mathematik und Physik*, Vol. 38 (1931), 173–198) misleadingly speaks of them also as corresponding to axioms of reducibility.

symbols), we have the rule that if f is a variable of type $(\alpha_1, \alpha_2, \ldots, \alpha_n)$, then $f(a_1, a_2, \ldots a_n)$ is well-formed if and only if $a_1, a_2, \ldots a_n$ are variables whose types are, in order, $\alpha_1, \alpha_2, \ldots, \alpha_n$.

We think of the propositional variables as included in the foregoing explanation by allowing the case $n = 0$, but for convenience we modify the notation as follows. If f is a propositional variable, we call its type 1_0, rather than $(\ )$, and we take f standing alone as being well-formed, rather than $f(\ )$.

Then the types are divided into numbered type-classes as follows. (We may speak either of a type or of a variable of that type as belonging to a certain type-class m.) The type 0 belongs to, or is of, the type-class 0. The type 1_0 belongs to the type-class 1. And beyond that, the type $(\alpha_1, \alpha_2, \ldots, \alpha_n)$ belongs to the type-class $m + 1$, where m is the highest type-class to which any of the types $\alpha_1, \alpha_2, \ldots, \alpha_n$ belong.

This accounts for the primitive symbols of the pure functional calculus of order ω. And for the pure functional calculi of finite order we specify the primitive symbols as follows. The pure functional calculus of order $2m - 1$ and the pure functional calculus of order $2m$ have the same primitive symbols, which are namely the same as those remaining from the primitive symbols of the pure functional calculus of order ω after deleting all variables of type-class higher than m.

The formation rules for all of these functional calculi are now evident, as being implicit in what has already been said. But for the functional calculi of odd order, the formation rule for the universal quantifier, that if M is well-formed then $(a)M$ is well-formed, must have the restriction that the variable a is not of the highest type-class.

For the pure functional calculi of odd finite order and of order ω we then take rules of inference as follows:

The rule of modus ponens, from $A \supset B$ and A to infer B.

The rule of generalization, from A to infer $(a)A$, provided a is a variable of such type that the result of the inference is well-formed.

The rule of substitution for individual variables, from A to infer $S_b^a A \,|$, where a and b are individual variables, provided that no bound occurrence of b results at any place at which b is substituted for a free occurrence of a (in other words, provided that there is no capture of the variable b).

The rule of substitution for propositional variables, from A to infer $\overset{\vee}{S}_B^p A\,|$, where B is any wff and p is any propositional variable.[14]

---

[14] $\overset{\vee}{S}_B^p A\,|$ is the result of substituting B for free occurrences of p throughout A, so that this is the same rule of substitution that is familiar in propo-

The rule of substitution for functional variables, from **A** to infer

$$\overset{\lor}{S}{}_{\mathbf{B}}^{\mathbf{f}(\mathbf{x},\,\mathbf{y},\,\ldots,\,\mathbf{u})}\,\mathbf{A}|\,,$$

where **B** is any wff, **f** is an n-ary functional variable, and **x, y, . . . , u** are n distinct variables of such types that $\mathbf{f}(\mathbf{x},\mathbf{y},\ldots,\mathbf{u})$ is well-formed.

As axioms there are first of all the axioms of extensionality (1), as given above, including the axiom (1₀) as one of them. Then there are the following axioms of quantifiers:[15]

(2) $\qquad\qquad p \supset_{\mathbf{x}} \mathbf{f}(\mathbf{x}) \supset\,.\,p \supset (\mathbf{x})\mathbf{f}(\mathbf{x})$

(3) $\qquad\qquad (\mathbf{x})\mathbf{f}(\mathbf{x}) \supset \mathbf{f}\,(\mathbf{y})$

In (2) and (3), p is the particular propositional variable, and **f, x, y** are variables of such type as to make the axioms well-formed, with the restriction in the case of (2) that **x** is not p.

After that we need only axioms of propositional calculus, and our present purpose is to minimize the number and the length of these. Perhaps the simplest choice is to take as the two final axioms:

(4) $\qquad\qquad\qquad p \supset\,.\,q \supset p$

(5) $\qquad\qquad\qquad p \supset q \supset p \supset p$

However, we shall also consider replacing the axiom (4) by:

---

sitional calculus. Here, however, it is necessary to impose restrictions analogous to those already described in regard to substitution for functional variables, and to understand $\overset{\lor}{S}{}_{\mathbf{B}}^{p}\,\mathbf{A}|$ as being simply **A** if one of the restrictions fails. There are two such restrictions, the first one being that no capture of variables shall result from the substitution, and the second one that **p** shall not have any occurrence in **A** as argument of a functional variable.

In connection with the second restriction, observe that we are here following the long-standing restriction on notation in the pure functional calculi, that each argument of a functional variable must be a single primitive symbol, hence a variable; as a special case of this, where e.g. h is a variable of such type that $h(p)$ is well-formed, nevertheless $h(f)$ and $h(p \supset q)$ are not well-formed. This is a divergence from the usage of Leśniewski's prototethic, but not an essential one.

[15] For brevity the axiom schemata (1), (2), (3) are here stated in such a way that they include obviously non-independent axioms, even for any particular choice of types of the variables **f, g, h, x, y, . . . , u** (or **f, x, y**). In the case of schema (1) it is not difficult to avoid this by restating in such a way that, for any such particular choice of types, particular variables **f, g, h, x, y, . . . , u** are prescribed. But in schemata (2) and (3) only **f** and **y** can be thus particularized; and **x** must remain an arbitrary variable of its type—unless a rule of alphabetic change of bound variable is added to the primitive rules of inference.

(6) $$p \supset [q \supset r] \supset .q \supset .p \supset r$$

We sketch a proof that the axioms (4) and (5) are sufficient for propositional calculus, in the presence of the other axioms stated.

By substitution for the functional variable h in (1_0) we get:

(7) $$p \supset q \supset .q \supset p \supset .r \supset r$$

Hence by substitution for q:

$$p \supset [p \supset q \supset p] \supset .p \supset q \supset p \supset p \supset .r \supset r$$

Hence by two applications of *modus ponens* we get the theorem,

(8) $$r \supset r ,$$

the first minor premiss being obtained by substitution in axiom (4) and the second one being axiom (5).[16]

By substituting p for q in (7) and using *modus ponens* (since $p \supset p$ is a theorem by substitution in (8)) we get:

(9) $$p \supset p \supset .r \supset r$$

Similarly from (7) (or from (9)) we get:

(10) $$r \supset r \supset .p \supset p$$

By substitution for the functional variable h in (1_0):

$$p \supset q \supset .q \supset p \supset .p \supset s \supset s \supset .q \supset s \supset s$$

Hence by substitution for the propositional variables:

$$p \supset p \supset [r \supset r] \supset .r \supset r \supset [p \supset p] \supset .$$
$$p \supset p \supset p \supset p \supset .r \supset r \supset p \supset p$$

From this by three applications of *modus ponens* we get the theorem:

(11) $$r \supset r \supset p \supset p$$

(The three successive minor premisses that are required are in order (9), (10), and obtained from (5) by substitution of p for q.)

---

[16] To get analogous results in a formulation without propositional variables the general plan is to use $F(x)$, $G(x)$, $H(x)$, and so forth in place of the propositional variables p, q, r, and so forth. Thus theorem (8) is replaced by $H(x) \supset H(x)$, and in its proof we use in place of (1_0) the case $n = 1$ in axiom schema (1). Then, e.g. the last two minor premisses in the proof, instead of $p \supset .p \supset q \supset p$ and $p \supset q \supset p \supset p$, will be $F(x) \supset_x .F(x) \supset G(x) \supset F(x)$ and $F(x) \supset G(x) \supset F(x) \supset_x F(x)$. For this purpose it does not matter whether axioms (4) and (5) are replaced by particular axioms such as $F(x) \supset .G(x) \supset F(x)$ and $F(x) \supset G(x) \supset F(x) \supset F(x)$ or whether they are replaced by axiom schemata.

By substitution in (4) we have:

$$(12) \qquad p \supset . r \supset r \supset p$$

Also from (4) and (8) we can prove:

$$(13) \qquad p \supset . r \supset r$$

In consequence of (11) and (12), and by using the extensionality axiom (1_0), we may replace p by $r \supset r \supset p$ in any context except that of an occurrence of p as argument of a functional variable. We omit details of this, as they are entirely similar to those of the last use of (1_0) which was made above. Equally we may use (11), (12), and (1_0) to replace $p \supset q$ by $r \supset r \supset . p \supset q$ in any context. Hence from the theorem $p \supset q \supset . p \supset q$ (which results from (8) by substitution) we get:

$$(14) \qquad r \supset r \supset [p \supset q] \supset . r \supset r \supset p \supset q$$

Now we prove the following derived rule:

Modified rule of modus ponens. From **C** $\supset$. **A** $\supset$ **B** and **A** we may infer **C** $\supset$ **B**.

For given **A** we have, by (12) and (13), $r \supset r \supset$ **A** and **A** $\supset . r \supset r$. Hence using the extensionality axiom (1_0) we may replace **A** by $r \supset r$ in **C** $\supset$. **A** $\supset$ **B**, so obtaining **C** $\supset . r \supset r \supset$ **B**. But (11) and (12) enable us, by another use of (1_0), to replace $r \supset r \supset$ **B** by **B**, so that we get **C** $\supset$ **B**.[17]

Having thus proved the derived rule, we substitute in (1_0) to get the following (first substituting for the functional variable h and then making a succession of substitutions for the propositional variables):

$$r \supset [s \supset r] \supset . s \supset r \supset r \supset .$$
$$r \supset r \supset [p \supset q] \supset [r \supset r \supset p \supset q] \supset .$$
$$s \supset r \supset r \supset [p \supset q] \supset . s \supset r \supset r \supset p \supset q$$

From this by first using *modus ponens,* with $r \supset . s \supset r$ as minor premiss (obtained from (4) by substitution), and then using the modified rule of *modus ponens,* with (14) as minor premiss, we get:

$$s \supset r \supset r \supset . s \supset r \supset r \supset [p \supset q] \supset . s \supset r \supset r \supset p \supset q$$

---

[17] Obviously we could use a variation of the same argument to prove the much stronger derived rule (not needed here) that, given **A** and **C** as premisses, we can replace any occurrence of **A** $\supset$ **B** by **B**, or of **B** by **A** $\supset$ **B**, within **C**, provided the result is well-formed.

In this we substitute s for r and then use (11), (12), and (1_0) to replace $s \supset s \supset s$ by s. The result is:

(15) $$s \supset . s \supset [p \supset q] \supset . s \supset p \supset q$$

Now (15) is close to the self-distributive law (†103 in *Introduction to Mathematical Logic*) ; in fact it differs from the self-distributive law only in regard to the order in which the antecedents are arranged. Moreover an examination of the proof of the deduction theorem in Sec. 13 of *Introduction to Mathematical Logic* shows that we may use it here almost unchanged. We have to modify only case 3 in the proof, replacing use of the self-distributive law by use of (15), and hence using the modified rule of *modus ponens* at certain points instead of the rule of *modus ponens*.

By substitution in (3) we have the theorem:

(16) $$f \supset p$$

At this point our proof that axioms (4) and (5) are sufficient for propositional calculus could be considered complete, as it is known that (4), (5), (16), and the transitive law of implication are sufficient —with *modus ponens* and substitution as rules of inference—and the transitive law is of course an easy consequence of the deduction theorem. But to make the connection with *Introduction to Mathematical Logic,* we indicate also the proof of

(17) $$p \supset f \supset f \supset p,$$

so that it can be seen directly that all the axioms of the system P_1 are theorems. Namely we get by substitution in (1_0) :

$$p \supset f \supset f \supset . f \supset [p \supset f] \supset . p \supset f \supset p \supset p \supset . f \supset p \supset p$$

But $f \supset . p \supset f$ is a theorem by substitution in (4), $p \supset f \supset p \supset p$ is a theorem by substitution in (5), and $f \supset p$ is (16). Hence we get (17) by three successive applications of the modified rule of *modus ponens*.

Now we turn to demonstration of the sufficiency of axioms (5) and (6) for propositional calculus, in the presence of the axioms of extensionality and the axioms of quantifiers. And for this purpose we follow as closely as we can the above treatment of axioms (4) and (5).

By substitution in (7) we have

$$p \supset [q \supset r] \supset [q \supset . p \supset r] \supset .$$
$$q \supset [p \supset r] \supset [p \supset . q \supset r] \supset . r \supset r,$$

and hence we prove (8) by two applications of *modus ponens*.

[210]

By substitution in (8) we have:

$$r \supset r \supset p \supset . r \supset r \supset p$$

Hence by (6):

$$r \supset r \supset . r \supset r \supset p \supset p$$

Hence (11) follows by *modus ponens*.

By substituting in (7) and using *modus ponens*, with (8) as minor premiss, we prove (10). Hence (12) can be proved by use of (6).

By substitution in (7) we have:

$$q \supset [r \supset r] \supset . r \supset r \supset q \supset . p \supset p$$

By (1_0), (11), and (12) we may replace $r \supset r \supset q$ by q, so that we have:

(18) $$q \supset [r \supset r] \supset . q \supset . p \supset p$$

Again by substitution in (1_0) we have:

$$q \supset r \supset . r \supset q \supset . q \supset r$$

Hence by (6):

$$r \supset q \supset . q \supset r \supset . q \supset r$$

Hence by (18):

$$r \supset q \supset . p \supset p$$

Hence by substitution for r:

$$r \supset r \supset q \supset . p \supset p$$

Hence again using (1_0), (11), and (12) to replace $r \supset r \supset q$ by q we have:

$$q \supset . p \supset p$$

From this last we get (13) by substitution, and we get (4) by use of (6).

From this point on, the treatment of axioms (5) and (6) may duplicate that already given for axioms (4) and (5). And as Peirce's law, axiom (5), is thus not used until after completion of the proof of the deduction theorem, we have the following separation property of the axioms:

[211]

Axioms (1_o) *and* (6) *are sufficient for the positive implicational propositional calculus. The addition of axiom* (5) *then yields the implicational propositional calculus. And the further addition of* (3) *yields the full propositional calculus.*

It would be of interest to determine what is the shortest axiom or the axiom with the smallest number of distinct variables which, in place of (6), preserves this separation property.

Finally, though we do not make a systematic treatment of independence questions in this connection, we cite the two following independence examples, which settle some of the most critical questions.

To show the independence of axiom (5) from axioms (1), (2), (3), (4) we use the truth-table for ⊃ which is shown in the table below in the column headed (5). The truth-value 0 is designated and 1 and 2 are non-designated. And the valuation rule for the universal quantifier is as follows:[18] For a given system of values of the free variables of (x)**M**, we give the value 0 to (x)**M** if **M** has the value 0 for every value of **x**, the value 1 if **M** has the value 1 for at least one value of **x**, and the value 2 in all remaining cases.

This same independence example (or model), since it falsifies axiom (6), shows that the axioms (1), (2), (3), (4), (5) do not have the separation property that was just stated above for the axioms (1), (2), (3), (5), (6).

To show the independence of (4) from axioms (1), (2), (3), (5) we use the truth-table for ⊃ that is shown in the column headed (4). The truth-values 0 and 1 are designated and 2 is non-designated. And

		(4)	(5)
p	q	$p \supset q$	$p \supset q$
0	0	0	0
0	1	0	2
0	2	2	2
1	0	2	0
1	1	0	0
1	2	2	0
2	0	0	0
2	1	0	2
2	2	0	0

[18] Other details of the intended model are the obvious ones and are omitted for brevity. The model may be varied somewhat, and in particular any non-empty domain of individuals will serve—the suggestion is immediate that the model may be simplified by using the unit domain.

the valuation rule for the universal quantifier is as follows: For a given system of values of the free variables of $(x)M$, we give the value 1 to $(x)M$ if M has the value 1 for every value of x, the value 2 if M has the value 2 for at least one value of x, and the value 0 in all remaining cases.

The independence of (6) from axioms (1), (2), (3), (5) is then obvious without further reference to independence examples.

ELEVEN

Algebraic Logic

and

Predicate Functors

W. V. QUINE

1
Algebra and Analysis

TRY TO THINK back over the years to the time, in school or in college, when you finished algebra and started the differential calculus. Algebra had been neat and clear. It was put together of clean-cut blocks. You substituted blocklike expressions for variables. Also, on the strength of previous equations, you substituted them for one another. The calculus, in contrast, was enveloped in fog. There were variables and there were constants, so-called. You had $dc/dx = 0$, where 'c' was a constant and 'x' a variable. But could you substitute? For the variables, no. For the constants, yes: $d9/dx = 0$. For the variables you could not even substitute on the strength of previous equations. You had $dx^2/dx = 2x$; still, given further that $x = 3$, you could not substitute and conclude that $d9/dx = 6$. You had $d9/dx = 0$.

The work leading to the present paper was supported in part by grant GS-2615 of the National Science Foundation.

Maybe some of you were given a better introduction to the calculus than I was. The thing can of course be made straightforward. We should view 'dx^2/dx' as expressing the application of an operator not to a number x^2 but to a function, square-of, to yield not a number $2x$ but a function, double-of. Using Frege's functional abstraction (in Church's lambda notation), we can put the matter clearly:

$$D \lambda_x(x^2) = \lambda_x(2x).$$

Even the identity '$d9/dx = 0$' should be seen as treating not of numbers but of constant functions: $D \lambda_x 9 = \lambda_x 0$. But even when it is thus clarified the calculus lacks the neat and blocklike character of algebra. We can put a name to the contrast now: it is that the calculus binds variables. The variable of functional abstraction is bound. This has long struck me as the great contrast between the spirit of algebra and the spirit of analysis: analysis binds variables.

We know how to reduce all use of bound variables to quantification. For instance '$\lambda_x(x^2)$' can be eliminated from any sentential context, say '$\phi \lambda_x(x^2)$', by explaining this whole as:

$$(\exists f)(\phi f \cdot (x)(f`x = x^2))$$

or, in terms more purely of set theory:

$$(\exists z)(\phi z \cdot (y)(x)(\langle y, x \rangle \epsilon z \cdot \equiv \cdot y = x^2)).$$

We can reduce all use of free variables to quantification too, if we like, since an open sentence has its uses ultimately only as a clause of various closed sentences in which its variables have become bound.

But in a way the opposite reduction is much more attractive, if it can be done: the elimination of bound variables in favor of just free ones. This would be a reduction of the analytic style to the algebraic style. Since all use of bound variables can be limited to quantification, the problem is that of algebrizing quantification. Whether or not this result would be practically useful, it should be theoretically significant as an analysis of the idea of the bound variable: an explanation of it with all the clarity of the discrete and blocklike terms and simple substitutions characteristic of algebra. It should, in addition, yield a deeper understanding of variables as such, bound or free; for, as I just remarked, free variables themselves are for binding in broader contexts. Thus the algebrization of quantification could prove illuminating in two ways: in analyzing away bound variables and in enhancing our understanding even of the free variables surviving in the algebra itself.

[215]

In part the algebrization of quantification is a step backward; for part of what quantification does was previously done algebraically by talking of classes in the manner of Boole and of relations in the manner of Peirce and Schröder. Instead of '$(x)(Fx \supset Gx)$' and '$(\exists x)(Fx \cdot Gx)$', one would treat the predicate letters as class names and write '$F \subseteq G$' and '$F \cap G \neq \Lambda$'. Instead of:

$$(x) \sim Fxx, \qquad (x)(y)(Fxy \supset Fyx), \qquad (x)(y)(z)(Fxy \cdot Fyz \cdot \supset Fxz),$$

one would treat the predicate letter as a relation name and write '$F \cap I = \Lambda$', '$\breve{F} \subseteq F$', and '$F \mid F \subseteq F$'. Here, then, we have some of the algebraic notations that help us get rid of quantifiers and their variables: '$\cap$', '$\subseteq$', '$=$', 'Λ', 'I', '$\smile$', '$\mid$'. The problem is to pick an assortment of such devices adequate to the general case.

2
Functional Abstraction

Schönfinkel succeeded in eliminating bound variables in 1924,[1] and his work took an interestingly different line. The best approach to his idea is through functional abstraction rather than quantification. We saw how the use of bound variables in functional abstraction could be reduced to their use in quantification; but the opposite reduction is possible as well. In fact the only devices we need besides functional abstraction are functional application, as in '$f'x$', and the identity sign '$=$'. These can be made to suffice if we follow Frege in taking true sentences as names of a certain thing $\top$, and false sentences as names of a certain thing $\bot$. A class then can be seen as a function that gives the value $\top$ when applied to the members and the value $\bot$ otherwise. Thus take the class of prime numbers. It becomes identified with the function f such that $f'x = \top$ for prime x and $f'x = \bot$ for other x. But wait: we can say also that (x is prime) $= \top$ for prime x and (x is prime) $= \bot$ for other x. So $f'x = $ (x is prime) for each x. So the function f is $\lambda_x(x$ is prime). We see from this example that

---

[1] Moses Schönfinkel, "Ueber die Bausteine der mathematischen Logik", *Mathematische Annalen* 92 (1924), 305–316. Translation and commentary in J. van Heijenoort, ed., *From Frege to Gödel* (Cambridge: Harvard University Press, 1967). Schönfinkel's line is developed in an extensive literature, largely by Curry. See H. B. Curry and Robert Feys, *Combinatory Logic* (Amsterdam: North-Holland, 1958).

functional abstraction does the work, in particular, of class abstraction; $\{x: x$ is prime$\}$ becomes $\lambda_x(x$ is prime$)$.

That much was already in Frege. Now I shall go on from there and show how functional abstraction, functional application, and identity can yield quantification. In view of what we just saw, the universal class V or $\{x: x = x\}$ can be defined as $\lambda_x(x = x)$; and thereupon the universal quantification '$(x)Fx$', with any open sentence in place of 'Fx', can be defined as $\lambda_x(Fx) = V$. The existential quantifier '$(\exists x)$' can then be explained in turn in the usual manner as '$\sim(x)\sim$', provided that we can define negation. To do this we first pick some arbitrary falsehood expressible in our notation; say '$(x)(x = V)$'. Then we define '$\sim y$' in general as '$y = (x)(x = V)$', taking advantage again of the fact that sentences are names and false sentences are names of the one object $\perp$.

In explaining how to define the two kinds of quantification in terms of functional abstraction, application, and identity, I have talked of the objects $\top$ and $\perp$, the two truth values. I have not used these symbols in the definitions, and I have not defined them. We can formally define them, though, if we like. We can choose again our arbitrary falsehood '$(x)(x = V)$' and define '$\perp$' as short for it, and '$\top$' as '$\sim\perp$'.

We can get all the truth functions. The trick is to get conjunction; everyone knows how to get the others from it and negation. The trick for defining conjunction is one that I have adapted from an early paper of Tarski's:[2] define the conjunction '$x \cdot y$' as '$(z)(x = (z^\prime x = z^\prime y))$'. My use of variables in conjunction here, and under negation earlier, looks odd; we have to remind ourselves that sentences now count as names. To see how conjunction as thus defined compels x and y to be $\top$, try taking z first as $\lambda_w x$ and then as $\lambda_w w$. We get $x = (x = x)$ and $x = (x = y)$ and so $x = \top = y$.

We have now seen that functional abstraction, application, and identity are enough for elementary logic—that is, enough for the truth functions, quantification, and identity. But they are enough also for much more. We have seen that class abstraction is at hand, as the special case of functional abstraction where the function's values are truth values. Equally, class membership is at hand; it is the special case of functional application where the function's values

[2] Alfred Tarski, "Sur le terme primitif de la logistique", *Fundamenta Mathematicae* 4 (1923), 196–200. Translation in Tarski, *Logic, Semantics, Metamathematics* (Oxford: Clarendon, 1956).

are truth values. For, recall the class f of all primes. We saw that $f'x$ was $\top$ for prime x and $\bot$ for other x; and this is precisely what we want $x \in f$ to be.

We have overreached ourselves. We wanted to see how the bound variables of quantification could be got down to the bound variable of functional abstraction. What we have found is that functional abstraction, along with the seemingly minimal auxiliary notations of application and identity, are enough for logic and set theory and hence mathematics generally.[3]

3

Combinators

What I want to trace next, proceeding from this notation, is Schönfinkel's elimination of bound variables. We define two specific functions:

(1) $$C = \lambda_x \lambda_y x.$$

(2) $$S = \lambda_x \lambda_y \lambda_z ((x'z)'(y'z)).$$

Conversely, as we shall find, all use of functional abstraction is eliminable in favor of C and S.

C is the function that carries any object into the corresponding constant function. $C'9$ is the constant function $\lambda_y 9$ whose value is always 9. And what is S? Words fail one. It is the functional which, applied to any function x, yields the functional which, applied to any function y, yields the function which, applied to anything z, yields what the function $x'z$ would yield when applied to $y'z$.

The content of equations like (1) and (2) can be put into a more convenient form by applying both sides. Thus (1) tells us that $C'x = \lambda_y x$, and hence that $(C'x)'y = x$. Similarly (2) tells us, after three such steps, that

$$((S'x)'y)'z = (x'z)'(y'z).$$

Further let us adopt a convention of Schönfinkel's for economy of parentheses in iterated functional application:

(3) $$a'b'c = (a'b)'c.$$

---

[3] The adequacy of this combination was noted at the end of my "Unification of universes in set theory", *Journal of Symbolic Logic* 21 (1956), 267–279.

So our two results now run thus:

(4) $$C'x'y = x.$$

(5) $$S'x'y'z = x'z'(y'z).$$

C and S, and all the functions compounded of them by functional application, have come to be called *combinators*. Example: $S'C$. What is it? By (5), $S'C'y'z$ is $C'z'(y'z)$. So, by (4),

(6) $$S'C'y'z = z.$$

Another example: $S'C'C$. By (6), $S'C'C'z = z$. Thus $S'C'C$ is the identity function. Abbreviating it as 'I', we have:

(7) $$I'z = z.$$

Another example: $S'(C'S)'C$. By (5),

$$S'(C'S)'C'w = (C'S)'w'(C'w)$$
$$\text{(by (3))} \quad = (C'S'w)'(C'w)$$
$$\text{(by (4))} \quad = S'(C'w).$$

Following Schönfinkel, let us refer to $S'(C'S)'C$ briefly as Z. So $Z'w$ is $S'(C'w)$. So

$$Z'w'y'x = S'(C'w)'y'x$$
$$\text{(by (5))} \quad = (C'w)'x'(y'x)$$
$$\text{(by (3))} \quad = (C'w'x)'(y'x).$$

So, by (4),

(8) $$Z'w'y'x = w'(y'x).$$

You see how mechanically the evaluation of combinators proceeds. You will find by further computation of the same sort that, where 'R' stands for '$S'(Z'Z'S)'(C'C)$',

(9) $$R'x'y'z = x'z'y.$$

Also, where 'W' stands for '$R'S'I$', that

(10) $$W'x'y = x'y'y.$$

As a convenient adjustment of detail, next, let us dispense with '$=$' in favor of the unit-class function ι. The two are interdefinable, since

$$\iota = \lambda_x \lambda_y (x = y), \qquad\qquad \iota'x'y = (x = y).$$

The advantage of this shift is a simplification of grammatical categories. There are now just variables and the letters for specific functions ($'S'$, $'C'$, $'\iota'$) and the $'\lambda'$ of abstraction and the inverted comma and parentheses of functional application. What we want to show is that the $'\lambda'$ can be eliminated.

4
Elimination of Variables

I shall prepare the way by first proving some things about terms that lack $'\lambda'$. By the *superficial* components of such a term I shall mean the terms that occur in it unenclosed in any parentheses when parentheses have been suppressed to the extent that convention (3) allows. Thus a formula has the form $\ulcorner\phi_1{}^\iota\phi_2{}^\iota \ldots {}^\iota\phi_n\urcorner$ where ϕ_1, ϕ_2, $\ldots$, and ϕ_n are its superficial components. Now consider a superficial occurrence of some variable, say $'x'$, in a term ς. We can assure that this occurrence is not initial to ς, since by (7) we can change $'x'$ to $'I'x'$. So ς has the form $\ulcorner\phi'x'\psi_1 {}^\iota \ldots {}^\iota\psi_n\urcorner$, where ϕ, ψ_1, $\ldots$, ψ_n can be complex. Now either $n = 0$, so that this occurrence of $'x'$ is already terminal to ς, or else the occurrence can be maneuvered into terminal position as follows. By (9), the beginning $\ulcorner\phi'x'\psi_1\urcorner$ of ς can be rendered $\ulcorner R'\phi'\psi_1'x\urcorner$, so that ς becomes

$$\ulcorner R'\phi'\psi_1'x'\psi_2'\psi_3' \ldots {}^\iota\psi_n\urcorner.$$

By (9) again, the beginning $\ulcorner R'\phi'\psi_1'x'\psi_2\urcorner$ of this can be rendered $\ulcorner R'(R'\phi'\psi_1)'\psi_2'x\urcorner$. So ς as a whole has now become:

$$\ulcorner R'(R'\phi'\psi_1)'\psi_2'x'\psi_3'\psi_4' \ldots {}^\iota\psi_n\urcorner.$$

Continuing thus, we push the occurrence of $'x'$ until it terminates the whole formula.

Such is the proof of

Lemma 1. If ς lacks $'\lambda'$ and has a superficial occurrence of $'x'$, then, roughly speaking, *that occurrence can be worked around to the end;* accurately speaking, *ς is equivalent to a term of the form $\ulcorner\eta'x\urcorner$* lacking $'\lambda'$ and lacking any added occurrences of variables.

This lemma was a matter of using the combinator R to push a superficial occurrence of $'x'$. The next is a matter of using Z to surface an occurrence of $'x'$.

Lemma 2. If ζ lacks 'λ' and contains 'x', then some occurrence of 'x' is superficial or, roughly speaking, *can be rendered superficial;* accurately speaking, ζ is equivalent to a term containing a superficial occurrence of 'x' and no 'λ' nor any added occurrences of variables.

Proof. An occurrence of 'x' in ζ is enclosed by, say, k pairs of parentheses. Say the term occupying the innermost pair is θ. The occurrence of 'x' is superficial in θ; so, by Lemma 1, θ becomes $\ulcorner \eta'x \urcorner$. This parenthetical expression $\ulcorner (\eta'x) \urcorner$ is situated subject to some functional application, $\ulcorner \phi'(\eta'x) \urcorner$; and this latter can, by (8), be rendered $\ulcorner Z'\phi'\eta'x \urcorner$, thus extricating the '$x$' from one of the k pairs of parentheses. By k such steps we bring 'x' to the surface.

Observe now how the two lemmas combine. If a term ζ contains occurrences of 'x' and none of 'λ', we can assure by Lemma 2 that an occurrence of 'x' is superficial; and then by Lemma 1 we can render it terminal, so that ζ reduces to the form $\ulcorner \eta'x \urcorner$. Then we reduce η similarly to the form $\ulcorner \theta'x \urcorner$, so that ζ becomes $\ulcorner \theta'x'x \urcorner$ and so, by (10), $\ulcorner W'\theta'x \urcorner$. This last has fewer occurrences of 'x' than ζ had, and one of them is terminal. Iteration of this process assures

Lemma 3. Any term lacking 'λ' and containing 'x' is reducible to the form $\ulcorner \eta'x \urcorner$ where η lacks 'λ' and 'x'.

Now we are ready to attend to 'λ'. Consider $\ulcorner \lambda_x\zeta \urcorner$, where ζ itself lacks 'λ'. By Lemma 3 we convert ζ to $\ulcorner \eta'x \urcorner$ where η lacks 'λ' and 'x'. But $\ulcorner \lambda_x(\eta'x) \urcorner$ is equivalent to η alone. In this way, given any term at all, we can eliminate each of its innermost 'λ's, and so, continuing outward, eliminate all its 'λ's. Such is our theorem.

Elimination of 'λ' means elimination of bound variables, since only 'λ' binds variables. Elimination of bound variables means also, in a way, elimination of free variables, since open expressions are wanted ultimately only for embedding in closed ones. So our vocabulary is down now to just the three constant terms 'S', 'C', and 'ι' and the inverted comma and parentheses of functional application. This, we see, is adequate for logic and set theory and hence for mathematics generally. This is Schönfinkel's result, except in detail. The detail is that he used something else instead of 'ι'.

Schönfinkel was the first to reduce analysis to algebra. He was the first to analyze the variable, by showing how to translate it contextually into constant terms. But his treatment is less pure than one could wish; it analyzes the variable only in combination with a function theory that is in effect general set theory.

5

Toward a Calculus of Concepts

In a paper of 1936 under the above title,[4] I showed how quantification could be dealt with in algebraic terms less powerful than Schönfinkel's. In calling the envisaged algebra a calculus of concepts, I was using the unhappy term 'concept' generally to cover truth values, classes, and relations. The truth values, two in number, were concepts of degree 0. Classes of individuals of some supposedly preassigned domain were concepts of degree 1. Relations of those individuals were concepts of degree 2 and higher, according as the relations were dyadic, triadic, etc. The degrees were mutually exclusive even to their null elements; the null concept of degree 0 was the truth value $\perp$, the null element of degree 1 was the null class, and so on up. The concepts were the elements of the envisaged algebra, the values of the free variables, which I shall now render 'X', 'Y', etc. Individuals figured only in the informal explanations.

I shall continue for a while to speak of X, Y, etc. as concepts, rather than as classes of sequences, for two weak reasons. One is that in this calculus the null concepts of different degrees are viewed as different. The other is that sequences of different lengths are not allowed under the same concept.

For any concepts X and Y of degrees m and n there was the *Cartesian product* $X \times Y$ of degree $m + n$, comprising all the sequences obtainable by concatenating sequences belonging to X with sequences belonging to Y. Further I assumed the Boolean *complement*, yielding, for each concept X of degree n, the complementary concept $-X$ of degree n. Further there was the *image*. Where the degrees of X and Y are 2 and 1, the image $X"Y$ has the familiar meaning: it is the class of all the things that bear the relation X to members of Y. Where X is of degree $m + n$ and Y is of degree n, more generally, $X"Y$ comprises all sequences $\langle x_1, \ldots, x_m \rangle$ such that $\langle x_1, \ldots, x_m, y_1, \ldots, y_n \rangle$ is in X for some sequence $\langle y_1, \ldots, y_n \rangle$ in Y.

A fourth and last operation was a *duplicating* operation, written 'I' but not to be confused with Schönfinkel's identity function.[5] Where

---

[4] "Toward a calculus of concepts", *Journal of Symbolic Logic* 1 (1936), 2–25. See also my abstract in the *Bulletin of the American Mathematical Society* 41 (1935), 338.

[5] I presented these four operations explicitly as basis in "Concepts of nega-

X is of degree n, IX comprises all sequences $\langle x_1, \ldots, x_n, x_1, \ldots, x_n \rangle$ such that $\langle x_1, \ldots, x_n \rangle$ is in X.

My present expository use of the sequence notation and the lower case variables 'x_1', 'x_2', 'y_1', etc. is foreign to the calculus of concepts itself. So are the symbols 'T' and '$\perp$' and the talk of degree. The notation of the calculus of concepts comprises only the capital letters for concept variables and the symbols for Cartesian product, complement, image, and duplication.

For a representatively devious example of the construction of other notions from these four, consider in its generalized form the notion of a *converse* of a relation. Where the degree of X is n, one of the $n - 1$ converses of X comprises the transposed sequences $\langle x_{i+1}, \ldots, x_n, x_1, \ldots, x_i \rangle$ such that $\langle x_1, \ldots, x_n \rangle$ is in X; and X has a different such converse for each $i < n$. But in fashioning the calculus of concepts I avoided numerals and appealed instead to concept variables themselves as measures of degree. So, instead of specifying this converse of X as the one that comes of breaking after the ith place, I specified it as the converse of X that comes of breaking after the degree of some other appropriately chosen concept Y. Nearly enough, the notation was '$\text{Cnv}_Y X$' and its definition was this:

$$(11) \quad ((I - (I(X \times Y)'' - (X \times Y)))''(I - (IY \times -Y)))''X.$$

Let us see why. For simplicity let us suppose the degrees of X and Y to be 2 and 1, and let us then see why (11) gives the familiar converse of X.

It is evident that when Y and Z are of equal degree, the image $IY''Z$ reduces to the Boolean intersection $Y \cap Z$. So, in particular, $IY'' - Y$ is the null concept in the degree of Y; hence the null class, since Y is of degree 1. So $-(IY'' - Y)$ is the universal class; call it V^1. Similarly, since $X \times Y$ is of degree 3,

$$-(I(X \times Y)'' - (X \times Y)) = V^3.$$

So (11) boils down to $(IV^{3''}IV^1)''X$. But IV^3 comprises all sequences of the form $\langle x, y, z, x, y, z \rangle$, and IV^1 comprises all pairs $\langle y, z \rangle$ such that $y = z$; so the image $IV^{3''}IV^1$ comprises all sequences of the form $\langle x, y, z, x \rangle$ such that $y = z$. In short, $IV^{3''}IV^1$ comprises all sequences of the form $\langle x, y, y, x \rangle$. But then the image $(IV^{3''}IV^1)''X$, in turn,

tive degree", *Proceedings of the National Academy of Sciences* 22 (1936), 40–45. In "Toward a calculus of concepts" I compacted three of the four artificially and uninterestingly into a single two-place operation.

comprises all pairs $\langle x, y \rangle$ such that $\langle y, x \rangle$ is in X; and this is just the familiar converse of X that we hoped (11) would give.

Let us next consider how to translate a schema of the ordinary logic of quantification, say:

$$(12) \qquad (x)\,(Fx \supset (\exists y)\,(Fy \cdot Gxy)),$$

into the calculus of concepts. With the predicate letters 'F' and 'G' changed to concept variables 'X' and 'Y', this clearly amounts to '$X \subseteq Y``X$'. Moreover, it is evident from the general explanation of image that, when any concepts $X$ and $Z$ are alike in degree, $X``Z$ reduces to a mere truth value: to $\top$ if X and Z overlap, and to $\bot$ otherwise. In other words, '$X``Z$' becomes a statement to the effect that $X$ overlaps $Z$. So '$X \subseteq Y``X$', which denies that X overlaps $-(Y``X)$, can be rendered:

$$(13) \qquad -(X``-(Y``X)).$$

Such, then, is a translation of (12) into the calculus of concepts.

However, the same (13) can be reached equally as a translation of any of the further logical schemata of the form:

$$(14)\ (x_1) \ldots (x_n)\,(Fx_1 \ldots x_n \supset (\exists y_1) \ldots (\exists y_n)\,(Fy_1 \ldots y_n \cdot Gx_1 \ldots$$
$$x_n y_1 \ldots y_n)),$$

including even the case, '$p \supset pq$', where n is 0. (13) can even be reached as a translation of certain non-sentential terms for classes and relations, e.g.:

$$\{z: (x)\,(Fzx \supset (\exists y)\,(\exists w)\,(Fyw \cdot Gxyw))\}$$

and in fact all of this form:

$$(15) \qquad \{x_1 \ldots x_m: (x_{m+1}) \ldots (x_n)\,(Fx_1 \ldots x_n \supset (\exists y_1) \ldots$$
$$(\exists y_n)\,(Fy_1 \ldots y_n \cdot Gx_{m+1} \ldots x_n y_1 \ldots y_n))\}.$$

The sentential cases (14) are merely the cases of (15) where $m = 0$.

Thus the calculus of concepts diverges from the ordinary logic of quantification in its aloofness from details of degree. Predicate letters in the schemata of quantification logic are of visible degree, shown by the number of appended variables, whereas degree in the calculus of concepts is left open. I proved in effect[6] that the logic of quantification and identity was translatable into the calculus of con-

---

[6] In "Toward a calculus of concepts". Anyone consulting that paper should be warned that 'α', 'β', etc. there play the role of my present 'X', 'Y', etc., whereas 'X', 'Y', etc. there range over sequences.

cepts to within this latitude of indeterminacy. It would have been natural and easy to add indices of degree to my concept variables and thus fix translation in full; but at the time I was more interested in the abstraction.

I devised no definitive proof procedure for the calculus of concepts. If one were to be devised, it should be devised for proving as theorems not just the formulas that come out true for all values of their concept variables, but all the formulas that designate universal concepts V^n for all values of their variables. This policy is wanted because of what was illustrated by (15) in relation to (13): in omitting degree we suppress any general distinction between sentential formulas and others. Some forms are unequivocally sentential, notably '$X"X$', but most are not.

A curious simplification of the calculus of concepts comes of admitting concepts of negative degree, as I showed in my paper of that title. Cartesian multiplication can thereupon be dropped as a primitive operation, for $X \times Y$ becomes definable as $X"((Y"Y)"Y)$; and the laws undergo a similarly gratifying reduction. But I never thought of a natural or interesting interpretation of negative degree.

The calculus of concepts contrasts with Schönfinkel's scheme in retaining free variables. These may indeed be reassessed as schematic letters (cf. Sec. 8 below), but they are not eliminable in favor of constants; for besides them there are only the four operation signs, which cannot make formulas by themselves. 'C', 'S', and 'ι', in contrast, were terms, proper names of three abstract objects; they were complete formulas as they stood, and they gave rise to the rest of Schönfinkel's formulas through functional application to one another, unaided by variables or schematic letters.

A related and more profound contrast is that we are not faced in the calculus of concepts with a runaway ontology, as Schönfinkel was. A denumerable universe of concepts would suffice, finite for each degree and denumerable over all.

6
Cylindrical Algebra

In 1951 and thereafter, Tarski and his pupils developed what they called *cylindrical algebra*.[7] Its elements are classes of infinite se-

---

[7] Alfred Tarski and F. B. Thompson, abstracts in *Bulletin of the American Mathematical Society* 58 (1952), 65f; Leon Henkin, "The representation

quences of the individuals of some domain. Its universe is, so to speak, the missing degree ω of the calculus of concepts and that only.

The algebra is presented as presupposing the usual Boolean algebra of classes along with the usual truth-function logic. It uses free variables for classes—let us say the letters 'X', 'Y', etc. In addition there are infinitely many constants 'd_{11}', 'd_{12}', etc., explained thus: d_{ij}, called a *diagonal element*, is the class of all infinite sequences whose ith and jth places match. Finally there are infinitely many operators 'C_1', 'C_2', etc. upon classes of sequences, and they are explained thus: C_iX, called a *cylindrification* of the class X, is the class that comprises all the sequences in X and, in addition, all the sequences obtainable from them by ringing changes on the ith place.

Toward seeing how this bears on quantification, think back on the concept of satisfaction in Tarski's *Wahrheitsbegriff*.[8] Suppose a quantificational language of the familiar sort, with its infinite alphabet of quantifiable variables 'w', 'x', 'y', 'z', 'w'', etc. A sequence of objects satisfies an open sentence ϕ of this language if ϕ comes out true when the first object of the sequence is assigned as value of 'w', and the second as value of 'x', and so on through the alphabet. Let X be the class of all the infinite sequences that thus satisfy ϕ. Now quantify ϕ existentially, using say 'y', the third variable of the alphabet. What sequences will satisfy $\ulcorner (\exists y)\phi \urcorner$? All those in X and more: all those that can be got from sequences in X by ringing changes on the third place. Thus the class of sequences satisfying $\ulcorner (\exists y)\phi \urcorner$ will be C_3X.

Such is the link between cylindrification and existential quantification. A more extended argument would of course be needed to show that cylindrical algebra fully accommodates the usual quantification theory. Indeed there is a difficulty in the way of showing this; for cylindrical algebra, like the calculus of concepts, preserves a certain abstractness in relation to the number of places in predicates.

Bernays, however, takes the further step of resolving this ab-

---

theorem for cylindrical algebras", in Thoralf Skolem et al., *Mathematical Interpretations of Formal Systems* (Amsterdam: North-Holland, 1955), 85–97. A somewhat similar plan has been advanced by P. R. Halmos under the name of "polyadic algebra" in his "Algebraic logic (II)", *Fundamenta Mathematicae* 43 (1956), 255–325.

[8] Alfred Tarski, "Der Wahrheitsbegriff in den formalisierten Sprachen", *Studia Philosophica* 1 (1935 for 1936), 261–405. Translation in Tarski, *Logic, Semantics, Metamathematics* (Oxford: Clarendon, 1956).

stractness by attaching numerical indices to the class variables, thus: 'X^1', 'Y^2', 'Z^1', etc.[9] True, the classes already all have the uniform degree ω, in the sense of being classes of sequences of that length. But what Bernays's indices indicate rather is *effective* degree, in this sense: a class is of degree n if only the first n places of sequences are relevant to it. That is, whenever two sequences are alike in their first n places, they are both in the class or both out. Bernays admits classes only of finite degree, in *this* sense, as values of variables. Note that, by this definition, degree is cumulative; classes of degree n are of all degrees $m > n$. Thus modified, cylindrical algebra is shown by Bernays to afford full translation of the ordinary logic of quantification and identity.

Limitation of the elements of cylindrical algebra to classes of finite degrees in this sense gives what Tarski and his pupils call *locally finite* cylindrical algebra. Once this limitation is adopted, no further power is lost by forgetting infinite sequences and simply viewing X^n as a class of sequences of length n. Degree ceases to be cumulative, and becomes substantially what it was in the calculus of concepts. There is the difference, though, that the null relations now all boil down to the null class. As for whether a class should now admit sequences of unlike lengths, this is really a question of style; but the negative decision seems more convenient. We can still get the benefits of any such mixed class by just thinking of its short members as prolonged in all possible ways to gain uniformity of length.

Bernays presents another algebra following this latter line. Its primitive ideas differ from those of cylindrical algebra. They are as follows. There is Boolean algebra as before, and there are the truth functions. Further there is the Cartesian product $X^m \times Y^n$. There is a class constant 'I' (that overworked letter), now designating the identity relation; that is, the class of degree 2 comprising all pairs $\langle x, x \rangle$. There is an infinite lot of *permutation functors* 'p_{11}', 'p_{12}', etc.; where $i, j \leqq n$, $p_{ij}X^n$ is the class of all the sequences obtainable from those in X^n by switching their ith and jth places.

Finally there is a *cropping* functor which has the effect of decapitating all the sequences in a class X^{n+1}, leaving a class of degree n which I shall refer to as $\mathbf{l}X^{n+1}$. Its members are the sequences $\langle x_1,$ $\ldots, x_n \rangle$ such that, for some x_0, $\langle x_0, \ldots, x_n \rangle$ belongs to X^{n+1}. My sym-

[9] Paul Bernays, "Ueber eine natürliche Erweiterung des Relationenkalküls," in A. Heyting, ed., *Constructivity in Mathematics* (Amsterdam: North-Holland, 1959), 1–14.

bol is meant to connote excision of the left column of X^{n+1}. Later we shall see an inverse functor of *padding*, $\mathsf{C}X^n$, which adds a left column to produce a class of degree $n+1$.

Bernays refers to the class $\mathsf{J}X^{n+1}$ rather as DX^{n+1} and calls the operation *Domainbildung*. One apparent reason is that $\mathsf{J}X^2$, or DX^2, is what Whitehead and Russell called the converse domain of the relation X^2. E.g., where X^2 is the love relation, $\mathsf{J}X^2$ is the class of the loved. Another reason is that, where the relation X^2 is a function, $\mathsf{J}X^2$ is its domain commonly so called: the class of its arguments. Tarski has called the operation *projection*, which is very much its geometrical force. Thus consider a class X^3 of triples $\langle x, y, z \rangle$. Each such triple can be viewed as the point having x, y, z as its coordinates in 3-space, and the class X^3 can be a solid composed of such points. The class $\mathsf{J}X^3$ then abstracts from the first of these dimensions—height, say. $\mathsf{J}X^3$ then is the two-dimensional shadow of X^3; it is the plane figure composed of those points $\langle y, z \rangle$ lying directly beneath points $\langle x, y, z \rangle$ of X^3.

7
Some Economies

Bernays notes that Cartesian multiplication becomes dispensable as soon as, with Tarski, we reconstrue each class X^n by prolonging its n-length sequences *ad infinitum* in all ways. For, you can thereupon explain $X^1 \times Y^1$ as $X^1 \cap p_{12}Y^1$; and the trick is easily generalized to $X^m \times Y^n$, which becomes

$$(16) \qquad X^m \cap p_{1(m+1)}p_{2(m+2)} \ldots p_{n(m+n)}Y^n.$$

Observe, however, that we can use this same trick without confessing to infinite sequences and without turning back to cumulative degrees. We can get the same effect while continuing to think of X^n as strictly a class of n-length sequences, if we just embellish the interpretations of '$\cap$' and 'p_{ij}' a bit. Instead of recognizing $X^m \cap Y^n$ only where $m = n$, as Bernays had done, we can recognize it generally; we can take it as the class of all sequences in X^m that begin with sequences in Y^n, or vice versa, according as $m \geqq n$ or $m \leqq n$. Instead of recognizing $p_{ij}X^n$ only where i, $j \leqq n$, as Bernays had done, we can recognize it generally. When $i \leqq n < j$, we can take it as $p_{ij}X^j$ where X^j is the class of all the j-length sequences that begin with sequences in X^n; that is,

$$(17) \langle x_1, \ldots, x_{i-1}, y, x_{i+1}, \ldots, x_{j-1}, x_i \rangle \, \epsilon \, p_{ij}X^n \cdot \equiv \cdot \langle x_1, \ldots, x_n \rangle \, \epsilon \, X^n.$$

Correspondingly, of course, when $j \leqq n < i$. Where $i, j > n$, finally, $p_{ij}X^n = X^n$. So now we are as free as Tarski to define $X^m \times Y^n$ away as (16).

Further economy can be gained by reviving Frege's idea of sentences as names of the truth values, and viewing the truth values as classes of degree 0. This enables us to treat existential quantifications more uniformly. The formula '$(\exists y)(\exists x)(\langle x, y \rangle \, \epsilon \, X^2)$' of ordinary notation would go over into Bernays's algebra in two dissimilar steps as follows: first to '$(\exists y)(y \, \epsilon \, \mathfrak{z}X^2)$' and then to '$\mathfrak{z}X^2 \neq \Lambda$'. Our new plan allows two uniform steps, issuing in '$\mathfrak{z}\mathfrak{z}X^2$', which counts as sentential because the degree is 0. Moreover, this new plan assimilates negation and conjunction to Boolean complementation and intersection. The two truth functions become merely the zero cases, $-X^0$ and $X^0 \cap Y^0$. The Boolean '$\subseteq$' and '$=$' are dispensable too, since '$X^n \subseteq Y^n$' comes down to '$\sim\mathfrak{z}\mathfrak{z} \ldots \mathfrak{z}(X^n \cap -Y^n)$' and '$X^n = Y^n$' comes down to '$X^n \subseteq Y^n \cdot Y^n \subseteq X^n$'. So the whole auxiliary apparatus of Boolean algebra and truth functions boils down now to '$-X^n$' and '$X^n \cap Y^n$' for the various $n \geqq 0$. This is not to say that the idea of individual identity drops out; it is with us in 'I'.

Further economy can be gained in the permutation functors. Far from needing Bernays's infinite lot, viz. 'p_{ij}' for each i and j, we can get all rearrangements of n things using just Bernays's 'p_{12}' together with a functor 'P' which puts the first thing last. I shall write 'p_{12}' simply as 'p' hereafter, and call it the *minor* permutation functor. It switches the first two places of sequences. 'P' I shall call the *major* permutation functor.

Toward showing the adequacy of these two, I shall begin by showing merely that they suffice to bring one arbitrary element of a sequence to the front without disturbing the others. Given $\langle 1, 2, \ldots, n \rangle$ and $i < n$, we want

(18) $$\langle i + 1, 1, 2, \ldots, i, i + 2, \ldots, n \rangle.$$

By i applications of 'P' we turn $\langle 1, 2, \ldots, n \rangle$ into $\langle i + 1, \ldots, n, 1, \ldots i \rangle$. Next, by a maneuver consisting of a step first of 'p' and then of 'P', we pull out the second element here (namely $i + 2$) and banish it to the end, getting

$$\langle i + 1, i + 3, \ldots, n, 1, \ldots, i, i + 2 \rangle.$$

Iterated $n - i - 1$ times, this maneuver delivers (18). Let us crystallize this observation in a convention of abbreviation, as follows: '$p_i X^n$' will stand for a string of $n - i - 1$ alternating repetitions of 'P' and 'p', followed by a string of i occurrences of 'P', followed by 'X^n'. Succinctly,

(19)   'p_iX^n' for ' $(Pp)^{n-i-1}P^iX^n$'.

Thus p_iX^n is the class of sequences resulting from those in X^n by bringing the $i + 1$st elements to the front. The reason I write 'p_i' for the transfer of the $i + 1$st element, rather than of the ith, is just not to waste 'p_1'. The subscript says how many places are leaped.

It is easy now to see how to get any desired permutation. Pick out, in the given sequence, the element that is destined for last place in the desired rearrangement, and bring it to the front, if it is not already there. Then do the same for the element that is destined for next-to-last place. At most n such applications of 'p_i', for the appropriate choices of i, suffice to build up the desired order from back to front.

We have now seen that 'P' and 'p' suffice for Bernays's $p_{ij}X^n$ wherever $i, j \leqq n$. We still have to provide for the odd case (17) where $i \leqq n < j$. (The further cases $j \leqq n < i$ and $i, j > n$, we saw, add nothing.) This can be covered by adding one more functor, the *padding* functor '$\mathfrak{c}$'. $\mathfrak{c}X^n$ is to be V $\times X^n$, hence the class of all sequences $\langle x_0, \ldots, x_n \rangle$ such that $\langle x_1, \ldots, x_n \rangle \, \epsilon \, X^n$. For note to begin with that the Cartesian product $X^n \times$ V is P$\mathfrak{c}X^n$. By applying the pair of functors 'P$\mathfrak{c}$' to X^n repeatedly, then, indeed $j-n$ times, we get what I called X^j two pages back where I was preparing to state (17). But we noted at the beginning of the present paragraph that 'P' and 'p' suffice for 'p_{ij}' in the application $p_{ij}X^j$. The result is precisely the $p_{ij}X^n$ of (17).

Let us ponder the relation of padding to cropping. Cropping is the inverse of padding; $\mathfrak{Jc}X^n = X^n$. Padding is an inverse of cropping; in general $X^n \subseteq \mathfrak{cJ}X^n$. Geometrically, just as $\mathfrak{J}X^3$ may be seen as the projection of the solid X^3 upon a chosen plane, so $\mathfrak{c}X^2$ comprises all the points that would project onto the plane figure X^2. $\mathfrak{c}X^2$ is the infinite right cylinder whose plane cross-section is X^2. Yet $\mathfrak{c}X^2$ is not Tarski's cylindrification. The latter—if for the sake of comparison we descend from Tarski's $\aleph_0$ dimensions to three—is an operation that carries solids into solids rather than plane figures into solids; it cylindrifies around a preexisting protuberance. The operation expressed by '$\mathfrak{c}$' might be distinguished from Tarski's cylindrification by the name of *hypercylindrification,* in allusion to the adding of a dimension, just as we speak of hypercubes, hyperspheres, etc. in 4-space. But the terms 'cropping' and 'padding' are the ones that become graphic when, turning away from geometry, we think of a class X^n rather as an n-column stack of sequences.

We saw, awhile back, how Tarski's cylindrification corresponded to existential quantification. We saw later how cropping, '$\mathbf{J}$', corresponded to existential quantification. Yet the two seem opposed; cropping is the inverse of hypercylindrification. I mention this as a curiosity.

My modification of Bernays's modification of Tarski's cylindrical algebra, then, has just these primitive notations: the Boolean functors '$-$' and '$\cap$', the cropping and padding functors '$\mathbf{J}$' and '$\mathbf{C}$', the permutation functors 'P' and 'p', the class constant 'I', and the free class variables with their indices. It is easy to compute the degree of a class specified in these terms, and to see when it goes to 0. The degree of $-X^n$, pX^n, and PX^n is n. The degree of $X^m \cap Y^n$ is $\max(m, n)$. The degree of $\mathbf{J}X^{n+1}$ is n and that of $\mathbf{C}X^n$ is $n + 1$. The degree of I is 2.

Schönfinkel's convention of parentheses, (3) above, reflects an important formal difference between his scheme and the present one. My '$-$', 'p', 'P', '$\mathbf{J}$', and '$\mathbf{C}$' offer scope for no such convention, for they are not names of functions. They are not terms at all, but functors, mere markers of operations. They attach to the ensuing term to produce a complex term which is accessible to further operations; they are not themselves operated upon. For them the association is unswervingly to the right, without benefit of convention or parentheses. What I am saying of this present algebra applies equally of course to Tarski's and Bernays's.

8

Predicate-functor Logic

The universe of the algebra that we have been considering has only to contain I and be closed under the Boolean operations, the permutations, cropping, and padding. A denumerable universe of classes, finite for each degree, is not too poor for these conditions. In fact there is no longer any need to view this algebra in set theoretic terms at all, however modest. This is not to say that it can be treated as an abstract algebra; that would be a trivial remark. My point is rather that we can treat these so-called free class variables simply as schematic predicate letters, on a par with those of the ordinary logic of quantification. We can rewrite 'X^n', 'Y^n', etc. as 'F^n', 'G^n', etc.: as schematic letters for n-place predicates or, where $n = 0$, for sentences.

There is no thought any longer of reference to classes nor to truth values. The functors '$-$', '$\cap$', 'p', 'P', '$\jmath$', and 'Γ' become functors on predicates and sentences, yielding predicates and sentences. 'I' becomes a two-place identity predicate, tantamount to '$=$'. We come to be doing what we may call *predicate-functor logic*.

When we thus shift our attitude, we find that our notation of predicate-functor logic is *just* adequate to the ordinary logic of quantification and identity; it goes no farther. I will now show how the translation proceeds, forwards and backwards.

Since Bernays has shown how his algebras accommodate the ordinary logic of quantification and identity, and I have shown how mine accommodates his, it is not strictly necessary now to show how to translate that ordinary logic into predicate-functor logic. Still I shall do so. To this end it will be convenient to adopt three conventions of abbreviation. One of them was already seen in (19), but should now be put thus:

$$\text{'}p_i F^n\text{' for '}(\text{P}p)^{n-i-1}\text{P}^i F^n\text{'}.$$

One of them restores the notation of the Cartesian product, thus:

$$\text{'}F^m \times G^n\text{' for '}F^m \cap \ \Gamma\Gamma \ldots \Gamma G^n\text{'}$$

to m occurrences of 'Γ'. The remaining one introduces the self functor:

$$\text{'}SF^n\text{' for '}\jmath(I \cap F^n)\text{'}.$$

To say that $SF^n x_2 x_3 \ldots x_n$ is to say that $F^n x_2 x_2 x_3 \ldots x_n$. I use the letter '$S$' because this functor is a generalization of the self functor so written by Peirce; there is no connection with Schönfinkel's S as of (2) above.

I propose to show that if a schema of the ordinary logic of quantification and identity is closed, that is, if it has no free variables of the quantifiable sort 'w', 'x', etc., then it can be translated into predicate-functor logic. Given any such schema, we begin by turning it into a certain normal form as follows. Translate all universal quantifiers into existential quantification and negation. Translate the scope of each innermost existential quantifier into alternational normal form and distribute the quantifier through the alternation. Thereupon each innermost quantifier comes to govern, at worst, a conjunction of atomic formulas with or without negation signs attached to them. Rewrite each identity using the predicate 'I'; '$x = y$' becomes 'Ixy'. Rewrite the negation sign '$\sim$' now as '$-$' each time, thus thinking of it as applying no longer to the atomic formulas but to the predicates, and as expressing the Boolean complement. Thus adjusted, the expression following each innermost quantifier is just a simple predication such as 'Ixy', '$-Iyz$', 'F^3zyz', '$-F^3xyz$', etc., or a conjunction of such. Next, if it is a conjunction, merge it into a single predication by forming the Cartesian product of the predicates and concatenating the strings of variables. For instance the conjunction:

$$-Iyz \cdot F^3zyz \cdot -F^3xyz$$

becomes:

$$(-I \times F^3 \times -F^3)\,yzzyzxyz.$$

So now each innermost quantifier governs just a single predication. Next we bring 'p_i' to bear upon this Cartesian product so as to permute the string of variables. The permutation wanted is that which brings all recurrences of the variable of the quantifier leftward. If our quantification is '$(\exists y)$' followed by the above example, it becomes:

$$(\exists y)\,p_6p_3\,(-I \times F^3 \times -F^3)\,yyyzzzxz.$$

Next we delete any repetitions of that variable by applying 'S' that many times to the complex predicate. Our example becomes:

$$(\exists y)\,SSp_6p_3\,(-I \times F^3 \times -F^3)\,yzzzxz.$$

Finally, prefixing '$\jmath$' to the complex predicate, we can drop the quantifier and its variable. Our example becomes:

$$\jmath SSp_6p_3\,(-I \times F^3 \times -F^3)\,zzzxz,$$

having once been '$(\exists y)\,(y \neq z \cdot F^3zyz \cdot \sim F^3xyz)$'.

We have now seen how to eliminate each innermost quantifier. Applying this method then to each surviving quantifier as it becomes innermost, we eliminate all quantifiers and hence all bound variables. In particular a closed schema goes over into a formula purely of predicate-functor logic.

Note that this way of translating innermost quantifications uses just these six devices of predicate-functor logic: '$-$', '$\jmath$', 'I', and the defined '$\times$', 'S', and 'p_i'. Nor is any additional provision needed for the truth functions, ultimately negation and conjunction, in which the quantifications may be embedded. For negation, as remarked, is covered by '$-$' in application to formulas of degree 0. Conjunction is similarly covered by '$\cap$', as remarked, but actually '$\cap$' is not needed for the purpose when we have '$\times$'. Applied to formulas of degree 0, '$\cap$' and '$\times$' both collapse to conjunction.

[233]

For translating from ordinary logic, therefore, the above six are a more directly useful stock of primitive notations than the ones we adopted; '×', 'S', and 'p_i' are more directly suited to the purpose than 'ɼ', 'P', 'p', and '∩'. But I would rather be guided by considerations of intrinsic simplicity than by those of ease of translation. I would seek maximum benefit from the shift of system rather than cling to vestiges of the old. The hope of gaining new insights from the shift of viewpoint is thereby increased.[10]

9

Reverse Translation

Translation in the opposite direction, from predicate-functor logic into the ordinary logical notation, is implemented by the following equivalences.

(20) $$-F^n x_1 \ldots x_n \equiv \sim F^n x_1 \ldots x_n.$$

(21) $$(F^m \cap G^n) x_1 \ldots x_{\max(m,n)} \equiv \cdot F^m x_1 \ldots x_m \cdot G^n x \ldots x_n.$$

(22) $$\mathrm{P} F^n x_2 \ldots x_n x_1 \equiv F^n x_1 \ldots x_n.$$

(23) $$\mathrm{p} F^n x_2 x_1 x_3 \ldots x_n \equiv F^n x_1 \ldots x_n.$$

(24) $$\mathbf{C} F^n x_0 \ldots x_n \equiv F^n x_1 \ldots x_n.$$

(25) $$\mathbf{J} F^n x_2 \ldots x_n \equiv (\exists x_1) F^n x_1 \ldots x_n.$$

(26) $$Ixy \equiv \cdot x = y.$$

Since the predicate-functor logic has no variables 'x_1', 'x_2', etc., any sentential formula of that logic will be of one of the forms $(20)-(21)$ with $m = n = 0$ or else (25) with $n = 1$. As we translate it inward by $(20)-(26)$, structure by structure, variables creep in through the 'x_1' position in (25). Example:

(27) $$\mathbf{J}(G^1 \cap \mathbf{J} - \mathrm{p}(H^2 \cap \mathbf{J}K^2)).$$

---

[10] Predicate-functor logic was the burden of my abstract in the *Journal of Symbolic Logic* 24 (1959), 324f, and of my paper "Variables explained away", *Proceedings of the American Philosophical Society* 140 (1960), 343–347, reprinted in my *Selected Logic Papers* (New York: Random House, 1966). In that version I took the Cartesian product and the self functor as primitive, instead of intersection, padding, and 'I'. Also there was a switch of direction: cropping and minor permutation operated on the ends of sequences rather than the beginnings, and major permutation was from right to left. Also the nomenclature and notation were different.

This is a case of (25) with $n = 1$. It becomes:

$$(\exists x)\,(G^1 \cap \mathsf{J} - \mathrm{p}(H^2 \cap \mathsf{J}K^2))\,x.$$

Here we see, after '$(\exists x)$', a case of (21) with $m = n = 1$. It becomes, with '$(\exists x)$' reattached afterward, this:

$$(\exists x)\,(G^1x \cdot \mathsf{J}{-}\mathrm{p}(H^2 \cap \mathsf{J}K^2)x).$$

The part '$\mathsf{J}{-}\mathrm{p}(H^2 \cap \mathsf{J}K^2)x$' here has the form (25), with $n = 2$. By (25), (20), and (23) it becomes:

$$(\exists y)\sim(H^2 \cap \mathsf{J}K^2)xy.$$

Thus the whole becomes:

$$(\exists x)\,(G^1x \cdot (\exists y)\sim(H^2 \cap \mathsf{J}K^2)xy).$$

The part '$(H^2 \cap \mathsf{J}K^2)xy$' here is a case of (21) with $m = 2$ and $n = 1$, and so becomes '$H^2xy \cdot \mathsf{J}K^2x$'. Its part '$\mathsf{J}K^2x$', finally, becomes '$(\exists z)K^2zx$' by (25). So the translation of the whole is:

$$(\exists x)\,(G^1x \cdot (\exists y)\sim(H^2xy \cdot (\exists z)K^2zx)).$$

Since the predicate-functor logic is just intertranslatable with the ordinary logic of quantification and identity, its elimination of variables may be seen as a purer analysis of the variable than Schönfinkel's. Actually both analyses bring out that the essential services of the variable are the permutation of predicate places and the linking of predicate places by identity. The permutation job is discharged in our predicate-functor logic by the functors 'p_i', and the linking job by the self functor 'S'. In Schönfinkel's approach the permutation job was discharged mainly by his combinator S (unrelated to the self functor) and the linking job by the combinator W. But the burden of the variable is less clearly divided and apportioned in Schönfinkel's scheme because his scheme bears so much further burden.

10
Existence and Singular Terms

The existential force of quantification, at any rate, is no essential or distinctive service of the variable; it is carried as well by the cropping functor 'J' and, for that matter, by the Boolean '$\neq \Lambda$'.

Care must be taken here against a possible misunderstanding. When a theory is given the usual quantificational form, the things that the theory accepts as existing are indeed the things that it accepts as the values of its variables of quantification. If a theory is given another form, moreover, there is no sense in asking what the theory accepts as existing except as we are in a position to say how to translate the theory into the usual quantificational form. I have long urged these points, and I continue to. When we switch to predicate-functor logic, such a mode of translation is available; we have just seen it. In the light of it, we find that the things that a theory in predicate-functor form accepts as existing are the things that satisfy its predicates; the things that any of its one-place predicates (complements included!) are true of. But then we note also this special further circumstance: the things that a theory in the usual quantificational form accepts as existing could *also* be described as the things that satisfy its predicates (and their complements). These are the same as the values of the quantified variables, for a theory in the usual quantificational form. So the characterization in terms of satisfaction of predicates does have the advantage of applying equally and outright to theories in quantificational form and theories in predicate-functor form, without having to be funneled through a translation.

It is well known that theories in ordinary quantificational form can get along without any singular terms beyond the variables of quantification. A name, say 'a', can be dispensed with in favor of a predicate 'A' that is true uniquely of the object a; for we can then paraphrase 'Fa' as '$(\exists x)(Fx \cdot Ax)$'. Complex singular terms can be dispensed with in a somewhat similar fashion. Practically the move is a poor one, since it sacrifices the natural and convenient steps of inference that consist in direct substitution of names and complex terms for variables. Theoretically it is of interest, as simplifying certain systematic formulations.

The elimination of quantifiers and their variables which the predicate-functor logic achieves is not, it will be noted, an elimination by restoration of names or other singular terms. Schönfinkel's procedure depended indeed on constant abstract singular terms, which named functions; but predicate-functor logic does not. There are no singular terms any more—neither variables nor the constants that might have been substituted for them. So what becomes of a theory's names, one may ask, when the theory is put into predicate-functor form? First they are dropped in favor of predicates, as just explained; 'a' in favor of 'A'. Then these predicates survive under the predicate-functor plan. What had been *one* way of handling names,

[236]

and a way having only theoretical interest, comes now to be *the* way. '*Fa*' goes into the predicate-functor idiom as '$\mathbf{J}(F^1 \cap A^1)$', via the intermediate stage '$(\exists x)(Fx \cdot Ax)$'.

It is in keeping with the motivation of the present study that a way of handling names that was of purely theoretical value and practically inconvenient in the quantificational setting should become mandatory in the predicate-functor setting. For the purpose of predicate-functor logic is itself theoretical: a deeper understanding of the variable. There is no thought of forswearing the practical convenience of quantification and the convenience of substituting names and complex singular terms for quantified variables.

11
Proof Procedure

Since the predicate-functor approach to logic differs so radically from the quantificational approach, and since it seems somehow more basic, one wonders how a simple and complete proof procedure for it might look, and what new light it might shed on logic.

Bernays presents axioms for one form of his algebra, and proves that they are complete. He presupposes a usual logic of truth functions, identity, and Boolean equations. To this basis he adds thirteen axioms or axiom schemata, mostly in the form of equations, governing cylindrification, degree, his permutation operators, and *I*.

Our predicate-functor logic calls rather for an autonomous proof procedure, presupposing no prior logic. Instead of undertaking to limit the theorems to schemata of degree 0 whose instances are true sentences, it is convenient to welcome as theorems all schemata of any degree whose instances are predicates satisfied by all sequences of that length.[11] As an infinite initial stock of axiom schemata, then, we may accept all tautologous Boolean functions; that is, all compounds built of '$-$' and '$\cap$' after the pattern of a truth-table tautology in '$\sim$' and '$\cdot$'. A natural rule of inference to adopt is the analogue, in these Boolean terms, of *modus ponens*; viz.,

$$\text{If } \vdash \zeta \text{ and } \vdash \ulcorner \zeta \supset \eta \urcorner \text{ then } \vdash \eta$$

[11] This and other features of the system were anticipated by L. Nolin, "Sur l'algèbre des prédicats", in the colloquium volume *Le Raisonnement en Mathématiques et en Sciences Expérimentales* (Paris: Centre National de la Recherche Scientifique, 1958), 33–37.

where the *implex* $F^m \supset G^n$ is defined as $-(F^m \cap -G^n)$. Further there is this quadruple rule:

If $\vdash \zeta$ then $\vdash \ulcorner p\zeta \urcorner$, $\vdash \ulcorner P\zeta \urcorner$, $\vdash \ulcorner \mathfrak{c}\zeta \urcorner$, and $\vdash \ulcorner -\mathfrak{z}-\zeta \urcorner$.

Also a rule of substitution for predicate letters is wanted, allowing substitution of predicate expressions of any degree for predicate letters of that degree. This rule includes the subsidiary rule, explained earlier, for computing the degree of a complex expression.

Some of the axiom schemata that suggest themselves, in addition to the Boolean tautologies, are these:

$$\mathfrak{z}I, \qquad (I \cap F^n) \supset pF^n, \qquad -\mathfrak{z}F^n \supset \mathfrak{z}-F^n, \qquad F^n \supset \mathfrak{c}\mathfrak{z}F^n.$$

Before stating further ones, it will be convenient to adopt as an abbreviation one more Boolean functor along with '$\supset$'. The *concourse* or symmetric quotient $F^m \# G^n$ is defined as $(F^m \supset G^n) \cap (G^n \supset F^m)$; thus it is $(F^m \cap G^n) \cup (-F^m \cap -G^n)$.[12] Just as '$\supset$' as main connective in an axiom does the work of '$\supset$', so '$\#$' does the work of '$\equiv$' or '$=$'. Provision would be made for a convenient metatheorem allowing replacement, anywhere, of one side of a proved concourse by the other.

Here, then, are some likely further axiom schemata.

$$F^n \# ppF^n, \qquad F^n \# P^nF^n, \qquad F^n \# P\mathfrak{c}F^n, \qquad F^n \# \mathfrak{z}\mathfrak{c}F^n.$$

Also there are these distribution laws, where $m, n > 1$:

$$p-F^n \# -pF^n, \qquad p(F^m \cap G^n) \# (pF^m \cap pG^n),$$

$$P-F^n \# -PF^n, \qquad P(F^n \cap G^n) \# (PF^n \cap PG^n).$$

A straggler to notice, among perhaps others, is '$pF^2 \# PF^2$'. A major agendum is a proof of the completeness of some such proof procedure, or, better, of some other and more instructively unified sort of proof procedure for predicate-functor logic.

---

[12] The names and symbols of the implex and concourse are from my *System of Logistic* (Cambridge: Harvard University Press, 1934).

TWELVE

On Pragmatics,
the Meta-Theory
of Science, and
Subjective Intensions

R. M. MARTIN

IN HIS *The Anatomy of Inquiry*,[1] Israel Scheffler, following Nelson Goodman in essentials, speaks of the "theory of science", or the "theory of scientific structure", as concerned with the problem of providing "a clear and systematic explanation of such terms as 'theory', 'law', 'explains', 'confirms', etc., which are themselves used both in describing the structure of particular scientific domains and in giving an overall structural picture of science." Such an explanation is not given *within* any particular science, and hence is not a "theory" in the same sense that the "theory" of relativity is, or the "theory" of mitosis in *Drosophila melanogaster*. It is rather the *meta*-theory of these and other areas of science of which Scheffler is speaking.

---

[1] New York: Alfred A. Knopf, 1963.

The meta-theory of science divides, conveniently and by common consent, into syntax, semantics, and pragmatics. Syntax tends to be rather cut-and-dried, being concerned exclusively with signs and their interrelations. Semantics divides into the theory of reference and the theory of meaning, and Scheffler wisely stays clear, for the most part, of the latter. Precisely what form the theory of reference takes that he is apparently using or presupposing, however, is not too clear. The word 'true' plays an important role in much of his discussion, but no hint is given as to how it is to be defined or otherwise characterized. Surely, however, an adequate characterization is sorely needed if we are to gain a clear "overall structural picture of science."

The theory of reference is intimately bound up with the topic of ontic commitment. Roughly we are ontically committed to the entities over which our variables are allowed to range.[2] Thus the problem of giving a suitable "ontological interpretation" of the language in which we talk of explanation, prediction, confirmation, meaningfulness, and the like, is a very basic one for the philosophy of science. "Ontological extravagance," to use Scheffler's apt phrase, is as much to be avoided as are confusion, error, or contradiction.

The exhibition of the logical form of scientific statements is presumably a part of giving an overall structural picture of science. Prior to such exhibition for science in general, is the exhibition for specific sciences. It is rather fashionable to pass over this latter as in some sense not interesting, and to jump ahead as though all problems therein had been adequately solved to the satisfaction of all. This is rarely the case, however, and fascinating and important problems remain as to the forms of significant (atomic) sentences in the special sciences.

When we turn to the *meta*-theory of scientific languages, we have the well-developed tools of semantics. But here too problems emerge as to *precisely* what forms to allow for the meta-sentences. Different forms give rise to very different kinds of meta-theory. Scheffler makes ample use of such notions as *logical truth* and *logical equivalence,* but with scarcely a hint as to how they are to be introduced. There is no reference to Carnap's writings on these, so we may assume that it is

---

[2] See especially W. V. Quine, *Word and Object* (New York and London: The Technology Press of the Massachusetts Institute of Technology and John Wiley and Sons, 1960), 242. See also the author's *Belief, Existence, and Meaning* (New York: New York University Press, 1969).

not to Carnap's *L-concepts* that he is referring.[3] The L-concepts or similar ones loom crucially in his explanation of *explanation* and of other notions, and we must thus be assured that satisfactory definitions are forthcoming in terms that are "philosophically intelligible" or "acceptable." In particular, if these terms are to be applicable to *inscriptions,* and not merely to shapes of expressions, suitable definitions must be given within an inscriptional semantics. It is not clear that such definitions have ever been given.[4]

It is not the aim here to discuss minutiae of Scheffler's essay, but merely to call attention to the very central role that semiotic plays in the philosophy of science. Scheffler rightly insists upon the *systematic* character of the theory or meta-theory of science, which, however, does not come easily but must be dug out of clinging mud. Syntax and semantics have been given a suitable systematic form in various alternative ways. In the author's *Toward a Systematic Pragmatics,*[5] an attempt was made to achieve some semblance of structure in pragmatics, wherein variables over the human users of language are introduced. Whatever its defects or shortcomings, this appears to embody the first fairly extensive effort in this direction.

For minimum clarity, then, in the meta-theory of science, both Goodman and Scheffler would no doubt agree, some hint at formalization is a *sine qua non* both at the object-language and meta-linguistic levels. It is not required that either object- or meta-language be explicitly formulated, so much as that it be reasonably clear how in principle this could be done. And the meta-language must, for both Goodman and Scheffler, include a pragmatics as a part. Presumably the more systematic we are in delineating just what this pragmatics consists of, the better.

In the Appendix to *Toward a Systematic Pragmatics,* the attempt was made to formalize a portion of Goodman's theory of "projectible predicates."[6] The notion of "projectible predicate" is a pragmatic

---

[3] See especially R. Carnap, *Introduction to Semantics* (Cambridge: Harvard University Press, 1946) and *Meaning and Necessity* (Chicago: University of Chicago Press, 1956). See also A. Tarski, *Logic, Semantics, Metamathematics* (Oxford: Clarendon Press, 1956).

[4] See, however, the author's *Truth and Denotation* (Chicago: University of Chicago Press, 1958) and *The Notion of Analytic Truth* (Philadelphia: University of Pennsylvania Press, 1959).

[5] *Studies in Logic and the Foundations of Mathematics* (Amsterdam: North-Holland Pub., 1959).

[6] See his *Fact, Fiction, and Forecast* (Indianapolis: Bobbs-Merrill, 1965).

one, and to get at the structure of the theory concerning it, we ought to be as clear as possible concerning the pragmatics in which it is couched. So far, so good, and to this neither Goodman nor Scheffler would presumably object.

In his "Faulty Formalization",[7] Goodman claimed that the definition of 'projectible predicate' suggested in *Toward a Systematic Pragmatics* is inadequate. The definition made use of 'Acpt' (for ('accepts') as the only pragmatical primitive. "In dealing with projection", however, Goodman urges, "some such notions as 'examine' and 'determine to be true' are needed along with 'accept'." This is a point we need not cavil at this late date, for notions akin to both of these play a significant role in the more extended pragmatics of *Belief, Existence, and Meaning*.

It is gratifying that Goodman finds in the suggested definition even a faulty formalization of one of his notions. One would not have been sure in advance that he would recognize it as providing a formalization of it at all. There were doubts as to whether 'Acpt' even remotely correlates with his use of 'accepts'. There were doubts whether the underlying theory of time-flow supplies what Goodman seems to need. There were doubts concerning the underlying semantics and syntax, and even concerning the object-language L. It seems that Goodman might be willing to consider first-order L's and their syntax —albeit presumably an inscriptional rather than a classical one— but that he would condone the use of semantical notions was not clear. That we have apparently gotten over all these hurdles, with some measure of apparent agreement, seems all to the good. Whatever defects emerge in the actual definitions suggested, we are at any event well on the way to achieving a framework that may be suitable.

Let 'X Tst a,t' express that person X is *testing* a at t in the sense of "examining" it in order to decide whether it is true or not. And let 'X B a,t' express that X believes a at t.[8] Now if a is true and X B a,t, then X presumably has "determined" a to be true. Goodman nowhere tells us very much as to just what 'determines to be true' is supposed to involve. Perhaps, in addition, some reference to the *evidence* for a is needed here. In the testing of a, suitable evidence must be found supporting a to X's satisfaction, at least to some extent. It is not clear, however, that the evidence need be explicitly brought in. If not, we

---

[7] *The Journal of Philosophy* 60 (1963), 578–579.

[8] These are simplified versions of notions discussed in *Belief, Existence, and Meaning*.

can perhaps say that X determines a (at t) to be true if and only if X Tst a,t, X B a,t, and a is true. Actually this is a little too simple, for some allowance should be made for the believing temporally to follow the testing.

If the evidence is to be brought in explicitly, we can let

(1)   'X Tst a,b,t'

express that X tests a at t culminating in the result b. The sentence b may merely restate what a states or state something stronger or weaker than what a states. In any case b is to express the result of the test. Similarly, let

(2)   'X B a,b,t'

express that X believes a on the evidence or "reason" b at t. Then X may be said to determine a as true at t if and only if there is a b such that X Tst a,b,t, X B a,b,t, and a is true. Here too, some allowance for the believing temporally to follow the testing is perhaps desirable.

We have been concerned here only with settling upon suitable logical (or linguistic) *forms* for systematic pragmatics. In general, the settling upon forms is not to be confused with the substantive analysis of what is conveyed or expressed by means of those forms. Essentially this distinction has been articulated by Donald Davidson.[9] Settling upon forms, however, is a necessary first step in analysis, without which the *analysandum* remains forever fleeting.

In systematic pragmatics an extensive theory of *subjective intensions* may be developed. A subjective intension, unlike an *objective* intension, *Sinn*, or meaning, depends upon a person and a time, upon you or me, now or then.[10] In the author's *Intension and Decision*[11] an outline of an integrated theory of intensions was given. Several objections against this have been raised. These divide conveniently into those concerned with subjective intensions (in Chap. II–IV) and with objective intensions (in Chap. V). In four previous papers the attempt has been made to answer in two quite different ways the objections against the latter.[12] Here therefore let us concentrate exclu-

---

[9] See, for example, his "Truth and Meaning," *Synthese* 17 (1967), 304–323.

[10] For an especially clear statement of this, see G. Frege's famous "On Sense and Reference" and "The Thought".

[11] Englewood Cliffs: Prentice-Hall, 1963.

[12] See "An Improvement in the Theory of Intensions", *Philosophical Studies* 18 (1967), 33–37, "On Objective Intensions and the Law of Inverse

sively on the former. John Vickers's comments being the most recent, let us begin with them.[13]

Vickers first remarks that whether "the theory of reference is identical with the theory of meaning or not, a full account of the reference of a class of expressions amounts as well to an account of their meaning." Much depends here upon what a *full* account consists in and what is meant by *identity* as between theories. Alonzo Church's theory of *sense*, for example, is surely not *identical* with a theory of reference, as Vickers suggests, nor is it a "referential theory" in just the sense that W. V. Quine's is, as he explicitly states. Of course names or expressions for senses designate senses just as expressions for classes, relations, or individuals designate respectively given classes, relations, or individuals—but this is a very different matter. Also Vickers claims that "paradigms" of accounts of theories of meaning are "Wittgenstein's account of truth functions, Frege's account of quantification, and Tarski's of the algebra of classes." But Vickers is surely wrong on all three scores. None of these is a theory of *meaning* in any strict sense, nor, for that matter, of reference.

The attempt to give an account of meaning via the notion of synonymy Vickers regards as the *syntactical* approach. But synonymy is *par excellence* a, perhaps *the*, key notion of intensional semantics. It is thus two steps beyond anything that should reasonably be called '*syntactical*'. Let us distinguish clearly syntax from semantics, and in semantics let us distinguish clearly the theory of reference from the theory of intension, sense, and the like. The latter area of semantics may be suitably built up, so we have contended in the papers cited, in terms of the former. But no more need be said about this here.

Once a viable theory of objective intensions, sense, and the like, has been achieved we are then in a position to study belief and other so-called "propositional attitudes". To attempt this latter without the former seems premature. It is to embark upon a voyage with no secure means of transport. In *Belief, Existence, and Meaning* we have attempted such a voyage using a suitable theory of intensions as a

---

Variation", S. Morgenbesser, P. Suppes, M. White, *Philosophy, Science, and Method* (New York: St. Martin's Press, 1969), "On Abstract Entities in Semantic Analysis", *Noûs* 2 (1968), 373–389, and "On Leonardian Intensions of Class-Terms", K. Lambert, ed., *The Logical Way of Doing Things* (New Haven: Yale University Press, 1969). See also *Belief, Existence, and Meaning*, Chap. VII.

13 *The Journal of Philosophy* 64 (1967), 193–200.

vessel. Thus, although this subject was justifiably neglected in *Intension and Decision*, it has not been neglected elsewhere.

Vickers mentions also the "psychological" theory of meaning in which one views "the meaning of an expression as the stimuli or responses that would elicit or be occasioned by it on the part of an appropriately attuned user of the language in which the expression is included." But this approach can boast of no conspicuous successes, he points out, and consists mainly of a "talk program." Is it not so also with other approaches? Vickers takes sides here prematurely, it would seem. A "wait and see" attitude was espoused in *Intension and Decision*. The door to the behavioral theory need not be closed, nor need it be accepted as the only one. Quine's theory is a kind of "blend" of the referential and behavioral, as Vickers points out. But it is misleading of Vickers to say that the theory of *Intension and Decision* is also a blend. Rather there the door is open to the behavioral approach. One can interpret the primitives behaviorily, or at least in part behaviorily, if one wishes, but one is not compelled to do so.

Vickers is incorrect in saying that according to me "the objective intension of an expression is roughly the class of expressions to which it is provably equivalent." The 'roughly' here conceals three errors. The intensions to which he refers are rather what are called '*quasi-intensions*', they are *not* classes, and they do *not* consist of expressions to which the given expression is provably equivalent. Vickers has obviously failed to note the difference between intensions and quasi-intensions, the purpose of the *virtual*-class technique, and the difference between the syntactical notion of provability and the semantical ones of *L-equivalence*.

In his *The Logic of Decision*[14] Richard C. Jeffrey has sketched a mathematical theory of decision that is *unified* in the sense that utility (or *subjective desirability*) and *subjective probabilities* are attributed to the same objects, namely, "propositions". We need not expatiate here against the use of unanalyzed propositions, for the attempt has been made elsewhere to give a rather full analysis of them as intensional constructs of a certain kind.[15] The theory sketched in *Intension and Decision* was likewise unified in essentially the same sense, where the "objects" are rather declarative sentences of some language-system *L* of first order.

Let us consider for a moment Jeffrey's account, where a subjec-

---

[14] New York: McGraw-Hill, 1965.
[15] In *Belief, Existence, and Meaning*, Chap. IX.

tive probability function *prob* and a subjective desirability function *des* play the fundamental roles. Let us adapt these notions as follows. Let

(3) $\text{prob}(a,X,t)$

be the measure of X's subjective probability at time t with respect to the sentence a. And similarly let

(4) $\text{des}(a,X,t)$

be the measure of X's desirability at t that a be true. Jeffrey gives four axioms governing these, to the effect that prob is a non-negative, normalized, and additive function and that $\text{des}((a \; vee \; b),X,t)$ under suitable circumstances depends in a certain way upon the prob and des values for a and b separately. (*'vee'* here is the structural description of 'v' for disjunction.)

Consider now

(5) $\text{prob}(a,X,t) > \text{prob}(b,X,t)$

and

(6) $\text{des}(a,X,t) > \text{des}(b,X,t).$

We have here, in Jeffrey's theory, two possible explicata for *preference*. On the one hand we can say that X prefers a to b at t provided (5). This gives us essentially the notion Prfr of Chapter II of *Intension and Decision*. Let us call this hereafter '*cognitive* preference', 'CogPrfr', so that X CogPrfr a,b,t now if and only if (5). In contrast to this we let 'X ValPrfr a,b,t' express (6). Here the preference is *valuative*. Both notions figure prominently in decision theory, as Jeffrey and others have shown.

Also we let

(7)   'X Acpt a,t,a'

express that $\text{prob}(a,X,t) = a$. Quantitative *acceptance* is thus identified with subjective probability. Also, to complete the inventory, we can let

(8)   'X Dsrbl a,t,a'

express that $\text{des}(a,X,t) = a$. (7) states that X accepts the sentence a at time t to degree a and (8), that X's degree of desirability of a at t is a.

In *Intension and Decision* (7) was introduced in terms of a certain primitive along with 'Prfr' construed in the sense of cognitive preference. Vickers, following Richard Montague,[16] construes it rather in the sense of valuative preference. But surely the very context Vickers quotes states plainly enough the other construal. Vickers's misreading here vitiates most of his subsequent comments.

For a full theory of utility and decision, we should presumably need all four locutions, those providing for (5) and (6) as well as (7) and (8). And of course these must all be appropriately differentiated both axiomatically and empirically. Here we could use Jeffrey's method or some alternative as a guide. In *Intension and Decision*, decision theory was used anyhow merely as a basis for building up the theory of subjective intensions. It was remarked that the particular basis chosen was merely one and that it might not be fully satisfactory. No doubt a better basis is forthcoming in terms of direct primitives 'Acpt' and 'Dsr' taken quantitatively.

It is customary in decision theory to suppress the arguments 'X' and 't' in (3) and (4) and hence in (7) and (8). But of course these must be brought in as soon as more than one person is considered and more than one time. In a general pragmatical meta-language such additional factors are surely needed, even though some notational complications result. One must distinguish between decision theory itself and the logico-philosophic analysis thereof. For this latter the wider resources of a full pragmatical meta-language are surely needed.

Montague, whose discussion Vickers echoes, remarks that my discussion of preference and degree of acceptance "is completely clouded by a failure to distinguish between value and belief" and that I appear "to feel that utility and belief have the same formal properties." But this is of course not the case. It is true that *Intension and Decision* was concerned primarily with the scientist at work, with his official scientific language, and with the relations between the two. In such a context it is not unreasonable to take utility and degree of belief as the same. The special kind of utility which a scientist in his official work has for a given scientific statement *a* should in a reasonable sense be just his degree of belief in it. In other words,

$$(9) \qquad \mathrm{prob}\,(X,a,t) = \mathrm{des}\,(X,a,t),$$

for such X, a, and suitable t. If this fails to hold, we might think the scientist lacking in objectivity, of letting his desires, or rather what he regards as desirable, get in the way of his better judgment. Of

[16] *The Journal of Symbolic Logic* 31 (1966), 98–102.

course one might say here that if (9) fails to hold, it is a matter rather of his judgment getting in the way of what he regards as desirable! In general, however, the des values tend to be more extreme, do they not?, than the prob values. Our des values depend in part surely on our normative valuations, whereas our prob values depend more on the sobrieties of past experience in which our norms are time and again violated.

Also it may be asked: what role anyhow should desirability play within the pragmatic description of the procedures of the scientist and of his relations to language? It is surely not clear *a priori* that it should play any role at all. It plays no part in the pragmatics of mere acceptance—Russell's "bare assent." Yet why not argue against the pragmatics of acceptance that acceptance is there confused with the desirable, just as in *Intension and Decision, degree of acceptance* was supposed to be confused with *degree of desirability?* Happiness, they say, consists in the extinction of desires. At any event the happiness of the scientist, *qua* scientist in his official work, may well be thought to consist in the identification of the values of his prob and des functions. The truth is, after all and however platitudinous it may sound, that which to the scientist is most eminently desirable. It is also that in which he most firmly believes. His degree of acceptance of any statement (in science) should reflect precisely then the extent to which he regards it as true, and this extent in turn is precisely the extent to which it is desirable for him.

Now it was nowhere suggested in *Intension and Decision* that utility and belief have the same formal properties, and it is unfortunate if this impression was given. Rather attention was there confined for the most part to the context in which (9) holds. This is no doubt too narrow a context for general purposes. It would be better to distinguish sharply prob and des and to proceed accordingly, as has already been suggested. And it is no doubt better to distinguish these, even if one wishes still to keep to the context of official scientific parlance.

Now as to the "rationality" of the patterns. It is difficult to be sure when a pattern is rational or not. The attitude of *Intension and Decision* was that all patterns are on a par before the tribunal of logic. There is a vast multiplicity of them, some of some "formal" interest perhaps, others not. Against whatever pattern one picks out and labels 'rational', one can be sure objections can be raised. The attitude in *Intension and Decision* was thoroughly catholic in this respect. If

[248]

you do not like one pattern or its label, either re-label it or formulate another with the same or a new label. And out of the plethora available, some are bound to approximate your favorite intuitive notion of rationality. And some are bound to appear counter-intuitive.[17]

Let us conclude with a few additional words concerning ontic or ontological extravagance, a topic that Goodman has happily and insistently brought to the fore. "A philosophic problem is a call to provide an adequate explanation in terms of an acceptable basis", he writes. "If we are ready to tolerate everything as understood, there is nothing left to explain . . ."[18] A most significant item in the "acceptable basis" is of course its ontic commitment. If we allow the basis to commit us to anything *quodlibet,* there is not much reason to do philosophic analysis, which "hardly exists without its restraints". One is reminded of Nadia Boulanger's dictum that "great art likes chains". Restraints are primarily ontic, notional and postulational restraint depending thereon fundamentally.

The kind of pragmatics discussed throughout is formulated with due attention to ontic restraint. The only serious competitor in the field seems to be that provided in a recent paper by Montague, in which ontic restraint is tossed to the winds.[19] For Montague's pragmatics to work, all manner of excess entities must be condoned: not only sets and models (suspect enough, as mathematical constructivists of all kinds have in effect repeatedly urged), but "possible contexts of use" (as contrasted with actual contexts of use), "complexes of relevant aspects of intended possible contexts of use", "possible objects", "possible interpretations", and therewith "possible worlds," etc., etc. With so vast an array of obscure entities at hand, "we are ready to tolerate everything as understood" and it is not surprising that in terms of them almost anything can be accomplished. The elegant mathematical detail takes the place of philosophical conscience and painstaking analysis. With all "possible worlds" at hand—whatever they are—the complexities of the one actual world or cosmos recede into the background. No "advance in clarification", to use Carl Hempel's apt phrase, is to be gained by such wholesale ontic extravagance. One man's logic is another's mythology, and it is doubtful that

---

[17] A technical discussion of patterns of belief is in preparation.

[18] *Fact, Fiction, and Forecast,* p. 31.

[19] In *La Philosophie Contemporaine,* Vol. I, R. Klibansky, ed. (Florence: La Nuova Italia Editrice, 1968), 102–122.

mythologic pragmatics will help to shed light on the structural problems of natural language for which it is apparently designed.[20]

In this paper (1) the meta-theoretic as well as (2) the pragmatic character of the "overall structural theory of science" has been emphasized, (3) improved foundations for the theory of subjective intensions have been sketched, and (4) attention has been called to the ontological extravagance and subsequent unacceptability of alternative forms for pragmatic theory.

[20] On the usefulness of non-mythologic pragmatics for the study of natural language, see the author's *Logic, Language, and Metaphysics* (New York: New York University Press, 1971).

THIRTEEN

Ambiguity: An Inscriptional Approach

ISRAEL SCHEFFLER

1
Introduction

WHAT IS AMBIGUITY? Under what conditions is a word ambiguous? We all claim a certain practical facility in spotting ambiguities, but the theory of the matter is in a sorry state. Logicians and philosophers typically concern themselves with ambiguity either as a defect in the arguments of others or as a hazard from which their own serious discourse is to be protected. Literary critics, alive to the rhetorical values of ambiguous expression, are not equally sensitive to the philosophical demands for clarity and system. General analytical questions thus remain for the most part unexplored, while commonly repeated explanations suffer from various grave difficulties.

A word is, for example, said to be ambiguous if it has different meanings or senses, or if it stands for different ideas. But ghostly entities such as meanings, senses, or ideas provide no more than the ghost of an explanation unless, as seems unlikely, they can be clearly construed as countable things whose relations to one another and to words are independently determinable. At best, such entities may be regarded as hypostatizations of the content of sets of synonymous expressions, the specification resting on the critically obscure notion of synonymy.

In more concrete vein, a word may be said to be ambiguous in having different dictionary readings, that is, in being correlated with different actual expressions in the dictionary. But which dictionary is to be chosen and how has it been composed? Are the principles by which its readings have been assigned clearly formulable; can we be confident that they themselves make no appeal to the lexicographer's unanalyzed judgments of ambiguity?

Further, we must ask in what the relevant difference of readings consists. Presumably, they are to be not merely different but non-synonymous; the proposed criterion of ambiguity thus presupposes, without providing an answer to the troublesome question of synonymy. Alternatively, it may be suggested that we consider not different actual expressions, but different abstract readings, a reading to be construed now as an intensional entity correlated with a set of synonymous expressions; the individuation of readings again hinges on synonymy, and the postulation of such purported entities takes us back to meanings or senses once more.

Moreover, the criterion at best falls short of providing a sufficient condition, for non-synonymous readings, however construed, may signify generality rather than ambiguity. For the word "caravan", for instance, we find the following two readings:[1]

(i) a group of travelers journeying together through desert or hostile regions.

(ii) a group of vehicles traveling together in a file.

Is it clear that these two readings signify the ambiguity of "caravan" rather than mark out two regions of its general, and unambiguous, application?

Finally, are the expressions representing the readings themselves assumed to be purified of ambiguity? Unless they are, we cannot take the lack of non-synonymous readings for a given word to betoken its freedom from ambiguity. On the other hand, to require the readings themselves to be unambiguous renders the criterion, as a whole, circular.

[1] *The New Merriam-Webster Pocket Dictionary* (New York: Pocket Books, G. & C. Merriam, 1964), 72.

2

Elementary Ambiguity

The proposals just considered have this in common: Between words and denoted things they interpose additional entities as the root of ambiguity—meanings or senses or ideas or readings—entities whose individuation or explanatory role is obscure, involving, at the very least, appeal to the controverted notion of synonymy. Can any progress be made by wiping the slate clean, renouncing such interposition altogether and restricting ourselves to words and ordinary things? In fact, will an inscriptional approach, considering word-tokens only and surrendering the notion of associated abstract types, enable us to advance the analysis of ambiguity? Such an approach has advantages that have shown themselves in other problem areas,[2] and it has one basic advantage: that the entities it requires are also acknowledged by other approaches, so that it presupposes nothing controversial for itself.

A simplified inscriptional account may be sketched, as follows: We treat written tokens only and, among these, attend only to predicate tokens. These, however, are given to us embedded in naturally occurring contexts which enable us, generally, to judge certain of their denotative relations. Then, for any two predicate tokens x and y, we ask:

(i) Are x and y spelled exactly alike, i.e. are they replicas of one another?

(ii) Are x and y extensionally divergent, i.e. does either one denote something not denoted by the other?

Given tokens x and y for which the answers to the above two questions are both positive, we now say they are ambiguous with respect to one another. Further, given simply x, we hold it ambiguous if there is some token y with respect to which it is ambiguous.

This account needs, of course, to be relativized to a discourse D to become effective, for, as it stands, it characterizes x as ambiguous

---

[2] See, for example, N. Goodman and W. V. Quine, "Steps Toward a Constructive Nominalism", *Journal of Symbolic Logic*, 12 (1947), 105–122; Chap. XI of Nelson Goodman, *The Structure of Appearance*, 2nd ed. (Indianapolis: Bobbs-Merrill, 1966); Israel Scheffler, *The Anatomy of Inquiry* (New York: Alfred A. Knopf, 1963), Part I, secs. 6 and 8.

if it has an extensionally divergent replica in some other language or remote context. The condition it sets is far too weak and, hence, satisfied by vastly more (perhaps all) predicate tokens than are ordinarily deemed ambiguous. That x fulfills this condition is compatible with its being perfectly unambiguous within the space of some restricted discourse of interest. We thus amplify the account by adding that x is ambiguous within a containing discourse D if, and only if, it is ambiguous with respect to some token within D.

The proposal just sketched is, to be sure, limited. It restricts itself to predicate tokens, and does not deal with other sorts of word-tokens nor with word-sequences of sentence length or more. It gives no account of syntactic ambiguities, but treats only ambiguity of a semantic sort. Yet it covers an undeniably important variety, of the same sort with which we have, in fact, been concerned from the beginning, and earlier accounts of which we found wanting in our previous discussion. We shall refer to the present proposal as providing an *elementary (inscriptional) notion of ambiguity.*

3
Aspects of Elementary Ambiguity

The idea of the above proposal is set forth by Nelson Goodman from the point of view of a primary interest in indicator terms:

> Roughly speaking, a word is an *indicator* if . . . it names something not named by some replica of the word. This is admittedly broad, including ambiguous terms as well as what might be regarded as indicators-proper, such as pronouns; but delimitation of the narrower class of indicators-proper is a ticklish business and is not needed for our present purposes.[3]

The inclusive category is, from the point of view of our present concerns, that of *ambiguity,* with indicators forming one subgroup of ambiguous terms, roughly distinguishable by the fact that extensional variation across indicator-replicas is related, in a relatively simple, systematic manner, to some contextual feature of these replicas. Thus, an "I" normally refers to its own producer and a "now" to a suitable time period within which its own production lies. Another subgroup is constituted by metaphorical terms, a metaphorical predicate within D roughly characterizable as having therein some replica

[3] *The Structure of Appearance,* p. 362.

with divergent extension related to its own in special ways, the latter literal counterpart providing, in some manner, a clue to application of the former.

Elementary ambiguity, as above explained, is distinguishable from generality in that a token ambiguous within D must diverge extensionally from some replica therein. If no such divergence exists, the fact that a token applies to many things signifies only that it is general, no matter how dissimilar these things may be, by whatever criteria of similarity may be chosen. That a "table" denotes big as well as little tables argues not its ambiguity but only its breadth of applicability. Though difficult to apply in certain instances, the distinction will nevertheless be effective in many others. In a "This book contains a table of contents on page 4", the constituent "table" token diverges extensionally from replicas denoting items of furniture. Philosophical disputes as to whether some critical term, e.g. "exists", *should* be construed as ambiguous, or merely general, hinge on theoretical considerations. The problem of settling the construction of a term for special theoretical purposes is different, however, from that of judging the issue of ambiguity versus generality as affecting ordinary terms within given discourses. At any rate, the purport of even the philosophical issue may be clarified by the distinction.

Elementary ambiguity will also be distinguishable from vagueness, where the latter is taken to involve a certain indeterminacy or ambivalence in deciding the applicability of a term to an object. For x, within D, may be unambiguous and yet vague relative to some object o, all its replicas within D being alike indeterminate respecting o. Conversely, x and y may be ambiguous within D, neither displaying vagueness relative to any o within our domain of consideration. Indicators provide the most striking, if not the only, examples, each of several "I" tokens within a given D being, we may imagine, clearly decidable in its denotation, which yet varies from that of each other replica within D.

Elementary ambiguity, therefore, does not altogether accord with usual understandings. It consists in extensional variation among replicas, each of which may, however, be perfectly definite in the way we apply it. Reverting to the language of types, we may say it is a feature of variability of the type rather than a species of variability characterizing the single token; moreover, the type variability may occasion no problem of decision. On the other hand, we often convey, in calling an expression "ambiguous", that there is some difficulty attaching to its interpretation in a given occurrence, some indecision infecting the single token. Such a point has been often noted. Hospers, for example, writes, "Sometimes, in fact, the very word 'ambiguity' is restricted so as to mean only *misleading* ambiguity . . .".[4] Richman distinguishes "semantical ambiguity", as the possession of more than one meaning by an expression, from "psychological ambiguity", as the occurrence of a semantically ambiguous expression in a context in which the intended interpretation is unclear.[5] Quine remarks that "ambiguity is supposed to consist in indecisiveness between meanings."[6] Having here renounced the notion of meanings, can we account for indecision respecting the individual token, a feature not implied by elementary ambiguity in itself?

To assimilate such indecision to mere vagueness would miss the crucial point that, as Richman puts it, "psychological ambiguity involves semantical ambiguity";[7] the indecision affecting the given token must be related to the fact that its type is ambiguous. But we have already mirrored type variability in the notion of elementary ambiguity, so our problem is to relate the indecision in question here to elementary ambiguity. Suppose then that z and y are replicas of x and extensionally divergent, hence ambiguous within discourse D containing both; let us, moreover, take D as containing also x. Now assume x embedded in a context that does not rule out its being extensionally equivalent either to z or to y. Let us, to simplify the example, also bar from D any further replica of x that is not extensionally equivalent either to z or to y. Now, to interpret x as extensionally equivalent to z or to y will enable a clear decision regarding x's extension. Either interpretation makes good sense of the relevant embedding context and, we may imagine, is simpler or more convenient than the assignment to x of a wholly new extension that makes equal sense. Either interpretation will enable us to understand what attribution is accomplished in the context in question by the presence of x. Yet we cannot in fact find sufficient reason in this situation to make up our minds, for the alternative decisions are equally reasonable. Note that if x is a predicate token attached to the name of an object o, our indecision relates not to the fact that o is said to fall within the

[4] John Hospers, *An Introduction to Philosophical Analysis* (New York: Prentice-Hall, 1953), 23. Cited in R. J. Richman, "Ambiguity and Intuition", *Mind*, 68 (1959), 87.

[5] Richman, *ibid.*, and see footnote, p. 87, where the point is credited to Bertram Jessup.

[6] Willard Van Orman Quine, *Word and Object* (New York and London: The Technology Press of the Massachusetts Institute of Technology, and John Wiley & Sons, Inc., 1960), 132.

[7] "Ambiguity and Intuition", p. 87.

extension of x, but rather to what the application of x accomplishes, i.e. what x's extension is: Is o, in particular, asserted to fall within the extension of z or of y? Here is an inscriptional example, readily generalizable, of what Quine calls "indecisiveness between meanings", the indecision being a matter of aligning x with one or another divergent replica, each providing in itself a definite clue to a plausible interpretation.[8]

4

A New Problem: Green Centaurs

So far, elementary ambiguity has been offered as an account of so-called type variability, and "ambiguity of occurrence" has been explained by elementary ambiguity coupled with an appeal to the relative richness of a token's available context. Is this the whole story?

Richman notes the following case, which presents us with a new problem. " 'Green centaur' ", he writes, "is an ambiguous term since it may be used to mean centaurs of a certain color, or centaurs of a certain degree of experience; the classes referred to, however, are both identical, both being empty."[9] Now imagine any two English "green centaur" tokens, x and y. Though replicas, they are not extensionally divergent, so lack elementary ambiguity. Faced, moreover, with such an unlikely sentence as:

In my dream I met some experienced zebras and a green centaur,

if we cannot decide which interpretation to place upon the "green centaur" token, it is no longer open to us to explain our indecision as we earlier dealt with ambiguity of occurrence. For we there required replicas of the undecided token with divergent extensions, whereas every replica of our undecided "green centaur" token, within our operative domain, has the same (null) extension. Thus we cannot suppose our present indecision to be a matter of aligning some token with one or another replica with divergent extensions.[10] If, moreover,

---

[8] The interpretation here proposed accords with the notion that ambiguity of occurrence presupposes "semantical ambiguity." Of course, there may be analogous cases where indecision concerns the alignment of x with divergent non-replicas of appropriate sort.

[9] "Ambiguity and Intuition", p. 88.

[10] Indeed, the two interpretations in question are themselves coextensive, so the indecision cannot be attributed to variable extension, independently of whether or not divergent replicas are available.

we find two sentences with sufficient context to resolve the indecision in question, say:

> (i) There were a yellow griffin, a purple unicorn, and a green centaur at the tea party,
>
> and
>
> (ii) Though most of the centaurs present were well-schooled in the social graces, there was also one green centaur, whose inexperience made him visibly uncomfortable,

we still need to account for our interpreting the "green centaur" token in (i) as differing in meaning from its replica in (ii), despite their extensional equivalence. In what does their unlikeness of meaning consist, failing elementary ambiguity?

It is worth noting here that the general problem of likeness of meaning (or synonymy) is the converse of the problem of ambiguity. The former concerns the conditions under which two words have the same meaning, while the latter concerns the conditions under which the same word has different meanings. While the first asks when two words have the same meaning, the second, we may say, asks when two meanings have the same word. In discussing the first problem, Nelson Goodman[11] reached the conclusion that no two words have the same meaning, but he was considering words as types. Further discussion of his ideas in papers by Richard Rudner,[12] Beverly Robbins,[13] and Goodman[14] dealt with the extension of these ideas to tokens. Since the problem of ambiguity is the reverse of that of likeness of meaning, it will be worth seeing if the inscriptional extension referred to bears on our present problem. We shall find that it does, and in unexpected ways.

5

Difference in Meaning

In dealing with ambiguity, we made some progress through appeal to extensional divergence, but encountered difficulty in cases where ambiguity persists without such divergence. Sameness of extension,

---

[11] Goodman, "On Likeness of Meaning", *Analysis,* 10 (1949), 1–7.

[12] R. Rudner, "A Note on Likeness of Meaning", *Analysis,* 10 (1950) 115–118.

[13] B. L. Robbins, "On Synonymy of Word-events", *Analysis,* 12 (1952), 98–100.

[14] N. Goodman, "On Some Differences About Meaning", *Analysis,* 13 (1953), 90–96.

we saw, does not in every case remove differences of meaning associated with different replicas. A parallel inadequacy forms the main problem to which Goodman's "On Likeness of Meaning" is addressed: Sameness of extension does not guarantee sameness of meaning in the case of *words*, i.e. types. The words "centaur" and "unicorn" differ in meaning though not in extension, for example.

To account for this fact, Goodman proposes that it is not only the extensions of the original two words themselves that we need to consider (so-called *primary* extensions) but also the extensions of their parallel compounds (so-called *secondary* extensions). A pair of parallel compounds is formed by making an identical addition to each of the two words under consideration; thus, adding "picture" to "centaur" and "unicorn", we have the parallel pair "centaur-picture" and "unicorn-picture". Now, although there are neither centaurs nor unicorns, there certainly are centaur-pictures and unicorn-pictures and, moreover, they are different. Though the original words have the same extension, the parallel compounds differ in extension. Goodman's idea is, then, that the difference in meaning between two words is a matter of either their own difference in extension or that of any of their parallel compounds. Terms, in general, have the same meaning if and only if they have the same primary and secondary extensions.

The proposal is further generalized to cover cases in which the addition of "picture" yields a term with null extension, e.g. "acrid-odor-picture" and "pungent-odor-picture" have the same (null) extension since neither applies to anything. Compounds can, however, be formed by other additions, and Goodman argues that "description" constitutes a suffix capable of yielding all the wanted distinctions for every pair of words P and Q. For any actual inscription of the form "a P that is not a Q" is a physical thing denoted by the compound "P-description", but not by the parallel compound "Q-description". And any inscription of "a Q that is not a P" belongs to the extension of "Q-description" but not to that of "P-description". Thus, "pungent-odor-description" and "acrid-odor-description" differ extensionally since the first, but not the second, applies to any inscription of the form "a pungent odor that is not an acrid odor", and vice versa. Thus, even if all pungent odors are acrid and acrid odors pungent, the terms "pungent odor" and "acrid odor" differ in meaning. It follows from this proposal, in fact, that "no two different words have the same meaning."[15]

[15] "On Likeness of Meaning", p. 6. In "On Some Differences About Meaning", *ibid.*, Goodman proposes other, and more easily applicable compounds to the same effect, e.g. "literal English—word".

Goodman's paper was intended to eliminate reference to images, meanings, concepts, possibilities etc., and to appeal only to the notion of extension or application to physical things. But the bearers of extension he there took to be terms, i.e. word-types, although, as he later acknowledged, wishing any final formulation of his doctrine to countenance only actual inscriptions or events, that is, what are commonly called "tokens". What, indeed, would be the result of extending his proposal explicitly to tokens? Would it, in particular, follow that no two tokens have the same meaning? This would, we may note, be even a stronger conclusion than the one suggested earlier, by the "green centaur" example. For what the latter showed was that there are instances in which replicas differ in meaning even when they have the same extension. The stronger conclusion that no two tokens have the same meaning under any circumstances clearly goes beyond the moral of the green centaurs. It implies that there is a type ambiguity that always remains even after elementary ambiguity is eliminated. Does this stronger conclusion, however, follow from Goodman's proposal reformulated for tokens?

Rudner argues that it does. In the statement S, "A rose is a rose", the fifth token but not the second is denoted by the term "PS_5", defined as "rose-description occurring in fifth place in S". It follows, says Rudner, that the second and the fifth token are different terms, but then, since Goodman concludes that different terms cannot have the same meaning, these tokens must differ in meaning, though they are replicas of one another.[16]

Now the above argument is vulnerable to the following criticism: While it indeed shows the first "rose" token and the second "rose" token in S to be different entities, it does not show that they constitute different terms or words, which would be required for them to instantiate Goodman's generalization that different *words* never have the same meaning. Rudner argues, to be sure, that "PS_5" is *prima facie* a predicate of words, not mere tokens, but this seems hardly to the point. It is not the *prima facie* application of "PS_5" that is decisive here, but rather whether the two "rose" tokens in question can be shown to fall under Goodman's generalization, through satisfying the specific considerations upon which it is itself based. This generalization, formulated for word-types, results after all from a special argument concerning primary and secondary extensions. The question is, therefore, not whether tokens are sometimes called "words", but

[16] "A Note on Likeness of Meaning", p. 116.

rather whether this special argument can be extended to the case of tokens by independent considerations. Such considerations are, however, not offered by Rudner. He remarks that "if one takes simply the position that inscriptions and parts of inscriptions are meaningful, one can maintain that no 'repetitive' inscription [such as "a rose is a rose"] is analytic; for no two of its constituent parts have the same primary and secondary extensions."[17] The latter point is, however, not demonstrated by his argument. It shows that a third predicate, "PS_5", has one but not the other of his "rose" tokens in *its* extension, but it gives no reason to suppose that these two tokens themselves do not have identical extensions, both primary and secondary.

A criticism of Rudner's paper was offered by Beverly Robbins,[18] who argued not only that Rudner had failed to deduce his strong conclusion from Goodman's proposal regarding word-types, but also that the strong conclusion does not, in fact, follow. Commenting on the passage from Rudner just quoted, to the effect that no two tokens have the same primary and secondary extensions, she raises the critical question as to the existence of relevant compounds in the case of tokens, the compounds being required for an assessment of secondary extension. Reference to secondary extension is, in turn, crucial, for since two tokens may obviously have the same primary extension, the strong thesis that no two tokens have the same meaning depends on their never having the same secondary extensions. And this, as suggested, depends on the extensional divergence of some of their parallel compounds. But what compounds are available in the case of tokens?

Unlike a word-type, whose compounds can always be supposed (on classical platonistic assumptions) to exist, a compound of a concrete token cannot be assumed to exist; the abstract word-type is repeatable whereas the token is not. If two tokens

> themselves are to be constituents of the compounds, then they must actually exist or have existed as so many marks or sounds within these compounds. . . . In general, if we stipulate that the compounds corresponding to two predicate-events [tokens] be formed by additions to the predicate-events themselves, then most predicate-events, being uncompounded, will lack secondary extension. Among such predicate-events, those with identical primary extensions will be synonymous, since they will also have the same secondary extensions by virtue of having none.

---

[17] *Ibid.*, p. 117.
[18] "On Synonymy of Word-events".

Robbins thus concludes that strictly to apply Goodman's criterion of likeness of meaning to tokens yields too many synonymous pairs, "e.g. any uncompounded 'centaur'-event and 'unicorn'-event, will have the same meaning".[19]

However, we can construe the compounding of a token not as its literal embeddedness within a larger token, but rather as the embeddedness of any of its replicas therein. As Robbins puts it, we can take the statement (for tokens I_1 and C_1) :

I_1 occurs in the compound C_1.

as saying:

Some replica of I_1 is part of some replica of C_1.

Such a construal obviates the difficulty that every "centaur"-token which is not literally a part of some compound must be said to have the same meaning as every such "unicorn"-token. For we can assume, or construct at will, a suitable compound, say a "centaur-picture" token containing a "centaur" replica as constituent, and we can equally assume or construct a "unicorn-picture" token containing a "unicorn" replica as constituent. The extensional divergence of these latter compound tokens would now show a difference of meaning not only between their actual first word-constituents, but also between every replica of one such constituent and every replica of the other. For by Robbins's extended notion of "occurrence within a compound", every token occurs within every compound of which it has a replica as a constituent.

By this extended notion, however, every two tokens that are replicas of each other occur in exactly the same compounds, the *replica* relation being reflexive, symmetric, and transitive. "Consequently", concludes Robbins, "if two such predicate-events have the same primary extension, they will also have the same secondary extensions. The two 'rose'-events in Rudner's example 'A rose is a rose' will, contrary to his contention, have the same meaning."[20] Commenting upon the Rudner-Robbins exchange in a later paper, Goodman concluded that the application of his thesis to tokens indeed does not yield the strong result that every two tokens differ in meaning, but "only that every two word-events [tokens] that are not replicas of each other differ in meaning."[21]

[19] *Ibid.*, p. 99.
[20] *Ibid.*, p. 100.
[21] "On Some Differences About Meaning", p. 92.

6
Implications for Our New Problem

To say that no two words have the same meaning is a denial of synonymy. To say, further, that no two tokens have the same meaning is an affirmation of an ambiguity so strong as to infect *all* replica-pairs whatever. Such an affirmation would account for our "green centaur" example by bringing it under a universal generalization: Two "green centaur" tokens differ in meaning simply because every two tokens differ in meaning. In generalizing ambiguity for all token-pairs, however, such an account fails to explain what is *peculiar* to our "green centaur" example, namely, that just those "green centaur" replicas that involve differing interpretations are thought to differ in meaning: Two such replicas, *both* construed as indicating centaur color, will *not* be taken to differ in meaning, whereas a pair in which one indicates color and the other degree of experience *will* be supposed to involve difference in meaning. The "green centaur" example, in other words, presents us with *particular* replica-pairs which differ in meaning even though they lack elementary ambiguity. To say that every two tokens differ in meaning is too strong a thesis to explain the particular ambiguity constituting our problem.

We have seen that this strong thesis cannot be supposed to follow from Goodman's criterion. What is the state of our problem, however, if we accept Robbins's arguments? Given two replicas with identical primary extension, they cannot diverge in secondary extension since they occur in the very same compounds. It follows that every two replicas with the same primary extension *must* have the same meaning; sameness of meaning for replicas depends solely upon sameness of primary extension. And this conclusion is in direct conflict with our "green centaur" case. For here we have replicas identical in primary extension, yet different in meaning. The situation thus turns out to be more complicated than had been supposed. Given replicas with the same primary extension, we can neither say (with Rudner) that every two of them differ in meaning, nor (with Robbins) that every two of them are alike in meaning. Some such pairs show same-ness whereas some show difference. But on what does this variation depend?

7
Derivative Constituent Ambiguity

One answer that suggests itself immediately is to take into account the extensions of word-constituents as well as compounds. Goodman's original criterion hinged on reference to the extensions of the two original words themselves, as well as to the extensions of their compounds. Applied to tokens, this criterion (as we have seen) cannot account for the "green centaur" case. But we need only to note here that replicas of the word-constituent "green" are characterized by elementary ambiguity, since some denote things of a certain color and others denote things of a certain degree of experience. Moreover, the particular difference of meaning between those "green centaur" tokens involving differing interpretations is exactly associated with difference of extensional assignment to the constituent "green" tokens in question. What is suggested, then, is a revision of Goodman's original criterion to include reference to word-constituents: Tokens are alike in meaning if and only if they have the same primary extensions, the same secondary extensions, and the same constituent extensions, where the latter clause is to be taken as requiring the same primary extensions for parallel word-constituents.[22]

In *Languages of Art*, Goodman suggests such a revision of his criterion as applied to sign-types, for independent reasons, namely, because restricted artificial languages may bar the free compounding characteristic of natural languages. Discussing his original criterion, he writes:

> As applied to natural languages, where there is great freedom in generating compounds, this criterion tends to give the result that every two terms differ in meaning. No such result follows for more restricted languages; and indeed for these the criterion may need to be strengthened by providing further that characters differ in meaning if they are parallel compounds of terms that differ either in primary or in parallel secondary extension.[23]

---

[22] The constituent extensions need to be primary only, for in the case of tokens with which we are here concerned, secondary extensions differentiate only among non-replicas, but if parallel constituents are non-replicas, the wholes will also be non-replicas, and thus already distinguished by the earlier reference to secondary extensions of the wholes. On the other hand, where the wholes are replicas, and also have the same primary extensions, they may be distinguished through the varying primary extensions of their parallel word-constituents.

[23] Nelson Goodman, *Languages of Art* (Indianapolis: Bobbs-Merrill,

The motivation for the proposal in this passage is to provide a suitable criterion for restricted languages, whereas our present motivation has been to take account of meaning differences among replicas, which share all their compounds. But the common general point is the need for a strengthening of the original criterion when limitations of one or another sort are placed on compounding. For word-types in languages with structural restrictions on compounding, reference to constituents is thus indicated. For tokens, where compounds of replicas are shared by all such replicas, and where compounding is thus powerless to differentiate among them, reference to constituents is equally indicated.

Once we take constituents into account, we can deal with the sort of ambiguity represented by the "green centaur" case, a case not dealt with by Robbins's treatment. She treats replicas with identical primary extension, arguing that they cannot differ in secondary extension, i.e. cannot occur in parallel compounds with divergent extension. Our "green centaur" case offers replicas with identical primary extension, but containing parallel constituents with differing primary extension. We have here, in other words, compounds lacking elementary ambiguity, but containing constituents possessing elementary ambiguity. We can thus now acknowledge, in extensional terms, the peculiar difference of meaning among certain compound replicas which have the same primary extensions. This sort of difference of meaning we shall refer to as *derivative constituent ambiguity*. Moreover, corresponding to the latter, which is another form of "type variability", we may also note a new sort of "ambiguity of occurrence", involving indecision as to the interpretation of a single token, whose context is too meagre to settle the extensional alignment of a constituent; this concept is parallel to that of our earlier notion of ambiguity of occurrence related to elementary ambiguity of the whole.

8

Derivative Compound Ambiguity

A critical case remains, however, yet to be considered, one that is beyond the reach of any of the notions so far developed. Consider first that derivative constituent ambiguity depends upon the separability

1968), 205, fn. 16. Secondary extensions of constituents are here included, since the context concerns types rather than tokens. (See footnote 22 above.)

of word constituents of given tokens. Can we not conceive of an ambiguity that remains even when such separability is not allowed? Imagine, for example, that every "green centaur" token has been learned initially as a single indivisible unit, and that no mastery of isolated "green" tokens has as yet been gained. It is, however, known that all "greencentaur" tokens are identical in extension, there being no greencentaurs. Thus, there is here no elementary ambiguity, nor is there, for lack of relevant separability, any derivative constituent ambiguity. (There can, further, be no ambiguity of occurrence in any of the forms so far distinguished.) Nevertheless, a form of ambiguity persists: the situation is here strikingly different from that involving, say, just "unicorn" tokens, which also lack elementary as well as derivative constituent ambiguity. What is this difference?

The contrast is seen immediately if we form compounds with "picture" tokens in each case. All "unicorn-picture" tokens have the same extension; on the other hand, "greencentaur-picture" tokens are marked by elementary ambiguity: Some of these denote what, from a more sophisticated standpoint, might be described as green-colored-centaur-pictures (or pictures of green-colored centaurs), whereas others denote what, from the same standpoint, might be described as immature-centaur-pictures (or pictures of immature centaurs), irrespective of the purported color of the depicted centaur. Given what sophisticates might describe as a picture of a green-colored but worldly-wise centaur or a picture of a yellow, baby centaur, it will be denoted by some but not all of the "greencentaur-picture" replicas. The point, in short, is this: even though indivisible "greencentaur" tokens *lack* elementary ambiguity, certain of their compounds, e.g. "greencentaur-picture" tokens, *do possess* elementary ambiguity.

Nor does this general sort of case depend upon our imagined circumstance in which the constituent of a compound ("green" in "greencentaur") has not yet been grasped as a separable unit. Suppose two novelists use the same name "Algernon" for their central characters in two fictional works. All replicas of the name within our given domain may then have the same (null) extension, and there are no word-constituents in any of these replicas. Yet "Algernon-description" tokens may display elementary ambiguity, some denoting portions of the one fictional work, and others denoting portions of the other. Myths employ the same name for purportedly different but actually nonexistent characters. Thus, "The child Linus of Argos must be distinguished from Linus, the son of Ismenius, whom Heracles killed with a lyre."[24] And Argus, the hound; Argus, son of Medea; Argus Panoptes; and Argus the Thespian are all to be distinguished[25] despite the sharing of a name with null extension and no word-constituents.

Recalling Robbins's argument against the efficacy of secondary extensions to distinguish among replicas with identical primary extension, we find that she does not make this critical contrast between compounds *with,* and compounds *without,* elementary ambiguity. Concerning the two "rose" tokens in a given "A rose is a rose", she argues that they must occur in exactly the same compounds, since to occur in a compound (by her extended notion) is to have a replica therein. Thus, given a compound containing a replica of the one "rose" token, this compound must also contain a replica of the other, the replica relation being transitive. "Consequently", she concludes, "if two such predicate-events have the same primary extension, they will also have the same secondary extensions."[26]

Now, in any case, replicas have the same secondary extensions. But such *sameness* of secondary extension does not imply that the extensions of the relevant compounds are the *same.* The compounds, although *shared* by all replicas of the constituents, may themselves *diverge* in extension, i.e. possess elementary ambiguity. The example Robbins deals with is one in which the relevant compounds ("rose-description" tokens) do not suggest such ambiguity, but the possibility of such ambiguity is nevertheless clear.

Consider, for example, replicas (unlike "rose" tokens) which differ in primary extension, e.g. two tokens T_1 and T_2, of the word "trunk", T_1 denoting containers of a certain sort and T_2 denoting certain portions of elephants. Since they are replicas, T_1 and T_2 have exactly the same secondary extensions, but such sameness clearly does not preclude elementary ambiguity of compound "trunk-picture" tokens, some of which denote certain container-pictures but not elephant-pictures, while some do just the reverse. Since T_1 and T_2 differ in primary extension, they *ipso facto* differ in meaning, so that consideration of their compounds is, for Robbins's purposes, superfluous. But the question that concerns us here is this: Given indivisible replicas with *identical* primary extensions, does the elementary ambiguity of their shared secondary extension contribute a new form

[24] Robert Graves, *The Greek Myths* (New York: George Braziller, 1957), Vol. 2, p. 212, sec. 147.
[25] *The Greek Myths.*
[26] "On Synonymy of Word-events", p. 100.

of derivative ambiguity to the original replicas? The "rose" example, to be sure, does not highlight this problem, but the examples introduced in the present section do raise the issue. The "greencentaur-picture" tokens, the "Algernon-description" tokens, the "Linus-description" tokens, and the "Argus-description" tokens display elementary ambiguity in spite of the lack of elementary ambiguity of their respective constituents. We thus have here, it seems, another form of ambiguity, flowing inward to the constituent from elementary ambiguity of the compound; we shall refer to it as *derivative compound ambiguity*.

9

Mention-Selection

Derivative compound ambiguity diverges, in a critical manner, from forms hitherto recognized: it fails to correlate differing extensions differentially with the ambiguous replicas in question. That is, given replicas R_1 and R_2, if they possess elementary ambiguity, they themselves differ in extension, while if they have derivative constituent ambiguity, some constituent of R_1 differs in extension from a parallel constituent of R_2. For derivative compound ambiguity, we cannot say the same thing. To be sure, the compounds of R_1 and R_2 differ in extension, but these divergent compounds cannot be differentially assigned to R_1 and R_2, for the latter two replicas occur in all the *very same* compounds, by Robbins's criterion.

It is true that extensional variation among compounds, which is here in question, has already shown itself significant in the case of non-replicas: Learning the difference in meaning between a "centaur" token and a "unicorn" token is *not* learning to associate different extensions with the latter pair or with their respective parallel constituents. Rather it is to learn to differentiate centaur-pictures from unicorn-pictures, centaur-descriptions from unicorn-descriptions, and so forth. But then, if learning the word "centaur" is learning how to apply also "centaur-picture", for example, then learning the indivisible word "greencentaur" is learning how to apply "greencentaur-picture" as well. And if the latter is plagued by elementary ambiguity, how can learning proceed coherently? If a child correctly withholds the term "centaur" from everything, it may still not be clear whether he is capable of correctly selecting centaur-pictures, and, until he can do this we may be unwilling to admit that he has gotten the whole point. Where elementary ambiguity infects the compounds, there are, so to speak, two or more points to be gotten. We may, by subsidiary indication, help to resolve the ambiguity, limiting relevant compounds (in teaching) to certain ones with homogeneous extension, or we may expect the child to learn to vary the extension of the compounds relevantly under variation of natural context. Moreover, in gauging his performance, we may ourselves be undecided as to which point he has gotten, with only limited sampling of his wielding of compounds. Analogously, given a fragment containing the name "Linus", we may be unable to decide whether it refers to the child Linus of Argos or to Linus the son of Ismenius, whom Heracles killed with a lyre. But "refers" cannot here be taken as "denotes" for, in either case, nothing is denoted. The question, it seems, is rather what "Linus-description" may have denoted, for the author of the fragment in question. Thus, in our finding "Linus" ambiguous, we are indirectly reflecting indecision as to the extension of "Linus-description" in this context.

Yet there is a residual problem in the case of replicas, which does not arise for non-replicas. A "centaur" token differs in meaning from a "unicorn" token since a syntactically distinguishable group of "centaur" compounds diverges extensionally from another such group of "unicorn" compounds. The notion of *parallel* compounds implies that they are syntactically distinguishable and assignable to the two tokens differing in meaning. And the latter condition fails for *replicas* differing in meaning. Though extensional variation among compounds may occasion a kind of indecision respecting single tokens, disrupting learning or interpretation in the process, these varying compounds cannot be syntactically associated with the replicas that occasion the indecision in question; it is thus not clear what constitutes a resolution of the indecision.

Raymond, a given student of the novel, produces an "Algernon" token, which leaves us undecided as to how he would apply the compound "Algernon-description"—whether, in particular, he would thereby denote portions of Jones's novel or portions of Smith's. Deciding after a while in favor of Jones, we take Raymond's compound "Algernon-description" tokens to denote portions of Jones's novel. Yet, how does this decision respecting the compound affect the status of Raymond's original "Algernon" token? It remains as true now as before that it occurs also in all those compounds that denote portions of Smith's novel. We have moreover, let us suppose, another student, George, who also produces an "Algernon" token and whose compound "Algernon-description" token denotes portions of Smith's rather than

Jones's novel. Let us call Raymond's "Algernon" token A_1 and George's A_2; let us call Raymond's compound K_1 and George's K_2. K_1 and K_2 have, then, been decided to be extensionally divergent, but we want to say that this divergence of the compounds also flows inward, affecting the "meanings" of A_1 and A_2. We want, in short, to differentiate the latter on the basis of K_1 and K_2, but this is precisely what we cannot do, for A_1 occurs in *both* compounds, and so does A_2.

Since syntactic features are incapable of making the wanted distinctions, to associate A_1 with K_1 but not K_2, and A_2 with K_2 but not K_1 is, in effect, to presuppose a new notion of parallel compounds which cuts more finely than syntactic distinctions will allow. We have seen that, where replicas are concerned, the very notion of parallel compounds, as originally conceived, *collapses* owing to the transitivity of the replica relation. What is needed then is appeal to some notion *other than* the replica relation.

We have already spoken of learning as providing some link between token and compound; the habits governing use of the token are associated with those governing use of the compounds. To wonder whether a given "Algernon" token is to be related to K_1 or K_2, it may now be suggested, is to wonder whether the habits governing the "Algernon" token in question are linked through learning with habits favoring K_1 or K_2. Can this account be made more specific? Can it, moreover, be freed from its dependence on the assumption of suitable compounds available to the producers of the original tokens? In the example of the "Linus" fragment earlier discussed, for instance, we imagined ourselves undecided as to whether the name referred to the child Linus of Argos or to Linus the son of Ismenius, and we characterized such indecision as concerning the denotation of "Linus-description" for the author of the fragment in question. But there may have been no such compound in the author's context and to talk, therefore, of linking his "Linus" habits with his "Linus-description" habits would thus be artificial.

A further consideration of the learning situation provides us with a clue. We noted that if a child withholds the term "centaur" from everything, we still do not judge him to have gotten the whole point until we are confident he can correctly select centaur-pictures. Now in his selection of such pictures, he does not, in fact, typically use the compound "centaur-picture", but rather the original term "centaur". We normally, moreover, ask him to point out the centaur *in* a given picture, and he is expected to apply the same term "centaur" to some appropriate region of the picture. Such quasi-denotative uses of the term we shall call *mention-selective,* for, though literally denoting neither centaur-pictures nor centaur-regions, it is here employed, in a manner reminiscent of metaphor, so as to select centaur-mentions in fact. In the case of "centaur", which has null (literal) denotation, its mention-selective employment seems clearly related to learning this denotation itself.

Mention-selective use is limited, however, neither to centaurs nor children. A child is often asked to point out trees, dogs, and automobiles, for example, in picture books and magazines. And in our own typical labelling of a picture of a man "Man" (rather than "Man-picture"), we ourselves apply the term "Man" to select not a man but a picture; we here apply the term not to what it denotes but rather to a mention thereof. Logicians have warned us so vehemently against confusing use with mention that we tend to overlook this employment of terms in actual learning and subsequent linguistic practice. The denotative and mention-selective uses are, it may be suggested, in fact intimately related, the one sometimes guiding the learning of the other and vice versa, the process resembling in significant ways the transfer phenomena characteristic of metaphor.

Consider the relation between the word "man" and man-pictures; the word is used not only to select men but to sort pictures of men. "Man" literally denotes men and "man-picture" literally denotes man-pictures, but "man" is also transferred and applied mention-selectively to man-pictures. If a person has mastered the conventional use of the term "man", he is normally expected to employ it properly not only in pointing out men but also in selecting man-pictures, and man-regions within such pictures. The habits governing his employment of "man" tokens in application to men are supposed, that is, to guide (and perhaps be guided by) his application of such tokens to man-mentions.[27]

Returning now to Raymond and George, the difference in meaning of their respective "Algernon" tokens does not lie in their primary extensions but rather in their mention-selective applications. That is

---

[27] In *Languages of Art,* Goodman stresses that labels or descriptions are themselves sorted by other labels, as well as effecting a sorting of elements themselves, the labelling of labels being independent of what these latter are labels for. "Objcts are classified under 'desk'. . . . Descriptions are classified under 'desk-description' . . ." (p. 31). What is presently being suggested is that the labelling of labels may be effected not by a new compound but by a habit-guided transfer of the original label itself. (See also *Languages of Art,* Part II, Sections 5–8, for treatments of metaphor and transfer.) Reverse transfers, we suggest, may also take place.

to say, A_1 mention-selects the extension of K_1; and A_2 mention-selects the extension of K_2. Given a portion of Jones's novel, or a suitable portrait of its hero, we ask whether Raymond or George would be prepared to apply an "Algernon" token to it by way of mention-selective transfer. Our indecision with respect to the "Linus" fragment, similarly, is an indecision as to what descriptions or pictures or other portrayals are mention-selected by its constituent "Linus" token. We ask, in effect, what mentions the author's habits led him, or would have led him, to point out by using this token or suitable replicas thereof. Analogously, too, for our indivisible "greencentaur" tokens; though lacking elementary ambiguity, they may vary in what they mention-select.

Derivative compound ambiguity, initially introduced as consisting in elementary ambiguity of secondary extension (i.e. of compounds), is thus reformulated as variation in mention-selection characterizing the original tokens themselves. Replicas, it is suggested, may vary in mention-selection despite their syntactical indistinguishability; we may estimate one, but not another, to be linked through mention-selection with some particular extension of an ambiguous compound of our construction. One non-compound replica may then, indeed, differ in meaning from another with the same primary extension, through differing in its mention-selection. If it be said that the concept of derivative compound ambiguity depends still for its *explanation* on the notion of extensionally divergent *compounds*, it is nevertheless not presupposed that either the concept or its explanation is shared by producers of the replicas we are concerned to interpret. *We* may judge by means of compounds available to us; we need not also attribute knowledge or employment of these compounds to the users whose replicas are in question. Yet, we may conclude that the extensional divergence represented by such compounds flows inward to differentiate the meanings of constituent replicas.

FOURTEEN

A Remark
on Deductive
Principles

JOSEPH S. ULLIAN

SOME TIME AGO, in an unguarded parenthesized clause that made its
way into print,[1] I promised to say something in support of Nelson
Goodman's view on principles of deductive inference:

> Principles of deductive inference are justified by their con-
> formity with accepted deductive practice. . . . rules and particu-
> lar inferences alike are justified by being brought into agreement
> with each other. . . . The process of justification is the delicate
> one of making mutual adjustments between rules and accepted
> inferences; and in the agreement achieved lies the only justifica-
> tion needed for either.[2]

[1] "Luck, License, & Lingo", *Journal of Philosophy* LVIII (1961), 732.
[2] Nelson Goodman, *Fact, Fiction, and Forecast*, Second Ed. (Indianapolis:
Bobbs-Merrill, 1966), 63ff.

Synoptically, for a canon to be valid is for it accurately to *codify* accepted practice. What is hard now is to see where this position needs support. Certainly Richard Rudner's pleasing parable about the imaginary philosopher "Aristotle"[3] sets the case so invitingly that there is little left to argue. But a promise is a promise, and this seems a good place to keep it.

Appropriately, I can draw on Goodman himself for a hint of the one objection to his own view that might still seem—to the hasty ear —to have a heartbeat. For Goodman once suggested that there might be thought to be an underlying problem something like this: "The notion of 'violation' or 'conformity' between rules and particular instances seems to involve principles of consistency. Thus it might be objected that the nature of the rules is the result of a put-up job, of the nature of the 'fit' required between rules and instances." So the objection, I take it, would have it that in looking to questions of conformity to rule we already load the dice, inasmuch as the very use of that notion predisposes us toward finding particular principles through already involving their employment.

But why should we object to such predisposition? Why should we demand impartiality in our search for valid principles? If certain principles are in some sense "built in" to the notions we find ourselves using, that would simply seem to count in their favor. All we care about is that the principles thus involved should receive appropriate recognition in our codification. And there is surely no bar to that.

The root issue is just that we reason even when what we reason about is our reasoning. As we well know, ascent to a metalanguage will serve us if we are content to reason about the reasoning *within* some system from a vantage point outside it. But here, in treating all our reasoning practices together, we have nowhere to ascend to. As W. V. Quine reminds us, "There is no . . . cosmic exile."[4] So we settle for coherence between what we find and what we use in finding it. For

---

[3] Paul Edwards, ed. *Encyclopedia of Philosophy*, Vol. 3, (New York: Macmillan, 1967) 371. Finding a world with deductive practices and discriminations but without codification thereof, Rudner's imaginary hero undertakes to fill the gap. He "eventually comes forward with such a codification. Using his codification people are enabled to make explicit their reasons for discriminating valid from invalid deductions by referring to the explicit rules which Aristotle has placed conveniently at hand. Of course no one would have paid any attention at all to these rules if they did not, with fair accuracy, reflect established practice—this is indeed what constitutes their validity as a set of rules."

[4] W. V. Quine, *Word and Object* (Cambridge, Mass.: M.I.T. Press and New York: John Wiley and Sons, 1960), 275.

it is true in any inquiry that what we find is in part conditioned by what we bring with us to the search. And if it be contended that some other way of initiating the search might have led to a different end product, we can reply that our search was, after all, only for *a* correct account.

Were our task that of reducing all our deductive principles to ones of more basic kind, then it would be simply hopeless. At best, we would meet the Achilles-and-the-tortoise difficulty that blocked the ill-nourished hope of reducing logical truth to convention.[5] As it is, we meet instead with the fact that our logical principles are central to our conceptual scheme, our frame of reference. Even in investigating them we can no more think them away than we can think ourselves away, and we set our task accordingly.

[5] Quine, "Truth by Convention", in *The Ways of Paradox and Other Essays* (New York: Random House, 1966), 97.

Implication & Modality

FIFTEEN

If-iculties

CHARLES L. STEVENSON

1

THE FOLLOWING EXERCISE is similar, in principle, to many exercises that can be found in elementary logic books:

> If you strike this match it will light; therefore, if you both wet this match and strike it, it will light. Is the argument valid?

A student is expected to test the argument by (say) the truth table, having first symbolized it as

$$S \supset L \quad \text{Therefore WS} \supset L$$

If he is a "good" student, he will find it to be valid. But he is not testing the English argument at all. He is mistranslating it into a simpler

From *Philosophy of Science*, Vol. 37, No. 1 (March 1970).

one and testing the latter. Nor do the usual symbols of logic permit a better translation of the English.

When logic countenances if-into-horseshoe translations of this sort, it readily teaches students how to manipulate the symbols of the propositional calculus. It prepares them, then, for understanding works on the foundations of mathematics that most of them will *not* go on to study. Meanwhile it gives them the impression that logic is trustworthy in helping them to argue validly in English—an impression that can turn out, as in the above example, to be erroneous.

In order to justify if-into-horseshoe translations, one would have to show that they (1) preserve the validity of valid English arguments, and (2) preserve the invalidity of invalid English arguments. But (2) is false, as is shown by the above example. And (1) is also false. For consider the following example:

> If this is gold it is insoluble in water; so it's not true that if this is gold it is soluble in water.

Here the "if's" lend themselves to an interpretation (not the only possible interpretation, but one that is quite appropriate to the context) that makes the argument valid. But with if-into-horseshoe translations it becomes

$$G \supset \sim S \qquad \text{Therefore} \sim (G \supset S)$$

which is invalid.

2

I give below a set of exercises that could "instructively" be added to any of our present-day texts:

> Prove the validity of the following arguments, after symbolizing them in the standard manner. Use the abbreviations indicated.
>
> (1) Logic is not confusing. So logic is confusing only if it isn't. (C)
>
> (2) If he dies tonight he will visit us tomorrow; because he will visit us tomorrow. (D,V)
>
> (3) It isn't true that if he breaks a mirror he will have bad luck. So if he *doesn't* break a mirror he will have bad luck. (M,B)
>
> (4) He is a former communist. So if he is smiling he has a bomb in his pocket, or else if he has a bomb in his pocket he is smiling. (C,S,B)

(5) If he won't propose to her unless he finds that she's wealthy, then he's mercenary. He will find that she's wealthy, but won't propose to her. So he's mercenary. (P,W,M)

(6) This is false: if God exists then the prayers of *evil* men will be answered. So we may conclude that God exists, and (as a bonus) we may conclude that the prayers of evil men will not be answered. (G,P)

(7) If this figure is rectangular and equal sided it is a square. Therefore, EITHER if this figure is rectangular and *not* equal sided it is a square, OR if this figure is *not* rectangular and is equal sided it is a square. (R,E,S)

(8) If it is seven o'clock you can hear the news report; and if you can hear the news report you have ears. Therefore: if it is seven o'clock you have ears. (S,L,E)

The possibility of such exercises shows us that the discrepancy between English "if's" and the horseshoe is far from being negligible. That is not a reason for distrusting the horseshoe, which is useful so long as it is taken to mean just what it is defined to mean; and it is not a reason for distrusting our English "if's", which in spite of their ambiguities are indispensable to our daily discourse. But it *is* a reason for distrusting the current logical pedagogy that leads students to take the two as being intertranslatable. So if symbolic logic is to help us in our English arguments (and that should surely be one of its functions) it needs to be supplemented: it needs to be provided with additional symbols (presumably with the introduction of one or more primitive concepts) that will preserve the meaning of our various "if's" with greater accuracy.

Lewis's strict implication is a step in the right direction: it spares us, for instance, from such absurdities as that of exercise (7) above. But it has its own "paradoxes" (better called "departures from English meanings of 'if' "), and is not intended to have any bearing on hypothetical propositions that are contingent. Accordingly, an even richer logic is needed.

In the present paper I shall point in the direction of such a logic. I cannot undertake to develop it in a complete postulational form; but I can at least call attention to certain English locutions by which the required postulates should be guided, and I can venture to state *some* of the postulates, using appropriate symbols.

I shall be indebted to the brief but insightful comments on implication made by W. E. Johnson /5/ and to an unpublished lecture

on implication given several years ago by H. P. Grice. /4/* It would
be an understatement for me to say that I am indebted to my colleague, Arthur W. Burks, for his work on "causal implications" /2/
and /3/, which he developed further in a manuscript that I hope will
be published in the near future. Without his work I would not have
known where to begin. But I shall nevertheless diverge from what
he says, partly because I hope to get a little closer to some of the
English "if's" than he does, and partly because I want to relate his
conceptions to those of Johnson and Grice. Perhaps my paper can best
be described as an effort to see certain aspects of Burks's work from
Johnson's and Grice's point of view.

3

"If" is used in various ways. It has non-implicational uses, as in "I
doubt if he'll come", or "His reply was oily, if you see what I mean",
or "If he is a bit too cynical, he is at any rate good company." And its
implicational uses (though the matter cannot easily be decided in advance) may be of different sorts, depending on the context in which it
occurs. It is well, then, to begin by examining "if" in a limited range
of contexts. If these contexts prove to throw light on its use in other
contexts as well, then so much the better; but even if they do not, they
may at least reveal how the word is *sometimes* used.

I shall here be mainly concerned with "if"-statements in which
only a contingent connection between the antecedent and the consequent is in question, the antecedent and consequent being also
contingent.

I shall be mainly concerned, further, with cases in which the antecedent does not purport to enumerate the entire set of conditions on
which the truth of the consequent depends. For example, suppose that
a man asserts,

If someone pushes the button the doorbell will ring.

When asked whether he is claiming that the ringing would depend
only on someone's pushing the button he is likely to say "No", adding
that it would depend on the wiring, for instance, and on the source of
electric current. But his initial statement may be true even though
it does not enumerate these other conditions. It will be true so long

* Numerals placed within / / relate to references following this essay.

as they are in fact fulfilled, along with similar conditions such as those involving the good repair of the button and the bell; and it will also, presumably, be as complete a statement as the purposes of ordinary discourse require. In subsequently giving *evidence* for the statement, of course, the man may *then* have every occasion to include evidence bearing on the wiring, the source of electric current, etc. And he may have every occasion to include evidence supporting generalizations about the manner in which these factors are related. But in giving that evidence he will be asserting other propositions, and not just reasserting his initial proposition.

As a symbol for my selected "if" I shall use a *doubled* horseshoe. Thus when substitutions for "p" and "q" yield contexts of the sort illustrated by the bell example, I shall want to translate "If p then q" into "p ⊃⊃ q." The problem, accordingly, will be to make the doubled horseshoe subject to the right sort of rules—rules that closely correspond to those that we implicitly follow (in our rational moments) when we use the English "if" that is in question.

I say "closely correspond," rather than "exactly correspond," because there are certain nuances of "if" that may not need to be formalized. Perhaps logic can safely neglect *some* aspects of its usage, just as it can safely neglect the distinction between "but" and "and." Perhaps it can neglect even more than that, transforming, for instance, certain presuppositions of our statements (in P. F. Strawson's sense of "presuppositions") into explicit meanings. But the doubled horseshoe, if it is to be useful, must be decidedly more "if"-like than the single horseshoe.

4

To understand what is required of the doubled horseshoe let us first make an observation (following W. E. Johnson, though with modifications) about the single horseshoe.

Let us consider any argument that has contingent premises and a contingent conclusion, and has the obviously valid form of *modus ponens*,

(1)
$$\frac{\begin{array}{l} p \supset q \\ p \end{array}}{q}$$

And let us assume that the person advancing the argument is asked to defend it by showing that its premises are well confirmed. Two lines of defense for his first premiss will then be closed to him, both being reminiscent of the "paradoxes" of material implication.

He cannot reasonably defend his first premiss by evidence that confirms the negation of its antecedent (i.e., that confirms ~p) ; for in that case he will *disc*onfirm his second premiss, and thus undermine the soundness of his argument as a whole. And he cannot reasonably defend his first premiss by evidence that confirms its consequent (i.e., that confirms q) ; for in that case he will be directly confirming his conclusion, thereby making his argument superfluous as a means of "reaching" his conclusion.

The only reasonable way in which he can defend the first premiss, then, is to give confirming evidence for it that is *not* confirming evidence for the negation of its antecedent, and *not* confirming evidence for its consequent. And in some cases, of course, that sort of evidence will be available. To realize that, we need only return to the doorbell example of the preceding section, though changing the "if" of that example into a horseshoe, and adding a second premiss. We then have:

(2) Someone will push this button $\supset$ the doorbell will ring
    Someone will push this button

    ───

                                    the doorbell will ring

where there may be evidence for the first premiss that leaves the truth or falsity of both its antecedent and its consequent quite uncertain— evidence that deals with the wiring, the source of electric current, and so on. Note that this evidence for the horseshoe-assertion is no different from that previously mentioned (Section 3) in connection with the corresponding "if"-assertion, and that it will relevantly include evidence for *generalizations* about wiring, electricity, etc.

When a proposition of the form $p \supset q$ is confirmed by evidence of this latter sort let us call the evidence "intensional." Thus

(A) A body of evidence that confirms $p \supset q$ is intensional
    just in case it does not confirm the stronger proposition,
    ~p, and does not confirm the stronger proposition, q.[1]

What has been said of a *modus ponens* argument can be repeated, *mutatis mutandis*, for a *modus tollens* argument. If the latter is to be

────────────────

[1] Throughout the paper I often drop needed quotation marks around sentences, statements, and statement forms, and also drop Quine's "quasi-quotes", and initial that's that transform sentences into noun clauses. My compromise with rigor simplifies printing and reading, and does not, I think, introduce any ambiguities that are not resolved by their context.

defended as sound and non-superfluous, *its* first premiss too must be confirmed by intensional evidence.

There is nothing about the meaning of a single-horseshoe proposition itself, of course, that prevents it from being confirmable by extensional (i.e., non-intensional) evidence, and by that sort of evidence only. For example, the proposition,

(3)   George Eliot was a woman $\supset$ George Sand was a woman

can be supported by excellent historical evidence—evidence that is entirely extensional, being entirely for the truth of its consequent. Such evidence, however, makes it unfit for use in *modus ponens* or *modus tollens* arguments of the defended sort that we have been considering.

Let us now compare and contrast the horseshoe with our selected English "if's"—"if's" that occur in thoroughly contingent contexts. We can readily see, I trust, that extensional evidence does not help to confirm any statement using such an "if." Relevant confirming evidence will not be evidence for the falsity of the antecedent, and will not be evidence for the truth of the consequent.

Now we shall want our *doubled* horseshoe, mentioned in the preceding section, to be "if"-like in this respect. So, apart from a qualification to be mentioned later, we shall want to specify that its confirmation is subject to the following conditions:

(B)   For contingent values of the variables that yield contingent propositions, any INTENSIONAL evidence that confirms $p \supset q$ to such and such a degree (making it more probable than not) will confirm $p \supset \supset q$ to the same degree; and there is no other sort of evidence that can confirm $p \supset \supset q$.

Let me spell this out a little, with attention to the remarks that I have just been making. As we have seen, when single-horseshoe propositions can be confirmed only by extensional evidence they close the way to their use in adequately defended *modus ponens* or *modus tollens* arguments. But *no* doubled-horseshoe proposition *can* be of that sort. Extensional evidence for a doubled-horseshoe proposition is ruled out from the start. If confirmable at all, it is confirmable by evidence that does not close the way to its subsequent use in an adequately defended *modus ponens* or *modus tollens* argument. The evidence that confirms it cannot disconfirm the second premiss of the argument, and cannot make the argument superfluous by directly confirming its conclusion.

These remarks do not yield a definition of "$p \supset \supset q$"; but by helping to show what it means to say, "$p \supset \supset q$ has been confirmed to such and such a degree", they help to show how a definition of "$p \supset \supset q$" might be devised.

5

I have remarked in passing that (B) just above may need to be qualified. Let me explain.

There can be no objection, of course, to a confirmation of a doubled-horseshoe proposition that depends on an appeal to an authority, since there may be good evidence that the authority has previously confirmed the doubled-horseshoe proposition and thus knows what he is talking about. But there is a curious *type* of authoritative evidence that I want to exclude as being irrelevant to a doubled-horseshoe proposition.

Suppose, for instance, that I find a historically ignorant but logically sophisticated Mr. Smith, to whom I assert the proposition about George Eliot and George Sand previously mentioned—repeated below for the reader's convenience:

(1)   George Eliot was a woman $\supset$ George Sand was a woman.

My own evidence for this assertion is purely *ex*tensional. But if Mr. Smith begins with evidence in support of my being a trustworthy authority on such a matter, then *the fact that I make* the assertion gives *him in*tensional evidence for its truth. That is to say, on the basis of my authority Smith has evidence for (1), but this evidence of his is not, like mine, evidence for the proposition that is the consequent of (1); and it is not evidence for the falsity of the proposition that is the antecedent of (1). According to (B) of the preceding section, then, Smith can assert, and on good evidence, an altered version of (1) in which the single horseshoe gives place to a doubled horseshoe. And so long as the doubled horseshoe is taken to be "if"-like, Smith can assert, and on good evidence, "If George Eliot was a woman, then George Sand was a woman." I myself, though Smith's authority, cannot assert the latter proposition on any sort of good (intensional) evidence; but Smith can.

My assertion of (1) would of course normally be unmotivated; for having evidence only for the truth of my consequent, I would be going out of my way to say less than I know. Still, I *could* make the assertion, perhaps just to introduce a discussion of logic.

Given the unusual context of my example there doubtless *is* a sense of "if" (a "temporary" sense, so to speak) that permits Smith to say, "If George Eliot was a woman, then George Sand was a woman." But I shall here be content to leave that sort of "if" without further analysis, and shall assume that the doubled horseshoe yields stronger propositions—propositions for which an authority's statement becomes relevant evidence only to the extent that it, in turn, is backed by non-authoritative (and intensional) evidence.

6

Before continuing my discussion of the doubled horseshoe, I must make some remarks that may at first seem a digression. I must ask the reader tentatively to share with me, with a "decently uncritical tolerance", two assumptions. I do not find them congenial assumptions, but I shall need them as *intuitive guides* to what must be said later.

One assumption is this:

(A)   It is practicable to speak of a conjunction of *atomic* propositions—i.e., a conjunction in which no conjunct is analyzable into simpler propositions.

For the purpose of throwing light on English arguments, this is an assumption rather than an established truth. For English, unlike the artificial languages discussed in logic, provides us with no *list* of atomic propositions; and any list that we suppose ourselves to be tacitly supplying will properly be open to suspicion.

When p and q are both atomic, then $\sim p$ and $\sim q$ are also to be considered as atomic. But $\sim (p \cdot q)$, with its initial negation sign, is not to be considered as a *con*junction of atomic propositions, since it is equivalent to the initially unnegated *dis*junction, $\sim p \lor \sim q$.

A further assumption is this:

(B)   The probability of a contingent proposition, p, relatively to a contingent proposition, e, can be equal to 1 (unity) even though e does not strictly imply p.

On occasion, probabilities that equal unity (which may also be called "certainty relationships") are interpreted more narrowly: they are taken to arise for a contingent p, relatively to a contingent e, only when the latter *does* strictly imply the former. But there is nothing in the probability calculus itself that requires such an interpretation; so it is not heretical, I trust, to suggest that there can be a broader interpretation of the probability calculus, permitting assumption (B) to be accepted.

Philosophers who feel that we can be "absolutely certain" of the truth of these or those empirical propositions—such propositions as *The moon did not collide with the earth in 1751,* or *Other people sometimes feel pain*—will find (B) more congenial than do the philosophers who think that empirical propositions can at most be "nearly certain." But having asked the reader to consider (B) only as an assumption to be used as an intuitive guide to what will be said later, I shall not attempt a defense of it.

It will be convenient to use a symbolic expression that is related to (B), namely, the expression "p/*e = 1", read, "In the extended interpretation of 'probability', the probability of *p*, relatively to *e*, equals 1." This simply adds a star to the familiar notation of Keynes, and does so as a reminder of the extended interpretation mentioned above. Thus:

(C) p/*e = 1 will be true, for a contingent *p* and a contingent *e*, not only when *e* strictly implies *p* but also in certain cases when *e* does not strictly imply *p*.

Two things should be noted in this connection.

In the first place, "p/*e = 1" refers to some sort of implication between *e* and *p*. This implication, however, is not the same as the one preserved by the doubled horseshoe; and since its symbol retains a connection with the probability calculus, it is not likely (particularly in the present, only half-formal discussion) to leave us perplexed about how it is to be used.

In the second place, from p/*e = 1 it does not follow that *p* can in practice be conclusively confirmed. The latter requires an *e* that can in practice be *found* to be *true*, whereas p/*e = 1 does not. Perhaps *e* is false, or perhaps it can itself be confirmed, in practice, only to this or that degree. It remains the case, however, that when *e* is confirmed to this or that degree, and p/*e = 1, then *p* will be confirmed to at least an equal degree.

Let me now introduce a further symbolic expression, to which the preceding remarks have been leading—an expression that will be of central importance throughout the remainder of the paper. It is "eGp", which can be read, "The proposition, *e*, is a *ground* for the proposition, *p*." Presupposing both assumption (A) and assumption

(B) above, I shall define it (though only for informal purposes) in this way:

(D)   eGp =Df.   (a) e and p are both contingent, and
                    (b) p/*e = 1, and
                    (c) e is strictly equivalent to a conjunction of
                         atomic propositions, and
                    (d) e⊃p

And *e* must not depend on an authoritative-saying-less-than-one-knows statement; though for simplicity I shall not mention that hereafter.[2]

Let me now explain why I have gone into these matters, which may seem remote from my topic. The reason is this:

I shall presently use expressions of the form "eGp" in defining the doubled horseshoe. And of course any such way of defining the doubled horseshoe would be absurd if the meaning of "G" (or "ground") were left mysterious. So the above remarks are intended to make "G", if still a little mysterious, at least sufficiently free from mystery to show promise of being helpful.

If I were placing "G" in a formal system—adding it, say, to Lewis's S5/6/—I could introduce it as a primitive term, and thus one not defined *within* the system. There would then be a need of my (1) interpreting it in a manner that suggested rules for its use, (2) systematizing the rules, and (3) checking the initial interpretation in the light of the rules, and the rules in the light of the initial interpretation, with such revisions of either as might prove necessary.

The above remarks are concerned only with the first, interpretive step. With regard to the second step I shall presently give some rules, though without attempting to be complete in doing so. I shall give them when I need to use them rather than attempt to axiomatize them in advance. And it will be my privilege, of course, to look ahead to a subsequent, third step, which includes the possibility of altering my informal interpretation of "G".

It is this latter possibility that makes me content, for the present, to let the meaning of "G" rest on assumptions. If its meaning is intel-

---

[2] It may at first seem that (d) follows from (b), and is thus superfluous in the definition. When *e* does not strictly imply *p*, however, there is no logical inconsistency (though there may be an error) in affirming p/*e = 1 and denying e⊃p. So (d) does not follow from (b); it is not superfluous, but serves to make the definition of "ground" slightly stronger. With regard to this point I am indebted to my colleagues, I. M. Copi and A. W. Burks.

ligible enough to suggest rules for its use, and if these rules, with the help of a definition, yield rules for the doubled horseshoe, then "G" will have served my purpose. The rules for the doubled horseshoe, thus obtained, can then be tested by their fidelity to those governing certain English "if's". And if they pass that test, I can *later* look back to the "G" that suggested them, in the hope of finding an interpretation for it that is less subject to philosophical controversy.

7

The definition of the doubled horseshoe in terms of "G" is this:

(1) $p \supset \supset q$ =Df.   There is some proposition, e, such that
                    (a) e is true, and
                    (b) $eG(p \supset q)$, and
                    (c) $\sim (eG \sim p) . \sim (eGq)$.

Stated as an equivalence, with the use of an existential quantifier, the definition becomes:

(2) $p \supset \supset q$ is strictly equivalent to $(\exists e) : e .$
            $eG(p \supset q) . \sim (eG \sim p) . \sim (eGq)$.

And stated in words, it becomes,

(3) $p \supset \supset q$ is true just in case there is some true proposition,
         e, that is a ground for $p \supset q$ but is not a ground for $\sim p$
         and is not a ground for q.

    I am speaking of a ground very much as I previously spoke of a body of evidence. Let me continue to do so by using the term "intensional ground", defined in a way that parallels (A) of page 284:

(4)   e is an intensional $eG(p \supset q)$, and
         ground for $p \supset q$ =Df. $\sim (eG \sim p)$, and $\sim (eGq)$.

The equivalences given by (2) and (3) can then be expressed:

(5) $p \supset \supset q$ is true just in case there is a true intensional
         ground for $p \supset q$.

    The similarities between ground and evidence are such that I might have dropped the term "ground" altogether and used the term *"conclusive* evidence" in its place. But the latter term would have been misleading, and for this reason: An expression of the form

"There is conclusive evidence, e, for p" strongly suggests that somebody now *has* the evidence—i.e., that somebody now *knows* that e is true. But an expression of the form "There is a ground, e, for p" can more easily be freed from that suggestion—an unnecessary and inconvenient suggestion, since when any e in question is true, probably true, known to be true, etc., it can be expressly specified as such. Note that just as p/*e can equal unity even though e is false, so e can be a ground for p even though e is false. A fortiori, e may be a ground for p even though e is not yet *known* to be true. Suppose, for instance, that no one now knows whether there is a true intensional ground for p⊃q, and hence that no one now knows whether p⊃⊃q is true. A man may nevertheless *guess* that p⊃⊃q is true; and his guess will not be wrong merely because of his present lack of evidence. Perhaps he has made a lucky guess—as may become known later on when the truth of an intensional ground for p⊃q has been discovered.

But *evidence* and *ground* remain related conceptions. When there is evidence (perhaps inconclusive) for the truth of an e that grounds p, then there is also evidence for p; and when such an e is known with certainty to be true, it is itself conclusive evidence for p.

I must now explain why I previously interpreted "eGp" in a somewhat complicated manner. (See (D), page 289.) I did so in anticipation of having to speak of an intensional ground in the course of defining "p⊃⊃q". Indeed, the term "ground" is useful almost exclusively in that connection.

Consider, for instance, just the expression, "eG(p⊃q)". Had I let this expression mean no more than "The contingent proposition, e, *strictly implies* the contingent proposition, p⊃q", then every contingently true proposition, p⊃q, would of necessity have had a true *intensional* ground. It would have had itself as such a ground in this unwanted sense: it would "ground" (i.e., strictly imply) itself without "grounding" the falsity of its antecedent and without "grounding" the truth of its consequent. So "ground" had to be given a stronger sense, in which the ground, e, was specified as equivalent to a contingent conjunction of atomic propositions. For the cases that interested me—those in which p⊃q is not *strictly equivalent* to an atomic *conjunction*—my strengthening step prevented e from being identical with p⊃q.[3] But it was too strong, permitting too few proposi-

---

[3] I say "for the cases that interested me" for this reason: Any proposition, p, is strictly equivalent to $(\sim p \lor \sim q) \supset p \sim q$. So when p is a true atomic conjunction, its single-horseshoe equivalent *will* be a true intensional ground for itself, guaranteeing the truth of $(\sim p \lor \sim q) \supset \supset p \sim q$. But it is

tions to have intensional grounds. So I reduced its strength by a further step: I no longer required p⊃q to be strictly implied by its ground, *e*, but instead required only that p⊃q/*e = 1.

Perhaps the conception of an atomic conjunction (and as I have previously remarked, I find it philosophically uncongenial) can derive a certain amount of clarity from its connection with our unanalyzed but practically useful conception of *evidence*. It is not altogether rash to claim that *basic* evidence can *always* be described by an atomic conjunction. We commonly do, of course, say that *s* is evidence for *p* in instances where we do not consider *s* to be such a conjunction; but that can be taken as a way of saying that any true atomic conjunction, *e*, which is the basic evidence for *s* is also basic evidence for *p*.

8

Let me now give some simple rules, both for "G" and for the doubled horseshoe. A rule obviously needed for "G", and suggested by the informal definition of it given as (D) in section 6 above, is the one that follows:

(R1)   e . eGp   strictly implies   p

And from this, along with standard steps, we obtain

(T1)   p⊃⊃q   strictly implies   p⊃q

Proof:

(1)	p⊃⊃q	(premiss)
(2)	(∃e): e . eG(p⊃q). ∼(eG∼p). ∼(eGq)	(by def.; see p. 290)
(3)	(∃e): e . eG(p⊃q)	(standard step)
(4)	e′ .e′G(p⊃q)	(standard step)
(5)	p⊃q	(by R1 above)

The converse of (T1) is of course fallacious. For even if we permit an inference from p⊃q to *There is a true ground for p⊃q*, we shall not be able to infer, further, that this true ground is intensional (as it

---

not necessary to exclude cases of that sort. The doubled-horseshoe proposition in question, curious though it is, can still be used in a well-defended *modus ponens* argument. It must itself be defended by evidence for *p*; but the second premiss in the argument, ∼p∨∼q, can consistently be defended by evidence for ∼q (with p∼q as a conclusion). The alternative possibility of a simpler *argument*, from *p* and from ∼q to p∼q, does not show that the *modus ponens* argument is superfluous. Similarly, in a *modus tollens* argument the second premiss, ∼(p∼q) can be defended by evidence for *q*.

must be for $p \supset \supset q$). I need scarcely add that I shall give no rule that justifies an inference from $\sim p$ to $p \supset \supset q$, or from q to $p \supset \supset q$.

Granted (T1) it is of course easy to prove such "if"-like theorems for the doubled horseshoe as these:

(T2)	$p \cdot p \supset \supset q$	strictly implies	q
(T3)	$\sim q \cdot p \supset \supset q$	strictly implies	$\sim p$
(T4)	$p \lor q \cdot p \supset \supset r \cdot q \supset \supset s$	strictly implies	$r \lor s$

The first step in a proof is simply one of inferring a single-horseshoe proposition from a corresponding doubled-horseshoe proposition, using (T1); and standard steps do the rest.

A further rule for "G," again suggested by the informal definition of page 289, is this:

(R2)   p is str. equiv. to q   str. imp.   eGp is str. equiv. to eGq

And from (R2), along with standard steps, we obtain

(T5) $p \supset \supset q$ is strictly equivalent to $\sim q \supset \supset \sim p$

Proof:
(1) $p \supset \supset q$ (premiss)
(2) $(\exists e) : e \cdot eG(p \supset q) \cdot \sim(eG \sim p) \cdot \sim(eGq)$ (def.)
(3) $(\exists e) : e \cdot eG(\sim q \supset \sim p) \cdot \sim(eG \sim \sim q) \cdot \sim(eG \sim p)$ (using (R2) and standard steps)
(4) $\sim q \supset \supset \sim p$ (def.)

And the proof holds also, *mutatis mutandis*, when read upwards.

For these simple theorems the doubled horseshoe behaves not only in an *"if"*-like manner but also in a single-horseshoe-like manner. And yet the doubled horseshoe entitles us to a little more than the single horseshoe in closely neighboring theorems. For example, $p \cdot (p \supset q)$ both strictly implies and is strictly implied by pq, whereas

(T6) $p \cdot (p \supset \supset q)$ strictly implies (one way only)   pq

where the left side properly suggests the reading, "q because p," as used in such a context as "The match lit because I struck it." The single horseshoe provides no symbolism for that sense of "because".

9

The following example illustrates a further difference between the single horseshoe and the "if"-regarding doubled horseshoe—a difference that particularly deserves attention.

Consider the English sentence, "If it is raining then there are no clouds in the sky, OR if there are no clouds in the sky then it is raining." Normally we should take this as expressing an empirically false proposition, both its disjuncts expressing falsehoods. But when the sentence is translated (i.e., mistranslated) into a single horseshoe symbolism the result expresses a proposition that is tautologically true. For we then have $(R \supset \sim C) \lor (\sim C \supset R)$, which is logically equivalent to $\sim R \lor \sim C \lor C \lor R$; and the latter, so to speak, *twice* proclaims itself to be a tautology.

When the above English sentence is translated into a doubled horseshoe symbolism, however, it becomes $(R \supset \supset \sim C) \lor (\sim C \supset \supset R)$. And there is nothing about my definition of the doubled horseshoe in terms of "G", or my informal (interpretive) definition of "G", that even remotely suggests that this latter proposition is a tautology. What the proposition tells us is this: Either there is a true intensional ground for $R \supset \sim C$, OR there is a true intensional ground for $\sim C \supset R$. And it is possible that both disjuncts are false. For to say of a material conditional that it has a true *intensional* ground is to say *more* about it than that it is true; and this "more" can fail to be true. So although it is logically necessary that at least one of the disjuncts in $(R \supset \sim C) \lor (\sim C \supset R)$ is true, it does not follow that at least one of them is true *and* has an intensional ground. To assert the latter (and thus to assert that $(R \supset \supset \sim C) \lor (\sim C \supset \supset R)$) is to make a possibly false statement, and one that, for the present example, actually is false, as we learn from experience.

10

Let us next consider symbolic translations of the *negations* of English hypothetical statements. Suppose Mr. A finds a large jewel that he mistakenly takes to be a diamond, and says, "If I sell this I'll suddenly become wealthy." And suppose that Mr. B, who knows about jewels, replies, "No, that isn't so." Presumably, Mr. B is saying, in effect, "It is not the case that if you sell it you will suddenly become wealthy", which we may abbreviate as

(a)   Not-(if S then W)

When "if" is translated into a single horseshoe this becomes logically equivalent to

(b) $S. \sim W$

which clearly shows that the translation is incorrect. In asserting (a),
Mr. B is not predicting that A will sell the jewel (and is perhaps about
to dissuade him from trying to sell it). Nor is he denying that A will
suddenly become wealthy; for he could consistently add to (a), "But
you will suddenly become wealthy for reasons that have nothing to do
with the jewel."

What is wanted, then, is a symbolic translation of (a) that, unlike (b), is logically compatible with ~S and logically compatible with
W. And we have that when (a) is translated as below by the doubled
horseshoe:

(c) $\qquad\qquad\qquad \sim (S \supset \supset W)$

For the latter tells us that there is no true intensional ground for
$S \supset W$. It is compatible, then, with the existence of a true *extensional*
ground for $S \supset W$. Further, it is compatible with the existence of a
true ground for ~S, and thus compatible with ~S; and it is compatible with the existence of a true ground for W, and thus compatible
with W. We have in (c), then, a weaker proposition than (b) for
translating (a), and one that is more faithful to (a).

At this point we may be inclined to ask, "How can a person know
that $\sim (S \supset \supset W)$ is true (or probably true)?" One way to know is to
find out that the *stronger* proposition, S~W, is true; for from this
$\sim (S \supset \supset W)$ follows. It follows because: $S \supset W$ follows from $S \supset \supset W$
(see (T1), page 292), and thus $\sim (S \supset \supset W)$ follows from $\sim (S \supset W)$,
the latter being equivalent to S~W. But that, in our example, was not
the way that Mr. B came to know $\sim (S \supset \supset W)$. Presumably, he had
much information about jewels, and none of this disclosed intensional
evidence for $S \supset W$. So assuming that he would have had such evidence
if it existed, he took his failure to find it as a good reason for saying
that there was no true intensional ground for $S \supset W$, and thus as a
good reason for affirming $\sim (S \supset \supset W)$.

11

In the sections immediately following the present one I shall want to
discuss some further rules that hold or fail to hold for the doubled
horseshoe. For that purpose it will be convenient to devise a symbolism that makes it easier to prove or disprove certain proposed
rules. The next few pages will be preparatory to the introduction of
the needed symbolism.

Let me define the symbol, "C," in this way:

(A) $\qquad\qquad\qquad$ eCp $\qquad$ =Df. $\qquad$ ~(eG~p)

Accordingly, using this definition and the definition of the doubled horseshoe, page 290, particularly (2), we have:

(B)

p⊃⊃q $\qquad$ is strictly equivalent to $\qquad$ (∃e) : e . eG(p⊃q) . eCp . eC~q

Here (i.e., in this context of (B)) "C" can be read "is compatible with"; but since "compatible" must then mean rather more than "logically compatible", I shall read it as "is ground compatible with."[4]

To continue: the probability clause in my informal definition of "G", page 289, suggests the important rule that follows:

(R3) $\qquad$ p str. imp. p′ $\quad$ is str. equiv. to $\quad$ eGp str. imp. eGp′
$\qquad\qquad$ provided that all variables are restricted to contingent
$\qquad\qquad$ propositions as their values, and e is an atomic con-
$\qquad\qquad$ junction.[5]

Now from (R3), writing ~p′ for p, and ~p for p′, we have (with same proviso):

$\quad$ ~p′ str. imp. ~p $\quad$ is str. equiv. to $\quad$ eG~p′ str. imp. eG~p

And transposing each of the strict implications just mentioned, we have:

$\quad$ p str. imp. p′ $\quad$ is str. equiv. to $\quad$ ~(eG~p) str. imp. ~(eG~p′)

And restating the right side of this strict equivalence by using definition (A) just above, we have:

(R3a) $\qquad$ p str. imp. p′ $\quad$ is str. equiv. to $\quad$ eCp str. imp. eCp′
$\qquad\qquad$ (with same proviso as that for (R3)).

---

[4] In itself, "C" has a rather weak meaning. Thus eC~p is equivalent to the *dis*junction of the negations of (a)–(d) in the interpretive definition of "G" suggested on page 289. But in contexts like (B) just above, where "G" and "C" both occur, various of the disjuncts in question cannot be true; and for these contexts a reading of "ground compatible" for "C" becomes not inappropriate. Note that the relation between "G" and "C" is *somewhat* similar to the relation between the square and the diamond in modal logic.

[5] The proviso is made stronger than it need be, to simplify exposition. It could read: "provided that e is a contingent atomic conjunction, and neither p nor p′ is necessary".

Let us now compare the statements below, which are logically equivalent, respectively, to $p \supset \supset q$ and to $p' \supset \supset q'$. (Cf. (B), page 296.)

(X) $(\exists e) : e . eG(p \supset q) . eCp . eC\sim q$

(X') $(\exists e) : e . eG(p' \supset q') . eCp' . eC\sim q'$

Under what conditions will (X) strictly imply (X')? The following conjecture (though I shall not attempt to prove it) seems to me thoroughly safe for cases in which (X) and (X') are both contingent. (X) will strictly imply (X') just in case the G-conjunct of the latter is strictly implied by the G-conjunct of the former and each C-conjunct of the latter is strictly implied by some *one* C-conjunct of the former. Moreover, by (R3) and (R3a) the strict implications between these conjuncts will hold true just in case there are corresponding strict implications between the propositions that occur to the right of the G's and C's. (They will hold true, accordingly, when $p \supset q$ strictly implies $p' \supset q'$, and p strictly implies p', and $\sim q$ strictly implies $\sim q'$.) So we have a test as to whether (X) strictly implies (X'), and thus a test as to whether $p \supset \supset q$ strictly implies $p' \supset \supset q'$.

Though somewhat complicated, these considerations lead to a very simple symbolism, which I shall now introduce:

(1)   "$p \supset \supset q$" can conveniently be written "$p \supset q \ \square \ p, \sim q$"

where the rectangle is to be understood as saying that some true proposition, *e*, is a ground for the proposition on the left of it and is ground-compatible with each of the propositions listed on the right of it. So in the above context the rectangle tells us exactly what (X) above tells us, and thus exactly what "$p \supset \supset q$" tells us in accordance with (B), page 296.

The convenience of the symbolism is best shown by examples of its use. Let us test the one-premissed argument form:

(2) $\dfrac{p \supset \supset q}{p \supset \supset qp}$

Rewriting premiss and conclusion by using the rectangle, we have

(2r) $\dfrac{p \supset q \ \square \ p, \sim q}{p \supset qp \ \square \ p, \sim (qp)}$

To test the inference we must first test whether the proposition on the left of the rectangle in the conclusion is strictly implied by the proposition to the left of the rectangle in the premiss. It clearly is, as a truth-table will show. Next, we must test whether each of the propositions listed to the right of the rectangle in the conclusion is strictly implied by some *one* of the propositions listed to the right of the rectangle in the premiss. That is in fact the case: the p in the conclusion is strictly implied by the p in the premiss, and the $\sim(qp)$ in the conclusion is strictly implied by the $\sim q$ in the premiss. So by the symbolism, based on the conjecture introduced immediately after (X) and (X') above, and on (R3) and (R3a), we have shown that our initial argument form, (2), is valid. We have tested an argument using doubled horseshoes by in effect using the truth-table three times.

The test is applicable only to inferences in which the premiss and conclusion are contingent. For the principles on which it is based include provisos about contingency.

Note that it is mnemonically very easy to write out a doubled-horseshoe proposition in the rectangle symbolism. On the left of the rectangle put the corresponding single-horseshoe proposition, and on the right of the rectangle put the propositions that would be needed, respectively, for a *modus ponens* and a *modus tollens* argument, separating them by a comma.

12

Let me now return to my very first example in this paper, where the validity of the following inference was in question:

(1)   If you strike this match it will light
       _____
       If you both wet this match and strike it it will light

I symbolize it below in both the doubled-horseshoe and the rectangle notation:

(2) $\dfrac{S \supset \supset L}{WS \supset \supset L}$ $\dfrac{S \supset L \;\square\; S, \;\sim L}{WS \supset L \;\square\; WS, \sim L}$

The rectangle notation immediately shows that the argument is invalid: of the propositions listed to the right of the rectangles, the WS in the conclusion follows from neither of the propositions listed in the premiss.

Stated in terms of *evidence* rather than in terms of *ground*—and as I have previously remarked, there is a close connection between the two—the situation is this: It may be the case (and presumably is the case for this example) that the only intensional evidence that can be obtained for $S \supset L$, and hence the only evidence of any sort that can be obtained for the premiss, $S \supset \supset L$, is also evidence for $\sim W$. Now this evidence will not be intensional evidence for $WS \supset L$, and hence not evidence for the conclusion, $WS \supset \supset L$; for so long as it is evidence for $\sim W$ it will also be evidence for $\sim (WS)$, and thus evidence for the negation of the antecedent of $WS \supset L$, as intensional evidence must not be. Thus in a possible (and presumably actual) situation the only sort of evidence that confirms the premiss of (2) will fail to confirm the conclusion—as in any one-premissed demonstratively valid argument is impossible. So (2) is invalid, and in that respect is a faithful translation of (1), which we see intuitively to be invalid.

Argument (2) can instructively be compared with

(3)
$$S \supset \supset L$$
$$\frac{WS}{L}$$

This latter argument is valid; but unless the match in question is of a curious sort, one of the premisses will be false.

13

We must next ask whether or not a doubled-horseshoe proposition can undergo partial transposition—i.e., whether a form of argument like the one below is valid:

(1)
$$\frac{pq \supset \supset r}{p \sim r \supset \supset \sim q} \qquad \frac{pq \supset r \ \Box \ pq, \sim r}{p \sim r \supset \sim q \ \Box \ p \sim r, q}$$

Quite evidently, it is *in*valid: of the propositions listed to the right of the rectangles, $p \sim r$ in the conclusion follows from neither *one* of the propositions listed in the premiss.

This may seem a decidedly un-*if*-like behavior on the part of the doubled horseshoe; but a moment's consideration will show that it is not. In English it is permissible, however odd, to make such a statement as:

(2)   If you strike this match and wear a hat, the match will light.

And this, given not unusual circumstances, will be a true statement. Our knowledge that the hat "has nothing to do with the situation" may make us demur if anyone asserts (2), but will lead us to say only

[299]

that the antecedent is needlessly strong, and not that the assertion is false. Now when partially transposed, (2) becomes

(3)   If you strike this match and it doesn't light, then you won't be wearing a hat.

And this is not a conclusion that we shall be entitled to draw from (2) ; we shall be entitled, rather, to say that (2) is true whereas (3) is false. In general, English tolerates an irrelevancy (like that about the hat) when it occurs as a conjunct in the antecedent, but not when its negation occurs alone in the consequent.

And yet (1) above, though invalid, has a valid analogue—valid because of a strengthened premiss. I shall write the strengthened premiss by using an additional symbol (an exclamation mark) in the antecedent, thus: "(p. !q) ⊃ ⊃ r". This expression is to be taken as meaning the same thing as "(∃e) : e . eG (pq⊃r) . eCpq . eCp~r . eCq~r". In the rectangle notation it becomes "pq⊃r ▯ pq, p~r, q~r". And in English it can be read, "If p and q (both being relevant) then r". We then have the following as the valid analogue of (1) just mentioned:

(4) $$\frac{(p.\,!q) \supset\supset r}{p\sim r \supset\supset \sim q} \qquad \frac{pq \supset r \;▯\; pq,\ p\sim r, q\sim r}{p\sim r \supset \sim q \;▯\; p\sim r,\ q}$$

It will be evident from the rectangle notation, moreover, that the doubled-horseshoe propositions given below are all strictly equivalent.

(5)   (p. !q) ⊃⊃ r   pq ⊃ r ▯ pq, p~r, q~r
        (p. !~r) ⊃⊃ ~q   p~r ⊃~q ▯ p~r, pq, ~rq
        (q. !~r) ⊃⊃ ~p   q~r ⊃~p ▯ q~r, qp, ~rp

These equivalences are of interest in showing that the strengthened doubled-horseshoe proposition, so far as partial transpositions are concerned, behaves just like a single-horseshoe proposition.

When in English we make statements of the form "If p and q then r", we normally try to eliminate irrelevancies of the hat type that (2) has illustrated; we usually expect it to be taken for granted that we have eliminated them *all*. So we usually expect our "if's" to behave like strengthened doubled horseshoes, not like ordinary ones. That is why our statements seem to us "obviously" equivalent to their partial transpositions.

When a proposition logically independent of the others occurs irrelevantly as a conjunct in an antecedent, as in (2), it is an *empirical* matter to show that it is irrelevant. And it is not always quite so simple a matter as (2) may suggest. A chemist, let us suppose, has dis-

[300]

covered that heat discolors a certain salt; but he has made all of his experiments under conditions in which the salt was also exposed to air. If cautious, he will say, "If this salt is exposed to heat *and air* it will discolor." He may suspect that the clause "and air" is irrelevant; but until he has made further experiments he had better not delete it, else he will transform a true statement that may merely have too strong an antecedent into one that may be false. English is not eccentric in permitting irrelevant conjuncts (or those that *may* be irrelevant) in an antecedent: it *usefully* permits them. And the same can be said of the (unstrengthened) doubled horseshoe.

14

We have been considering conjunctive antecedents. Let us now turn to conjunctive consequents, with special attention to a context that is rather unusual. Suppose that we are speaking to a man whom we consider too vain, and that in order to deflate him we say,

(1)   If you die tomorrow, the earth will continue to revolve and your heirs will rejoice.

We should then be surprised, I trust, at being held responsible for having logically implied.

(2)   If you die tomorrow, the earth will continue to revolve.

That is to say, feeling that the antecedent of (2) has nothing to do with its consequent, we should be half-inclined, at least, to deny it, and without retracting (1).

Indeed, we are likely to accept (2) only for a sense of "if" (though there definitely is such a sense) in which an implication is being *denied* rather than affirmed. In this sense "if" is short for "even if"; and the latter term can be defined with reference to a more standard "if" in this way:

(A)   "q, even if p" has the same meaning as "q, and not-(if p then ~q)"

where the definiens often means the same as "q.~(p⊃⊃~q)". So (2) becomes plausible only when its "even if" sense of "if" can be eliminated by the following expansion of it: "The earth will continue to revolve; and it is not the case that if you die tomorrow the earth will stop revolving."

But I doubt that (2) follows from (1) (if I may put it so) even if its "if" is interpreted as an "even if".

Net result: there is an implication *affirming* sense of "if" in which an inference of the form, "If p then q and r; therefore if p then q", is invalid.

The doubled horseshoe preserves this sense of "if"—the following form of inference being shown invalid by the $\sim (qr)$ and $\sim q$ of the rectangle notation:

(3) $$\frac{p \supset \supset qr}{p \supset \supset q} \qquad \frac{p \supset qr \ \square \ p, \sim (qr)}{p \supset q \ \square \ p, \sim q}$$

But this form of inference, like that discussed in the preceding section, has a valid analogue. To state it let me introduce a further symbol—this time a doubled exclamation mark, as in "$p \supset \supset (q!!r)$", with a meaning that can be defined in the rectangle notation thus: $p \supset qr \ \square \ p, \sim q, \sim r$. In English its meaning is best preserved by the explicit conjunction, "If p then q, and if p then r." The valid analogue of (3), with a strengthened premiss, can then be stated:

(4) $$\frac{p \supset \supset (q!!r)}{p \supset \supset q} \qquad \frac{p \supset qr \ \square \ p, \sim q, \sim r}{p \supset q \ \square \ p, \sim q}$$

Note that (1) above, if symbolized in the manner of (4) rather than of (3), becomes empirically false, and is not likely to be asserted in a context that makes such a symbolization appropriate; but most English hypothetical statements can appropriately be so symbolized.

From the present example, and also from the one in the preceding section, it will be evident that the doubled horseshoe, when *un*strengthened, gives a very weak sense of "if". But it can easily be strengthened, and therefore remains useful.

Here is a further example in which the use of an unstrengthened doubled horseshoe is appropriate: Knowing that Jones is stupid, and not knowing whether or not he is a professor, we might be inclined (speaking to someone who suggested that Jones *might* be a professor) to say:

(5)   If Jones is a professor he is a stupid professor.

But we would not, I trust, want to be held responsible for the seeming logical consequence:

(6)   If Jones is a professor he is stupid.

Much depends here, however, on the tone of one's voice in making the statements. Is the "if" in (6) an "even if"? Or alternatively, does (6) just mean, "I grant you that Jones *may* be a professor, but in any case he is stupid"?

But taking both (5) and (6) to be implicational uses of "if," and symbolizing them as below, we find that an inference from the former to the latter is invalid (as disclosed by $\sim$(SP) and $\sim$S):

(7)

$$\frac{P \supset \supset SP}{P \supset \supset S} \qquad \frac{P \supset SP \ \square \ P, \sim(SP)}{P \supset S \ \square \ P, \sim S}$$

The recurrence of the antecedent in the consequent here makes the premiss unusually weak—so weak that it can validly be deduced from *S*, subject only to the innocent assumption that there is a true ground for *S* that is ground-compatible with *P* and ground-compatible with $\sim P$. In the rectangle notation:

(8)

$$\frac{S \ \square \ P, \sim P}{P \supset SP \ \square \ P, \sim(SP)} \qquad \text{(This conclusion} = P \supset \supset SP.)$$

15

Is the doubled horseshoe transitive? In other words, are inferences of the sort below valid?

(1)

$$\frac{\begin{array}{l} p \supset \supset q \\ q \supset \supset r \end{array}}{p \supset \supset r} \qquad \frac{\begin{array}{l} p \supset q \ \square \ p, \sim q \\ q \supset r \ \square \ q, \sim r \end{array}}{p \supset r \ \square \ p, \sim r}$$

Previously, the rectangle notation has been used only for one-premissed arguments; so we have as yet no rule for using it to test this two-premissed argument. But we may judge the argument in the following way:

If (1) is valid, then the truth of the premisses must be sufficient to establish the truth of the conclusion under all possible circumstances. Now a particularly "stringent" circumstance will arise when there is only one true ground, *e*, that makes the first premiss true, and when this *e* is also a ground for *r*. In that case the (non-superfluous) first premiss will not entitle us to the conclusion; for the conclusion requires a true ground that is *not* a ground for *r* (i.e., one that is ground-compatible with $\sim r$). The above argument is *in*valid, then, for that reason. Similarly a particularly "stringent" circumstance will arise when there is only one true ground, e', that makes the second premiss true, and when this e' is also a ground for $\sim p$. In that case the (non-superfluous) second premiss will not entitle us to the conclusion; for the conclusion requires a true ground that is *not* a ground for $\sim p$ (i.e., one that is ground-compatible with p). The above argument is invalid, then, for that reason as well.

To be valid the argument must have strengthened premisses. In the rectangle notation the first premiss must have at least an additional $\sim r$ to the right of the rectangle, and the second premiss must have at least an additional p to the right of the rectangle. That will prevent the premisses from being true under the "stringent" circumstances mentioned above. But to take account of still other "stringent" circumstances (which I need not pause to mention) the premisses must be strengthened even further, and in a way that can be annotated thus:

(2)

$$p{\supset}q \; \Box \; p, \sim q$$
$$q{\supset}r \; \Box \; q, \sim r \quad \Big| \quad p, \sim r$$
$$\overline{p{\supset}r \; \Box \; p, \sim r}$$

Here the perpendicular line, together with the p and $\sim r$ to the right of it, affirm that the *conjunction* of the grounds for the premisses is ground-compatible with p and also ground-compatible with $\sim r$. This strengthening is necessary and sufficient for the validity of the argument-form. The premisses of (2) can also be stated as below,

(3)　$(\exists e,e') : e.e'$　.$eG(p{\supset}q).eCp.eC{\sim}q$　.$e'G(q{\supset}r).e'Cp.e'C{\sim}r.$
　　　$ee'Cp . ee'C{\sim}r,$

where the first line simply restates the premisses of (1) and the second line adds the strengthening introduced by (2).

In most English arguments of the form "If p then q and if q then r, therefore if p then r" we restrict ourselves to cases where (2), rather than (1), is an appropriate translation; and that is why we get the impression that "if" is transitive.

An English example in which "if" is presumably to be translated in the manner of (1), and thus behaves intransitively, will be found in exercise (8), page 281. Here is another example:

Speaking of a girl who is lazy, a professor remarks,

(a) If I pass her I'll be ashamed of myself.
Someone asks him, "If she gets down to work will you pass her?"
He replies in the affirmative, saying,

[304]

(b) If she gets down to work I'll pass her.

And he then becomes embarrassed, feeling that he is forced to the conclusion,

(c) If she gets down to work I'll be ashamed of myself.

But he should not become embarrassed, since he is not, presumably, prepared to strengthen (a) in a way that would make the conclusion follow.

Stated in terms of evidence, rather than of ground, the oddity of the example can be explained thus: The only evidence that can be found for (a), presumably, is also evidence for *she will not get down to work*. And if this evidence is transferred to the conclusion it will not, as required, be intensional evidence for the conclusion, but instead will be extensional evidence for the falsity of its antecedent.

16

The doubled horseshoe must not, of course, be expected to behave like *all* the "if's" in English. It has been specially devised to translate contingent hypothetical statements in which both the antecedent and the consequent are also contingent. So when used to translate "If it rains then it rains", for instance, it makes this necessarily true statement appear to be a contradiction. That is to say, since "ground" has been interpreted (page 289) in a way that suggests the rule,

(R4)   eGp   strictly implies   p is contingent

It follows that $R \supset \supset R$, which ascribes a true intensional ground to the tautology, $R \supset R$, is necessarily false. So "If R then R" must be translated in some other way (to be mentioned presently). I am here limiting my attention to hypothetical statements that deal only with contingencies—statements that impress me as needing special attention because they are typical of the premises and conclusions of every-day arguments.

In so limiting my attention I am, no doubt, treating as *meanings* of "if" certain contextual suggestions attending the term that could alternatively be said, in Strawson's sense, to be *presupposed* in the course of using it.[6] Thus when a man says, "If I strike this match it

---

[6] See /7/, pp. 175–179. I may be stretching the term "presupposition" somewhat, though not enough, I trust, to obscure Strawson's meaning or my own.

will light" (which *is* to be symbolized by the doubled horseshoe), he may be simply presupposing that his statement is contingent, not asserting that it is. But the presuppositions that attend "if's" are so varied that it is convenient, in my opinion, to use symbols that *make* them become meanings. With different presuppositions the "if's" will behave in accordance with different rules, and that is a reason for taking them to be different "if's".

With regard to presuppositions, and their connection with the doubled horseshoe, let us consider the following context: *If p then q,* [*and a contingent connection between a contingent antecedent and a contingent consequent is in question*]. And let us interpret the bracketed part of the context either (a) as being expressly stated or (b) as making explicit a presupposition of the unbracketed part, where the presupposition is so obviously to be attributed to the speaker that it can safely be treated as included in what he meant. Now the doubled horseshoe is expected to provide translations only for statements like these (and not all, even, of them, though certainly for those that are most typical of our everyday discourse).

Suppose, then, that someone were thoroughly muddled, saying, "If it rains then it rains" with the claim or obvious presupposition of contingency just mentioned. Such a person, and only such a person, might fairly be credited with giving the sentence a meaning that the doubled horseshoe could symbolize—the "to be rejected" nature of his assertion being then properly made evident by the rules governing the symbol.

Consider next these "oddities" in English:

(a) If it doesn't rain then it will rain.
(b) If 2+2=5, then Alger Hiss was guilty.
(c) If I take my umbrella, it will either rain or not rain.

Here (c) is acceptable when its "if" is understood as an implication denying "even if". But for implication affirming senses of "if", all three propositions might just as well as not be translated by the doubled horseshoe; for that will make them out as necessarily false, as they normally are taken to be. What is important is that we get safely rid of them. And the *single* horseshoe, of course, does not enable us to do that: it makes (a) a hard way of saying that it will rain, and thus a contingent statement; and it makes (b) and (c) both a priori true.

It is possible, using the doubled horseshoe, to define a weaker "if"-regarding symbol that at once can translate "If R then R" into a true statement and translate (a), (b), and (c) into false statements. Letting this weaker "if"-regarding symbol be "$\supset \# \supset$", we may define it:

(A) $p \supset \# \supset q$ =Df. $(p \supset \supset q) \vee (\Box (p \supset q) . \sim \Box \sim p . \sim \Box q)$

Such a symbol is still restricted to translations from English in which the contingency of the antecedent and consequent is affirmed (or obviously presupposed), but is no longer restricted to cases in which a contingent relation *between* the antecedent and consequent is affirmed. It should be noted that the modal part of the definiens requires a "rational intensional evidence," so to speak, for $p \supset q$.

There are certain "if"-sentences, such as "If $p \vee \sim p$ then $\sim (p \sim p)$", that are appropriate for use in speaking of the relation between axioms and theorems in a formal system, or between certain theorems and others that are proved by them. A proper symbolization of these sentences has been sought by A. R. Anderson and others /1/, in the hope of avoiding the "paradoxes" of strict implication. Whether that is possible, and how useful it would be if possible, I cannot say. The doubled horseshoe, of course, with its emphasis on contingency, is far removed from these perplexing "if's".

I suspect that my doubled horseshoe is more "if"-like than the symbol "ec", as defined by my colleague Arthur Burks /3/—though the two are in many respects alike. He uses another symbol, "npc," that is extremely close to *some* English "if's"—contingent "if's" that are stronger than those to which my doubled horseshoe and his "ec" are intended to be faithful. Perhaps I can define an equally strong "if"-like symbol in the following manner, writing it as a tripled horseshoe:

(B) $p \supset \supset \supset q$ =Df. $p \supset \supset q . \sim (\exists r) : (p . ! r) \supset \supset q$

That is to say, a tripled-horseshoe proposition, when true, is a true doubled-horseshoe proposition to which no conjunct can *relevantly* be added in its antecedent. (Cf. p. 300.)

17

My remarks have been exploratory, intended more to raise questions than to answer them. So perhaps I can properly end with some further questions, supplemented by conjectures.

What is to be said of propositions of the form $(x) : Px \supset \supset Qx$, or of the form (x) : Px ⊃⊃⊃ Qx? Both will be stronger than (x) : Px ⊃ Qx, since neither will follow from ∼ (∃x) Px, or from (x) Qx. So perhaps the quantified tripled horseshoe, like Burks's quantified "npc", will be useful in stating laws of nature; and perhaps the quantified doubled horseshoe will be useful in stating generalizations that depend on the facts, as well as the laws, of nature—such generalizations as *all brakeless trains are dangerous.*

Shall expressions of the form e′G (eGp), dealing with grounds for ground-relations, be provided with special rules that make them reducible to simpler expressions? For example, just as □□p is sometimes taken to be reducible to □p, so, perhaps, e′G (eGp) can be taken as reducible, with certain provisos, to eGp. Or more plausibly : perhaps e′G (e . eGp) can be taken as reducible to e′Ge . eGp.

A decision about e′G (eGp) will have a bearing on cases in which one doubled-horseshoe proposition has another as its antecedent or consequent, as in p⊃⊃ (q⊃⊃r) or in (p⊃⊃q) ⊃⊃r. In accordance with the definition of the doubled horseshoe, each of these will include a ground-symbol within the scope of another; but perhaps they will prove, given acceptable postulates, to be equivalent to propositions in which that is not the case. Perhaps p⊃⊃ (q⊃⊃r) can be properly taken as equivalent to (∃e) : p⊃⊃e . eG^i(q⊃r)—where "eG^i" abbreviates "is an intensional ground for". And perhaps (p⊃⊃q)⊃⊃r can be handled in a parallel but somewhat more complicated manner.

For doubled-horseshoe propositions that have a strengthened conjunctive antecedent (see p. 300), a not dissimilar question arises with regard to exportation. Unquestionably, (p.!q) ⊃⊃r exports to p⊃⊃(q⊃r); but does it, with innocent provisos, also export to p⊃⊃(q⊃⊃r)?

Finally : will the doubled horseshoe help to provide an analysis of hypothetical statements that are expressed in the subjunctive mood?

References

1. Anderson, A. R. and Belnap, N. D., "Tautological Entailments", *Philosophical Studies,* Vol. 13, 1962.

2. Burks, A. W., "The Logic of Causal Propositions", *Mind,* Vol. 60 (1951).

3. Burks, A. W., "Dispositional Statements", *Philosophy of Science,* Vol. 22 (1955).

4. Grice, H. P., "Implication" (unpublished).

5. Johnson, W. E., *Logic,* Vol. I, Chap. III (Cambridge, England, 1921), 38–47.

6. Lewis, C. I., and Langford, C. H., *Symbolic Logic* (New York, 1932).

7. Strawson, P. F., *Introduction to Logical Theory* (London, 1952).

SIXTEEN

On What

Could Have

Happened

MORTON WHITE

1

FOR LONGER than some people know, or others care to remember, philosophers have been concerned to elucidate sentences of the form, "That did not happen but it could have happened," especially philosophers who wish to show that such utterances do not conflict with determinism. For example, G. E. Moore says at one point in his *Ethics:* "It is impossible to exaggerate the frequency of the occasions on which we *all* of us make a distinction between two things, neither of which *did* happen—a distinction which we express by saying, that whereas the one *could* have happened, [the] other could not", and Moore adds that this distinction "is *the* one which we mean to express

I regret that I was prevented, for personal reasons, from preparing a new paper in time for inclusion in this volume. Therefore, I am very grateful to the editors for consenting to reprint a paper of mine which reflects, I believe, the salutary influence of Nelson Goodman on my philosophical work. The paper appeared originally in the *Philosophical Review*, Vol. LXXVII (January 1968), 73–89.

by saying that the one was possible and the other impossible".[1]

In illustrating this distinction, Moore tells us that he did not walk a mile in twenty minutes on (I add a date) January 1, 1910, and that he did not run two miles in five minutes that day, but that he could have performed the first action though he could not have performed the second. Furthermore, Moore tells us, a certain cat could have climbed a tree that day but a certain dog could not have climbed a tree that day, though neither did climb a tree that day. Moore also cites the case of a twenty-knot steamer which did not steam twenty knots that day but which could have, and contrasts it with the case of a fifteen-knot steamer which did not steam twenty knots that day but could not have.

In producing these illustrations, Moore aims first of all to show that whereas a determinist may want to say that all the mentioned non-happenings, so to speak, are necessary, in another sense of the word "necessary" they are not. Moore also has the more specific aim of showing that some non-happenings like his not walking a mile in twenty minutes on January 1, 1910, are not necessary, in order to show that some human actions are voluntary and in what sense they are. Understandably, Moore devotes himself more assiduously to the second task in his *Ethics* and says comparatively little about the first. He tries to tell us what the sense is in which he could have performed an action even though he did not perform it, but there is little discussion of what it means to say that other kinds of non-happenings are possible. Yet the more general problem is of great philosophical interest, and I venture to say that if we are not clear about it we will not be as clear as we should be about the more special problem that arises in ethics. For this reason I wish to address myself in this paper to the general concept of what could have happened or what could have been the case, and to say a few fundamental things about it which I think deserve notice. One of my ultimate aims is to use the conclusions of this paper in an effort to clarify ethical or free-will "could have"-sentences, but that will have to wait for another time.

2

If we are to discuss the more general concept of what could have happened, we shall find it useful to add another sort of illustration to

---

[1] G. E. Moore, *Ethics* (New York: Oxford University Press, 1949), 127–128.

Moore's list of things that did not happen but that could have happened. Let us suppose that a certain match did not light on January 1, 1910, but that it could have lit. Once again the determinist may want to say that the match's not lighting is necessary, but a philosopher like Moore may wish to say that there is another sense of "necessary" in which the match's not lighting is not necessary since there is a sense of "could have" in which it could have lit. If we keep in mind illustrations like this, we shall be able to avoid thinking about some of the irrelevant features of Moore's illustrations about cats, dogs, steamships, and human beings as we concentrate on the general concept of what could have been the case.

While we are freeing ourselves from the need to concentrate on some of the irrelevant features of Moore's illustrations, we may also observe a peculiarity of Moore's comments on his illustrations—comments which may also stand in the way of our focusing on the relevant uses of "could have" and "could not have". When Moore says that a particular cat could have climbed a tree that day, he supports his assertion merely by pointing out that as a rule cats can climb trees. Similarly, when he says that a particular dog could *not* have climbed a tree that day, he defends that assertion merely by pointing out that as a rule dogs cannot climb trees. Presumably, it is by means of a similar argument that Moore would have defended his assertion that a particular twenty-knot steamer could have steamed twenty knots on a particular day whereas a particular fifteen-knot steamer could not have. Yet if the sentence "Jemimah could have climbed a tree that day" is supported merely by pointing out that Jemimah is a cat and cats can climb trees, it is not the sort of context of "could have" that I am primarily concerned with, nor, I might add, the sort that Moore should have been concerned with in his *Ethics*. For suppose that Jemimah had a broken leg on January 1, 1910. In that case Jemimah could *not* have climbed a tree that day, even though Jemimah is a cat and cats can as a rule climb trees. For this reason we must make explicit our concern with those "could have"-sentences which are the denials of sentences like "That cat could not have climbed a tree that day", when it is understood that the latter sentence may be uttered by one who knows full well that as a rule cats can climb trees, or simply that that cat had that ability during the period in question.[2]

---

[2] I find an analogous distinction made by Jonathan Edwards between what he calls a *"general and habitual* moral inability" and a *"particular and occasional* moral inability". See his *Freedom of the Will, The Works of Jonathan Edwards*, ed. Ramsey, Paul (New Haven: Yale University

That Moore ought to have been concerned with this sort of "could have"-sentence, and not with one that merely expresses a general capacity of a cat, a man, or a steamship is evident from the fact that he is concerned in his *Ethics* with the conditions under which we may properly pass moral judgment. Clearly, it is not enough to know that Moore had the general capacity to walk a mile in twenty minutes if we are planning to condemn him for *not* performing that action on a certain day. If we know that he had a broken leg on that day and that having the broken leg prevented him from performing the action, we withhold our moral judgment of his failure, even though we know that men as a rule can walk a mile in twenty minutes, or that he could. The moralist's "could have"-sentence, if I may call it that, is not one that follows from a statement about a general capacity that men as a rule have, nor is it one that follows from a statement about a general capacity that a particular man like Moore may have had at a certain period in his life.

Moreover, in spite of the fact that we do not pass moral judgment on a match for not lighting, we sometimes say of a match that it could have lit, while using "could have" in the same way as we do when, as moral judges of Moore's failure to walk a mile in twenty minutes on a certain day, we say that he could have. Matches can as a rule light but the one in question may have been wet and hence could not have lit. The logical moral is once again that A's having some general capacity or ability to x is not sufficient for showing that A could have x'ed in the sense of "could have x'ed" with which we are concerned. This is true independently of whether A is a person or an inanimate object, and independently of whether x'ing is a human action or a piece of behavior on the part of an inanimate object.

3

In order to deal with our "could have" more perspicuously, it will be useful to adopt a familiar notation, encouraged by Moore's statement that his distinction between what could have happened and what could not have happened may also be expressed by using the words

---

Press, 1957), I, 160. This seems to be related to Austin's distinction between saying that a man could have done something "in the full sense" and saying that he had an ability. See J. L. Austin, "Ifs and Cans", *Philosophical Papers*, eds. Urmson, J. O. and Warnock, G. J. (New York: Oxford University Press, 1961), 173.

"possible" and "impossible". Let us prefix the word "possible" to a past-tense singular sentence enclosed in parentheses when we wish to say that what that sentence reports or records could have been the case, and also prefix the word "necessary" in an analogous way when we wish to say that what the sentence in parentheses records was bound to have been the case. In what follows we shall also use the dash as a denial or negation sign and the dot as a sign for conjunction. Reference to the past will therefore be made in the sentence enclosed in parentheses, whereas the words "possible" and "necessary" are to be used tenselessly, just as the expressions "It is true that" and "It is the case that", may be used tenselessly when prefixed to sentences about the past. Sometimes we shall use capital letters with subscripts "S_1," "S_2," and so forth, in place of sentences like "Moore walked a mile in twenty minutes on January 1, 1910" and "That match lit on January 1, 1910". Such parenthesized sentences will not only be in the past tense and singular because of our primary interest in what *could have happened,* but it is well to limit ourselves to third-person sentences in order to avoid certain irrelevant problems that have arisen in discussion of Moore's first-person examples.[3]

Using the notation mentioned, we may say that the general problem to which we address ourselves is to elucidate possibility sentences which may, but do not always, appear in true sentences having the form:

(A) $-S_1 \cdot \text{possible } (S_1) \cdot - S_2 \cdot - \text{possible } (S_2)$.

By contrast, the determinist would assert, for all p of the kind under consideration,

(B)   If $- p$ then $-$ possible (p),

and would therefore deny (A). Hence our task is to elucidate the conjunction "$-S_1 \cdot \text{possible } (S_1)$" appearing in (A), so as to show how (A) could be true and yet not conflict with the thesis of the determinist as expressed in (B).

4

The central thesis of this paper is that "could have"-sentences of the kind we are interested in are elliptical and may be elucidated in two

---

[3] I have in mind some of Austin's remarks in "Ifs and Cans", esp. pp. 159–160. See Sec. 9 below for further discussion of this point.

main ways, both of them consonant with a desire to provide an elucidation of (A) that will not conflict with determinism as formulated in (B). But before I say what those two ways are, I must point out that when trying to elucidate an elliptical sentence like "— S_1 · possible (S_1)" we must keep in mind a distinction, rightly insisted upon by Austin among writers on this subject, between expansion and analysis.[4] Expansion is the process whereby we convert an elliptical sentence into a complete sentence, and it is enough to say here that analysis is a process whereby we take a complete sentence and offer another complete sentence as its equivalent. Thus, certain probability theorists first advise us to expand sentences of the form "The probability that a is P is n" into complete sentences of the form "The probability that a is P relative to a's being Q is n". Then they say that such complete sentences are equivalent to complete sentences of the form "The limit of the relative frequency with which Q's are P is n."

The two modes of expanding "— S_1 · possible (S_1)" are as follows. One converts "— S_1 · possible (S_1)" into a contrary-to-fact conditional of a certain kind, and the other converts it into the denial of a factual conditional of a certain kind—that is, the denial of what may also be called a singular "because"-statement. Therefore any conclusion that one method of expansion is preferable to another in a given context—like the ethical—must be defended on grounds over and above the fact that it allows us to make peace with determinism. Naturally, if "—S_1 · possible (S_1)" is thought to require expansion into a contrary-to-fact conditional, the analysis of that conditional will, in general, be different from the analysis of the denial of a factual conditional. Therefore, if we think of elucidation as a process of expansion-*cum*-analysis, we see why the original elliptical sentence may be elucidated in two distinct ways. Once these two patterns of expansion-*cum*-analysis are before the moral philosopher, he may then decide which of them is to be used on "could have"-sentences in which we justify the passing of moral judgment on actions—that is, "could have"-sentences which express voluntariness. I now turn to a detailed presentation and discussion of these two modes of expansion and the analyses that go with them.

5

If we say "—Match a lit on January 1, 1910 · possible (match a lit on January 1, 1910)" and represent this by:

[4] *Ibid.,* pp. 162 ff.

(1) $-S_1 \cdot$ possible (S_1),

our first pattern of expansion dictates that we expand this into something of the form "If S_2 had been the case, then S_1 would have been
the case." But what is the false sentence "S_2"? That all depends on
what is in the mind of the speaker. It may be "Match a was struck on
January 1, 1910" or it may be "Match a was dry on January 1, 1910"
or it may be some other sentence. The possibility of several first-
pattern expansions of (1) is parallel to a similar possibility in the
case where we may be expanding probability sentences and using
different reference classes. But just as we would not say that this
possibility of several expansions in the case of probability sentences
shows that the *word* "probability" has different meanings, so we
should not say that the word "possible" or the phrase "could have"
means different things in the elliptical possibility sentence. What is
true is that one elliptical possibility *sentence* may be understood in
two different ways depending on which contrary-to-fact conditional
appears in its correct expansion.

It may be said that a three-part conjunction of the form "$-S_1 \cdot$
$-S_2 \cdot$ If it had been the case that S_2, then it would have been the case
that S_1" is redundant because the last of the conjuncts implies the
other two. In that case the sentence into which (1) is expanded may be
written as follows, since a contrary-to-fact conditional expresses a
necessary connection between the denial of its antecedent and the denial of its consequent:

(2) $-S_1 \cdot -S_2 \cdot$ necessary (if S_2 then S_1).

This in turn may be transformed into:

(3) $-S_1 \cdot -S_2 \cdot$ —possible— (if S_2 then S_1),

and further logical transformation will yield:

(4) $-S_1 \cdot -S_2 \cdot$ —possible $(S_2 \cdot -S_1)$.

We have now reached the point where our elliptical possibility
sentence (1) has been expanded into a complete sentence which contains the *denial* of a possibility. The expansion, therefore, involves,
among other things, putting a negation sign into the sentence where
one was not present before. Yet it should be insisted that the process
in question *is* expansion of a complicated sort, quite analogous to the
expansion recommended by the probability theory mentioned earlier.[5]

[5] Austin, in "Ifs and Cans", considers only one sort of expansion and that

The point is that when anyone asserts something elliptical like (1) he means to assert something complete like (4). People will put different sentences where "—S_2" is, depending on what they have in mind, but one *pattern* of expanding (1) is revealed in (4). We may call "—S_2" the reference sentence by aping the terminology of the probability theorist.

Nelson Goodman has pointed out that the denial of a contrary-to-fact conditional is what he calls a semifactual like "Even if S_2 had been the case, (still) —S_1 would have been the case"—semifactual because the antecedent "S_2" is false and the consequent "—S_1" is true. He also points out that such a semifactual is the contrary rather than the contradictory of the contrary-to-fact conditional of which it is a denial.[6] This is made perspicuous by writing the semifactual as:

(5) $-S_1 \cdot -S_2 \cdot$ possible $(S_2 \cdot -S_1)$,

because here we see plainly that (5) is the contrary of (4), rather than its contradictory. An interesting consequence is that the sentence "Moore's not walking a mile in twenty minutes was voluntary" will, on certain philosophical treatments of it, be the contrary of "Moore's not walking a mile in twenty minutes was *not* voluntary."

6

Let us now turn to another pattern of expanding (1) which we may call second-pattern expansion. Here, instead of saying as we do in the case of first-pattern expansion that S_1, which is not the case, would have been the case if S_2 had been the case, we say instead that —S_1 was not necessitated by some state or event recorded in a true sentence "S_4" which the speaker did not make explicit.[7] For example, we may

---

is different from those under consideration in this paper. In effect he considers only the view that "possible (S_1)" must be expanded into "If S_2 then possible (S_1)." In rejecting that view, he does not show that "possible (S_1)" is not elliptical, but at best that it is not elliptical for "If S_2 then possible (S_1)", where the conditional is causal.

[6] Nelson Goodman, *Fact, Fiction, and Forecast*, Second Ed. (Indianapolis: Bobbs-Merrill, 1965), Chap. 1, Sec. 1.

[7] This approach to elliptical possibility sentences is a corollary of a familiar approach to elliptical necessity sentences. Thus W. V. Quine says that "the adverb 'necessarily' applies only by ellipsis to particular events or states, and properly rather to whole conditional connections: 'Necessarily if p then q.'" "Necessary Truth", *The Ways of Paradox and Other Essays* (New York: Random House, 1966), p. 51.

say that the match's not lighting was not necessitated by its being white (for whatever reason). In that case a sentence like (1) is expanded into:

(6) $-S_1 \cdot S_4 \cdot -$necessary (if S_4 then $-S_1$),

which may be logically transformed into:

(7) $-S_1 \cdot S_4 \cdot$ possible $-$ (if S_4 then $-S_1$),

which may be transformed into:

(8) $-S_1 \cdot S_4 \cdot$ possible $(S_4 \cdot S_1)$

Here the contrast with the first pattern of expansion may be seen most dramatically, since the third conjunct of (8) asserts a possibility whereas the corresponding conjunct in (4) asserts an impossibility, though the same contrast is already portrayed in the contrast between (2) and (6), which are formulated by the use of the word "necessary". Furthermore, the denial of (6) is its contrary, namely,

(9) $-S_1 \cdot S_4 \cdot$ necessary (if S_4 then $-S_1$).

This is equivalent to what Goodman calls a factual conditional because "$-S_1$" and "S_4" are thought to be true. It may be read "Since S_4 is the case, $-S_1$ is the case", or "Because S_4 is the case, $-S_1$ is the case", and also be called a singular "because"-statement.

That we have here a pattern of expansion may be seen by noticing that there are many sentences other than "S_4" which could have been used as reference sentences in other situations in which a possibility was elliptically asserted. Once again, therefore, it is misleading to think that the *word* "possible" changes its meaning as we move from one second-pattern expansion to another. In illustration of a similar point we may point out that an expression like "5 is greater" may be expanded on one occasion into "5 is greater than 4" and on another into "5 is greater than 3," depending on what the speaker had in mind when he uttered the elliptical expression. The phrase "is greater" will, however, retain the same meaning throughout.

7

A first-pattern expansion of (1) normally leads to a contrary-to-fact conditional, but because every contrary-to-fact conditional is equivalent to an indicative which is its contrapositive, we may express such an expansion by replacing "if S_2 then S_1" in (2) above by "if —S_1, then —S_2," to get:

(10)   —S_1 • —S_2 • necessary (if —S_1 then —S_2).

Formula (10) may now be instructively compared with formula (6), since in each case the first two conjuncts are thought to be true. We can see plainly now that (10), the first-pattern expansion of (1), yields after some obvious logical transformations the *affirmation* of a certain factual conditional, whereas (6), the second-pattern expansion of (1), yields the *denial* of another factual conditional.

We may now summarize what we have said about the two patterns of expansion by distinguishing two relations between p and q, where p and q are both false. We may say that p is *I*-possible relative to q if and only if the denial of p necessitates the denial of q. Thus, considering a match which did not light and was not struck, *it was lit* is *I*-possible relative to *it was struck* if and only if *it was not lit* necessitates *it was not struck*. It should be observed that this statement of necessitation contains two true statements as components. We may also say that p is *II*-possible relative to q if and only if the denial of q does not necessitate the denial of p. For example, in the case of a white match which did not light, *it was lit* is *II*-possible relative to *it was not white* if, and only if, *it was white* does not necessitate *it was not lit*. Here the denial of necessitation contains two true statements as components. It may be said that these are not expansions because the word "possible" has disappeared. But we know that we can easily restore it by replacing the expression "The denial of p necessitates the denial of q" by its equivalent, "—possible (—p • q)", in the case of first-pattern expansion. Similarly, in the case of second-pattern expansion we may put for "The denial of q does not necessitate the denial of p" the expression "possible (—q • p)."

So far we have said nothing about how to analyze the complete affirmations and denials of possibility into which we have expanded elliptical possibility sentences. Therefore we have not reached the stage of elucidation corresponding to that in which the probability theorist equates "The probability that a is P relative to a's being Q is n" with "The limit of the relative frequency with which Q's are P is n". Let us now sketch an analysis of necessity sentences from which the reader can easily derive the analysis of the relevant complete sentences containing the word "possible".

Here it must suffice to say that I favor an approach modeled on Goodman's treatment of contrary-to-fact conditionals. The statement "Necessary (if p then q)", in the case where "p" and "q" are true, is true just in case there are true statements of relevant conditions such that "p" and those true statements lead by law to "q".[8] This approach to factual conditionals may be distinguished from one presented by Quine, who says in answer to the question "What does it take to qualify a connection as necessary?" that it is a generality.[9] When a man who knows that a certain individual had spots says, "Necessarily, Leo had spots", he may mean on certain occasions what should be expanded into "Necessarily, if Leo was a leopard then Leo had spots" or, in our notation, "Necessary (if Leo was a leopard then Leo had spots)". This complete statement, as I understand Quine, is true if and only if all leopards have spots. Unlike Quine, however, I think that a sentence of the form "Necessary (if p, then q)", where the substituends for "p" and "q" are singular sentences of the kind illustrated earlier, may be true even if the generalization which stands to it as "All leopards have spots" stands to "Necessary (if Leo was a leopard, then Leo had spots)" is not true. "All leopards have spots" is what I have elsewhere described as superficially related to "Necessary (if Leo was a leopard, then Leo had spots)."[10] Therefore, I think that "Necessary (if match a was struck yesterday, then match a lit yesterday)" is true even though it is false that all matches light when they are struck. In other words, it is proper to say that *one* of the so-called jointly sufficient conditions for a certain state or event necessitates that state or event.

8

Now that we have presented two ways of expanding elliptical sentences like (1) into complete sentences, and have outlined analyses of those complete sentences, we see that either one of these ways of expanding-*cum*-analyzing sentences like (1) will do a job described earlier. Either one of them will elucidate possibility sentences and impossibility sentences that may appear in true sentences like (A) above, without forcing the abandonment of what may be called de-

---

[8] *Ibid.* See also my *Foundations of Historical Knowledge* (New York: Harper and Row, 1965), ch. III.

[9] *The Ways of Paradox*, pp. 48–51.

[10] *Foundations of Historical Knowledge*, pp. 63–66.

terminism. If we say "*p* is *I*-possible relative to *q*", meaning that —*p*, which is true, necessitates —*q*, which is true, we are obviously not denying that something necessitates —*p*. And if we say "*p* is *II*-possible relative to *q*", meaning that —*q*, which is true, does not necessitate —*p*, which is true, once again we are not denying that something necessitates —*p*. So we cannot decide which expansion to use simply on the basis of finding out which of them accords with a desire like Moore's to find a sense of "possible" (and hence of "necessary") which is not deterministic in the sense of (B) above.

Furthermore, when the determinist says that Moore's *not* walking a mile in twenty minutes on January 1, 1910, *A*'s cat's *not* climbing a tree on January 1, 1910, the twenty-knot steamer's *not* steaming twenty knots on January 1, 1910, and match *a*'s not lighting on January 1, 1910, are all necessary, he too speaks elliptically. Only *his* elliptical sentence, "Necessary (—match *a* lit on January 1, 1910)", is to be expanded according to a pattern which is neither our first nor our second. His elliptical sentence, it would appear, should be expanded into a complete existential sentence which is equivalent to "Something necessitated (—match *a* lit on January 1, 1910)." In that case, however, we see that he uses the word "necessitated" *in his complete sentence* as it is used in the expansions of elliptical necessity sentences according to our first or second patterns.

This is a convenient place at which to observe that the existence of the first two patterns of expansion mentioned is closely connected with the difference between a semifactual conditional like "Even if that match had been struck, it still would not have lit" and a factual conditional like "If (or since) that match was wet, it did not light." The first pattern of expansion leads from "possible (that match lit)" to the denial of the semifactual conditional, whereas the second pattern of expansion leads from the same elliptical sentence to the denial of the factual conditional. Sometimes when we say that that match, which did not light, could have lit, we mean to disagree with someone (real or imagined) who has said, for whatever reason, "Even if that match had been struck, still it would not have lit", whereas on other occasions we mean to disagree with someone (real or imagined) who has said, for whatever reason, "If (or since) that match was white, it did not light." Perhaps the fact that both expansions of "possible (that match lit)" lead to the denial of a certain kind of sentence containing "if" makes more comprehensible the linguistic phenomenon to which I am calling attention.

9

Having made the main positive points of this paper, I should like now to mention some questions that remain, and to draw certain implications from what I have said.

A. I want to repeat that I have not here addressed myself to the problem of how we should elucidate "could have"-sentences that are used to express the voluntariness of an action. In particular, I have not tried to say whether the first pattern of expansion or the second must be used in such cases. That question is too large to be treated here. I do think, however, that an answer to it would help clarify the muddy waters in which discussions of so-called positive and negative freedom have for so long been submerged. It may be that *positive* freedom is linked with our first pattern, which transforms a "could have"-sentence into an *affirmation* of a particular necessity, and *negative* freedom with our second, which transforms a "could have"-sentence into a *denial* of a particular necessity.

B. Even though I do not argue that sentences of the form "Moore could have *x*'ed" must be expanded into "Moore would have *x*'ed if Moore had chosen to *x*", where the latter sentence is a causal conditional, I do want to call attention here to two questionable arguments *against* this mode of expansion-*cum*-analysis, both of them employed by Austin.

One argument that Austin uses may be plausibly leveled only against the view that first-person sentences of the form "I could have *x*'ed" are to be expanded into "I should have *x*'ed if I had chosen to *x*." Because this argument exploits the peculiarities of first-person sentences, it does not affect third-person sentences like "Moore would have *x*'ed if he had chosen to *x*." That is to say, it does not show that such third-person sentences are not causal in the sense in which "It would have lit if it had been struck" is causal. I would also observe that because moral judges are primarily concerned to make third-person statements of voluntariness in order to determine whether their third-person moral judgments are applicable, the behavior of first-person sentences of the kind that Austin fastens on is of comparatively little interest to them. We can see this by comparing "I shall if I choose" with "Moore will if he chooses". Even if the first be non-causal, as Austin maintains it is, it does not follow that the second is. And the second is what counts when the moral judge is trying to decide whether the action about to be performed by Moore is voluntary. Returning to the alleged contrast between "I should have if I had chosen" and "Moore would have if he had chosen", I think we can say that it is less obvious than that between "I shall if I choose" and "Moore will if he chooses". In the latter case one may plausibly argue as Austin does that "I shall" is not an assertion of fact but an expression of intention, and in that way challenge the view that "I shall if I choose" is causal. But that argument is not available when one is dealing with "I should have if I had chosen", and I do not think that Austin offers others that do the trick. In any case, the crucial point is that Austin's arguments concerning first-person conditionals, whether valid or not, fail to show that the corresponding third-person conditionals are not causal.

C. Another argument employed by Austin is directed at the view that sentences of the form "Jones could have x'ed" may be transformed into sentences of the form "Jones would have x'ed if Jones had *tried* to x", a view which he regards as having only some plausibility by contrast to the wholly, as he thinks, implausible view that "I could have x'ed" may be transformed into "I should have x'ed if I had *chosen* to x".

I agree that the kind of "could have"-sentence that Austin has in mind here is *not* susceptible to first-pattern expansion, but only because it is the sort of "could have"-sentence that expresses a general capacity and hence is illustrated by Moore's example about A's cat, which kind of example we set aside in Section 2 above. It does not follow, however, that the sort of "could have"-sentences treated in this paper cannot, on some occasions of their use, be properly expanded according to the first pattern into sentences of the form "He would have x'ed if he had tried to x."

I would argue that "Jones could have sunk that ball" may be expanded on *some* occasions of its utterance into the conjunction "—Jones sank that ball · —Jones tried to sink that ball · If Jones had tried to sink that ball, Jones would have sunk that ball." Naturally, if Jones on some other occasion did not sink a ball and had *tried* to sink it, we cannot expand the "could have"-sentence uttered on that occasion in the same way. The expansion of that "could have"-sentence might, however, read "—Jones sank the ball · That blade of grass deflected the ball · If that blade of grass had not deflected the ball, Jones would have sunk the ball." The fact that on the other occasion we can mean this by a "could have"-sentence shows that Austin is right in saying that there are occasions on which we utter sentences of the form "Jones could have x'ed" whose meaning is not rendered

[323]

by a contrary-to-fact conditional with "tried" in the antecedent. But Austin goes further and seems to say that there are "could have"-sentences, which are uttered on occasions when it would be wrong to use *any* first-pattern expansion. For that reason, I believe, he is thinking of a different kind of "could have"-sentence, namely one that expresses a general capacity or ability.

After Austin points out, as I would say in my terminology, that some "could have"-sentences are not first-pattern expandable by using reference sentences containing the word "tried", he says: "It is not that I should have holed it if conditions had been different: that might of course be so, but I am talking about conditions as they precisely were, and asserting that I could have holed it. There is the rub." So it looks as though Austin would reject *all* expansions like the one using "That blade of grass deflected the ball" as a reference sentence. We can see more clearly what Austin may be driving at by considering his further statement, "Nor does 'I can hole it this time' mean that I shall hole it this time if I try or if anything else: for I may try and miss, and yet not be convinced that I could not have done it; indeed, further experiments may confirm my belief that I could have done it that time although I did not." Now we may ask: what use of "y could have x'ed" may (1) lead us to say that such a sentence is not expandable according to our first pattern no matter what the reference sentence, (2) lead us to say that such a sentence is maintainable in the face of y's failures to do x upon trying, and (3) lead us to say that the sentence may be confirmed by further experiments of the kind mentioned by Austin? I suggest that it may be the very use misleadingly employed by Moore in his illustration about A's cat. Moore, it will be recalled, defended his assertion that A's cat could have climbed a tree on January 1, 1910, simply by pointing out that cats can as a rule climb trees. Presumably, therefore, he was relying on the fact that A's cat had the general capacity to climb trees when he said that A's cat could have climbed a tree on a certain day. This sort of sentence, which asserts a general capacity, or rather one of its supposed consequences, is the sort of thing that Austin seems to have in mind in his perplexing footnote about putting. Such a "could have"-sentence may be true even if y tries to x and fails, and it may be confirmed by further experiments. But what could it be that those further experiments might establish in the golf example? Simply that y can sink, say, two-foot putts. And this is the counterpart of "y can climb trees", which, as I have said earlier, is not to be confused with the sentences for which I have proposed the above expansion patterns.

[324]

That this interpretation of Austin is correct may be seen from the footnote in question, since he says there that "enshrined" in the "can" and "could" he has in mind there are "traditional beliefs", according to which "a human ability or power or capacity is inherently liable not to produce success, on occasion, and that for no reason (or are bad luck and bad form sometimes reasons?)." Clearly, then, Austin thinks that "Jones could have sunk that putt", as he understands that sentence in the footnote, expresses an ability or power or capacity that Jones had at the time in question, much as Moore thought that "A's cat could have climbed a tree on January 1, 1910" expresses a capacity that A's cat had, or that cats as a rule have. It is a further question, of course, whether there is always a reason why a man who has a capacity and who tries to exercise it, fails. Austin seems to say no but does not argue seriously for his view.

In any case, it seems to me that even though some "could have"-sentences are not expandable according to our first pattern—or according to our second, I might add—this in no way undermines the main thesis of this paper, according to which there are two main ways of expanding the "could have"-sentences with which I have been concerned here, both ways compatible with determinism as conceived by Moore. The further question about how "could have"-sentences which are expandable according to the first or second patterns are logically related to those expressing capacity or opportunity has not been raised in this paper. But obviously it must be raised by anyone interested in "could have"-sentences expressing voluntariness.

Writings of

Nelson Goodman

Books

A Study of Qualities (Ph.D. thesis), Harvard University (ms.) (1941) (An earlier version of parts of *The Structure of Appearance*).

The Structure of Appearance, Harvard University Press (1951). Second Edition, Indianapolis: Bobbs-Merrill (1966).

Fact, Fiction, and Forecast, Athlone Press, University of London (1954), Harvard University Press (1955). Second Edition, Indianapolis: Bobbs-Merrill (1965).

Languages of Art: An Approach to a Theory of Symbols, Indianapolis: Bobbs-Merrill (1968).

Problems and Projects, Indianapolis: Bobbs-Merrill (1971).

Articles

"The Calculus of Individuals and its Uses" (with H. S. Leonard), *Journal of Symbolic Logic,* 5 (1940), 45–55.

"Elimination of Extra-Logical Postulates" (with W. V. Quine), *Journal of Symbolic Logic*, 5 (1940), 104–109.

"Sequences", *Journal of Symbolic Logic*, 6 (1941), 150–153.

"On the Simplicity of Ideas", *Journal of Symbolic Logic*, 8 (1943), 107–121.

"Descartes as Philosopher", mimeographed, Boston: Cartesian Research Bureau (1946).

"A Query on Confirmation", *Journal of Philosophy*, 43 (1946), 383–385.

"On Infirmities of Confirmation-Theory", *Philosophy and Phenomenological Research*, 8 (1947), 149–151.

"The Problem of Counterfactual Conditionals", *Journal of Philosophy*, 44 (1947), 113–120. (Also reprinted with slight changes in *Fact, Fiction, and Forecast*.)

"Steps Toward a Constructive Nominalism" (with W. V. Quine), *Journal of Symbolic Logic*, 12 (1947), 105–122.

"The Logical Simplicity of Predicates", *Journal of Symbolic Logic*, 14 (1949), 32–41.

"On Likeness of Meaning", *Analysis*, 10 (1949), 1–7.

"Some Reflections on the Theory of Systems", *Philosophy and Phenomenological Research*, 9 (1949), 620–626.

"An Improvement in the Theory of Simplicity", *Journal of Symbolic Logic*, 14 (1950), 228–229.

"New Notes on Simplicity", *Journal of Symbolic Logic*, 17 (1952), 189–191.

"On a Pseudo-test of Translation", *Philosophical Studies*, 6 (1952), 81–82.

"Sense and Certainty", *Philosophical Review*, 61 (1952), 160–167.

"On Some Differences about Meaning", *Analysis*, 13 (1953), 90–96.

"Axiomatic Measurement of Simplicity", *Journal of Philosophy*, 52 (1955), 709–722.

"Definition and Dogma", *Pennsylvania Literary Review*, 6 (1956), 9–14.

"The Revision of Philosophy", *American Philosophers at Work*, Sidney Hook, ed. (New York: Criterion Books, 1956), 75–92. See also "The Significance of *Der logische Aufbau der Welt*" (1963), below.

A Study of Methods of Evaluating Information Processing Systems of Weapons Systems, monograph, University of Pennsylvania, The Institute for Cooperative Research: Project Wescom DA36–039 SC 63143 (1956).

"A World of Individuals", *The Problem of Universals*, University of Notre Dame press: Notre Dame, Ind. (1956), 13–31.

Determination of Deficiencies in Information Processing, monograph, University of Pennsylvania, The Institute for Cooperative Research: Project Wescom DA36–039 SC 63143 (1957).

"Letter to the Editor", *Mind,* 66 (1957), 78.

"Parry on Counterfactuals", *Journal of Philosophy,* 54 (1957), 442–445.

"Reply to an Adverse Ally", *Journal of Philosophy,* 54 (1957), 531–533.

"On Relations that Generate", *Philosophical Studies,* 9 (1958), 65–66.

"The Test of Simplicity", *Science,* 128 (1958), 1064–1069.

"Recent Developments in the Theory of Simplicity", *Philosophy and Phenomenological Research,* 19 (1959), 429–446.

"Positionality and Pictures", *Philosophical Review,* 69 (1960), 523–525.

"The Way the World Is", *Review of Metaphysics,* 14 (1960), 48–56.

"About", *Mind,* 70 (1961), 1–24.

"Condensation versus Simplification", *Theoria,* 27 (1961), 47–48.

"Graphs for Linguistics", *Proceedings of Symposia in Applied Mathematics,* American Mathematical Society, 12 (1961), 52–55.

"Safety, Strength, Simplicity", *Philosophy of Science,* 28 (1961), 150–151.

"Faulty Formalization", *Journal of Philosophy,* 50 (1963), 578–579.

"The Significance of *Der logische Aufbau der Welt*", *The Philosophy of Rudolf Carnap,* P. Schilpp, ed. La Salle, Ill.: Open Court (1963), 545–558. This is a slightly different version of "The Revision of Philosophy" (1956), above.

" 'About' Mistaken", *Mind,* 74 (1965), 248.

"Comments", *Journal of Philosophy,* 63 (1966), 328–331.

"Merit as Means", *Art and Philosophy,* Sidney Hook, ed. New York University Press (1966).

"The New Riddle of Induction: Foreword", *Journal of Philosophy,* 63 (1966), 281.

"The Epistemological Argument", *Synthese,* 17 (1967), 23–28.

"Science and Simplicity", *Philosophy of Science Today,* Sidney Morgenbesser, ed. New York: Basic Books (1967), 68–78.

"Two Replies", *Journal of Philosophy,* 64 (1967), 286–287.

"Uniformity and Simplicity", *75th Anniversary Lecture,* Geological Society of America (1963), GSA Special Paper 89 (1967), 93–99.

"Art and Inquiry" (Presidential Address, American Philosophical Association, Eastern Division), *Proceedings of the American Philo-*

sophical Association, 1967–1968 Yellow Springs, Ohio: Antioch Press, 5–19.

"Reality Remade", *l'Age de la Science,* 1 (1968), 19–40.

"The Emperor's New Ideas", *Language and Philosophy,* Sidney Hook, ed. New York University Press (1969), 138–142.

"Memorial Note" (on Henry Leonard), *The Logical Way of Doing Things,* K. Lambert, ed. Yale University Press (1969), ix–x.

"A Revision in the *Structure of Appearance*", *Journal of Philosophy,* 66 (1969), 383–385.

"Some Notes on *Languages of Art*", *Journal of Philosophy,* 67 (1970), 563–573.

"An Improvement in the Theory of Projectibility" (with Robert Schwartz and Israel Scheffler), *Journal of Philosophy,* 67 (1970), 605–609.

"Seven Strictures on Similarity", *Experience and Theory,* Lawrence Foster and J. W. Swanson, eds., The University of Massachusetts Press (1970), 19–29.

"Professor Gibson's New Perspective", *Leonardo,* forthcoming.

Reviews

"Review of Kaplan, 'Definition and the Specification of Meaning,' " *Journal of Symbolic Logic,* 11 (1946), 30.

"Review of Hans Reichenbach, *Elements of Symbolic Logic*", *Philosophical Review,* 58 (1948), 100–102.

"Review of William Craig, 'Replacement of Auxiliary Expressions,' " *Journal of Symbolic Logic,* 22 (1957).

"Review of Hilary Putnam, 'Reds, Greens and Logical Analysis,' " *Journal of Symbolic Logic,* 22 (1957).

"Review of Urmson's *Philosophical Analysis*", *Mind,* 67 (1958), 107–109.

"Review of E. H. Gombrich, *Art and Illusion*", *Journal of Philosophy,* 57 (1960), 595–599.

"Review of David Armstrong's *Berkeley*", *Philosophy and Phenomenological Research,* 23 (1962), 284–285.

74
75
76
79
81
83
86
88